Lakes and Empires in Macedonian History

Lakes and Empires in Macedonian History

Contesting the Waters

James Pettifer and Miranda Vickers

BLOOMSBURY ACADEMIC
LONDON • NEW YORK • OXFORD • NEW DELHI • SYDNEY

BLOOMSBURY ACADEMIC
Bloomsbury Publishing Plc
50 Bedford Square, London, WC1B 3DP, UK
1385 Broadway, New York, NY 10018, USA
29 Earlsfort Terrace, Dublin 2, Ireland

BLOOMSBURY, BLOOMSBURY ACADEMIC and the Diana logo are trademarks
of Bloomsbury Publishing Plc

First published in Great Britain 2022
Paperback edition published in 2023

Copyright © James Pettifer and Miranda Vickers, 2022

James Pettifer and Miranda Vickers have asserted their right under the Copyright,
Designs and Patents Act, 1988, to be identified as Authors of this work.

Cover image: Aerial view of the Prespes Lake in Northern Greece.
© VASILIS VERVERIDIS / Alamy Stock Photo

All rights reserved. No part of this publication may be reproduced or transmitted
in any form or by any means, electronic or mechanical, including photocopying,
recording, or any information storage or retrieval system, without prior
permission in writing from the publishers.

Bloomsbury Publishing Plc does not have any control over, or responsibility for, any
third-party websites referred to or in this book. All internet addresses given in this
book were correct at the time of going to press. The authors and publisher regret
any inconvenience caused if addresses have changed or sites have ceased to
exist, but can accept no responsibility for any such changes.

Every effort has been made to trace copyright holders and to obtain their permissions
for the use of copyright material. The publisher apologizes for any errors or omissions
and would be grateful if notified of any corrections that should be incorporated
in future reprints or editions of this book.

A catalogue record for this book is available from the British Library.

Library of Congress Cataloging-in-Publication Data

Names: Pettifer, James, author. | Vickers, Miranda, author.
Title: Lakes and empires in Macedonian history: contesting the waters /
James Pettifer and Miranda Vickers.
Description: London; New York: Bloomsbury Academic, 2021. | Includes
bibliographical references and index. |
Identifiers: LCCN 2021007671 (print) | LCCN 2021007672 (ebook) | ISBN 9781350226135
(hardback) | ISBN 9781350226142 (ebook) | ISBN 9781350226159 (epub)
Subjects: LCSH: Psarades (Greece)–History. | Prespa, Lake, Region–History. |
Borderlands–Macedonia. | Human geography–North Macedonia. |
North Macedonia–History. | North Macedonia–Historical geography.
Classification: LCC DF951.P745 P47 2021 (print) | LCC DF951.P745 (ebook) |
DDC 949.5/62–dc23
LC record available at https://lccn.loc.gov/2021007671
LC ebook record available at https://lccn.loc.gov/2021007672

ISBN: HB: 978-1-3502-2613-5
PB: 978-1-3502-2617-3
ePDF: 978-1-3502-2614-2
eBook: 978-1-3502-2615-9

Typeset by Deanta Global Publishing Services, Chennai, India

To find out more about our authors and books visit www.bloomsbury.com and
sign up for our newsletters.

For the people of Psarades/Nivica,
Past, Present and Future

Contents

List of illustrations	viii
Preface and acknowledgements	ix
Maps	xvii

1	The Prespa Lakes: Ecology and human geography	1
2	The Prespa Lake communities: From prehistory to the Ottoman conquest	13
3	The Prespa Lake communities in the Ottoman Empire, 1380–1863	31
4	Prespa and the struggle for Ottoman Macedonia, 1863–1914	47
5	New nations and new borders divide the Lakes, 1914–23	65
6	Nivica becomes Psarades: The construction of Greek Macedonia, 1924–39	79
7	Prespa during war and Axis occupation	91
8	Freedom and civil conflict, 1945–9: The centrality of Prespa	101
9	Exile and return: The Cold War years, 1950–90	117
10	The Lake world: Conflict in Albania and Yugoslavia, 1991–2001	129
11	The Prespa Lakes: Peace and environmental crisis, 2001–18	145

Appendix A: Place-name usage in late Ottoman and twentieth-century Prespa	155
Appendix B: Religious and ethnic identities in Prespa villages in RM	157
Appendix C: Some non-Greek terms in Prespa and Ohrid region	159
Appendix D: The Macedonian toponym	160
Notes	161
Select bibliography	205
Index	215

Illustrations

1	Golem Grad Island in Great Prespa Lake	3
2	Psarades village depicting the receding water level of Great Prespa Lake	6
3	Agios Achilleos Island in Lesser Prespa Lake	24
4	Interior of a house in *Nivica* in 1905	51
5	Soldiers in late Ottoman Prespa	57
6	The First World War French fort opposite Psarades	69
7	Andartes fighters in Prespa during the Civil War	107
8	The house in Psarades where Democratic Army leader Markos Vafeiadis stayed in 1948	111
9	Refugee children in Hungary after 1949	113
10	Pushtec village and Maligrad Island in Albanian Prespa	137
11	The old fishing house in Psarades in 1960	141
12	The old fishing house in Psarades in 2013 showing the dramatic fall in water level	142

Maps

1	Prespa region	xvii
2	Greek Prespa	xviii
3	North Prespa	xix

Preface and acknowledgements

Macedonia, past and present, ancient and modern, has always been on the border of Mediterranean history and maritime empires not far from the sea, 200 kilometres from the waters of the Thermaikos Gulf, a world of lakes, mountains, dense forests and wetlands.[1] It is the only region of Greece and its northern neighbours where lakes and a major river, the ancient Axios, now the modern Vardar, play a significant part in the landscape and ecology. Yet to the lake riparian dwellers, the lake is their sea. Villages surround the southern Balkan lakes, along with a few towns like Ohrid.

This book explores the history of Psarades, once Ottoman *Neverska*, medieval *Nivica*, a village in Macedonian Greece on the shore of Great Prespa Lake, in the context of the wider history of the region that culminated in the division of Macedonia in late Ottoman and post-Ottoman times. This division has been central to the political and economic life of the Balkan region ever since, starting with the crises immediately before and leading to the First World War. Although so remote, the Prespa and Ohrid regions reflect the main developments in Balkan history and were central to the northern territorial expansion of twentieth-century Greece. Psarades/Nivica was frequently involved in the protracted and violent conflicts over the future of Macedonia in the twentieth and early twenty-first centuries, and Prespa was in its time a centre of support for the Internal Macedonian Revolutionary Organization (IMRO) and then the anti-Axis resistance and communism during and after the Second World War. It remains a nodal point in the region today. The Prespa and Ohrid Lakes lie high in the mountains where the three borders of Greece, Albania and what is now in official quarters called '*North Macedonia*' meet, with a harsh winter climate, and in the Nazi occupation and Greek Civil War period the Prespa region was known as 'Frontier Corner'. Climatic and environmental factors, along with epidemic diseases, are also important determinants in the history.[2] We also explore the development of international borders in the region in the post-Ottoman years and the different movements of population around Prespa focussed on Psarades. It is also the history of a changing environment and increasingly an ecological crisis.

Psarades produces no wine and grows no grain, olives, cotton or tobacco, and for centuries it has lived primarily off the fish from the lakes, so it is both an untypical Greek village and a typical Greek fishing community, situated in the landlocked central southern Balkans, yet not far from the sea. Deep contradictions in modern Greek history lie at the heart of the Psarades story. The village lies on the south side of Great Prespa Lake, in what is known in Macedonian as Lower Prespa, *Dolna Prespa*.[3] The district of Upper Prespa/*Gorna Prespa* comprises the town of Resen, once Ottoman *Resna*, and the villages on the northern shores of the lakes in Albania and what became in 1991 Republic of Macedonia, after the end of Yugoslavia. There has been regional involvement here in all the major conflicts of the late nineteenth and twentieth centuries, and extending into the twenty-first century, where in 2001 there was serious violence near the lakes in the city of Bitola, once Ottoman *Manastir*, ancient Heraclea Lyncestis. Regional history is the history of a peasant society, where only a very small proportion of the population lived in towns until the very late Ottoman period, and a strongly egalitarian rural society was based on the lakes. Subsistence and pastoral agriculture and the forests have always formed the material basis of existence. It has been a hard and difficult life. Pre-modern agriculture was based primarily on physical drudgery, *ponos*, and hand tools, but we do not know very much about the nature of many aspects of that pre-modern peasant life other than the prevailing conditions of scarcity and frequent food deficit,[4] where as John Berger has written:

> The peasant ideal of equality recognises a world of scarcity and its promise is for mutual fraternal aid in struggling against this scarcity and a just sharing of what work produces.[5]

Within this southern Balkan lakeside society, poverty has always been the norm until the late twentieth century but ameliorated in Psarades by the very rich fish harvest of the lake, as to a lesser extent in other small piscatorial settlements in all three Lakes littoral nations. The roots of this rural society are very ancient indeed. Macedonia was well populated in the Neolithic and Bronze Ages. Ancient and Byzantine history around Prespa has been very important in determining current settlement patterns and human geography, and the monuments surviving from those periods also play a central role in modern national identities. Thus, our account starts in prehistory and antiquity where recent archaeological work has transformed understanding of the deep past.

Our field research in these villages started as long ago as 1992, and throughout the succeeding twenty-nine years we have been sustained in sometimes difficult material conditions, particularly on the Albanian side of the Lake region in the 1990s and in Psarades by the generous help of those resident there to whom we owe a profound debt. The simplest aspects of daily life were very difficult in the Yugoslav wartime days, for everybody, whether resident or visitor, and necessities were often in very short supply. Traditions of hospitality were always maintained and what was available was shared. The way of life based on traditional Balkan pastoralism and aquaculture has continued in many ways little changed over centuries and embodies values based on organic agriculture, hunting and gathering in the forests, and sustainable fishing in the lakes. As such it represents a beacon of light in a region where environmental concern has not always been strong, particularly among urban elites in the capital cities. Within agriculture, sheep remain the key pastoral animal, as they have always been in Macedonian history from the earliest times.

Our methodology with the oral history has been close to that of the anthropologists – Prespa is a society where written history is often bitterly disputed and oral memory is central. We have made many visits over a long period rather than the single period of uninterrupted residence that the anthropologists tend to favour.[6] Thus, the text is in many senses a microhistory where Prespa history embodies the most important elements in Macedonian and the wider south-east European history in many different historical periods, but it is not a society with 'microecology'.⁷ The main factors causing environmental change are traced but not to make a 'ecohistory' divorced from the economic, political and military realities that have dominated post-Ottoman Macedonia. Ornithology and the unique bird life of the Lakes have been central to recent somewhat positive Prespa developments since the end of the Cold War and are discussed in the final chapters of the book. The chapters most focussed on the environment and contemporary Prespa have been initially drafted by Miranda Vickers and the history of the ancient, Ottoman and modern periods up to 1990 initially by James Pettifer.

The deep past of Macedonia is important in Prespa history, and many features of the physical landscape and recent history cannot be understood without reference to much earlier epochs, in particular the period of the Roman imperial system, the arrival of Christianity and the long sunlit afternoon of late antiquity. Modes of production and settlement patterns that originated then continue in recognizable forms today in many places. All the lake communities have a significant relationship with fishing and in some like Psarades it has always been central to economic life. Bean production has always been in all epochs after the Iron Age the mainstay of Prespa field agriculture. Prespa societies are very complex, if small, with every village having a unique history, and their complexities relate closely to the geostrategic position on the lakes and then the wider cross-currents of regional and international history.

Empires are central to this reality, as Macedonia was in antiquity the crucible for the spread of Hellenism outside Greece, followed by the Roman Balkans, the Ottoman centuries and the modern world. Every village has a different history and particularly in Gorna Prespa religious affiliation also determines resident's perspectives of outside powers affecting Balkan politics. People from the complex of ethnic and national identities in Macedonia across the tense international borders have shared their thoughts and often painful recollections about their often very contested twentieth-century histories, sometimes their political exile and now their current lives. The different military and security forces of the three riparian countries have also had an important role to play in the history, given the international strategic importance of the nearby so-called Monastir Gap in twentieth-century World Wars and the troubled contemporary Balkans. The vast majority of these personnel have been both courteous and professional, and frequently very helpful, particularly the Greek police in and around modern Psarades.

We have also endeavoured to investigate the Byzantine and Ottoman heritage, and the relationship of these imperial systems to modern Prespa social and political development, mainly through the growth of the important Ottoman centres of Resna/Resen and Manastir/Bitola and the subsequent decline of the Ottoman *ciflik* farming systems linked to the weakening Empire and the development of modern market-driven agriculture. Empires have also brought major changes to the natural environment, with land clearance for large-scale cereal growing under the Romans followed by widespread deforestation in the Ottoman centuries.

We have obviously used many secondary sources but would like to highlight the most important. Like all students of the Ottoman regional history we owe a great debt to Halil Inalcik (1916–2016) in Turkey, Heath. W. Lowry in Princeton, and to Bernard

Lory whose history of Manastir/Bitola (*La Ville Balkanissime: Bitola, 1800-1918*) is likely to change many perceptions of the history of south-west Macedonia as a geographical entity in the late Ottoman years. Nada Boskovska's study in Zurich, *Das Jugoslawische Makedonien 1918-1941: Eine Randregion zwischen Repression und Integration*, is of equal importance in the post–First World War period when the inhabitants of the northern shores of the lakes were becoming, generally very unwillingly, citizens of the *banovina* of South Serbia within the first Royalist Yugoslavia. At the same time the Macedonian people of the villages within newly expanded Greece faced enforced Hellenization, or exile. All students of the ancient history of the region owe a profound debt to Vera Grazdenova-Bitrakova and her Skopje archaeological team who have revolutionized understanding of the early ecology and landscape of the lakes, and the drafting of the second chapter of this book would not have been possible without their work.

Many historical events can only be understood in relation to the lake riparian environments, where the wealth from the fish harvest has always saved the inhabitants from the chronic food deficit that affected most of Macedonia in earlier centuries. Psarades and the other lakeside villages thus form, in Horden and Purcell's terms, a 'virtual sea', where the lakes take on the role of a microsea, embodying in part the wider qualities of the Mediterranean as an avenue of provision, economic exchange and subversion of externally imposed state and national units. The lake thus, like Euripides sea, represents a cleansing force, an ideal of freedom from national state coercion, particularly enforced taxation, in all historical periods. To some extent this transnationality has been recognized in the late twentieth century. The unique ecology of the Prespa region benefitted from the declaration of a transnational forest Park. This has brought advances in wildlife protection, a reduction in hunting, better fish conservation and the opportunity to develop minor small-scale ecotourism. It has not slowed the economic decline of Psarades/Nivica, with deculturesation caused by US- and EU-led globalization, central state pressures, rural depopulation, EU agricultural policies, school closures, transport cuts and growing unemployment/emigration, the latter particularly evident since the Greek financial crisis broke in autumn 2009. The villages on the Albanian and northern Macedonian sides of the lake have been somewhat more economically resilient, although from a lower material base standard of living.

Ecological change is central to the modern narrative. The Prespa Lakes have been under serious stress in the years since our studies began, with a major drop in water levels which – if it continues – will threaten the viability of Psarades/Nivica as a fishing and tourism village. In Lake Ohrid most fishing has been banned, and the lake may lose its UNESCO world heritage site designation. The change in the Prespa Lakes water levels has complex causes but is undoubtedly generally linked to climate change where warmer winters have led to a major reduction in regional snowfall and thus the overall precipitation around the lakes and mountains.

Difficult issues face many residents. The human rights issues of those in northern Greece (including some residents of Psarades/Nivica) who see themselves with a partial Macedonian and/or Bulgarian identity remain unresolved although immediate Greek state coercion on language usage and other human rights issues in Greece is much less pronounced than in the last generations.⁸ Vlachs have no educational provision in their language except in primary schools in some places in Macedonia. The increased international interest in the region has brought a better understanding of the unique ecology, where, for instance, it has been discovered that over half of all European bat species live within a few miles of the lakes. This research has also brought considerable advances in the sources available to the historian. The study of pollens, timber, fish species and the climate and forensic archaeology generally have improved understanding considerably of the hitherto obscure period of late antiquity and the early Bulgarian and Byzantine periods where there are limited written sources.

In the modern period we have sought to show the society and its history principally focussed on modern Psarades/Nivica but with exploration of the complex patterns of historical time at work, where at one level the life of the people has many resonances with the life of distant historical periods when Prespa was prominent in the region in the Bulgarian and Byzantine clerical and monastic settlement of Prespa but where modern borders from the Treaty of Versailles era and then the Cold War aftermath still dominate life.

During the last hundred years, some of the most dramatic and important military and political struggles of the twentieth-century Balkans have taken place around Prespa, as in the struggle of the people for freedom under the Nazi occupation and then in the Greek Civil War period. In this context this very small group of riparian villages' fate has been centrally intertwined with the fate of regional powers and transnational empires. Prespa played a key part in the Greek Civil War, particularly in the 'Third Round' between 1947 and 1949. Democratic Army commander General Markos Vafeiades stayed for a period in the Greek Civil War in a house in Psarades in 1948, and the headquarters of his communist military force and their hospital can still be seen today in a cave near Lesser Prespa Lake. Ironically, perhaps, it has become a tourist attraction (and sometimes a winter residence for brown bears). Beyond the 'official' Greek narrative derived from Cold War events there are many secret histories of the region, particularly in respect of villages which until 1939 saw themselves with a primary Vlach/Romanian, Albanian or Macedonian/Bulgarian identity and consciousness. Modern Greek historical memory has been subject to very similar processes as those described by Maria Todorova concerning distortions of popular memory in Turkey, where 'The Turkish modernity project tended to discount the everyday experience (including memories) of ordinary persons in its attempt to create a single national identity within a historically multicultural geography'.⁹

The diverse histories of many Prespa-region villages have continued in the main as oral tradition, but the innovative scholarly work of Larry Koroloff in Canada on his family-origin village of Drenoveni, modern Greek Kranies, south of the immediate Prespa Lake region in the Koreshcha district near Kostur/Kastoria, has been very helpful. It has a very similar history to the Macedonian-speaking (until 1939) Prespa-region villages. The Greek national narrative from the Cold War has in general been mechanically reflected in all European Union publications, and also the United States, often to the serious detriment of rational debate and understanding of the history.

On the ultimately insoluble questions of regional onomastics, toponyms and place-name use, we have throughout only used the terms appropriate to the periods we are discussing. See Appendix D for details on toponymic evolution. The division of geographic Macedonia in 1912 and after to benefit the growth of the modern Greek and Yugoslav states by the late nineteenth and early twentieth-century imperialist powers – principally France and Britain – has formed the current borders across the lake. The relatively relaxed borders existing in the pre-1939 period through Greek and Yugoslav hegemonies became markedly changed as a result of the Cold War and the ex-Yugoslav wars, and some practical difficulties remain for the traveller up to the time of writing. These have been substantially worsened by population movement control connected to the Covid virus pandemic. The hegemonic power of the United States has, after 1947, become the main imperial influence on political elite in the region today, particularly in Skopje but it is often marginal outside the capital cities.

The 'linguistic turn' is not a theoretical construct of Western academic historians in Macedonia. There have been some important linguistic changes in some regional towns nearby the Lakes since 1990. The speaking of Greek in Korca/Koritsa in Albania as a primary language has declined considerably with population movement from the long-resident Greek minority, although many of the remaining inhabitants still understand and speak some Greek as a result of periods of work in Greece. Albanian which was a lingua franca around the lakes in the late Ottoman period in many villages and in Resna/Resen and Manastir/Bitola with many Albanophone Ottoman officials in post then suffered a steep decline. It has staged something of a recent revival in Greek Prespa with migrant workers from Albanian villages coming to work as stone masons and in the bean harvest in the summer. Human rights for the minority having a Macedonian cultural identity living in Albanian Prespa have improved somewhat in recent years.[10]

In Greece the Macedonian regional language known as 'Slavika' by the Greek government and most Greeks can be heard spoken in some Greek localities, particularly in rural areas, where it was not spoken publicly at all, in any circumstances, when we first began to visit and study the area after 1992. Turkish is understood in a few villages north of the Greek border and by a small minority of people in Resen, Bitola and Ohrid, and up the Radika river valley north of Ohrid. We have not found it used in Greek Macedonia around Prespa nowadays, although twenty-five years ago a few very old people of Asia Minor Greek descent did understand it.

In the August panigiri festival when exiles return to their Patrida villages, Bulgarian/Macedonian songs and bands can now be heard in some places in Greek Prespa.[11] Roma have little or no collective cultural presence in the Prespa region, except in one small district of Resen and two in Bitola. Roma traders traverse the region selling fruit, vegetables and household goods, much as their ancestors, as licensed pedlars, did in Ottoman times. Resen Roma speak a dialect of Macedonian. Vlach is still spoken in some villages, particularly Pili and Vronderon in Greek Prespa and some villages around Bitola north of the border although the situation of the language is rather fragile. The language carries on in oral usage largely through women within the family. Few people can write it.

Many Prespa Greek-Macedonian villages have had several different names since the end of the Ottoman period, usually as a product of new political masters, political impositions from Athens, population movements and twentieth-century border changes, which are indicated where they first appear in the text, and an Appendix gives further references. This is also the case with some Prespa villages in Albania, for example Liqenasi/Pushtec. In Royalist Yugoslavia and socialist Macedonia centrally imposed name changes were unusual. For a view on the development of the wider regional issues and international relations as they developed after 1990, see James Pettifer (Ed), *The New Macedonian Question* (London and New York) 1998, Hugh Poulton *Who Are the Macedonians?* (London, 1996), Miranda Vickers's *The Albanians: A Modern History* (London, 1996) and other works listed in the Select Bibliography. This is intended to provide readers with further relevant leads into the history but does not attempt to cover the vast and complex secondary literature in many languages on the modern New Macedonian Question. Little has changed since the end of the Cold War in most political realities except environmental protection. For ease of reference by non-specialists, book names in foreign languages in the Bibliography have been written in the Latin script. In general the scholarly apparatus in the footnotes has been kept to a reasonable minimum, for the same reason. There are many arcane and very complex controversies in Macedonian history, some relevant to Prespa history, others less so.

We would like to thank the following who have been kind enough to assist us, either with research materials or by comment on parts of the text – Anton Panev, Professor Aleksandar Grebanarov and the staff of the Macedonian Scientific Institute in Sofia; in Oxford, Averil Cameron, Mirela Ivanova, Alexandra Vukmanovic, Robert Evans, Tom Buchanan, Bryan Ward Perkins, Peter Frankopan, Judith Curthoys, Steven Archer, Jonathan Shepard and other colleagues, my pupil Lycourgos Sophoulis, the late Tom Winnifrith in Shipston-on-Stour on Vlach matters, Tom Urquhart, Julian and Julia Hoffman, Pippa and Revd Robin Blackall, and Susan Comely on ornithology, the Oxford Union Library, the Nuffield College, St Cross College and Christ Church libraries, the Bodleian Library, particularly Stuart Ackland in Maps, the Firestone Library in Princeton University, the Library of Congress in Washington, DC, Nick Balamaci in New York City, the School of Slavonic and South East European Studies Library in London, the late Nina Smirnova in Moscow, Evgeny Koloskov in Saint Petersburg, Basil and Steffi Kondis and the Institute of Balkan Studies (IMHA) and Society for Macedonian Studies libraries in Thessaloniki, Adil Nurallari and Xhevdet Shehu in Tirana, Kico Stavre and the Gjorgi family in Pushtec, the Association of Greek Civil War veterans in Skopje, John Phillips in Rome, in Switzerland Nada Boskovska in Zurich and Christian Zindel in Aargau, Larry Koroloff in Toronto, Kyril Drezov in Keele, Sasha Uzanov in Melbourne, Steve and Tina Playford and Jared Wiencke in Adelaide, George Liakopoulos in Jena, Albulena Halili in Tetovo, and in Skopje and Ohrid, Chris Deliso, Melina Grizo, Vera Grazdenova-Bitrakova, Gordana Silanovska-Davkova, Biljana Vankovska and the Macedonian National History Institute in Skopje.

Germanos Papadopoulos in Psarades was kind enough to share his outstanding photographic collection from his East European childhood in exile with us. Local Macedonian oral discourse has naturally focussed on memories of conflict and childhood displacement and the struggles in Prespa life under first Nazi occupation, then Civil War, political exile and afterwards successive Cold War governments in Greece. The recollections of Costas Giankopoulos and his family were also particularly evocative and helpful, as were the textual comments of Ljubica Stojkovska. In terms of the future, we do not know what the impact of the coronavirus pandemic will be on the region, except to say that it devastated most tourism in 2020.

We are profoundly grateful to all local residents, some sadly now passed away, who over a long period have accepted us into their lives and debated their very complex history with us. This book is dedicated to all of them, past and present, with deep gratitude.

James Pettifer
Miranda Vickers
Oxford and Ealing, 2021

Photograph and Map acknowledgements

P.3 Golem Grad Island, Alamy Stock Images, P.6 Psarades Village, Getty Images, P.24 Agios Achilleos Island, Alamy Stock Images, P.51 Nivica, out of copyright, P.57 Soldiers in Late Ottoman Prespa, Collection of G. Papadopoulos, P.69, First World War French Fort, Miranda Vickers, P.107 Andartes fighters in Prespa, National World War II Museum, Athens, open content, P.111 Vafeiades house in Psarades, Miranda Vickers, P.113 Refugee Children in Hungary, Collection of G. Papadopoulos, P.137, Pushtec, Getty Images, P.141, Old Fishing House in 1960, Collection of G. Papadopoulos, P.142 Old Fishing House in 2013, Miranda Vickers. Map acknowledgement, Sebastian Ballard.

Maps

Map 1 Prespa region.

Map 2 Greek Prespa.

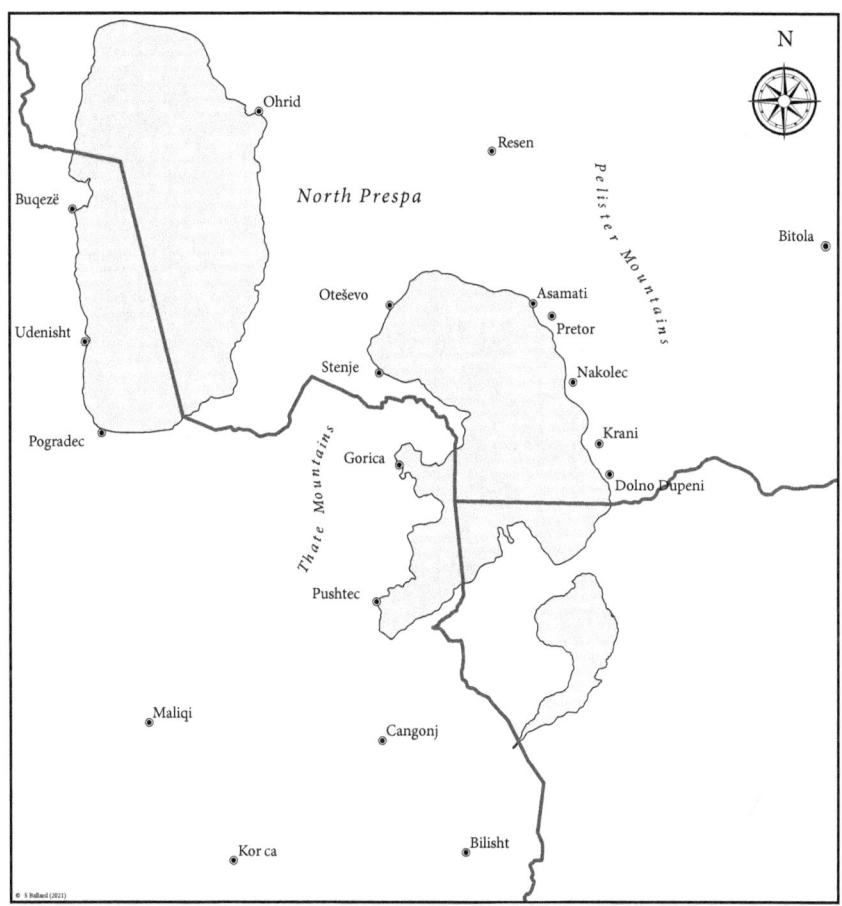

Map 3 North Prespa.

1

The Prespa Lakes

Ecology and human geography

In the far north-western of Greece where the country meets its northern neighbours is one of the most remote and least known regions in Europe. Until the late 1980s the Prespa marshes, forests and scrubland were an unfrequented semi-wilderness, traversed only by transhumant shepherds and a handful of tourists, either serious birdwatchers or students of Byzantine art. In the harsh winter months, typified by the Bulgarian meaning of Prespa, *snowdrift*, there were no travellers at all. The few settled communities were living virtually self-sufficient lives as they had for centuries. The 4,650-hectare Prespa National Park, 853 metres above sea level and surrounded by mountains, contains two remote and beautiful lakes. The larger known as Megali or Great Prespa has a surface of 285 square kilometres with a maximum depth of 54 metres and the smaller Lake Mikri or Lesser Prespa has a surface of 47 square kilometres and a depth of 12 metres. Great Prespa Lake is divided between Albania, Greece and the Republic of Macedonia/Former Yugoslav Macedonia (until the name change to 'North Macedonia' in 2018) while Lesser Prespa is shared only between Greece and Albania. The waters of the two Lakes connect the shores of the three countries and bind them together geographically. The region is home to approximately 24,000 people: 5,600 in Albania; 17,000 in 'North Macedonia' and 1,560 in Greece. In Albania there are twelve Prespa lakeside villages belonging to two municipalities: the Municipality of Pushtec, based in Pushtec village, which includes nine villages, and in the Municipality of Devoll, there are three villages around Lesser Prespa. North of the Greek border in western Macedonia there are forty-four settlements, with the largest town being Resen, which has 8,748 inhabitants. In Greece there are eleven villages belonging to the Municipality of Prespa, which look southwards towards Kastoria/*Kostur* and Florina/*Lerin* as their urban centres.[1]

The two Prespa Lakes are nowadays divided by a narrow strip of land but were not always separate and did not have the same dimensions as today. Around a thousand years ago an isthmus was created by the accumulation of sediment carried by the Agios Germanos stream and so created Lesser Prespa Lake, which flows into Great Prespa through a narrow channel 1,000 metres in length. The rugged limestone peaks and immense sombre forests of dwarf oak, fir, beech, juniper and black pine are home to an abundance of wildlife, including the European brown bear, jackals, wolves, lynx, otters, wild boar, hare, chamois, wildcats, tortoises and the Egyptian vulture. The Prespa region has over 200 species of birds, many from rare or declining populations within Europe. Prespa is the last stronghold of the Dalmatian pelican, containing the largest breeding colony in the world, and saving the pelicans was the trigger for the modern National Park. Also present are the golden oriole, the glossy ibis, the hoopoe and the largest colony of Pygmy cormorants in Europe. In the waters of the Lakes there are eleven species of fish, of which the Prespa carp, sardines and trout are the most important.

The ancient juniper forests are of considerable ecological importance containing 800 different species of plants, many unique to the region which, surrounded by mountains over 2,000 metres high, is virtually cut off by snow during the harsh winter months. In the spring thaw the meadows are carpeted with wild flowers, including many rare orchids, as well as the endemic species of cyclamen *Centurea prespana*.

In summer bears come down from mountain caves to feed on berries and other fruit. The mountains, some still snow-capped in June, drop sheer into the Lakes, fringed with white shingle beaches and reedbeds with forest paths winding through the dense vegetation. Caves in the lakeside cliffs house thousands of bats. Prespa is also home to a unique species of small cow, one of the last (still living) representatives descended from Neolithic Stone Age cattle.[2] As a result of the area's high natural biodiversity and the threat from post–Cold War commercial development pressures, in 2000 the region was declared a Trans-National Park managed by the three riparian nations which includes the whole Prespa Lakes watershed. This decision built on initiatives which had first been taken by Titoist Yugoslavia, when the tourist club 'Prespa' was established in Resen as long ago as 1954 to further the study of the environment by youth movement members.[3] The Park is protected under the Ramsar Convention for Conservation as a wetland of international importance. UNESCO has declared Prespa as an example of Outstanding Universal Value of harmonious coexistence between humans and nature.

In the northern sector of Great Prespa Lake is the mysterious, densely wooded island of Golem Grad. It was given as a gift to King Alexander of Yugoslavia by King Constantine of Greece in 1922. Covering an area of more than 20 hectares, it is also known as Snake Island due to the large number of reptiles, some poisonous, that inhabit its dense undergrowth. The island is uninhabited and has been so since a small monastic community left in the mid-twentieth century. There are, however, many ancient ruins, often overgrown by undergrowth, including the remains of Hellenistic buildings and the fourteenth-century church of St Demetrios. In Lesser Prespa is the small wooded island of Agios Achilleos with its Bulgarian Empire and Byzantine remains. There are no cars allowed on the island, so to view the buildings and lake marshes, visitors cross an 850-metres-long wooden pedestrian bridge. This tiny village, with just twenty-one inhabitants, contains the ruins of several Byzantine-period churches, the most significant being the basilica built by the Bulgarian Tsar Samuil before the collapse of his Empire.

After the Balkan Wars (1912–13) and the post–First World War border settlements, Prespa Lake region of historic Macedonia was divided with the northern area becoming a part of the newly established Kingdom of Yugoslavia, the south-western part was incorporated into the newly created state of Albania and the south-eastern corner

Illustration 1 Golem Grad Island in Great Prespa Lake.

became part of Greece. The Greek Civil War from 1946 to 1949 brought enormous political and social turbulence to the Prespa Lake region, whose predominantly Macedonian-speaking population suffered very severely and in its aftermath official Greek policy led to either enforced exile or assimilation. Those fighting on the losing side in the Civil War were forced to become refugees and their citizenship and property were confiscated by the Greek state. Some villages were laid waste and the last remaining Slavic, often Bulgarian origin names of the Greek region's villages that had survived the name-changing decrees of 1926, were changed to Greek names in the 1950s. During the Cold War, and until as late as 1980, the entire Prespa region was considered a military area by the Greek state, with special permission being required for entering the area.

Prespa has been a site of human inhabitation for at least 4,000 years. Since the late 1970s there has been a significant drop in the water level of both Great and Lesser Prespa. In the areas of land that have been reclaimed from the Lakes, recent archaeological discoveries include earthenware pottery, stone tools and wooden boats that date back to the Neolithic and Middle Bronze Age together with roads and buildings from the Roman Empire. Historically, the Prespa region has been subject to various waves of occupation by Romans, Goths, Bulgarians, Serbs, Byzantines and Ottomans, giving the area a rich but also infinitely complex cultural heritage. After the collapse of the Byzantine Empire in the Balkans in the mid-fourteenth century, five centuries of Ottoman rule followed. With Prespa so remote, the Ottoman imperial rule outside the main towns was often inefficient and Prespa always has had a strong open Orthodox Christian presence, with the survival of churches, monasteries and the remains of numerous hermitages some with impressive frescos dating from the fourteenth century.

The local population is concentrated in villages around the two Lakes, where houses are built in a traditional style from stone and clay bricks with roofs of straw or red stone tiles. Prespa's three main traditional occupations are fishing, animal husbandry and various agricultural activities, particularly the production of the region's high-quality beans in Greek Prespa. These giant white beans are made into *fasolada or gigantes* – a national dish which provides the main source of income for farmers. Most of Prespa's Macedonian settlements north of the Greek border are situated along the shore of Great Prespa where there are fifteen villages: Dolno Dupeni, Ljubojno, Brajcino, Kranj, Slivnica, Kurbinovo, Asamati, Grncari, Ezerani, Perovo, Pokrvenik, Otesevo, Leskoec, Stenje and Konsko. The majority population of these villages is Christian Orthodox Macedonian; however, some have a mixed population with Muslims and a few Turks. Asamati's inhabitants are divided almost equally between Albanian-speaking Muslims and Orthodox Slavs, while Krani and Grncari are around 70 per cent Muslim and 30 per cent Orthodox. Asamati's origins are unique. During the Middle Ages, the Prespa region was part of the Bulgarian Empire under Tsar Samuil. After the Battle of Kleidion in 1014 during the Bulgarian-Byzantine wars, some of Tsar Samuil's soldiers, who were each blinded in one eye, were settled in a village on the shore of Great Prespa. The Byzantines called the village *Asamati*, meaning 'settlement of the one-eyed people'. Kurbinovo became widely known when Pablo Picasso visited the village during a Yugoslav peace conference at Ohrid in the 1960s. Many northern Prespa villages have preserved their traditional Macedonian architecture, in particular Brajcino, Ljubojno and Dolno Dupeni.

The largest town in the Prespa region is Resen, Ottoman *Resna*, which was a significant point near the Roman Via Egnatia road linking *Dyracchium* – modern Durres in Albania – with *Constantinople*. The town is known for its apple orchards and has a multiethnic Macedonian, Roma, Albanian and Turkish population. The Albanian inhabitants first settled in *Resna*/Resen at the beginning of the nineteenth century, while most of the town's current Turkish-speaking population are descended from either Turks settled in strategic areas under Ottoman rule or ex-Ottoman soldiers or the descendants of local Turkified Slavs. The majority of the Macedonian identity population originates from the villages in the Lake Ohrid area who settled in *Resna* during the middle of the nineteenth century. North of modern Resen the city of Bitola is an important centre of education, trade and regional government. Once Roman *Heraclea Lyncestis*, on the *Via Egnetia*, and medieval and Ottoman *Manastir*, it occupies a key position on the east-west transport routes linking the Adriatic with the interior of the southern Balkans.

Along the Albanian shore there are seven villages: Bezmisht, Gorice, Gollombec, Shulline, Pushtec, Zaroshe and Rakicke. The most prominent of these villages is Pushtec (called *Liqenas* in communist Albania), which is well known for its two Byzantine churches, both containing frescos from the twelfth century.[4] The majority-ethnic Macedonians exist in some isolation speaking a dialect closely linked to Bulgarian. These remote lakeside villages, reached largely on poor dirt roads, remain largely self-sufficient from mainstream Albania with the population engaged in small-scale agriculture, fishing and animal husbandry as they have done for centuries. They benefit from a much larger area of fertile arable land than the Greek side of Great Prespa Lake at Psarades.[5]

Despite the intentions of all three neighbouring countries to protect and conserve Prespa's unique ecosystem, in 2006, a joint Albanian-Greek study raised the alarm about the drying of Lesser Prespa in the Albanian sector of the Lake. The study argued that Lesser Prespa risked being turned into a muddy marshland if it continued to be drained in order to irrigate the agricultural businesses in the Plain of Korca. The ebb of the Lake and the reduction of the water level have produced lavish vegetation mingled with mud, creating a vast expanse of marshland. This has led to a change in the environmental quality of the area with major economic effects. Over the past twenty years south-east Albania has been characterized by massive emigration. Around Korca and Prespa this has left the remaining inhabitants in difficulty due to the poor water resources caused by the drying of Lesser Prespa. According to the study, the deviation of the Drin river bed from its discharge into Lesser Prespa in the mid-1970s has dramatically reduced the environmental, social and economic importance of the Albanian part of the Lake.[6]

In the Greek Prespa region there are thirteen villages surrounding both Great and Lesser Prespa Lakes. For many years, the Greek Lake region was an under-populated, military sensitive area. The entire region remained little developed until the 1980s, when it gradually became promoted as a tourist destination, although numbers today remain very small. The villages are split into those surrounding Great Prespa – Psarades, Vrondero and Pili – and those around Lesser Prespa – Agios Achilleos, Agios Germanos, Laimos, Milionas, Plati, Kallithea, Lefkonas, Karies, Oxia and Mikrolimni. The largest village in Greek Prespa is Laimos, with around 250 permanent residents and together with nearby Agios Germanos making a larger semi-urban centre. It is also the administrative centre of the area. Agios Germanos, with its many well-preserved traditional houses and eleventh-century Byzantine church, is the most frequented by visitors. The village contains a Visitors Information Centre of the management body for the Prespa National Park with details of wildlife and walking trials, as well as a permanent exhibition of the region's environment and culture.

In the mountains overlooking the Lakes are the ruins of numerous abandoned villages, prominent reminders of the ravages of twentieth-century war and regional political conflicts. In Daseri, near Pili, all that remains are the wall of the school and the stone bases of the houses. In Agathoto are the ruins of a small church, hidden behind rocks and trees. Almost nothing remains of the Latsista settlement, situated among the hills behind the village of Mikrolimni at the tip of Lesser Prespa. Kranies, across the lake, where only a few houses remain, lies a few kilometres further on. Sfika, in the mountains above Oxia, was once quite a large village as can be seen from the size of the church, the ruins of which are hidden deep in the forest.[7]

The Prespa region is home to four main ethnic/national groups, who see their primary identity as Greeks, Vlachs, Roma or ethnic Macedonians. The latter are the Prespa region's largest ethnic group. Their ancestors came to the southern Balkans during the Slav and Bulgarian migrations after the fifth and sixth centuries AD. They speak the Slavonic linguistic family Macedonian language that evolved in Yugoslavia from common linguistic roots. Those living in the Albanian and Greek villages often speak both Albanian and Greek. Some older generation inhabitants can also speak Hungarian and Czech fluently, owing to their youth in exile after the Civil War. The ethnic Greek population is to a minor extent comprised of people who arrived from Asia Minor during the population exchanges following the First World War and those Vlach Greeks who moved to Prespa from Thessaly and other parts of Greece during the 1950s.

Illustration 2 Psarades village depicting the receding water level of Great Prespa Lake.

As the Ottoman Empire began to disintegrate in the late nineteenth century, the diverse peoples of Macedonia found themselves caught between Greece and Bulgaria for their sympathies and allegiance. During the Balkan Wars of 1912–13, Greece occupied the territory, now known as the Greek province of Macedonia, and under the Treaty of Bucharest (1912) it became part of the Greek state. After these wars and the First World War, the Slav-speaking population of Prespa and northern Greece generally was greatly reduced. At least 80,000 people were forced to flee to Bulgaria and to the new Turkish Republic under the post-Treaty of Lausanne population exchanges after 1922. The population exchange between Greece and Turkey in 1922 involved the expulsion of more than 40,000 Muslims from Greek Macedonia, thus further altering the population structure of the region. At the same time, the Greek government settled around 560,000 Christians from Turkey and another 50,000 from other parts of Greece, throughout Greek Macedonia, including the Prespa region.[8] The modern Greek state has never acknowledged the existence of any minorities in Greece other than the Treaty of Lausanne protected Muslim minority in Thrace and therefore a substantial proportion of Prespa's population are officially referred to as 'Slavophone-Greeks'. It is impossible to calculate accurately the number of Slavic-speakers or descendants of ethnic Macedonians in Greece. Historian Leonidas Embiricos estimates that more than 100,000 still live in the Greek region of Macedonia, though only 10,000 to 20,000 would identify openly as members of a minority and many others are proud Greek nationalists.[9]

With the creation of the Albanian state in 1912, several thousand Macedonians inhabiting the Prespa Lake's shore villages were incorporated into that new state. There are no accurate estimates of the exact number of Macedonian-speakers in Albania at that time or during communist times between 1945 and 1991. Estimates range from 4,000 according to the then leader Enver Hoxha in a speech to the 7th Congress of the Albanian Party of Labour in 1975 to over 100,000 in a book published in Skopje in 1983.[10] While the latter figure is certainly an exaggeration, most independent observers put the figure at between 10,000 and 20,000 people, but this usually includes the Slav *Gorani* people who live in the north near the Kosovo border with Albania and are not connected to the Prespa people. With the collapse of communism in 1991, many *Gorani* fled Albania for Yugoslavia. Since then many more inhabitants have left their Prespa villages to live in Tirana or other Albanian towns. Those who have remained living along the shore of Great Prespa live by fishing and small-scale farming.[11]

Prespa also has a sizable Vlach population. The Vlachs are among Europe's last semi-nomadic pastoralists who have managed to preserve many aspects of their traditions – if not always transhumance life – in the more remote mountainous regions of the southern Balkans. Speaking a language derived from Latin, which is akin to modern Romanian, Vlachs trace their decent from remnants of Roman garrisons stationed in the region. Today, an estimated 90,000 Vlachs live in scattered communities in the southern Balkans, with the majority in different parts of Macedonia. Many have urban lives in the towns of the central and northern Balkans where they have become largely assimilated into the broader community.

The Prespa Vlachs live in the villages of Gopes, Istok and Maloviste in the northern sector of the Lake region, in the villages of Agios Germanos, Kallithea, Pisodheri, Pili and Vrondero in the southern part and in the village of Pojan and other neighbouring villages in Albania. Since the 1920s, large numbers of Vlachs have emigrated to Germany, Australia, America and Canada where today their émigré groups preserve their culture through folk tales and Vlach songs. These organizations provide a valuable forum for Vlachs throughout the world to communicate and encourage debate on their culture and history. For those who remain in the Balkans, maintaining a true Vlach identity is increasingly difficult.[12] In Albania, the post–Second World War process of agricultural collectivization destroyed traditional patterns of nomadic pastoral life, forcing many Vlachs to find work in the country's newly established industrial centres. Some fled to Greece to escape Albanian communism. Many Vlachs nowadays speak Albanian with greater fluency than Vlach. In an effort to halt the decline of their language, which under communism never had any official recognition, a Vlach Association was formed in Tirana in 1990. It now has over 15,000 members and today many Vlachs hold important posts. A former Albanian ambassador to London, Pavli Qesku, is of Vlach descent.

There are several Vlach villages in the region of Bitola, but today these have a fraction of their pre-war population following large-scale emigration to Australia and Canada. During the 1970s greater mobility caused further break-ups of extended Vlach families, as many more young people moved to the cities of Prilep, Bitola and Skopje, where today, high in the concrete tower blocks, it is possible to hear mothers shouting to their children in Vlach. As young Vlachs settle in the larger towns and cities of the Balkans, they hear wildly confusing stories about their origins, although most families retain their old houses and use them as summer retreats. The widely repeated Greek version claims that Vlachs are descended from Greek women who married Roman soldiers. This theory seems improbable because the children would surely have learned their Vlach mother tongue from their mother's laps and not from their often absent soldiering fathers. Many Albanians believe Vlachs are descended from Thracians who lived alongside them during Illyrian times. The Romanians are convinced that Vlachs are of pure Romanian ethnicity, having somehow found themselves cut off from the main body of their kinsmen south of the Danube. Scholars are as yet unable to determine what exact connection the Vlachs had with their supposed Roman ancestry and when, if ever, Vlachs became distinct from Romanians.[13]

The development of a purely Vlach national consciousness has been greatly hindered by the fact that Vlachs were historically taught to use the alphabet of the country in which they lived.[14] Thus Vlachs living in Greece use the Greek alphabet, those in Albania and Romania the Latin alphabet, while Macedonian Vlachs use the Cyrilic script. According to a British scholar of the Vlachs, Tom Winnifrith, there is considerable controversy over the choice of developing a distinct Vlach alphabet noting:

> At every Vlach conference there are arguments about the alphabet. The Vlachs are only just beginning to organize themselves but already they have split into three groups with one in favor of the Greek alphabet, another for using the standard Romanian alphabet, and a third advocating a Latin script using diacritical signs to denote unique Vlach sounds.[15]

For the present time, the Vlachs remain a people divided not only by frontiers but also by internal dissent. Despite the energetic efforts of the various émigré and Balkan Vlach associations to preserve their language and customs, there is much uncertainty surrounding the long-term future of the Vlachs. Greek school life continues to erode Vlach speech and migration to the towns in search of permanent jobs has meant a decline in the annual spring trek back to highland pastures.

Further south in the Pindus villages, many young Vlachs are barely conscious of being Vlach, identifying themselves instead as Greek. In the remote villages of Greek Prespa, however, the Vlachs live a marginal, pastoral existence on the very edge of contemporary Greek society. Here some elements of their traditional culture and way of life still continue, but without transhumance, and the Vlach dominance of the increasingly prosperous and valuable bean harvest has brought more economic stability and money into these villages. With no particularly strong religious identity linked to a national agenda, traditional pagan beliefs have been superseded by often devout Orthodox Christianity. A few shepherds still wear the characteristic heavily woven goat's-hair capes, which were much prized as trading items. Many elderly women have a black cross tattooed on their forehead to ward off the evil eye and tell stories of witches and curses to the young. With their parents working long hours and often away from their villages, children are brought up by grandparents from whom they learn Vlach customs and the language with its distinctive hissing sounds, which has earned them the name 'Tsintsars', by which they are known throughout the Balkans.

In springtime, hillsides along the Greek-Albanian border echo with sheep bells as flocks come up from the plains. Until very recently a Vlach shepherd ran a large herd of goats on the hills around Psarades. The returning Vlachs create a buzz of activity in their isolated villages, which nowadays are only inhabited during the long winter by a few elderly people. Rugs and blankets are unpacked, wood is chopped, ovens are lit, and produce and gifts are exchanged. Mid-summer weddings are planned. In the evenings, homes smell of the Vlachs' favourite dish – *pitau* – layers of thin pastry soaked in butter and filled with leeks, baked in an iron dish and served with dark-red wine. For centuries Vlachs spent the summer months wandering with their animals through the forested hillsides then retiring to lowland areas when the snow comes in November.

Few parts of Greece are so little known by many Greeks as Prespa with its many depopulated villages becoming wild and empty as its young people leave in search of work. The population density is the lowest of any part of Greece. This has led to an increase in wolves that are hunted by fewer shepherds and at night can be heard howling near the villages. Their evocative sound reinforces the sense of remoteness in this area so far removed from Athens and mainstream Greece. The route from Florina to the village of Psarades passes through vast forests and then bean fields around the shores of Lesser Prespa and along the tortuously narrow road winding ever higher into mountains before descending down to Psarades. As the last village in Greece, within walking distance from the three neighbouring borders, Psarades encapsulates all the historic, geographic, ethnographic, ecological and political elements that characterize the entire Prespa region.

Throughout the twentieth century until the Civil War the village population was around 600 but the 2011 census recorded just eighty-three inhabitants. Historically, the village was called by its Bulgarian name of *Neverska*, which became *Nivitsa* in the late nineteenth century. It was renamed Psarades by Athens in 1926, along with many other villages in the region. Until 1982 it was very difficult to reach the village as it lay within the Greek army-controlled security zone that reached as far as 'Wolf's Pass', five miles to the south. For many years a special military permit was required. The only road to the village through the dense mountain forests was a rocky track which was eventually asphalted by 1978. Psarades has many ancient stone and oak beam houses with roofs of straw or stone tiles built in the classic Macedonian style with overhanging balconies and livestock mangers below. Like almost all Greek Prespa villages, many houses have long been abandoned and are in severe decay due to war and depopulation but some, particularly those near the Lake side, have recently been restored in the traditional style. On the outskirts a few prosperous looking houses were built during the 1930s by retiring returnees from America. Psarades has an imposing church built in 1893 with funds from a Russian diplomat who enjoyed visiting the village to hunt wildfowl.

Until 1989 there was a military free-fire zone across the Great Prespa, which forced the Albanian and Macedonian fishermen to stay inside their own sector of the waters. With the collapse of communism in Albania in 1991, Albanians from the villages along the Albanian Lake shore began to cross the Lake at night to steal the high-quality monofilament Greek fishing nets. In response, the Greek authorities established a special police patrol unit to monitor the lake. At the same time, Albanian illegal migrants began to wander through the forests surrounding Psarades on their way south in search of work. The villagers took to releasing their fierce wolf-like dogs at night to scare off the migrants. During this turbulent time, against the backdrop of the Yugoslav wars, there was heightened tension in this sensitive border region. In order to emphasize the Greek identity of the area, in 2002 a hastily erected monument, placed in the centre of Psarades village square, stated that 'Macedonia was and always will be Greek.' Nowadays, with somewhat better ethnic relations, a few Albanians work and live in Psarades as builders and shepherds, along with Vlach families who have established small shops.

Over the past twenty years Psarades has become a destination for birdwatchers, with the development of lakeside tavernas serving carp and *belvitsa*, fresh lake fish, or sell them dried, *tsironka*. The majority of visitors are Greek coach parties, many organized by the Church. There is basic accommodation in the few small pensions that have recently opened yet foreign tourist numbers rarely exceed thirty at any one time during the summer months. The annual village *panigiri*, or saint's day, is in mid-August when the village's Diaspora relatives arrive for the major annual event, mostly from Australia and Canada to visit their ancestor's graves. The *panigiri* is a lively occasion with much eating, drinking and dancing in Psarades square and the renewing of old acquaintances. Every year, however, fewer Diaspora arrive as the younger member's ties with the 'Old Country' weaken, but numbers of Macedonians who live in other parts of Greece are returning for the church service and in the evening the big street party in front of the war memorial.

As regional military tensions and the threat of marauding Albanians have receded, a new threat for the future of the village has emerged. As a result of an earthquake, an underground fissure exists in the bed of Great Prespa, adding to the problems caused by climate change. The Lake is now receding at the rate of around 2 feet a year. A decade ago the water covered the meadow at the edge of Psarades where today cattle and goats graze. Opposite this meadow lie the crumbling walls of the village's traditional vegetable plots. Now that the Lake has shrunk, the people have abandoned their old allotments for narrow, more fertile strips of land on the drained marshland reclaimed by the receding water. This is the only real benefit of the receding Lake water. Without the appealing view of the waterside, many of the tavernas no longer attract customers.

This book is not only about the people, history and environment of the Prespa region but also about real and invisible borders and the acceptability of those borders to those living around them. The national borders of north-western Greece, Albania and Macedonia, alongside many in the Balkans, have never coincided with the cultural and ethnic borders between the populations living alongside them. This corner of South-eastern Europe has always been a politically sensitive region. Although the three states cooperate in the management of the area's ecology and tourism, the state borders remain rigidly enforced. Aside from the main national border cross-points which are not part of the Prespa Lakes region, there is no border-crossing point at all within the National Park area.

Ever since the Second World War Prespa's borders had been sensitive military areas, closely sealed and guarded. The local population became separated from their traditional markets and grazing lands with families left divided and dispersed through forced eviction. It was hoped that the creation in 2000 of a Trans-National Prespa Park would result in the cooperation of the three border countries to promote not only an ecological sustainable environment but also a reconciliation of all the communities bordering the Lakes. It remains to be seen if this will be the case in the current climate of political tensions in the southern Balkans and around the eastern Mediterranean generally, together with the return of traditional border controls as a result of the Covid-19 pandemic. The Macedonian dilemmas remain, as they always have.

2

The Prespa Lake communities

From prehistory to the Ottoman conquest

Part One

Prespa and ancient empires

The Ohrid and Prespa Lake shores have been inhabited since the first human settlement in the Balkans and as part of the landscape of Macedonia have been subject to environmental change in all historical periods.[1] In prehistory, the hunting and gathering culture of the Neolithic and Bronze Age world was based on the rich fish and avian life of the lakes and the vast surrounding marshlands with plentiful game and timber resources in the deciduous forests. The Prespa Lake region has always had the quality of a wilderness, an Arcadia, simultaneously – as Simon Schama has written of Arcadian visions: *a place of bucolic leisure but also of primitive panic, a place without law, government or a state*.[2] This wilderness material world in antiquity was ideal then – as now – for an economy and society based primarily on foraging, and fishing from the lakes, and organized agriculture was probably slow to develop.[3] As George Thompson has written, in the very earliest societies, agriculture, which had spread to the Balkans from the Middle East in Neolithic times, was predominantly a woman's task, like spinning. This was linked to the survival of matriarchy and cultural conservatism.[4] This ultra-conservative world continued around Prespa and Ohrid lake wildernesses through the times of the Illyrian tribal societies into classical antiquity and Byzantium. An urban settlement known today by Macedonian archaeologists as *Lynk* developed on the site of modern Bitola before the Roman conquest in 168 BC.[5] After this, large-scale agriculture first began on the open plains to the north-east of Prespa in and around what became the city of *Heraclea Lyncestis*, a few miles south of the modern city. This was based predominantly on the labour of slaves.[6]

Much of the Prespa and adjacent regions in antiquity nevertheless remained a *terra incognita*, without defined property rights other than field grazing conventions.[7] The question of agricultural property rights was an obsessive concern of the Roman ruling elite throughout both the Republican and Imperial period, as illustrated by the writings of Cicero on the subject.[8] The exact development of landownership on the fertile plain east of *Heraclea* and south to the Prespa Lakes is unknown, but there can be little doubt that the original smallholdings developed for Roman army veterans and colonists on the republican model after the Roman conquest coalesced into much larger estates as time went on.[9] The large agricultural estates were surrounded by an ill-defined mountainous forested wilderness and marshland. South-west Macedonia today remains the most densely forested part of the region, with the remote Pelister Mountain and Mavrovo region and regional forests a barrier to travel and commerce until very recent years. The Romans built the Via Egnetia across the region linking the Adriatic and Constantinople, but not far away from it the landscape remained impassable wilderness and that remained the case until the modern period. In Greek Macedonia, the first asphalt road linking the Prespa villages with the town of Florina/*Lerin* was not constructed until 1978. To the north of the lakes, modern roads were first built under Yugoslav communism after 1955.

The wild mountainous landscape although apparently unchanging and outside time with lakes stretching to the vast horizons has undergone many changes since human settlement began. The Prespa Lakes were long believed to be much larger and deeper than they are today but recent archaeological research by Professor Vera Grazdenova-Bitrakova and her team in Skopje has revealed this was not the case, and their aquatic dimensions have varied considerably over the centuries, and these environmental changes have determined the possibilities of human settlement.[10] There was always limited fertile land around them and only a small population could be supported. The earliest human inhabitants would have been able to grow food grains along the lake margins but lived mainly from the waters and the forests.[11] Recent geomorphologic and archaeological research has now conclusively demonstrated that in the Early Neolithic period, the two modern Prespa Lakes were probably then one and formed a single vast mass of water, an inland sea which submerged most of the surrounding present-day arable land and marshes.[12] Human life would only have been possible high on what are now the slopes of the Galicia and Thate Mountains that now overlook the Lakes.[13]

The entire Prespa Basin and the contemporary Resen Plain stretching to modern Bitola/*Manastir* were then under water or deep marshland. There are no sites showing human habitation from the Middle Neolithic, when the warming climate encouraged the lake water levels to rise even higher than in the earlier epoch. Settled communities around the lakes are thought to date from about 4500 BC, when agriculture spread southwards to the southern Balkans. The substantial island of Golem Grad on the west side of Great Prespa Lake offered a relatively secure prospect for life and the earliest discoveries showing human occupation date from there. The coastlines of the lakes rose far up the Galicica mountain slopes, as maximum climate temperatures were reached. Only settlements built over the water were possible near the shores, the so-called *Palafites*, wooden houses built on poles above marshland that have been found on Lake Kastoria and elsewhere in the southern Balkan lakes, and recently near modern Nakolets village on the north-east side of Lake Great Prespa.

In the Late Bronze Age the waters retreated rapidly, a development which may have been caused, like recent water losses, by earthquakes opening up new fissures in the Prespa Lake bed and causing more water to flow through the underground channels into the Ohrid Basin. These channels have been studied in the twentieth century and form the basis of the lakes interconnections up to the present day, although Ohrid also has its own primary water source in the hundreds of tiny underground springs on the south side of the lake near Sveti Naum monastery. In 2005 the ancient site of *Asamati* was explored by RM archaeologists, near modern Asamati village on the eastern shore of Great Prespa, which revealed a group of prehistoric houses dating from the Late Bronze Age in a compact space.[14] Ceramic evidence shows several small settlements in the region of the shore that were connected by trade to Kastoria, in Greece, rather than later material which indicates links with Ohrid cultures of the Aegean Bronze Age. Strong late Mycenaean influences are present in the next period to the south of Prespa but are not found in Prespa itself, and the region remained a stronghold of Illyrian tribal cultural conservatism throughout the Iron Age.

The Illyrian tribal region known as *Paeonia* to the north-east of the lakes was on the northernmost fringe of the Greek consciousness in the Homeric period, with a single Paeonian – origin individual mentioned in Homer, Pyraechmes in Book Two of *The Iliad* – who fought with the Trojans and was killed in battle by Patroclus. Significantly, as Hammond points out, a later commentator noted his father was called *Axius*, the name for the ancient Greek *Axios* river, now the modern River Vardar flowing north-south to meet the sea near Thessaloniki/*Solun*. Upper (northern) Prespa was then on the borderland between the Dassaretes tribes while Lower (southern) Prespa was part of the Orestis grouping.[15] In this period the lake waters continued to recede steadily, which also resulted in an increase of fertile land around Lake Maliqi, to the south-west of the Prespa complex near Korca/*Koritsa* (finally drained fully under Albanian communism). In this period, Lesser Prespa Lake also had a western outflow, a small river which flowed westwards through the Tren gorge on the RM border into Albania to feed into what is now the River Devoll and was also linked to Lake Maliqi, near modern Korca/*Koritsa*. The Tren gorge itself has extensive evidence of very early human settlement, mainly cave paintings, although their dating has been subject of recent academic debate.[16] It is unclear when this little river finally dried up, and Lesser Prespa Lake came to be what it is today. The existence of this prehistoric river with the now lost link to the Adriatic Sea through the River Devoll may account for the unique fish life in the modern Prespa Lakes.

Archaeological discoveries on the north side of the lake at Plocite and elsewhere indicate a considerable development of settlements in the period between the third and first centuries BC, with a marked drop in the level of the lake waters and an increase in human population.[17] The area also began its long engagement with outside empires, firstly with the Kingdom of Macedon and then with the struggles of the Romans against the Illyrian tribes. Prespa region had been very important in the military campaigns of Alexander the Great, when Macedon was expanding to the west and into the Illyrian tribal regions.[18] In 424 BC a combined force of Spartans and Macedonians was defeated by the Illyrians in the Battle of *Lychnidos*. The water level was then substantially lower than it is today, with surrounding reedbeds dominating the landscape. The society that the Roman legions would have found when they arrived in the region after 168 BC would have been of a long series of very small fishing and hunting villages built of wood with often tiny strips of cultivable land along the lake margins on the edge of vast marshlands and swamps. The caves above the lakes that are now the sites of Byzantine and Post-Byzantine churches would have been likely to be the sites of local cults, as throughout the Illyrian world.¹⁹ The social structure of these communities would have been based on the conventions of Illyrian tribal life in wider Pelagonia. With the isolation and conservatism of the Prespa wilderness lands, older tribal peoples who had always lived there gradually began to be integrated into the Illyrian tribal identity that was forming in the later Iron Age.²⁰

The landscape itself was changing rapidly in this period. The lake levels continued to fall very quickly into Roman times, as shown by work on the Roman villa remains in Pretor village, and submerged lakeside buildings at Krani, very near the current Greek border north of Agios Germanos (*German*). This drop in the water level produced more arable land, particularly in the more northern lake littorals, and permitted a rise in population. Roman sites here were revealed by recent drops in the lake water level after centuries of obscurity in the lake bed. It is possible several smaller lakes existed in Roman antiquity rather than the two lakes of Great Prespa and Lesser Prespa we see today, a memory which is also preserved in Macedonian oral tradition and in folksongs. A paved Roman road has been found near the shore village of Erezeni well below the modern lake waters, demonstrating the low level around 250 AD in the Roman period, much lower than the shoreline today. Systematic economic exploitation of the fish resources was developed by the Romans, as carp were introduced to lakes in the southern Balkans, starting from the Danube Basin in the first century AD. The carp has remained a mainstay of the Prespa region food supply and local trade potential for the lake dwellers ever since, and a product (given it can survive in fish tanks or wrapped in wet reeds for quite long periods while transported) that could be exported to nearby urban communities, bringing the lake dwellers into the Roman monetary economy.²¹

The time when the Lakes began to rise again and assume their present form and size and depth is described by archaeologists as 'the great enigma' of this early history. The tenth-century Christian structures built by the Tsar Samuil on the island of St Achilleos in Lesser Prespa Lake would suggest a lake level then somewhat above the present twenty-first-century levels of the lake.²² The water level we see today may have been achieved by the early Middle Ages, and probably dates from around the twelfth century AD, shown by the establishment of modern villages like Agios Germanos (*German*), named after a Byzantine saint. It is noteworthy, though, that the Byzantine and medieval remains of these villages and the surviving buildings are nearly all 'upper villages' at the top of stream valleys well above current lakeside settlements. Thus Agios Germanos has become the 'upper village' in Ottoman and post-Ottoman times above the small and much later Ottoman-era lakeside settlement of Laimos that is below it and merges with it.

An early minor Roman road probably built about 100 AD runs south from the Via Egnetia along the east side of Great Prespa, crossing the modern Greek border near Agios Germanos.²³ After the foundation of the second Yugoslavia in 1944, a small border crossing with Greece on the modern road was opened here that was closed down in 1967. The ancient and the modern road routes were in essence the same, and ran down the side of Lesser Prespa Lake before turning inland towards the modern Greek and predominantly Vlach village of Pisoderi and then on to Florina, medieval *Fioerintina*, Bulgarian/Macedonian *Lerin*. Little is known of Florina/*Lerin* in either classical or Byzantine times other than it was the site of the *Fortress of Chierenon*, which is mentioned by Byzantine chroniclers. Florina has in all epochs been in essence a garrison town.

In the wider Macedonian context, on the much more densely populated hills to the north of the lakes and the foothills of the Pelister Mountains west of modern Bitola, the agricultural economy was dominated by transhumance pastoralism, as illustrated in Herodotus's tale of the origins of the Macedonian kingdom in very early times.[24] Here, on the uplands, animal husbandry of horses, sheep and goats were the main activities, as they still are in many places today, although as elsewhere in the Balkans nowadays, traditional pastoralism with its rich folk and musical culture is threatened by EU-origin subsidized meat imports.[25] The rich plains around modern Bitola, originally the Roman town of *Heraclea Lyncestis*, became important centres of grain and cereal cultivation under the Romans, and it is likely the men and women of the Prespa Lakes and forests worked in seasonal labour gangs both as free labourers and as slaves as part of the very difficult annual task of reaping the harvest and gathering in the grain that dominated the annual economic cycle on the plains.[26]

In the early period of ancient Greek colonization of the Balkans energies had been focussed on the maritime coasts, and (unless they had important mineral resources) internal regions such as Prespa and Ohrid were very much left to themselves, with their difficult land communications, limited fertile land and severe winter weather. In Pseudo-Scylax's *Periplus*, or Coastal Passage, written around the mid-forth century BC, there is a quite well-informed picture of the Balkan Adriatic coastline but no sense of the author having any knowledge or interest in the interior. In contrast, the Romans brought major advances to the southern Balkans interior, focussed on road and bridge construction but perhaps most clearly symbolized in Prespa by the introduction of the carp in the lakes, and organized bean cultivation around the lake margins, a crop that has remained central to the Prespa rural economy in all historical periods ever since.[27] There can be little doubt that the modern ex-Yugoslav state farms with thousands of acres devoted to bean and fruit growing were originally Ottoman *cifliks* and before that farms developed on Byzantine and Roman estates, although there is little in the way of sources to inform historians of the exact developments.

Modern Greek historiography has continued to shape the general narrative of regional history in Western universities, so that right up to the end of the Cold War, old concepts based on an almost binary opposition between Greek urban civilization spreading into the 'tribal' interior from the coasts and southern cities have predominated, often written with little regard for who has actually inhabited the Prespa regions in different historical periods. The periodization of Prespa history and also Ohrid in school and university textbooks has been dominated by notions of a Byzantine civilization of a fairly fixed nature that was crushed by the Ottoman conquest. The tendency towards this distortion has been accentuated by the post-Civil War historiography in Greece emphasizing the Slavophone people north of the modern border as dangerous 'Others' bent on destabilizing or communizing Greece.[28] Remote regions like Prespa were and to some extent still are seen as without significant history between the end of the Roman Empire in the Balkans and the construction of the churches and monasteries by Tsar Samuil in the period of his Bulgarian Empire, which were subsequently absorbed into 'Greek' Byzantium and in some guidebooks are not referred to as of Bulgarian origin at all.

In reality the entry of the Prespa region into classical antiquity is essentially a product of the growth of the Kingdom of Macedon, where the lakes lay on the uncertain and difficult to defend borders of ancient Pelagonia. Recent archaeology has shown that in the Neolithic period Macedonia was quite heavily populated, with villages every few miles over the entire region, but climate change in the late Neolithic and early Bronze Ages sent this society into very rapid decline. Archaic *Scupi* on the site of modern Skopje was a major centre from very early antiquity, its importance resting on the regional control exercised from its hilltop *Kale*, a massive fortress controlling the *Axios* river valley that dominated the transport route north into what is now modern Kosovo where mining at Trepca and Novo Berde/*Artana* and elsewhere was beginning.[29] With settlement concentrated in Upper Prespa, south of modern Resen, the inhabitants were under the domination of the Dassaretes tribal confederation before being fully integrated into the Macedonian kingdom.[30] Stability of a kind only ensued after the Roman conquest of the Balkans after 168 BC but not immediately. The history of Ohrid and Prespa became closely involved with the struggles of the Romans to either placate or suppress the Illyrian inhabitants. It was not until 9 AD with Tiberius's great victory over the Pannonian Illyrian tribes who still held sway in the central and northern Balkans that the southern regions could become fully integrated into the Roman world, and peace of a kind prevailed for nearly 300 years. It was, as the nineteenth-century German historian Theodore Mommsen observed, '*a small war but one with great consequences*'.[31] After this battle the Illyrians never again seriously threatened the *Pax Romana*. *Salona*/Split on the Adriatic coast became a focus of Adriatic Roman rule and economic life. In the interior change was slow. As elsewhere the overwhelming majority of the population remained in villages.

In the post-Neolithic communities, as in ancient Thrace, in Macedonia the sheep was the key farm animal. The animals provided milk and meat, and wool for weaving clothes, the latter important in the often harsh Macedonian winter. Sheep (and goats) could cope with the winter months much better than cattle or pigs. Prespa lay not far from the economically central Via Egnetia linking *Dyracchium*, modern Durres on the Adriatic with *Constantinople*, modern Istanbul. The Via Egnetia was the first Roman road built in the Balkans and became a main artery of the Roman world linking Italy with Constantinople and what became the eastern provinces of the Empire. The cities that grew up along it soon developed their own regional trade and economic patterns. *Heraclea Lyncestis*, later Ottoman *Manastir* and modern Bitola, was then the nearest important city to Prespa and established a cultural ascendancy in this part of Macedonia that remained until the border and political changes in the early twentieth century.

The Prespa mountain forests and lake villages nevertheless remained in considerable isolation in what was seen by the Roman colonists as a vast and sinister wilderness, the home of dangerous wild animals, which in those days included not only the modern fauna – wild boar, lynx, poisonous snakes, wolves and brown bears – but also lions, panthers and aurochs. The late antique Roman mosaic pavements at ancient *Heraclea* show a world of a hunting-fixated aristocracy continuing into the early Christian era.[32]

The growth of large agricultural estates on the uplands around *Heraclea Lyncestis* also demanded, as Banarji has pointed out, in the context of Roman Egypt, 'stable working communities', and finding and consolidating this workforce – enslaved or free – was a major challenge in a society dominated by nomadic pastoralism and hunter-gathering of wild animals and forest crops.

Vast and probably largely uninhabited forests remained to the north of the lakes, in what are now the Pelister Mountains and to the south-west in Lower Prespa in what is now Greek Macedonia. This view of the region as a hard wilderness is echoed much later in the writings of eleventh-century Byzantine clerical luminary Theophlyact of Ohrid, who saw himself exiled by the emperor in Constantinople into a primitive Bulgarian-dominated semi-wasteland.[33] In the early centuries, before the Via Egnetia was constructed there was little in the way of roads except ancient forest tracks that were often impassable in the winter, and this remained the case until after the Second World War. The mountain forests were also an ideal place of refuge for outlaws, bandits and escaped slaves in all historical periods. Macedonian lions were popular in Roman circuses and gladiatorial contests, some no doubt hunted down in the Prespa and Ohrid forests, and there were many Macedonian gladiators. All local Prespa transport of heavy goods would have been by water on the lakes, with wood, a monopoly that had been held by the Macedonian kings, as the main export under the Romans, linking to the Via Egnetia. Pickled and dried fish were also an important source of income for the lake regions. The forest people were a source of slaves for the estates of the Macedonian aristocracy, as they continued to be under the Romans.

It is unclear how these Lower Prespa border regions were ever fully subdued by the Macedonian rulers in Pella and Vergina, and written sources for the mechanisms of many aspects of Balkan life in antiquity are lacking, unlike the relative wealth of information for Roman Egypt and North Africa. Outside the few towns, the rural population's lives were dominated by timeless agricultural customs, with the farm year starting in the autumn after the setting of the Pleiades stars on 7 November and culminating with the rising of the star Sirius about 20 July. The Prespa and Ohrid regions did not have the important mineral resources of the northern Macedonian ranges in the Sar Mountains on the border of modern Kosova and so did not receive much official attention for that purpose. It is clear that as the classical period faded into late antiquity the rural production systems were breaking down and the coercive power of the imperial state focussed on the garrison towns rapidly declined.

A major event that affected the entire southern Balkan region was the crushing defeat of the Roman forces of Emperor Valens in 378 AD by the Goths in the Battle of Hadrianopolis (modern Edirne in Turkish Thrace). After it Goth incursions rapidly increased over the region.[34] Yet by the fourth century AD the Balkans had been governed from Rome for three hundred years, and many of the material cultural features recognizable in the modern world were established and have remained, such as agricultural irrigation channels, fish farming, land terracing and marsh drainage. But stability was not to last. After the catastrophe for Roman power at Hadrianopolis, the Goths and their Germanic allies went on a long migration through Greece and the southern Balkans and passed back northwards through the Ohrid and Prespa region in about 397 AD. In 441 Attila the Hun and his forces sacked the important

Roman fortress city of Naissus, modern Nish in Serbia, and much of the eastern part of the region was at their mercy. To the west the Byzantines survived longer. As Averil Cameron has written, in the fifth-century Dyracchium, modern Durres was walled, as was Saranda, and modern excavation at Butrint shows the continuation of some civilized Roman urban life. But it was not to last. The Slavs by the late sixth century overran Macedonia and northern Greece and went on to attack Thessalonika.[35] The old order was dying.

As in the contemporary world, Lower Prespa stood on the northern border of Hellenism. In the lands covering roughly what is now the modern Greek state as far north as Thessaly, Greek was universally spoken and Roman colonies planted in cities such as Corinth had long been Hellenized. The Roman agricultural writer Varro and the Byzantine author of the *Geopontika* (*Farmwork*) treatise written in the tenth century provide some insights into the world of rural life at the time, with beans a key crop, as nowadays around Prespa, which the *Geopontika* author notes, 'should always be sown in muddy soil', although he also writes that cultivation near lakes was to be undertaken carefully as the environment was unhealthy. Bean cultivation in antiquity was associated with superstition, and he notes one Amphiakos abstained from eating them as a protest against the practice of divination, *oneiromancy*, associated with beans, foretelling the future from dreams after bean consumption. It is reasonable to assume that the lake caves and often hidden shrines were centres of sorcery and pagan survivals in the developing Christian world.[36] The rural world provided a difficult life, as shown in the poetry of Virgil where the fruits of hard work were always threatened by a difficult climate and endemic diseases, such as *ignus sacer* (probably anthrax), which destroyed both livestock and people. In urban centres like *Heraclea Lyncestis* a different world existed, the world of 'comfort', described by Bryan Ward Perkins where there was production and sale of sophisticated and varied goods and food products, many brought long distances by trade. As the collapse of Rome proceeded, gradually the complexity and comforts of urban life declined and died, and the entire Prespa region reverted to the norms of rural life.[37] In many real senses it has remained in that condition ever since.

To the north of a line which roughly corresponds to the limits of the cultivation of the olive, the Macedonian population was much more culturally and linguistically mixed than south of it and in the west Latin was the main language of the cities. In the east Thracian was spoken in the rural areas and Illyrian in a large area in the west corresponding to modern Albania and nearby borderlands. The Prespa Lakes were on this borderland, as they have been on so many others throughout history, and this background accounts for the current use of Greek, Bulgarian/Macedonian and Vlach and Albanian as living languages in the lakeside communities today. In the third century the region had begun its long security decline, with invading Goths breaking through the imperial defences on the Danube and raiding down into the southern Balkans as far as Athens. They were followed in the next hundred years by other invaders from the north and the east and most importantly by the Visigoths who although failing to take Constantinople remained at large in the Balkans and many settled there, establishing local power centres outside imperial control. The once secure Roman cities in the lakes region like *Heraclea Lyncestis* – even on the major route of the Via Egnetia – saw rapid population and economic decline and a cessation (apart from some Christian church building) of public building activity, with all settlement increasingly concentrated around a fortified acropolis.[38] The time of the fourth century and onwards was also a time of famine and epidemics, and a lack of grain crippled life in the towns. There were five major epidemics in the fourth century, rising to ten in the fifth century and eight in the sixth century. Diphtheria and malaria were probably prevalent in swampy areas like the Prespa Basin. The so-called Justinian Plague of bubonic plague that had spread from Egypt in 541 had started in Constantinople and spread over all Europe reaching Britain and Scandinavia by perhaps 549 left much of the late antique Balkan countryside deserted with serious labour shortages. Recent academic debate stimulated by the Covid pandemic crisis has focussed on how far the epidemic brought a general catastrophe to the region.[39] Climate change was also playing an important part in the historical development. A cold and wet climatic period from about 500 to 900 AD compounded the people's difficulties. This has recently been characterized by historians as 'the Late Antique Little Ice Age', when the years between 530 and 680 saw successive and serious harvest failures.[40] In these difficult circumstances, the churches and shrines around the lake were more than ever a Christian society in microcosm, surrounded by a very uncertain, declining and problematic hinterland.

As Robert Browning observed, it was often difficult for local rural people to choose between loyalty to Constantinople with the imperial scourges of massive tax and manpower demands and the claims of the Goth and Slav 'barbarians', who needed certain types of craftsmen and agriculturalists in their new communities and above all sought fertile land – which could be made available. The real decline of imperial power nevertheless continued and *Heraclea* was destroyed by the Ostrogoths in about 470. Once broken patterns of trade between these cities and their hinterlands would never be restored, and there is every reason to believe the lake areas sunk into decline and obscurity with early Roman Prespa settlements like Pretor and the large villa site near modern Krani quickly abandoned. Traditions of servitude established under the Empire did not disappear, the world described by Peter Brown as one where 'poor farmers who could not emigrate did what little they could do: they handed themselves over to the rich in return for protection'.[41] The result of this transition from formal slavery to peasant serfdom has plagued the region ever since, with modern Balkan clientism and mafiadom traceable in origin to ancient and medieval landholding and employment practices.[42]

Little would have changed in the autarchic world of the villages and rural areas in the forests around the lakes with the onset of the Slav invasions in the sixth century, but the appearance of numerous Slav origin place names many of which survive today does indicate comprehensive Slav settlement of the Ohrid-Prespa region generally. Slavonic agriculture was essentially simple, focussed on grazing on common land and shifting patches of cultivation in cleared forests. A centre known by Slavicists as *Berzitia* developed around what is now modern Devoll in the Korca/*Koritsa* region of Albania to the south-west of Lesser Prespa Lake. Little is known for certain about the reception of these new peoples, but the *Berzitia* tribes came under the suzerainty of Bulgaria in about 864. The traditional model of explanation is long obsolete where the Slavs were seen as 'barbarian' enemies laying waste a functional urban civilization, and it is likely some Slav tribes may have settled fairly peacefully and built their villages on areas of what had become a very depopulated countryside. In what is now modern 'old' Greece the agricultural economy was surviving better than in the Macedonian north, with a continuing demand for exports of oil and wine, and on a common-sense basis it is reasonable to assume the Prespa salted and dried fish trade would have continued at a low level but severely restricted by the decline in urban markets and the often dangerous and uncertain road transport capacity as disorder and banditry plagued the Via Egnetia.

Slav settlement accelerated in the later sixth century after 548 when the northern invaders devastated the western Byzantine lands as far away as *Dyracchium* (modern Durres) on the Adriatic, and in 559 Macedonia was thoroughly laid waste. By the end of that century, Slavs were settling in the Balkans in very large numbers, and Latin speakers, the antecedents of the modern Vlachs and also remaining Illyrian tribes in remote regions in what is now Albania and speaking proto-Albanian had taken to the mountains as refugees from conquest.[43] There can be little doubt that majority Vlach villages near Prespa like Pili at Prespa and Pisoderi on the road south-east to Florina/*Lerin* owe their origins to this period. Some scholars, principally Nicholas Hammond, have identified modern (majority Vlach) Pisoderi as originally a Roman way station, *Pisodendron*, on the now largely defunct mountain link road from Prespa that ran around Mount Vitsi to the Via Egnetia. The settlement was later occupied by these Vlach pastoralists with their Latin-derived language who were undergoing a modicum of urbanization. Many of the early Slav names that survive today, like *Pushtec* on the Albanian shore of Great Prespa, and *Neverska/Nivica*, modern Psarades and many other villages in Lower Prespa in Greece originated in that period. The etymology of *Nivica* probably derives from the Slavonic term for the species of sardine found in the Prespa Lakes.[44] There were also many more Slavonic place names in Lower Prespa on the Greek side of the modern border until the Greek name-changing enforced after the new Yugoslavia came into being, with 1926 a high point for this Athens government imposition on these communities. This process came to an eventual conclusion during and after the Greek Civil War (1943–49) and its aftermath in the 1950s.

Part two

The Bulgarian Empire in the Prespa region

Byzantine rule over remote areas such as Prespa had always been uncertain and largely nominal, with the decline in security along the Via Egnetia a key factor in economic decline. The Slav tribes lived in small units, but the needs of trade brought the Slavs into contact with the Greek-speaking – if declining – towns to the south and south-west, and Greek merchants traded with the Slav rural settlements.[45] Christianization first took place in the Greek language and a small semi-aristocracy was forming in the Slav world which welcomed many aspects of Hellenization, but in Macedonia, far fewer urban centres remained functional than in the Peloponnese and the south, and the Vardar/*Axios* river valley was dominated by Slav tribes who were pagan and whose main occupation was piracy and raiding. In the second half of the ninth-century Ohrid grew rapidly as a clerical centre, under the church leadership of St Clement and St Naum, and became central to the foundation and spread of Panslavonic Christianity. This growth must have augmented the limited religious life of the Prespa hermitages around the lake. Naum died in 910, and Clement died in 916.[46] In the more northern Balkans including much of the Prespa regions, the coalescence of the Slavs with the expanding Bulgarians who had become Christian was leading to a new political reality where the Bulgarian Empire offered a separate focus to Byzantium.[47] Reviving Byzantium was making incursions westwards into the eastern regions of Bulgarian control and as a result the importance of the western Bulgarian Empire increased.[48]

In the aftermath of the disastrous Russian invasion of Bulgaria and the destruction of Preslav in 972, the western part of the Bulgarian Empire although depopulated and devastated fell under Byzantine control.[49] In the west Samuil, an emerging *boyar*, successfully led a revolt against the Byzantines and for a time made Prespa his centre of government, and a 'town' grew up although it would have been nothing to compare with what Preslav had once been.[50] The church of Saint Achilleos on the island in Lesser Prespa Lake was built then by Samuil, along with some other churches and monastic retreats. There were close links with the Bulgarian clerical and secular settlements in Ohrid and *Vodena* (modern Edessa). The symbolic significance of these events and buildings cannot be overestimated, not only for the immediate Prespa region but for all Macedonia. As Fine has pointed out, the new Patriarchate which Samuil established in Ohrid provided linear continuity between the world of the First Bulgarian Empire based on Preslav and the developing Bulgarian church in the region, and this see was to remain until the Ottoman Sultan abolished the Archbishopric of Ohrid in 1767. The relics of the saint Achilleos had been transferred from Larissa to Prespa after Samuil had conquered Larissa in 986.[51]

The Prespa Lake region had always lain roughly along the line of the northern Mediterranean world, the boundary of practical olive cultivation lying a little way to the south, but now it became the practical boundary and border of Bulgarian influence in what eventually was to become, centuries later, late-modern northern Greece.[52] The modern national identities obviously did not exist then but the human geographic, ethnic, and linguistic and ideological factors that have formed them were coming into place, a further illustration of the seminal role of late antiquity and Byzantium in later political issues and military conflicts.[53] Modern historiography and diplomacy has seen the ideology of the New Macedonian Question as based upon irreconcilable differences about the time of Alexander the Great and classical and Hellenistic civilization but the role of late antiquity and Byzantium in forming distinct modern identities has been unjustly neglected. If Samuil's world at Prespa was small and provincial compared to that of Constantinople, it was nevertheless Christian and Bulgarian in what is now northern Greece and would always represent a challenge to the preferred Greek narrative of a largely uninterrupted transition from classical antiquity to Greek Byzantium, a 'good Christian world' based on Greek cultural hegemony that continued in late Byzantium and was destroyed by the Ottoman conquest.

Illustration 3 Agios Achilleos Island in Lesser Prespa Lake.

The prosperity of Bulgarian Prespa did not last long. As Steven Runciman has written: '*In 1003 Basil struck in Macedonia.*' The emperor focussed then on the Ohrid and Prespa regions in his struggle to rid Byzantium of the Bulgarian threat and by 1019 the struggle was over.[54] When the Byzantines quelled the rebellion of the Bulgarian Tsar George Voitech in 1073, their German and Norman mercenaries destroyed Samuil's palace at Prespa and burnt down the town – if that is the correct word for what must have been mostly widely small scattered settlements around the lakes. Food shortages continued to dominate life in the region, in Ohrid a hundred years later in 1103 when Theophylact was the bishop there he hesitated to hold a church synod at Prespa as he was not sure whether there was sufficient food for the local clergy attending.[55] The major monastic settlements here and at Prespa did nevertheless set a kind of frontier. To the west, the influence of the archbishopric of Ohrid has been central to Christian identity under Bulgarian and then Byzantine rule, and then in all succeeding historical periods before its abolition by the Ottoman Turks in 1767.

Some writers have speculated that Samuil may have been in Prespa when he died in 1014, and the tombs discovered on the island in Lesser Prespa in 1995 were certainly of important individuals from the Comitopoulos family who were closely associated with Samuil. The Byzantine historian Skylites records that after a mopping up operation against Samuil's successors the Byzantine emperor visited Prespa and built a fortress by the lake. The location of this fortress is unknown, but it is possible it may be the *kale* ruined hill fortress dating from Byzantium near modern Kallithea village on Great Prespa Lake eastern littoral. In 1072 the last remains of Samuil's buildings were looted and Prespa once more disappeared into mountainous obscurity to later become a boundary of the Serbian Empire of Stefan Dusan in the middle of the fourteenth century. The culture of the local inhabitants had been and remained very backward, and after the Serbian tsar's victory in the eleventh century the local inhabitants of these regions clearly did not live in a monetary economy, paying their taxes in kind, not coin. The emperor in Constantinople reduced the title of Theophylact's successor to Archbishop, from Patriarch.

The main material inheritance of the earlier Byzantine centuries and the Bulgarian hegemony has been Prespa monasticism and the cave shrines around both lakes, the richest part in what is now in Greek Macedonia on the north-facing shores of Great Prespa Lake. It is likely the cave shrives were visited by pilgrims, particularly important for the Slav population after the collapse of Samuil's rule. Although nothing is known the details of the first coherent human settlement on the modern site of Psarades/*Nivica*, it must have been in connection with the shrines that were developing in the caves a few hundred metres to the west of the village along the south side of Great Prespa Lake. Pilgrims wishing to visit the region would in all probability have followed the forest tracks – only passable in summer – running from the Via Egnetia and associated minor roads or come in by boat, as tourists do today. The relationship between very early Christian monastic and earlier hermetic settlements has been very actively debated in modern academia, but the lack of sources for Ohrid and Prespa has made clear understanding difficult. It is probable pagan cult centres existed around the lakes in late antiquity and these were certainly later augmented by the Slav water deity *German*, centred on modern Agios Germanos village. Local oral tradition embodies views of the cave churches as developing from sites of early Christian refuge against imperial persecution, but no archaeological evidence has yet emerged to prove this thesis.[56] What is certain is the difficulty of reaching them, and the absence, unlike Ohrid, of any institutional framework of religious hospitality to succour the traveller. In the first century AD the Roman historian Tacitus pointed out how inaccessible most of the lands of *Germania* were, so 'in general the country is made terrible by its primeval forests or hateful by its bogs'.[57] This was also the world of much of the Prespa forests until the mid-twentieth century. Travel was on foot for the vast majority of pilgrims along forest tracks where an absolute maximum of 4 miles per hour by a fit young person could be achieved or perhaps twenty miles a day if on horseback in the summer months.[58]

Prespa in the later Middle Ages

In tracing the ancient and medieval outlines of modern borders and conflicts the apparent obscurity of not only the Prespa and Ohrid regions but the entire world of the Byzantine southern Balkans is deceptive. As Edward Luttwak has written the region was of some strategic importance to the medieval Byzantine emperors but not as central to their concerns as the eastern borderlands. This has remained the case up to the modern period and in the main focus of military activity in twentieth-century wars. The central Balkans was also rich by comparison and has remained ever since a centre for the provision of crops and raw materials, timber, sheep meat, fish, salt and other commodities. The dense forests to the south of the lakes were only used as monastic hunting lands, and the first clear source reference to the existence of *Nivica*, modern Psarades, is found in King Stefan Dusan's *gramota* in 1346, where it is described as a hunting forest. The Serbian ruler had undertaken major military campaigns in the Ohrid and Prespa regions in previous years, in 1329 plundering the lake region and attempting but failing in a siege of Ohrid itself.[59] The Serbs prioritized the economic exploitation of the lakes, and in 1334, the *Nivica* fishery and that at modern Nakolets was given by the Byzantines to Stefan and then the rights were passed on to what became the great monastery at Treskavec, north of modern Prilep.[60] At the same time, Christian building increased. A chapel in the cave Church of Askitirion above Lake Great Prespa has an inscription dated 1373 listing the names of monks. The Church of Panaghia Eleousa was built by a local Serbian vassal ruler, Kral Vlasin, reputedly in 1410. An inscription found on Golem Grad Island refers to the same Kral Vlasin building a small church there in 1369. In the same record, seventy fishermen are mentioned as living on the Great Prespa lakeside in Nakolec village.[61] Some of the lake commodities, for example leather, were important for the Byzantine army, as they remained important for the army of the Ottoman conquerors after 1350. The earliest records of Vlach transhumance pastoralism also date from the Byzantine period. The Serbian geographer Jovan Cvijic considered there were two main migration routes of the flocks from the Prespa-Ohrid area, the 'old route' to what is now the Albanian lowlands in the Llaberia region of Albania and the much longer lived route south-east to Thessaly.[62] As the practical power of Constantinople waxed and waned, and the economic and political strength of Venice in the Adriatic grew, Prespa remained a centre of clerical life and monasticism, if only as a place of refuge from the piracy and disorder of much of the Mediterranean littoral and the growing power of the Ottomans, particularly after the first capture of Salonika in 1387 by the forces of Sultan Murad I. After the death of Dusan in 1355, the church on Mali Grad island was endowed, and in 1371 the region came under the rule of Ottoman vassal King Marko until his death in 1395.[63]

It is unclear to what extent, if any, the Prespa region had been affected by adherents of the Bogomil dualist heresy which spread throughout the region in the early medieval period.[64] All oral tradition and many Macedonian songs and poems point to a very strong tradition of folk medicine and herbalism, linked to non-established religious practice, suggesting the Prespa caves were haunts of mystics and healers of various kinds.[65] In his seminal work published in 1949, Dimitri Obolensky suggests that the focus of Bogomils' activity was in what is now central northern Macedonia and that south of the Via Egnetia it had few active adherents. In the absence of new sources, these questions are never likely to be satisfactorily answered, but the strong element of Bulgarian Christianity in the great period of Prespa influence under Samuil – who was in any case a controversial and rebellious figure seen from Constantinople – would have encouraged religious dissidence of a more general kind, and some elements in Bogomilism seem to survive at least in part in the very strong folk traditions embodied in later Bulgarian Orthodoxy.[66] The Balkan countryside in late antiquity and the medieval period was, in Peter Brown's phrase, 'rich with local gods', some thinly disguised local shrines dating from classical or pre-classical antiquity that had undergone several changes of religious identity in later periods. Cults linked to local seers and practices of divination were common, and 'wise women' in particular, who combined fortune telling with medical work, dream interpretation, prophesies of the future and herbalist knowledge. This tradition has continued in Bulgaria, particularly in the Pirin mountains in Bulgarian Macedonia to the present day, to the extent that a 'wise woman' like Granny Vanga in Petrich region became one of the best-known individuals in communist Bulgaria and has subsequently become after her death the central figure in a major new Orthodox cult with hundreds of thousands of followers worldwide, particularly in Russia. Many places are still linked to a particular seer or oracular prophet, such as Rubnik in south-west Bulgaria, near Petrich, the site of Granny Vanga's prophesies and now her booming posthumous cult.

To the west within the Byzantine domains the emergence of the Despotate of Epirus which included *Koritsa* (modern Korca) in its lands meant that for the first time after the fall of Rome, Prespa region was significantly influenced by a power that looked towards the west. In this period any central control of the Via Egnetia had broken down, with different sections of the road held by different powers, the most important central section which included the Prespa region held by the Serbian ruler Stefan Dusan.[67] The main objective of all these rulers was to extract as much tax revenue as possible from passing traders and travellers, and banditry was endemic. The important salt and salted fish trading between the lake basin and *Constantinople* that had continued for centuries must have dwindled in scale in this period as the vicinity of the road had become a region of intermittent violent combat. The tendency, always strong in Balkan societies in all periods of disorder, to return to agricultural and material self-sufficiency in local communities grew, accentuated by the divisions around Prespa and Ohrid into many different ethnic and linguistic groups.

The only substantial *urbs* near Prespa – at least by the standards of the time – was *Manastir*, modern Bitola, with its key strategic position controlling the only pass over the Jaballica mountains westwards into what was then the theme of *Dyracchium* and the road to the Adriatic. Judging by the relatively well-preserved sections of the Via Egnetia that can still be seen today on and near the Quaf e Thanes pass on the Macedonian border with Albania it is possible the road had been maintained and used around here for much longer periods than in some other sections.[68] There are few sources of reliable information available on what medieval *Manastir* was like or how large it was; it was not an important clerical centre, unlike nearby Ohrid, and there is little evidence of new public buildings being constructed in Byzantine times, unlike the rapid growth in *Manastir/Toli* after the Ottoman conquest. The medieval centre had grown up around a river bridge a few miles north of the overgrown ruins of *Heraclea Lyncestis*. Nevertheless, trade continued both north-south through what is now known as the Monastir Gap, the open wide valley in the mountains leading down to modern Florina/*Lerin*, and down towards the Gulf of Corinth, and to the south-west to the large and important Byzantine town that Kastoria/*Kostur* had become. The valley of the Black Drin to the north towards Serbia and Bosnia was also an important trade route – although very slow and insecure compared to Quaf e Thanes and the Shkumbini river valley, eventually reaching Shkodra on the Adriatic via the linked White Drin river valley. A sign of the importance of this route is the surviving massive monastery of St John Bigorski with its large guesthouse where the roads from Ohrid and *Manastir* meet going northwards.

In terms of the effects of the growth of Byzantine society on the immediate Prespa vicinity, remains of primitive roads have been found linking the then tiny villages south of modern Agios Germanos village and running along the hillside well above the present lake levels as far as modern Greek Karies village (*Binovo*), where it divided, one track running down to the lakeside via modern Microlimni (*Ldvik*) to Kranies (*Drenovo*) and through difficult lakeside marshes and forests to the Tren Pass at the end of Lesser Prespa and then down to Korca/*Koritsa* in Albania. The other branch ran eastwards a few miles to the modern village of Antartiko, *Zhelovo*, a centre of Slavonic and Bulgarian life for centuries before its near total destruction by the Greek National Army in the Civil War in 1949 as a reprisal for the pro-communist and pro-Macedonian support there. This and other roads which were only usable outside the winter months such as the track leading east from Agios Germanos between Mount Varnoudas to the north and Mount Vitsi to the south which eventually met the main north-south route between *Manastir* and *Lerin* (modern Florina) indicates a continuing vitality in local trading and pilgrimage throughout the late Byzantine period.

The imposition of Greek language and culture was a primary task for the Church, and it is possible to trace exact correspondences between minor clerical urban centres that were successfully established in Byzantium such as Agios Germanos – and the absence of much Greek culture in the surrounding countryside, which remained firmly and loyally Slavonic and centuries later looked for leadership towards the Bulgarian Exarchate when it was established in the late-nineteenth century. In the main these centres of Greek Orthodox Christianity were on the more valuable lowland lands, while the Bulgarians dominated the mountains in an often uneasy relationship with Vlach pastoralists. The human geography of mid-twentieth-century conflicts is thus based on settlement patterns that originally emerged in late antiquity and Byzantium, and also illustrates the limitations of the modern controversies about the Macedonian identity if conducted exclusively about the ethnicity of Alexander the Great. Although concentrated in northern Greece, these issues of ethnicity and religious identity are not confined there. Almost as far away from the northern border of Greece as is possible to be on the Greek mainland, in the Mani region of the Peloponnese south of Kalamata, above the town of Kardamyli in the high Tayetos Mountains, villages like Saidona and Prastia have local shrines dedicated to Slavonic-origin saints and kings, Samuil in particular, and by no coincidence these villages were a centre of support for the communist-led ELAS (Ellenikos Laikos Apeleftherotikos Stratos) *andartes* and then the Democratic Army in the 1944 to 1949 period. The Hellenic coastal lowlands dominated by olive cultivation (as shown in the writings of Patrick Leigh Fermor and other contemporary authors) were usually a stronghold of the Right, often the Far Right and fascists. Family inheritance is very important for olive growers, given the very long lead times before olives become productive, while pastoralism works to an annual cycle and requires collective labour.

As Evelyne Patlagean observes in 'Un Moyen Age Grec', the family and social structures of medieval Byzantine society evolved from the key period of late antiquity, and it is indisputable that they have remained important ever since. External imperial modernizing forces have at intervals ever since sought to change the nature of southern Balkan society but in the main the old structures of material and daily life have shown remarkable vitality, embodied in the rural world of the Prespa and Ohrid basins today, and many other mountainous/remote Balkan regions where foreign commercial influences are weak.

The Ottoman conquest which began in the fourteenth century was the first attempt to secure the Balkans by organized external imperial military power since the Roman invasions around 168 BC, and Bulgarian expansionism in the eighth and ninth centuries, and it set the scene for the next centuries. Church leaders sought external help to resist but none was forthcoming, despite the heroic Christian stand at the Battle of Kosovo Polje in 1389. The Muslim theocratic empire was ill-equipped to deliver much of what it promised to the inhabitants, particularly those who sought to resist Ottoman pressures for conversion from Christianity. The Ottomans did, however, very quickly restore the settlement patterns and economic focus of the Roman-originated towns, already beginning to prosper in the late medieval period, and in a surprisingly short time, the small settlement on the site of modern Bitola, just north of the ruins of *Heraclea*, became growing Ottoman *Toli*, subsequently the great garrison city of *Manastir* and the administrative centre of a large *vilayet*. It was also not long before the problems of agricultural production, transport and trade to support a growing urban populations that had developed in late antiquity in the vicinity soon reappeared and were accentuated, as in the Byzantine *fis* tax regime, by the draconian and often violent fiscal extortions of the new Ottoman masters. A pattern was set of rebellion and distrust by the majority Macedonian and Vlach rural and mountain populations against the foreign-dominated towns that has continued in different forms ever since. Equally the crisis in secure transport on the roads, such as they were, was acute which as Michael Whitby has pointed out meant

> the Balkans were transformed from a relatively prosperous region, in which the Roman state invested considerably in terms of roads and their accompanying services – bridges, forts, garrisons and administrators – into a no-man's land where even official travellers under escort might be waylaid.[69]

This endemic disorder would need to be transformed by the new Ottoman masters of the region, although it is arguable whether not only they or their Byzantine predecessors or any of the later empires ruling the southern Balkans have succeeded in this objective. Medieval Prespa became and remained a *metochia*, a monastic outpost in a surrounding world of endemic disorder and violence. It did not have the substantial surrounding areas of fertile land around Ohrid which gave rise to large monasteries like St Naum or St John Bigorski based on the Athonite model, and Prespa churches and foundations remained very small, and vulnerable to external disorder.[70] The environmental constraints of the Prespa region were dominant and led to marked cultural conservatism, and only the public works of empire, principally the Roman Via Egnetia, had ever modified that reality. The world of the illiterate peasantry seemed unchanging, with the only source of education and knowledge being the Church and the monasteries where frescos illustrated the lives of the saints to the population. Yet it was soon to be subject to a dramatic transformation, as the Ottoman conquest gained momentum, and the Prespa Lakes, like the rest of the southern Balkans, were soon to be absorbed into a theocratic empire which like Rome in 168 BC was not based on Christianity. It did not take long for the devils, ghosts and demons that haunted the minds of the inhabitants of the ancient and Byzantine forests to be transformed in the minds of the medieval peasants into actual devils, in the form of the often brutal Ottoman soldiery and the incomprehensible religion of rule they wished to impose.

3

The Prespa Lake communities in the Ottoman Empire, 1380–1863

Then through a plain country we came to a great place, well peopled Manastir, or Toli, and pleasantly seated.
– Edward Brown, A Brief Account of Some Travels, London, 1673

Kastoria – where the Byzantine Empire has never ended.
– H. Brailsford, Macedonia – Its Races and Their Future, London, 1906

The early Ottoman centuries

A material life based on the fish from the lakes, forest game and associated pastoral agriculture provides continuity in Prespa material life from antiquity to the present day. The changing seasons and the vagaries of the weather dominated daily life in the huddle of lake inlet huts on Great Prespa that was to become *Nivica*/Psarades, the world the Roman poet Virgil describes:

> Just when the wind of an impending storm begins to blow, perhaps in the inlet channel, there are signs of swelling and heaving in the water.[1]

Yet the knowable space in the minds of the peasants changed considerably in different periods. After the decline of Rome, the rural communities of the southern Balkans which had been a part – if a very minor and insignificant part – of an empire covering much of the immediate Eurasian world slipped into greater and greater obscurity. In the fragmenting territories of the Byzantine Balkans the political and psychological space had also shrunk and continued to shrink for hundreds of years. The arrival of the Ottoman Empire brought a reopening of consciousness and material possibility to include distant realms and states. The repair of the Via Egnetia provided a means of reaching them. If inhabitants converted to Islam careers in very distant places indeed were available. The conquest was one of the major discontinuities in the political, economic and cultural superstructure that has punctuated history in the Balkans, and as imperial rule of the southern Balkans from Constantinople became established an entirely new administrative and financial system was imposed.[2] It also brought a reorientation of the economic and social life of Ohrid and Prespa, as well as a new political and economic system, with a decline in the importance of the towns like *Kostur* and *Fiorentina*, and the new dominance of *Manastir*, modern Bitola, and *Resna*, modern Resen, both to the north of Great Prespa. *Turkey-in-Europe* was being born.

The Prespa forests had been used by the forces of Albanian national hero Skanderbeg to harry and disrupt the Ottoman conquest, as had those in his native Dibra in modern north-eastern Albania.[3] The Ottoman conquest brought new demands on the forests that would disrupt Prespa society in fundamental ways, where exploitation for wood was an imperial priority.[4] The early stages of the Ottoman expansion were marked as Inalcik and other Turkish economic historians have established by the imposition of a rigid economic and fiscal system, and a complex categorization of all economic activity, as part of what can be regarded as a centralized statist and highly authoritarian economy. The empire was financed by an increasing burden of taxation on the peasantry and traders.[5] The remote landscape and terrible transport difficulties did not present such an obstacle to the Ottoman practical power with a vast invading army as they did later in the period of imperial decline. The registration of the population and their assets was rigorous and went down to the enumeration of everything that the people owned, even domestic animals as minor as rabbits and chickens. The Ottoman Turks' central interest was the conquest of substantial tracts of fertile land, *timars*, to set up as estates for new proprietors on the Roman model of retired soldier's settlements and to provide tax revenue, grain, meat, beans, rice and other foodstuffs, along with wool and leather for the voracious military machine. The Ohrid region was a priority for the conquerors with its large clerical estates that fell to the army in 1391, some to be quickly converted into *sipahis*, Christian landlords controlling *timars*. After 1400 as much as two-thirds of all southern Balkan agricultural production was destined for the army under the Ottoman economy.[6] In terms of the Prespa and Ohrid Lakes and those who lived around them, taxation of the fish catch was a central Ottoman concern. Prespa and Ohrid Lakes became *khass*, entities under the direct control of the Sultan. There are few sources to indicate the details at Prespa but central taxation was likely to have been similar to the Ottoman system on the lower Danube where about a third of the revenue went to the Ottoman state, a third to local religious institutions in the *vilayet* and a third to the fisherman and his family.[7] The lake waters became state property and were placed under the control of local officials, often in alliance with urban merchants, thereby increasing the rate of economic exploitation of the fishermen. This system continued in various forms until the end of the empire in the twentieth century with the venerable Monastery of Sveti Naum on Lake Ohrid the meeting place of the urban guildsmen from *Resna* and *Manastir* who controlled the fish trade. Ohrid remained a centre of civilized urban life, as the mid-nineteenth-century traveller Mary Adelaide Walker describes:

> The Serai of Ochrida, standing on the brow of a hill, commands a magnificent prospect of the town, with the lake beyond, sleeping in the hollow of the lofty encircling mountains.[8]

The peasants became *reaya* and subject to a series of vicious and burdensome taxes, complete control of their movements and the hated *devshirme*, the so-called blood tax, where Christian children could be removed from their parents and taken for slavery and re-education as Muslims in Constantinople. Only in the towns was the situation for Christians a little easier, as, for instance, in Ohrid, where in return for unpaid service for the military and maintenance of the fortress, they were released from some tax obligations. In Ohrid Walker notes the use of Sveti Naum monastery as a place where on 20th June each year, there was 'a great fair, a matter of profit as much as piety', where 'the Turks were eating up the resources of the monastery without scruple'.[9]

The enormous army of Sultan Murad preceded by elephants, hundreds of musicians playing howling zurnas and imams reading the Koran had swept westwards into Thrace in 1357, terrifying the inhabitants. Most fled with their animals into the countryside and the hills. The lands around Prespa and Ohrid immediately prior to the Ottoman conquest were the lands of the Albanian feudal Musachi family, extending to the town of *Kostur*/Kastoria, which was taken by the Ottomans in 1385.[10] The Ottoman army followed a route close to the coast as far as Salonika and then turned northward inland up the Vardar River valley towards *Vodena* (modern Edessa) and ultimately to *Skupi*, modern Skopje, which later became the important Ottoman city of *Uskub*. The army was led by the shock troops of the *Akinci*, a semi-irregular force that disrupted enemy defences, such as they were. The object of conquest was not simply or primarily rapine and plunder (although contrary to the neo-Ottomanist historiography fashionable in some quarters both would surely have taken place) but the rapid establishment of a settled southern Balkan society for long-term integration into the Empire, as studies of the speedy construction of forts (often based on Byzantine structures) imarets (the public feeding stations), mosques and bath complexes show.[11] In the Ottoman conquest in the east, the army was conquering in many senses a pre-existing Islamic society apart from the severely diminished Byzantine lands around Constantinople but in the west, in the Balkans, there were no existing Islamic institutions at all and they were imposed on a 'top down' basis. The development of functioning urban centres was the priority. Garrison posts were placed at regular intervals along the main roads, some of which later grew into significant towns like Gianitsa, south of modern Edessa in Greece.

The imposition of the Ottoman administration of the southern Balkans outside the main towns was a gradual process and was conducted in the main along the well-established route of the old Via Egnetia. There is little in the way of sources to indicate the state of life along the road in the last stages of Byzantine and then Serbian control of the Ohrid and Prespa areas other than evidence of some church construction by the Serbian Empire of Stefan Dushan in Ohrid and activity in the Prespa cave shrines. These would have been 'frontier' churches along the lines of the churches at Svac in Montenegro and other southern borders of the Serbian-controlled realms.[12] There was no local state in the modern sense, in the defining areas of providing security and being capable of raising taxation, and Ohrid and Prespa lay on the invisible and confused boundary line between the domains of the Despotate of Epirus to the south-west and the endemic disorder on the border of the Serbian Empire to the north. Neither power was capable of resisting the Ottomans for long, and after the 1389 Battle of the Field of Blackbirds in Kosova the Prespa and Ohrid basins were under the control of the Porte by 1395. The conquest needs to be understood in context; over much of the ex-Byzantine lands in Epirus, Thrace and Macedonia there were few or no organized military forces capable of resistance, and in very remote and rural areas such as the Prespa Lakes and forests there would have been none.[13] In the towns, and Manastir, Ohrid, the situation was more complex. Local people looked to the church for leadership, and many church leaders saw their interests lying in collaboration with the new masters. The Ottomans in turn needed administrative capacity and were prepared to integrate some Orthodox Christians into the new system of government.[14] The experience of Ohrid and Prespa areas differs here, by the time of the Ottoman conquest the main Prespa churches had long been in ruins or isolated monastic refuges in caves above the lakes, whereas Ohrid was a much larger and functional late Byzantine urban and religious centre – if in decline like most late Byzantine towns in the Balkans – with an educated elite and substantial Christian institutions that could be integrated into the imperial system. Struga at this time was marginal, a very small town linked to the bridge over the river *Raketa*/Drin and living by money exacted from travellers.

Throughout the history of the Prespa and Ohrid basins, there has been a dialectic of interacting pressures on the lake's rural society between the south, focussed initially on Lake Kastoria with its specifically Byzantine urban development, and the northern centre that was *Heraclea Lyncestis* in antiquity and developed into *Manastir* under the Byzantines. Then it was a small Byzantine *urbs* but became a burgeoning and substantially Islamic city under the Ottoman Empire. Trade routes ran down first to Kastoria and also to *Fiorentina*, modern Florina/*Lerin*, and then south through the rich plains of Thessaly to Corinth and the Peloponnese. To the north, trade was to Serbia, and to Venice via the Drin valley passes in Albania to the Adriatic and then north to the nascent Hapsburg lands. The Ottoman conquest also firmly restored the importance of the trade to the east, above all to rapidly growing Constantinople, the largest city in the world. In the west the key link was with Dubrovnik/*Ragusa*. Papal and Venetian influence was strong nearer the Adriatic and dominant in trading centres like Kotor but minor or non-existent in what is now modern Macedonia to the east of Ohrid and Struga. In western Macedonia and surrounding regions there is little reason to believe there was any substantial trade interaction between Christians and Muslims prior to the Ottoman conquest, along the lines explored by Molly Greene in pre-Ottoman and Ottoman Crete.[15] The conditions in the maritime Mediterranean where those of different faiths had interacted continuously through trade were very different from those of the inland southern Balkans in the immediate post-conquest period.

In terms of the Prespa region, this means above all that economic reintegration was re-established with *Resna* and *Manastir* where fish and other exports from the lakes could be quite quickly conveyed in dried and salted forms with the restoration of what had been minor arterial roads leading up to the Via Egnetia, and the use of the higher road to Resen that had been developed in Byzantine times passing through modern Agios Germanos/*German* in Greece north to Resen. Much of the local transport was by boat across the lakes, using the little inlet port of Pretor on Great Prespa, originally a Roman foundation. The Ottomans restored what had been the main trade routes dating from antiquity by restoring reasonable security on the roads and the physical reopening of old routes. To the north the medieval Serbian road system in central and northern Serbia was relatively advanced and functional with its different classifications between tracks and the large roads, *Via Magna*. Most of the latter focussed on east-west trading routes for minerals and the mineral ore to *Ragusa*, modern Dubrovnik. Some aspects of the Serbian system of road guards, *strazishte*, were adopted by the Ottomans, with important villages, the *derbeni*, ordered to provide watchmen for the roads. Little of this system had been functional in the Serbian southern 'new lands' like Ohrid and Prespa regions conquered by Tsar Dushan to the south of the Sar Mountains, but it was not long before the small garrison posts established by the Ottoman conquest began to grow into new villages and local administrative centres. An early beneficiary of the Ottoman dispensation was the rise of *Starova*, an urban centre that is now part of the modern Albanian town of Pogradec, on the south side of Lake Ohrid, where a pre-existing Byzantine fortress was rebuilt and a trading *urbs* grew up below it. The Turkish traveller and chronicler Evliya Celebi visited in November 1670 and noted its prosperity, describing 'the sweet town of Pogradec' with 'great houses by the lake' on his journey across southern Albania to Constantinople.[16]

In Prespa the early Ottoman military camp at what is now modern Kallithea village with its good defensive situation on the small *kale* hill above the north-south Great Prespa lakeside road grew into the main Ottoman garrison centre.[17] Villages grew more prosperous as security improved.[18] The Ottomans took over and developed the small Byzantine fort there. In general, prior to the conquest, anarchy and violence had prevailed away from the Via Egnetia, and local bandit leaders extracted tribute from the mostly Vlach herdsmen who ran the mule and horse caravans. Throughout this period, the centre of gravity of Serbia was moving north to Belgrade and Smederevo and the southern lands like Ohrid/Prespa were left more or less to their own devices.

In comparison the trade routes down towards *Salonika* had to pass through the mountainous and remote forests south of Mount Vitsi east of Great Prespa on bad mule tracks where security was often also very poor. Movement in the winter on this route was often impossible, whereas the northern route based on the old *Via* Egnetia east of *Manastir* was generally passable all the year round. The Ottomans also facilitated and encouraged trade along the main roads as goods moving there could be easily monitored and taxed. Kastoria/*Kostur* was in a different position, with alternative road routes to *Salonika*, via Kozani and Veroea, and also westwards into Epirus and then towards the Adriatic. With its own ample supplies of fish, timber and game and independent routes to the *Salonika* market and port, the town had little motive to trade with the much bigger lakes to the north. The focus of trade and religious and social influence was with the *sandjak* of Korca and the Devoll and the Shkumbini river valleys. Lake Maliqi near Korca was then still a major inland lake and surrounded by a wilderness of marshlands and swampy forests and was an obstacle to all transport until it was eventually drained in the mid-twentieth century.

In the years after the Ottoman conquerors established their government and regional power, the *Manastir* region comprised a single *vilayet* which in turn was subdivided into *sandjaks*. *Manastir* comprised the subsidiary *sandjaks* of Prizren, Dibra and *Scutari*, modern Shkodra, each subdivided into the *kazas* of *Manastir*, *Pirlepe* (Prilep), *Fiorentina* (Florina/Lerin) and *Ohrid*. From the point of view of the local peasant populations this meant that they were faced with an imposed foreign administration and a directed economy and fiscal system of considerable complexity whose affairs were conducted in a language very few could understand. The priority of the Ottomans was the extraction of taxation revenue and the supply of military requisites and manpower from the population, and it did not take long before what were the positive aspects of the conquest in terms of the improvement of travel and general security and the restoration of urban life in old centres (or in the case of *Manastir*/Bitola a few miles north from the ancient *Heraclea Lyncestis* site) transmuted into rural Christian resentment and endemic rebellion.

The Ottoman policy in the immediate post-Conquest years involved using the principle of *istimalet* – goodwill – to an accommodation with the local population, so those who did not resist the new masters were rewarded, but there were serious limits to how far this system could be successful in rural and mountain western Macedonia. As Heath. W. Lowry has pointed out, *istimalet* was most successful immediately where there were military issues to decide in urban areas, the peaceful surrender of forts in particular where compliant local defenders could be quickly rewarded; it was not a useful tool of government where endemic disorder and local anarchy prevailed and there was no real political authority for the Turks to negotiate with over pacification.[19] Within a few years of establishing their formal authority, like both ancient and more modern conquerors of the Balkans, the Ottoman Sultans were to discover the limits of their real power and this realization soon led to neglect of remote and thinly populated regions like Prespa. In the wider Balkan history, the abandonment of Ottoman plans to invade and govern modern Montenegro is usually cited as a 'legendary', even an unique Balkan military achievement of the Montenegrins but in fact many smaller areas were de facto abandoned by the Ottomans over the more mountainous and remote parts of the entire Balkan region. In central Greece the remote *Agrapha* (unwritten) lands in the Evretania nomarchy around modern Karpenisi are an example of an area where for centuries the Ottoman tax collector had little or no presence.[20] In the case of Prespa the inhabitants had a partly pre-monetary economy based on self-sufficiency and rich local resources that was to an extent immune from the attentions of the tax collection officials.

The chronic underpopulation of the Ohrid and Prespa region also hindered the onerous tax demands of the Ottomans, worsened considerably by endemic malaria on the marshlands, other epidemics and above all the region-wide outbreak of plague in 1500 that spread to Constantinople itself where it took the lives of perhaps a third of the population. As in late antiquity, periods of some social and economic progress in Ottoman times could be quickly undermined by disease-led depredations and population loss.

In response, in order to try to pacify the population and alter the religious composition towards Islam, substantial numbers of Islamic settlers, mostly from eastern Anatolia, were moved into the southern Balkans. Some of these people, like the *Yorucks* in the eastern hills around Radovis in Macedonia and the Turkish-speaking villages in the west and in Bulgaria, have maintained Muslim/Turkish/Albanian religious and cultural identities to the present day. In and around Prespa they are nowadays represented by Turko-Albanian villages like Krani, north of Agios Germanos, and Cernje, on the Albanian side of the modern lake. The scale of this immigration into the Balkans which began soon after the conquest and continued intermittently, for different reasons, until the collapse of the *vilayet* in the First Balkan War in 1912 was considerable. The Ottoman/Turkish presence lasting to the end of the empire during the First World War is often underestimated, in the main by Balkan and regional historians with national agendas that generally seek to downplay the Ottoman influence in their societies. The available data shows a consistently large 'Turkish' population was maintained throughout the centuries in the *Manastir vilayet* and lasted until the Empire collapsed. Thus, as late as 1897, 400 years after the conquest, the Russian consul in *Manastir*, Rostkovski, estimated the population composition of the *vilayet*, as follows:

Ottoman Turks 78,867
Albanians 226,436
Greeks 109,423
Vlachs 53,227
Jews 5,600
Slavs 291,592

No doubt these figures are substantially 'guesstimates' and highly speculative in detail, and the Russian consul no doubt had his own reasons to inflate the Slav numbers but they do indicate certain general realities that are also borne out in the data and subjective observations of other contemporary observers. In the earliest years of the empire a clearer picture of post-Ottoman conquest society around the lakes begins to appear with the Ottoman Empire census documents (*tahir defterri*) that were discovered in the archives in Istanbul in the 1950s. These show a very detailed study by the Porte of the economic resources of the Balkan region, enumerating mills and grain production comprehensively and also studying the population of individual *sandjaks*, with a particular focus on the number of married people and unmarried males in a locality. The documents do not have an exact date but can be placed in the period of Sultan Murad II (1421–51) and were probably compiled around 1440. The census focussed heavily on the larger towns, for example the *Manastir* document only records the society in the town itself with nine quite closely surrounding villages. The Prespa and Ohrid villages do not appear in the documents at all. As the editor of the first edition of the documents published in stages over many years in Skopje points out, the focus is thoroughly imperial, on the 'domaines feudale plus riche' where the commodities of most immediate interest to the Sultan's army were produced. These were the traditional fertile plain lands to the east of *Manastir* stretching hundreds of miles towards Prilep and across the Vardar valley and then the dry eastern Macedonian uplands into what is now modern Pirin Bulgaria.[21] The modern traveller coming from Ohrid to Prespa region notices this when as the road runs down the mountains from Resen to Bitola, grain silos suddenly appear in the landscape.

Other natural boundaries were also important. In the conquest period and for hundreds of years afterwards, central Macedonia was bisected not merely by the Vardar River but also by the very wide marshlands either side of most of its upper length. The register that was produced covering the *sandjak* of Kastoria, probably around 1480, is of great later relevance to the study of Prespa region population composition as the forty-eight villages surrounding the city are recorded in more detail than those around *Manastir*, and without exception have Slavonic not Greek names and more detail is given on the inhabitants than in some other records, where the overwhelming majority of place names and personal names are Slavonic. In terms of more modern historical issues, the picture is confirmed, as with early medieval Ohrid, of a strong Greek/Byzantine presence through the church and a Greek-speaking and literate elite in the urban centres but very much less Greek influence in the surrounding Macedonian/Bulgarian, Albanian-speaking and Vlach populated countryside and rural areas, a picture the contemporaries of Theophylact of Ohrid would have immediately recognized four centuries before. The data recorded for the *sandjak* of *Fiorentina*, modern Florina/*Lerin*, is heavily focussed on heads of households, a sign that the largely forested wilderness around the garrison town was seen mainly as a source of manpower for the army and forced labour for the harvest on the plains to the north near *Manastir* itself rather than having significant local agricultural inputs. The historical continuities nevertheless remain, as Heath. W. Lowry points out, in the southern Balkans: 'almost all the commodities that the Ottoman registers show as taxed in 1490 are still being produced at the beginning of the twenty first century'.

In military terms, the control of territory evolved around control of fortresses, and smaller strongpoints, but the lands around Prespa did not have any of much significance, apart from the hillfort below Kallithea, whereas Ohrid did, in the shape of the majestic castle of Tsar Samuil in the middle of the old town. Equally there were (and are) no large Prespa churches or monasteries with very significant landholdings, unlike a major monastery like Sveti Jovan Bigorski north of Ohrid and the numerous Christian foundations in the town itself, and the historic monastery of Sveti Naum on the south fringe of the Ohrid lake. In and around the town there was a stable Christian elite who could be induced to join the Ottoman system, around Prespa there was not.

The later Ottoman centuries

In the later Ottoman centuries the early command economy had broken down with its rigid neo-feudal designations, and conventional capitalist relations had begun to replace the early central statism. Major changes began in the sixteenth century and continued in the seventeenth century. Small centres around Prespa benefitted, with the first mention of Ottoman *San Germanos*, modern Agios Germanos, recorded in a 1662 document.[22] Land grants made by the Porte strengthened the economic power of the *vakuf* Muslim religious foundations in the towns and steadily encroached on free grazing lands and smallholdings of the Orthodox peasantry. In what has been called 'the pastoralist revolution' changes in agrarian production patterns started that were very limited at first but culminated in the years of railway construction in the nineteenth century. A new middle class of agricultural traders were becoming established in the towns and soon became integrated into the imperial tax collection system.²³ Animals that had only been kept for meat and wool for centuries began to be important as sources of cheese, with improved transport enabling milk products – even a primitive butter – to be exported well outside the originating rural area.²⁴ More luxury crops such as grapes were grown. Transhumance Vlachs began to become more settled. Trade itself changed, fairs became important for regional life and the town of Struga, *Uststruga*, grew very much as an Ottoman creation with an important fair and a majority Albanian and Turkish-Muslim population. East-west trade grew, with the road running alongside the riverbed of the little River Devoll fed from Lesser Prespa Lake becoming more important.²⁵

Many of the fairs attracted Greek traders from what is now modern Greece to the south and laid the first foundations for Greek trading supremacy in many Turkey-in-Europe towns in the Ottoman period.²⁶ Little is known about the state of the Prespa villages in the immediate post-conquest years, but the absence of any material remains of buildings dating from that time would indicate a low level of material life and probably a very small population. The oldest stone houses in *Nivica*/Psarades and other Prespa villages date from the later Ottoman period. The fall of Constantinople in 1453 may have encouraged movement of population to wilderness areas, and some monks may have moved in to inhabit the cave churches around the lakes and/or lived on Golem Grad Island. The isolation of Prespa region would also have been accentuated by the development of the *Manastir/Fiorentina* road and significant numbers of Muslim settlers moving to the vicinity, something that can be seen in the survival of Turko-Albanian Muslim villages along the modern main roads like Medzitlija near Bitola that trace their origins to post-conquest immigration. But the lakes and forests remained a territory of endemic and extreme poverty and intermittent rebellion.

Outside the towns where the Ottoman garrisons remained an effective and dominating presence, rural and forested Prespa remained, as it had always been, the terrain of the bandit and the *haiduk*, a dangerous and unpredictable wilderness. Nevertheless, the village life of little Nivica was developing with the village designated in the 1530 *cadastre* of *Rumelia* as within the *kaza* of Bilisht and having sixty-nine hearths (houses) a similar size to that of modern Psarades, with a total revenue of 4,101 *akces*.²⁷ Such development as took place in the sixteenth and seventeenth centuries was focussed on the northern Upper Prespa villages most adjacent to *Resna*/Resen. Apart from fish transport routes, the Ottomans began to develop small *ciflik* farms created from land drainage in the lake vicinity for rice and for fruit growing, so laying the foundations of an industry around Resen that continues to the present day. In the wider economic world of the Empire, these fruit plantations were insignificant, and wool, salt, fish and leather exports always headed the list of commodities moving from the Balkans to the eastern parts of the Empire every year. A fort was constructed to control the lakeside road on Bouskani hill near Lefkona village. As the sixteenth and seventeenth centuries wore on, conversions to Islam became the norm in many areas, and it appeared the Sultan's rule would be eternal. This period had also seen an economic boom in the region, focussed on ports like *Ragusa* but also spreading to the town like *Manastir* on the flourishing trade routes.

Major changes came to the southern Balkans as the original rigidities of the Ottoman system broke down under the influences of Mediterranean trade and western economic penetration.²⁸ Struga continued to grow as a main trade route town on the Drin route to the Adriatic and in the eighteenth-century-imported goods began to appear in the local fairs. In Prespa the little village of *German*, modern Agios Germanos, was of Byzantine origins but the original settlement was very ancient. *German*, the precursor of Christian Saint Germanos, was a primitive Slavonic deity connected with rain, water and water divination, venerated in an appropriate position near the lake crossings. The road running on the lakeside below Agios Germans was an Ottoman creation, crossing to the north what is now the Greek-Macedonian border to the modern village of Dolno Dupeni and then running north towards *Resna*/Resen. The later Ottoman centuries saw significant development on this side of the lakes. A continuing immigration of Turkish-speaking people took place into the Prespa villages, with Turks 'planted' in communities such as at *Saouftsi* on the southern outskirts of the modern village of Laimos and at *Soukofski* on the western side of Agios Germanos. A small fortress was built on the hill immediately south of *Orovnik*, modern Lefkonas, near Lesser Prespa Lake, which became an Ottoman administrative and military centre with its commanding position of the lakeside road that ran down to Korca through the Tren defile, as nowadays a small track does, much used by illegal Albanian migrants to Greece. The settlement had a substantial Turko-Albanian population, as well as Macedonian Slavs, and Vlachs, and a local Pasha lived a little higher up the hill near the modern, now mixed Vlach/Greek-Macedonian village of Kallithea. With its Byzantine origins and higher position up the hills, Kallithea has always kept its original Greek place name. The Pasha chose somewhere – as so often with residences of senior officials – with a fine situation and perhaps healthier than the marshlands in the immediate vicinity of the lakes. The substantial official residence and administrative buildings of the late Ottoman economic boom time in Macedonia linked to the arrival of the railway from Salonika to Florina still stand in the middle of Kallithea and is an atmospheric memorial to those years.

   Ottoman agricultural practice here focussed on harnessing the waters of the strong streams that ran in winter down the hills through these villages above the lake into a complex system of irrigation channels which were used for rice and bean cultivation on the lake wetlands. Some remnants of this today can be seen around the Lefkonas lakeside and below modern Karyes/*Binovo* village. A now largely overgrown and disappeared track ran as a mule caravan route across the hills eastwards from *Binovo* to the large village of *Orovnik* and then linked with the remains of the old Via Egnetia to the Vlach trading and pastoral centre of Pisoderi, ancient *Pisodendron*, on the road to *Vodena*/Edessa.²⁹ There was an Ottoman trading post and tiny port on the southern edge of Lesser Prespa Lake to the south at *Laga*, modern Microlimni. Another Ottoman military post was at the hill village of *Rehova*, a mile east of modern Vrondero on the boundary of the old *sandjak* of Korca. *Drenovo* as a later centre of communist support in Prespa was destroyed at the end of the Greek Civil War when the site was 'renamed' Pyxos after 1949 on an entirely artificial basis as the original village was left deserted with no inhabitants. It was on the hill just south of *Grazdeno*/modern Vrondero and is now a small scrubby landscape of sad ruins and the occasional Vlach herdsman with sheepfolds. A monument to the female military fighters of the communist Democratic Army has recently been erected there. The Korca *sandjak* boundary extended northwards in a loop to enclose most of the villages now in Albania on the western margins of Great Prespa Lake, also, as far north as modern Konsko and Bezmishta villages north of Pushtec.[30] In Albania, unlike Greece, these Macedonian/Bulgarian bilingual villages with Albanian as the current primary public-use language have kept their original Slavonic-origin place names. Thus, original Ottoman administrative divisions that in themselves had often become less and less functional as any kind of meaningful internal boundary as the Empire declined nevertheless have had significant influence on modern borders and settlement patterns. In their turn the Ottoman boundaries had been based on earlier Byzantine and ancient Roman models, as noted by the French Consul General in Salonika, Cousinery, immediately after the establishment of the modern Greek state in the 1820s. Travelling in the region to pursue his antiquarian and neoclassical interests, he noted: '*la division de la pays, etablie par les Romains après la conquete*'.[31]

The physical landscape was also changing, but it was seen by very few foreigners indeed. The Macedonia travelled by an adventurous and learned man like Cousinery with an official role in *Salonika* and servants, a dragoman and some money was still very confined. He only seems to have visited a number of main towns outside Salonika, Serres, Veroia, Edessa/*Vodena*, Pella and Phillipi. The well-drawn map of Macedonia in his book only shows the central lowlands and a few places like *Gradisca*, modern Gevgelia, on valley passage routes northwards. It is doubtful if a man in his position would have ever visited the dangerous and unruly western Macedonian mountains or maybe not have ever heard of Prespa. The late medieval world described by Fine had continued throughout the Ottoman centuries in the hills, where powerful families might have some degree of dominance over their local area and exercised some power over other smaller families but in a climate of chronic instability and intermittent violence.[32] There is one passing mention of Lake Ohrid in Cousinery's account but no suggestion he ever went there. The obscurity of Prespa continued in the later nineteenth century.[33] The English poet and artist Edward Lear travelled in the region in 1847, following the Via route between Ohrid and *Resna*/Resen but makes no mention of Prespa in his diaries.[34] He did though enjoy a visit to *Akhridha*/Ohrid and to *Manastir*/Bitola where he noted:

> The natural beauties of Manastir are abundant. The city is built at the western edge of a noble plain, surrounded by the most exquisite shaped hills, in a recess or bay between two high mountains between which magnificent snow-covered barriers is the pass to Akhridha. A river runs through the town, a broad and shifting torrent crossed by numerous bridges, mostly of wood, on some of which two rows of shops stand, forming a broadly covered bazaar.

Lesser Prespa Lake was known in late Ottoman times as *Lake Ventrok* and until the middle of the twentieth century was significantly larger than it is now. Nineteenth-century Bulgarian maps show the now mile-wide modern sandy causeway near Agios Acheillos Island separating the two lakes as hardly existing, and whatever degree of detailed accuracy they may have is an indicator of the somewhat higher level of the lake waters at that time. The modern causeway, across what is known in Greek as

Megala Kampos, the great field, has grown continually since and is now over a mile wide, with ever-widening marshland on the lake Lesser Prespa littoral. At the end of the Greek Civil War in 1949, according to Greek military maps, it was a narrow strip of land barely capable of taking mechanized vehicles or the columns of hapless refugees fleeing from Greece into Albania by this route.

Nevertheless, the modern village of Psarades/*Nivica* owes its origins to the improvement of trade and transport in the later Ottoman period, and began to obtain a permanent presence in Prespa as a very small fishing and trading centre. With its tiny harbour *Nivica* developed strung along the Great Prespa Lake inlet, and very near the important rock ikons and cave churches. The village no doubt caught and sold fish by the only available mule caravan route down to Korca and also to Kastoria. Dried salt fish was in ready demand everywhere in the southern Balkans and elsewhere for winter food. The village looked southward towards what is now modern Greece and to the Korca *sandjak* unlike the more developed villages on the roads to Resen which relate to the northern plains of central Macedonia. The lakes then provided a kind of Braudelian freedom, whose water unifies communities. The Ottoman peasant was tied by law to the land of the *timar* holder and he and his family could not move anywhere without the landowners permission which given the chronic labour shortages was rarely granted. In contrast the fisherman had to range far and wide over the Prespa Lakes and fishing was not merely economically vital but also a means of cultural and material and ideological exchange. Goods other than fish could be moved in the fishing boats. In these conditions, following the familiar Balkan pattern, smuggling and tax evasion across and around the lakes were endemic. Crime in the region often brings freedom from the economic and fiscal demands of external empires. The Ottoman inheritors of the Byzantine *fisc* had little chance of following regional trade movements efficiently, particularly when the local garrisons were increasingly composed of locally recruited irregular troops, often ill-fed and badly paid and subject to bribery. Ottoman coin discoveries made in and around Psarades and other lake villages indicate integration into the wider monetary economy and show the profits of fishing and smuggling. In the later Ottoman centuries around the lakes government authority to enforce what were the original *sandjak* internal frontiers became more and more nominal. Thus the ground was laid for a Prespa Lake village political and economic culture of subversion, economic criminality and rebellion against the central government entrenched in the towns. The lakes also provided much faster and more efficient transport than the land, particularly in the wetter and colder times of the year when road conditions deteriorated to the point of impassability. The Ottoman-period irrigation channel systems that are still visible at modern villages such as Karies not only benefitted agriculture but also helped prevent the creation of new marshlands every winter as the roads were inundated. Live animals and meat could be transported on small boats from outlying villages on the lakes into town markets to the north and traded for imported Western goods from the Adriatic which increasingly dominated the fairs from the mid-eighteenth century onwards.

The life of the region around the Lakes in the late nineteenth century was dominated by the seismic effects on the regional economy of the railway construction, first linking Salonika with *Uskub*, modern Skopje, and Kosovo, and then after 1892, the opening of the *Salonika-Manastir* line. By 1897 an astonishing number of 242,000 passengers was carried on this line in a single year of operation.[35] With the railway came the foreign missionaries, the American Protestant Council opening its first branch in *Manastir* as early as 1873.[36] The Orthodox church sought to adapt to the changing population realities.[37] Prespa and western Macedonia generally did not share in the economic boost for farmers in eastern Macedonia associated with the boom in cash revenue from growing the very profitable new crop of tobacco, but local worthies were nevertheless beginning to adopt more modern patterns of capitalist agriculture. Robert Walsh, a British traveller in 1829, noted the world of a local Ottoman magnate in Macedonia, Osywn Aga, '*who applied himself to farming on the European plan. He built a fine residence, with extensive offices attached and in a very short time converted the wild country with a rich Demsene, and most abundant and profitable farms*'.[38]

The railway also permitted the transport of heavy commodities, such as gravel, sand and fertilizers that mules could not carry, at least in quantity. Although in one sense the lakes remained in their traditional mountain obscurity, in others the late industrial revolution that the railways and farm machinery improvements brought to the southern Balkan region transformed their future. Railway construction always had a strong military dimension and what later became known in the First World War period as the 'Monastir Gap', where the line ran between Florina and *Manastir*/Bitola began to appear in the thinking of the Great Powers. The *Pax Ottomanica* had lasted over 400 years and Turkey-in-Europe which included all of Macedonia that had been an ill-governed but passive space began to change. Modern nationalism fed by the decisions of the Congress of Berlin in 1878 and the establishment of the Bulgarian Exarchate after 1870 led to the development of the modern Macedonian Question, the contest between Bulgaria, Albanians, Serbia and Greece for control of the declining Imperial lands. In 1893 IMRO, the Internal Macedonian Revolutionary Organisation, was founded by a mixture of Bulgarians, Macedonians, Greeks and Albanians in *Salonika* and began a military campaign against Ottoman rule of the region which has been seen by some of its more critical historians such as Duncan Perry as the foundation of the first modern terrorist organization. It was a clandestine body financed in part by voluntary contributions and partly by violence and extortion, and assassination of opponents was a central modus operandi. After centuries of obscurity, modern revolutionary politics arrived in Macedonia in a particularly violent and coercive form and the region became a byword in the Western press for random violence and disorder.

The secret underground IMRO was strongly supported on the north side of the Prespa Lakes where prominent revolutionary leaders emerged in *Manastir* and *Resna*/Resen, and in 1894 on the occasion of the dedication of the new church of Cyril and Methodius in Resen a three-day-long revolutionary congress of IMRO was also held. There was strong IMRO support in *Manastir* itself among the population, resentful of the economic burdens placed on them by the predominantly ethnic Greek and Jewish domination of local business and trade, and the arrival of Greek and foreign-dominated banks and local moneylenders. The revolutionary movement spread southwards to the villages around the lakes focussed on those where the Bulgarian church had gained most support in the intense inter-religious competition in the previous generation. There was a very close link between IMRO and the Bulgarian Exarchate church in these struggles, to the extent that senior IMRO leader Damjen Gruev, a member of the IMRO Central Committee, also initiated the retraining of ex-Greek clergymen to perform the liturgy in Bulgarian. The head of IMRO on the northern Great Prespa Lake littoral, Pande Jonov-Suztov from Pretor, was appointed to head the campaign for the 'Bulgarisation' of the church in the Prespa Lake villages.[39] Substantial amounts of Bulgarian and in some cases Russian money were available to IMRO and the results can still be seen nowadays in some places as in the surviving very large church in Psarades itself and in surrounding villages like completely ruined *Orovo* near Vrondero. The strongest support for IMRO was a little to the south of lake Lesser Prespa, in the *Korescha* villages in the hills towards Kastoria/*Kostur* such as *Drenoveni* where local leader Dono Kirkov was a legendary figure in 1903 in the Ilinden Rising.

Technology assisted and may have 'made' some aspects of IMRO. The flintlock pistol had improved technically in the late nineteenth century and became a weapon that facilitated assassination as a tactic, where the assassin could stand some distance away from the target figure. Assassination, Bulgarians, Macedonia and IMRO became more or less synonymous in the Western newspapers. Flintlocks were cheap and could even be cloned from American and German manufacturer's originals by local blacksmiths. They were also light to carry around and so ideally suited to the basic unit of IMRO military organization, the *ceta*, a small group of armed men and sometimes also women based in the hills and could move easily in contrast to the cumbersome and badly organized Ottoman soldiers based in lowland garrison towns. The *ceta* had in a certain sense always existed in the vast Prespa forests, in the form of bands of outlaws, the *klephts* of the Greek mountains, but with IMRO and new technology had acquired good regional organization by educated and dedicated revolutionaries and much better weapons. IMRO also had that key element for underground warfare, the support, or at least tolerance of a neighbouring kinship state, Bulgaria. From about 1840, where in a general sense the Ottoman peace still prevailed and then after 1870 when the railway brought an economic boom throughout Turkey-in-Europe, by 1900 material conditions had deteriorated. After the Ilinden Rising in 1903, violent conflicts over Macedonia continued in different forms at regular intervals through the twentieth century. The hitherto obscure Prespa region, on the invisible borderland between the end of olive cultivation and the forests and wasteland to the north, suddenly was thrust into the centre of first regional and then international conflict. The transformation in the daily lives of the people should not be underestimated. It was possible for a Macedonian family with long-lived grandparents to live in no less than six different government/state structures in the late nineteenth and the twentieth centuries without ever leaving their village.

Politics which in the mid-nineteenth century had only been a pursuit of the very few educated men who left to a city were gradually brought into every village and every household, and intense ideological struggle over religion and national identity affected every family, the origins of the 'Balkan' political culture which modern international organizations find very hard to reconcile with contemporary technocracy and positivist ideology. The country was also at increasing odds with the town, and modern class and ethnic politics appeared, as the processes of industrialism and trade disproportionately benefitted the mainly Greek-speaking economic elite in the towns, while the predominantly Macedonian/Bulgarian/Vlach peasantry in the countryside suffered a heavier and heavier economic burden. The authority of the local *Cadi* officials in regional towns that had suffered continual population loss throughout the nineteenth century was continually weakening, along with their links to the Pasha in Salonika. Conflict within the Ottoman system was also accentuated by increasing emigration, particularly after 1880, and a consequent decline in the taxation base with serious labour shortages affecting the central agricultural task of bringing in the summer harvest.[40] In a sign of the conflicts to come, at Prespa the existing late Byzantine church at Agios Germanos was extended with a new church building that was opened for worship in 1882. Yet it was far from clear what its future might be, with only the Vlach pastoralists in the local population in the vicinity firmly committed to the Constantinople Patriarchate while most people of Macedonian or Bulgarian identity and speaking that language looked towards the Bulgarian Exarchate and ultimately towards Tsarist Russia. As ever, religion was to form the basic dividing line of conflicts in the Balkans.[41]

4

Prespa and the struggle for Ottoman Macedonia, 1863–1914

The Prespa region remained in its customary obscurity as the declining Ottoman world in the Balkans entered its final phase and remained, in the words of the eighteenth-century historian Edward Gibbon, within *'very obscure countries'*, where the *'whole country is still infested by tribes of barbarians, whose savage independence irregularly marks the doubtful limit of Christian and Mahometan power'*.[1] Yet events that were central to the future of the entire Ottoman Empire were developing in towns near Prespa and Ohrid, particularly *Manastir*/Bitola and *Resna*/Resen. IMRO, the generic name, the International Macedonian Revolutionary Organisation, after its foundation in *Salonika* in 1893, was about to transform the political landscape in and around *Manastir*/Bitola. The lake region was beginning to attract the attention of educated independent travellers, like Mary Adelaide Walker in her book *Through Macedonia to the Albanian Lakes*.[2] The world of a relatively egalitarian peasant society dominated by the Ottoman statist economy that had existed in the early years after the conquest had become a world of considerable economic differentiation, with local capitalists who became prominent citizens, *kocabasis*, rivalling the Ottoman state officials, the *rical*, for dominance in particular areas.[3] The little village that is now modern Psarades was then still known by its name of *Neverska*, and although only a scattering of small houses by Lake Great Prespa inlet was beginning to enter the wider history of the region as the contest between the Great Powers and their local state followers began to intensify. Education and religion were key battlegrounds as each participant sought to establish ideological hegemony.[4] The clerical struggle to become dominant was the central motor of new Balkan nationalisms, and in many senses, the Patriarchate in Constantinople became transformed during the nineteenth century into an agent of the Greek nationalists agenda.

In the 1901 survey of Greek schools in the region conducted by the Ecumenical Patriarchate in Constantinople, no less than 2300 *Neverska* residents were recorded, all of them denoted as Vlachs. There is no evidence of any mosque existing in the village in this period, unlike many nearby villages around the Lakes. *Neverska* was, though, a subject for intense inter-Orthodox competition through education and church adherence between Romania, Greece, Bulgaria and Serbia. The figure of 2300 people does not simply relate to the population of *Neverska*, which all other evidence shows as only having about six hundred inhabitants at that time but the Constantinople clerical estimate clearly includes nearby villages like Pili and Grazdeno. The Vlachs at that time were generally loyal adherents to the Constantinople Patriarchate.[5] All the available evidence suggests that *Neverska*/Psarades was a linguistically and ethnically mixed community. The Hapsburg traveller and pioneer Albanologist Von Hahn had visited *Manastir* in his *Reise von Belgrad nach Salonik* in 1861, following in the footsteps of his compatriot Muller who had recorded in 1838 that he found the town with 9,000 Bulgarian Christians, 4,500 Greeks, 1,200 Roman Catholic Albanians, 1,400 Jews, and 2,200 *Zigeuner* (Roma).[6] *Neverska* had also been visited by the pioneering German ethnologist and linguist Gustav Weigand, a teacher at Leipzig University, in his *sommerreise* research journey in the Balkans in June 1889 that began near *Resna*, modern Resen, on a *chiflik* owned by his Turkish friend Robi. Weigand was beginning his definitive work on the grammatical structure and philology of the Vlach language and its relation to modern Romanian, most of which later came to be focussed on the Meglen Vlachs living in the central Macedonian mountains.[7] Travelling from Ohrid towards the Meglen in these borderlands he noted *Neverska* as a significant place, and he stayed with a prosperous Vlach family living there called Gjorgi Dimitri Tsohoko. He writes the people wore Bulgarian costumes and sung Bulgarian songs, and as elsewhere in his published work he recorded folklore extensively, particularly the strength of vampire and werewolf legends in the Vlach communities. Unfortunately, Weigand had little interest in religion and records nothing about whether the villagers looked to the Constantinople Patriarch or to the Bulgarian Orthodox Exarchate for religious leadership, or whether anybody at all spoke Greek. The circumstances in which he went there on his journey would suggest that *Neverska* had substantial Vlach connections, if not a majority population, as Psarades does today, and in an interesting glimpse into the security functioning of the late imperial system he observed a security *kulla*, a watchtower on a road by the lakes, occupied by twenty Ottoman soldiers who were there to protect the mule caravans. He also noted the generally appalling state of the roads.

Other newly committed academics from different countries focussed elsewhere in the Prespa and Ohrid regions, with their different 'national' agendas. The role of Russia was becoming more important, and as Jelavitch has pointed out, 'In any attempt to form a Balkan front, the Russian emphasis was bound to be on Serbia and Bulgaria.' Two talented and energetic Russian diplomats/intelligence agents, Hartwig in Belgrade and Nekludov in Sofia, were in the region after the failure of the 1903 Ilinden Rising and it was not long before a Russian Consulate was in operation in *Manastir*/Bitola, which also covered the strategic Prespa region.[8] In his survey taken after the Balkan Wars, the Serbian geographer Jovan Cvijic noted the significant Albanophone-majority communities to the immediate south-west of Prespa, and a large and significant community in the villages on the northern fringe of Lake Great Prespa, immediately south of *Resna*, modern Resen.[9] The English author and humanitarian activist Edith Durham visited one of these Great Prespa villages, Nakolets, now in RM, in the immediate aftermath of the Ilinden Rising in 1904, seeing it as a 'wretched little fishing village', where the

> people had fled to the island of Grad during the insurrection, so had escaped; but the village had been robbed, their fishing tackle destroyed, they had an outbreak

of smallpox and were in great distress. It was a miserable hole of a place, but possessed a large new church that was surprisingly fine. One day, said the people enthusiastically, that great and good man the Russian consul had come with some friends to shoot birds. He had stayed a week, paid them lavishly, and had asked if they would like to have a church of their own. Here was the church.[10]

The Russian consul was clearly following in the Orthodox tradition of building 'frontier' churches to define political influence, and in the prevailing Panslavist atmosphere where the Russian Tsar saw his role as leading the freedom struggle of the South Slavs, it was not long before the first Russian archaeologists appeared and started to study Golem Grad Island in the lake. In the wider region, *Manastir vilayet* was the epicentre of the anti-Ottoman struggle that culminated in the Young Turk Revolution of 1908, and many of the Young Turk leaders either came from *Manastir* and Ohrid or learned their political skills there in the developing political struggle for Macedonia after the Congress of Berlin. The city of *Manastir* was not far away from Prespa, about five hours on a horse from the lakes, and the villages became rapidly drawn into the growing political turmoil in the region. The *Manastir vilayet* was the heart of the developing revolutionary movement, and the Prespa villages played their full part.

The Berlin Congress had taken place against a background of progressive capitalist economic development where the Industrial Revolution was finally reaching the southern Balkans. In a landmark initiative, the Ottoman government began, after 1830, the standardization of time measurement throughout the Empire, something closely linked to industrialization and factory production.[11] A new and fairly wealthy middle class was emerging, as elsewhere in Europe. *Manastir* was an attractive objective for Greek irredentist expansion, with its classical origins, importance in Byzantium, modern trade significance and a growing Greek trading community. The Greek military, particularly after the coup d'etat of 1909, was developing an internal political narrative of expansion into *Turkey-in-Europe* which was almost entirely focussed on towns, whether *Manastir, Salonika*, or distant Melnik, in modern Bulgaria.[12] Yet the Greek project was to founder on the fact that the members of the new urban bourgeoisie were often far from interested in becoming Greek, but many had a strong Macedonian/Bulgarian national consciousness. In London, British Foreign Secretary Sir Edward Grey expressed his fears about the Greek army, writing, 'We should discourage further loans to the Greek government if the money is wanted for armaments. If they get money to spend on armaments they will rush to war and bankruptcy.'[13]

In the little town of Ottoman *Resna*, modern Resen, just to the north of Great Prespa Lake the Tatarchev family were successful bankers, yet one of the children, Hristo, born in 1869 was to become the first leader of the Macedonian-Adrianopole Revolutionary Committee, the first Internal Macedonian Revolutionary Organisation.[14] The acute contradictions in the political identity of IMRO, sometimes seen as a legitimate popular movement and at other times the first modern terrorist organization inspired by Bulgarian irredentism, can be seen through the background and personality of Tatarchev. At one level a successful professional man who had completed his medical studies abroad in Zurich and Berlin, he was also a dedicated revolutionary who was gaoled and exiled by the Ottoman authorities. He operated in an ambience where the political self-awareness of the labyrinthine complexity of ethnic settlement in Ottoman Macedonia was beginning to be better understood. IMRO gained an early foothold in *Nivica*/Psarades with an organizer called Spiro Hristov, who like most local underground activists worked through the local monasteries, in his case at Podmocani, both for personal security reasons and to tie in the local clerics and monks to the Bulgarian Exarchate.[15]

In this period fairly reliable information begins to become available on the ethnicity and religion of those living in the Ohrid and Prespa lakeside littoral.[16] This came to the British and American public from sources as disparate as the writings of, and about, Greek nationalist leader Pavlos Melas, Bulgarian nationalist writers, the records kept by the Hapsburg, British, Russian and other Consulates in *Manastir* and competing religious institutions. This was augmented by the observations of Edwardian journalists and others who witnessed the developing struggle for Ottoman Macedonia.[17] Clerical records, often a mainstay for the late Ottoman historian, are scanty given that at this time the bishopric of Ohrid and Prespa was based in distant Krushevo.[18] Other important sources are in the study of popular culture, most of all the discoveries of musicologist and folk song collector Jane Sugerman, on the nature of Ottoman 'survivals' in the oral tradition among the ethnic Albanian and Albanophone communities she studied in Upper Prespa villages in late Titoist Yugoslavia. These records all show an important reality that has often been absent from traditional analysis of the Macedonian Question after the Congress of Berlin, in that the number and general presence of Albanian speakers around the lake and in Macedonia generally was much higher than has been generally thought, particularly in the villages with a mixed Turkish and Albanian-speaking population on the north side of Lake Great Prespa and nearer *Resna*/Resen.

Concrete earlier evidence for this view can be found in the work of the Bulgarian ethnographer Vasil Kunchov, who recorded when he visited *Nakolets* in the 1890s, just over the north side of the border on Lake Great Prespa, that there were about 300 residents, the majority Bulgarian-speaking Orthodox Christians but many others whose primary language was Turkish or Albanian.[19] Pili, which is now Vlach-dominated, was then a Turkish-majority village, linked to the long-standing Ottoman garrison post on the track running by the Lake Lesser Prespa towards Albania. *Nivica*/Psarades is mentioned in these sources in different contexts, primarily as a target for a small Cretan military band led by one 'Captain Nikoyannis' of originally about ten men that established itself there by 1905 when the village was attacked by Ottoman forces.[20] It is likely that the savage reprisal massacres by the Ottoman army against the population around the lakes after the failure of Ilinden in 1903 had reduced that population in *Nivica* considerably and made the village an easier target for Greek irredentists. The Cretan irredentist adventurers knew, on the wider canvas, that *Manastir vilayet* was where the struggle for Macedonia would be decided and must have seen the strategic importance of little *Neverska*/*Nivica* on Great Prespa Lake with its secure protected inlet, water transport trade and harbour. Their band survived an Ottoman assault and the capture of a local leader called Silaki, and according to the Hapsburg Consul in *Manastir* had grown to about a hundred men by the following year.[21]

Illustration 4 Interior of a house in *Nivica*. M. E. Durham: The Burden of the Balkans, London, 1905.

As the village was then only a hamlet with a few hundred inhabitants, at least some of whom were probably bilingual or trilingual with Greek, Albanian and Macedonian/Bulgarian, the 100-strong Greek band was large enough to dominate it. Psarades/*Nivica* originally became Greek through irredentist violence, conquest and guerrilla warfare, epitomizing Karakatsidou's Macedonian book title *Fields of Wheat, Hills of Blood*. In the background was the use of the Greek bands by the Church to promote Hellenization.[22] In the Ilinden period, the transformation of *Nivica* began, to be constructed as twentieth-century Psarades, the 'Last Village in Greece'.[23] The very limited amount of fertile/cultivable land at *Nivica* in Lower Prespa would have precluded the survival within the peasant/fishermen working community of a declassed layer of ex-Ottoman minor officials who later had been able to secure post-Ottoman 'ownership' of small farms and occasionally landed estates, the '*Kolojare*' families that Sugerman describes as having an influential role in all Upper Prespa communities in the twentieth century. *Nivica* was nevertheless not immune from the arrival of the Industrial Revolution in late Ottoman Macedonia. In the third quarter of the nineteenth century, Macedonia and the rest of Turkey-in-Europe was undergoing a period of sustained economic and social transformation linked to the growth of *Salonika* as an international trading port and manufacturing centre, the opening of major new mines in the Sar Mountains and the rise of the lucrative tobacco industry where Macedonia did and still does grow the finest quality leaf.[24] Trade in fish was facilitated by the construction of the first railway from *Salonika* which opened in 1872 and ran north up the Vardar valley via *Vodena*, modern Edessa, to Skopje/*Uskub* and then north into Kosovo to terminate in the important mining town of Mitrovica. In the little fishing settlement of *Nivica* the huddle of little houses by the lake with their balconies hung with drying and repaired nets would have looked as picturesque then as they do now but were on the point of new relationships with the capitalist market.

Within a days walk of *Nivica* there were numerous communities on the lake littoral of extraordinary ethnic, linguistic and religious diversity. The songs and oral traditions of many Prespa Albanians suggest a pattern of Albanian emigration to Prespa from Ottoman southern Albania, perhaps accentuated by the destruction of *Moschopolis*, modern Voskopja near Korca, in the wars between the *beys* after the death of Ali Pasha Tepelena in 1822 and its later sacking by the armed band of Albanian guerrilla leader Sali Butka (1852–1938) in the early twentieth century. The lake land and its forests were performing their traditional role of refugee haven in times of trouble and oppression.[25] Life on the littoral was often poor and insecure but long-standing cultural identities were not threatened until the Industrial Revolution and draconian and nation-state enforced changes brought by twentieth-century borders and wars. The Sultan in Constantinople had little or no interest in which church was ascendant among the Christian majority in remote places, only that they remained peaceful and paid due taxes. The lake was at much higher level than it is now and early photographs show it lapped the muddy street that ran along the *Nivica* strand, houses sometimes flooded, and the little village would have been full of children playing, at a time when Prespa families were fecund and families with six or eight children were common. Vlach shepherds ran large flocks on the dry upper hillside, then as now nicknamed *Africa* by inhabitants.[26] It was a world of almost total illiteracy and all memory was oral. All lived under the distant and arbitrary rule of the Sultan and the often burdensome demands of church leaders and monastic estates for a share of their produce. The towering presence of Mount *Vicho*/Vitsi loomed on the eastern horizon, treeless above the winter snowline and an icy wilderness subject to vicious blizzards from November to April. In many respects life had changed little for centuries.

Yet in the lowlands of Macedonia nearby the world was changing rapidly. Small steam- and water-powered textile factories were developing in Vlach villages around *Manastir*. Railway construction marked the most important infusion of foreign capital, initially French, Belgian and Austrian, into Turkey-in Europe since the Tanzimat reform period around 1830. In 1885 work began on an extension railway line from Skopje to link with the central European rail network via Vranje, Nis and Belgrade. The dream of a comprehensive Balkan rail network directly linked to northern Europe that had haunted rulers throughout the later nineteenth century seemed to being realised.[27] In 1893 a second line linking Salonika with *Manastir* via Florina/*Lerin* was opened, an event of great significance for all the territory near the line, including the Prespa and Ohrid regions. In the first year of operation, over 42,000 passengers used the line, which had been financed by speculative capital itself based on rumours of new mines and mineral wealth waiting to be exploited in the *Manastir vilayet*. Promoters claimed it was as extensive as the rich mines in the Sar Mountains to the north, like *Trepca*/Mitrovica and Artana/*Novo Berde* in Kosovo. Mineral wealth in the *Manastir* region was actually completely mythical but in the frenzy of late nineteenth-century railway speculation rumour was enough for the capital to be raised to build the line. The only functioning mine in the region, the small coal mine that was opened in

1850 by the Ottomans at Drenovo village, a few miles from Korca, was far from the new railway line. The vast lignite coal deposits south of Florina/*Lerin* that have been exploited in Greece in the mid-twentieth century were unknown.

The dominant themes of this era of Macedonian history were industrialization, urban growth and rural depopulation. Emigration of workers to the United States and Canada grew rapidly with the first large concentrations of Macedonians growing in cities like Toronto, Columbus and Cleveland Ohio, and Chicago where they worked in the stockyards and throughout Indiana. Ethnic Albanians tended to go to New England, particularly Massachusetts. Emigration to Australia began a little later, focussed on the boom town of Melbourne. Peasants also moved to the growing factories in rapidly expanding *Salonika* and to new towns like Gevgelia that were almost entirely a product of the construction and opening of the railway. Life in the city brought more money but exposure to new threats, with *Salonika* in the grip of intermittent fever and cholera epidemics throughout the nineteenth century, such as the recurrent outbreaks that sabotaged English artist Edward Lear's planned visits to Mount Athos for so many years.

Labour shortages affected the rail construction, so that over 2,000 Italian labourers with construction skills were imported to work on the final stage of the Florina-*Manastir* line through the difficult mountainous terrain. Those who remained and mostly settled in Gevgelia became the basis in some communities for the small Uniate church accepting Papal authority that developed in the town and still exists today. In the main, *cifliks* in Turkey-in-Europe were small, often only a few hundred acres at most and those in the vicinity of the Prespa Lakes were on the whole much smaller. Hitherto the appalling state of the roads had limited agricultural and fish trading opportunities but the railway transformed this situation, particularly in respect of the rapidly rising demands for food in *Salonika*. Carp, as a plentiful Prespa fish since it had been introduced in Roman times, was in strong demand in the *Salonika* Jewish communities. The ease of trade helped break down the remains of the cumbersome and inefficient Ottoman tax collection system, but the insatiable demands of the *ciflik* owners (generally absentee landlords in cities as far away as Constantinople) and the Porte itself for revenue led to draconian economic pressures on the peasant and smallholding population. Commerce at local level was usually in Greek or Jewish hands (in the towns) and could involve usury and debt bondage. The majority Slav-speaking population of the rural areas who looked towards the Exarchate in Bulgaria and ultimately Russia for religious leadership suffered dual patterns of economic exploitation. The arrival of the railways and the nascent Industrial Revolution it brought to the few towns was a recipe for serious intensification of conflict in the rural areas where the overwhelming majority of the population lived, in an atmosphere of rising economic and social expectation but a brutal exposure to developing capitalism.

The mechanisms of the *millet* system of religious communities provided the Macedonian clergy with an opportunity to build their own independent authority in the localities and often to look eastwards – *Ex Oriente, Lux* – for clerical leadership to Sofia and Moscow rather than towards the Greek Patriarchate in Constantinople[28] This benefitted Bulgarian nationalists which with their 'own' churches were able to build up nationalist support through religious adherents. It inhibited, though, the Albanians who as overwhelmingly Muslim in the *Manastir vilayet* remained much closer to the dying Ottoman system. The old religion of rule that had benefitted many Albanians for centuries had become a handicap and a burden.

In the Lesser Prespa community of *Nivica*/Psarades, visits by the Russian consul in *Manastir* became a regular feature of life, he was a keen wildfowler and he spent so much time there that funds were made available to build the church, which can still be seen on the same site in its restored state today. Intense religious competition brought material gains for the Prespa villages, and once a church was built, the schoolroom soon followed. There was equally intense competition in school education, with Bulgarian, Romanian and Greek foundations vying for influence around Prespa and in Ohrid, and in Prilep augmented by Serbian interests. English reporter Allen Upward saw *Neverska* as a definitely Patriarchist village by 1906, although he was a British philhellene who may not have been an objective observer with the only quoted source for his view an assertion of the Patriarchist Bishop of Florina.[29] In reality the population almost certainly also had many Exarchist adherents. *Manastir* and the Prespa-Ohrid regions had become a focus for international diplomatic activity in Turkey-in-Europe generally with major powers like French, Austria and Britain establishing a diplomatic presence there and opening small embassies, so that even nowadays in Macedonia, Bitola is known as 'The City of the Consuls'. The intensifying final crisis of the Ottoman Empire was more and more focussed on the region. International media interest was growing with some of the most graphic coverage of the Ottoman army massacres in and around *Manastir vilayet* in 1903–4 appearing in the *Detroit Free Press* and the *New York Times*.

Earlier in the nineteenth century there had been attempts by the central government in Athens to foment unrest in the north and their efforts had borne some fruit with the activity of klephtic bands often led by adventurers, sometimes criminals. The Epirus Revolt of 1854 had hardly touched western Macedonia as it was focussed on Arta and other coastal regions. The scale of the territory and the relative efficiency of the Ottoman military (augmented by Albanian irregulars) brought failure. Although the expansion of Greece proceeded steadily until the acquisition of Thessaly in 1881, it slowed after it and suffered a major setback in 1897 with the defeat in Crete. The Prespa and Ohrid region was caught, as it has been many times before in history, between the pressures of Hellenism from the south, with its strongly bourgeois 'urban' social basis (the 'polis'), and 'Greek' cultural/religious identity meeting the very diverse and decentralized world of Turkey-in-Europe and its very mixed overwhelmingly peasant-smallholder populations. This was exemplified by Kastoria/*Kostur* with its numerous monasteries and churches in and around the city with a strongly Hellenic urban population and Greek-speaking Christians of *bey* rank dominating trade. But the city was surrounded by a massive Bulgarian and Macedonian speaking hinterland, particularly to the north in the large villages stretching up to Lesser Prespa Lake in the upland region known as *Korescha*.

In the background was intensifying social disorder and random violence throughout the Ottoman Empire in the Balkans. In western Macedonia, the social order had been close to breakdown as early as the time of Greek independence in 1821 and as Apostolos Vacalopoulos points out, at that time 'persecution, robbery and violent crime were to continue throughout the nineteenth century', to accelerate with the new social and political crisis after the failure of the Ilinden Rising in 1903 and the accelerated and brutal period of Ottoman military repression that followed it. Although involved in one of the first conflicts of the new twentieth century, the Greek and Bulgarian governments both relied on the nineteenth-century relic of the *ceta*, the military band, led by a charismatic individual revolutionary to advance their interests: yet only ten years later major organized armies were to take the field to fight in the Balkan Wars in 1912 to 1913. Modern political ideas were beginning to influence the mass of rural peasants, as the American journalist Albert Sonnichsen was to note a few years later. Seeing the influence of the 1905 Russian revolution among the Exarchist adherents, he recorded: '*Occasionally a young fellow would rise during the discussions and expound on the doctrine that even then was penetrating into the masses of the cities – socialism.*'[30]

A Greek narrative – Pavlos Melas

The Ilinden Rising in 1903 in Macedonia against Ottoman rule which could have brought a major territorial expansion of Bulgaria in the region caused alarm in Athens, and the activity of Greek armed bands was encouraged and financed by the central government. In Greece a climate was developing in all spheres of intellectual life inspired by the poetry of Kostis Palamas (1859–1943) where the long-distant conflicts between the Byzantines and the Bulgarians for control of the southern Balkans became paradigms for contemporary struggles between modern Greece and modern Bulgaria over the declining Ottoman Empire in Macedonia. Once again the inheritance of late antiquity, Byzantium and the early medieval period reasserted itself in current history. In one of his best-known works, *The King's Flute*, Palamas wrote of Prespa with its 'unforgettable lake' as a terrain that was spiritually Greek and, whether he intended to or not, placed it upon the national irredentist agenda.[31] In reality scholars disagree whether the poet ever even went to Prespa but at the time this did not matter. The poet was to become a legislator of the new irredentism and struggle for Greek expansion in the north. One of the main Greek heroes of the struggle for Macedonia Pavlos Melas was to get to know Prespa well and the activity of his unit brought modern Greek paramilitary irredentist nationalism to the lakes for the first time. From a wealthy Epirus trading background, the Melas family were supporters of the *Ethniki Amina* (National Defence) movement which espoused the 'Great Idea' of expansionist irredentism. In 1897/8 during the Cretan crisis Melas (as a regular Greek army officer) had moved north to the then border with the Ottoman Empire in Thessaly. The scale of the Greek defeat in Crete in 1897 came as a shock to the nation which had seen steady national expansion and the acquisition of more territory over the previous two generations.[32] Melas's father was said to have died of grief over what had happened.

The Greek irredentist's response to the threat posed by the Ilinden Rising was to attempt to open a front in Macedonia. Greek opinion was alarmed by the formation in 1904 in Prilep of a renewed revolutionary organization by the Bitola Revolutionary District of IMRO. The Greek response was not only a secular nation building project but involved the active collaboration of the Greek Orthodox church, which was in serious difficulties in many places, with the famous Byzantine-origin monastery on

Golem Grad Island in Great Prespa Lake reduced to a single monk, one Callistos, by 1903. Melas and his brother set up an underground organization to try to staunch the clerical advance of the Bulgarian Exarchate and against what they saw as IMRO's anti-Greek and anti-Turkish positions. His activity fell on fertile soil. The Bishop of Kastoria Germanos Karavangelis was already smuggling small arms and munitions from the Kastoria churches and monasteries into western Macedonia, and by 1902 a relative of Pavlos Melas had become Greek Consul in *Manastir*. After many vicissitudes Melas led a band in spring 1904 into Macedonia and began the armed struggle for territory there, under the military plan produced earlier by the Greek Consul General in Salonika, Lambros Koromilas, who became the architect of the military side of what Greeks now know as the period of the *Makedonikos Agonas*, the struggle for Macedonia.

The numbers then involved on the Greek side were small, all volunteers, and a central problem they faced was the widespread popular support for the Bulgarian Orthodox Exarchate and IMRO in many of the villages. By the third week in March 1904 Melas had reached the important Greek monastery of Tsirlovo, in Kastoria, and received the backing of the local Greek clerical hierarchy and then moved along the dangerous and difficult winter route across the slopes of Mount *Vicho*/Vitsi towards *Manastir* and Prespa. Their target village was Bulgarophone *Zhelevo*, modern Andartiko, and it became a focus for bitter contest between the Greeks and Bulgarians in the first years of the twentieth century just as it was later fought over and partly destroyed in the Greek Civil War. The visit of Melas and his men to *Orovnik* and Prespa is graphically described in a letter of Melas to his sister, where the region between *German*/Agios Germanos village was dominated by an IMRO *ceta* of about thirty armed men who had just escaped from *Manastir* prison. Melas was unprepared for the hostile early spring weather and a fierce north wind off Lake Great Prespa, and heard from the family of thirty-six people he was lodging with how the Turks had sent troops to Prespa after 1903 to try to disarm the villagers. In a candid account, he notes how many of the villagers had Albanian as their primary language and how few spoke Greek.[33] He does not appear to have made any effort to meet any Exarchist sympathizers, and as an IMRO band was about to descend on them from the hills, they retreated from the Prespa area. It was nevertheless a salutary and educational period, and the Melas experience, particularly his subsequent 'martyrdom' a few months later in the emergency, has always influenced the Greek military mindset. The question is bound to arise as to why Melas went this difficult and remote route in the winter at all? The answer must surely be that his mission was primarily one of a military intelligence nature, to see how far the growing power of IMRO could be opposed in the northern mountains and how many active anti-Exarchist activists could be found and supplied with small arms. In the harsh and unfavourable Macedonian conditions his tiny band could only expect death, as duly came to him the following year. His activity nevertheless laid the foundation for Greek expansionism around the Prespa Lakes, with a Greek band in November 1905 reported as attacking and plundering *German*, modern Agios Germanos, four miles from *Nivica*, and carrying off local women, one of whom was killed.[34] The old Byzantine-origin village of Agios Germanos with its strategic position controlling the lakeside road north to *Resna*/Resen was seen as a priority for conquest by both sides.

Illustration 5 Soldiers in late Ottoman Prespa.

Orovnik is modern Lefkonas/Kallithea, a major village on the east side of Lake Great Prespa five miles south of Agios Germanos and the operation there for Melas and his men suggests that although it was the centre of Ottoman administration at Prespa, the Sultan's authority had collapsed there post-Ilinden and the rural surrounding region was being captured by IMRO and the Bulgarian *comitadjis*. In 1904 it was attacked by the early Greek nationalist militia leader 'Captain Kotta', who failed to overthrow the Turkish garrison force. In late Ottoman times the village also had the Albanian name of *Popeli* indicating significant Albanophone settlement there.[35] The savage violence committed by the Ottoman troops in *German*/Agios Germanos against civilians suspected of holding weapons after Ilinden in 1904 had only brought further support for IMRO. The villages along the eastern Great Prespa Lake shore north of Agios Germanos in what is now RM were very divided ethnically and also by religion. Some like Krani with its mosque had a substantial Albanian and Turkish presence with a conservative Islamic ethos, while others nearby like Dolno Dupeni were entirely Orthodox, pro-Bulgarian and pro-IMRO with a long tradition of revolutionary activism. The language issue was important and linked to religion. Some visiting journalists like H.M. Brailsford saw most of the Macedonian population as able to understand some Greek although virtually no one was able to write it, but it is possible his view of the widespread understanding of the language was distorted by spending most of his time in the towns.[36] The role of Greek armed force as seen from Athens should be to protect the villagers from IMRO terrorists and that could only succeed with large and ruthless applications of force. There is a direct transference of this rhetoric and official Greek military thinking from fighting IMRO in the early twentieth century to the anti-communist struggles of the 1940s and 1950s, perhaps unsurprisingly as the Greek army faced many of the same structural problems as its Ottoman predecessor.

Melas had few followers, and perhaps like many middle-class Greeks, particularly those from Athens, the islands, and the Peloponnese, had little accurate idea of the scale of the landmass and wild mountainous nature of rural Macedonia and Turkey-in-Europe or its population diversity. The romantic dreamers and theorists of Greek irredentism were always faced with a compelling and insoluble problem, the shortage of unredeemed Greeks awaiting liberation and integration into the expanding Greek state.[37] In addition to the competing interests of Romanians, Bulgarians and the resident Turks and Greeks in some places like the western districts of *Manastir* itself there were large numbers of nationalist Albanians who were, correctly, anticipating the declaration of Albanian independence that was to come in 1913 ten years later. Most were Muslims and many had minor roles in the imperial administration and had little instinctive sympathy for the nationalist agendas of the Greeks. Melas discovered, as a romantic nationalist adventurer, what many other Greek and foreign soldiers did later in the twentieth-century Balkans that the Prespa region is an essential boundary nowadays just as it was in late antiquity and Byzantium between the Greek speakers of the Mediterranean south and their northern neighbours. Melas's campaign saw many later setbacks in the lawless IMRO-dominated hills and he was forced to return to Athens in the early autumn, although by then the Macedonian Struggle had received the support of the Greek monarchy.

New Greek leaders were soon to emerge around Prespa. A Cretan adventurer, Captain Vardas, hailing from the little town of Sphakia had first gone to fight in Macedonia in November 1904 and in an interview given to the English journalist Allen Upward in 1906 explained that he came because 'I was stirred up to go by the outrages committed on Greeks. Refugees from Macedonia had arrived in Athens, many former chiefs of Macedonian bands who had been driven out by the Bulgars'.[38] His statement may be true in one sense, but it was also designed for the ears of an English philhellene; in reality increasingly the Greek state and church were promoting a military campaign to capture the lands of the Ottoman *vilayets* throughout Macedonia.

A Bulgarian IMRO narrative – Lazar Pop Traikov and Dono Kirkov

A days' ride south of modern Microlimni on Lesser Prespa the modern village of Kranonias, once *Drenoveni*, occupies an exposed situation on the *Koreschka* hilly plateau between the Prespa Lakes and Kastoria.[39] Most of the modern village straggles along the main road linking the Prespa region with Kastoria to the south-east. Little remains of old *Drenoveni* as a functional village, about half a mile away, although some old people eke out a living with their sheep among the many ruined and semi-ruined timber and mud brick houses. Some are scarred with numerous bullet holes and signs of fires. The ruins of *Drenoveni* are a testament to the violence of the struggles for twentieth-century Macedonia. In Ottoman Macedonia this village was an important centre for the Exarchists with an overwhelmingly Bulgarian Orthodox population, and in 1903 the Ilinden Rising in this part of Macedonia was declared in the village. In the division of the land into IMRO revolutionary provinces, *Kostur*/Kastoria came under the province of Bitola, *Manastir*. One of the main *ceta* leaders from *Drenoveni* was Lazar Pop Traikov, and in his band a very young man called Dono Kirkov fought against the Ottomans. It was the beginning of a long revolutionary and Bulgarian nationalist career for Kirkov that lasted until his death near Prespa in 1944. Unlike many of his comrades, he survived the failure of Ilinden and its bloody aftermath, although Traikov did not. Lazar Pop Traikov as *ceta* leader was murdered, allegedly on the personal order of the gunrunning Greek Bishop of Kastoria, Germanos Karavangelis, who later displayed a photograph of his severed head in his office.[40]

In the years after Ilinden the Prespa region was never far from the eye of the growing interlocking Balkan and Ottoman crises. The Young Turk movement which in 1908 sought modernization and partial democratization of the Empire had many adherents among the Ottoman office corps based in the Balkans who were acutely aware of popular dissatisfaction with the Sultan and his rule and who felt ill-equipped to defend the ossified edifice of the Empire. The Young Turk movement was in many senses born in Macedonia and many of its leaders had served in, or did still serve in, *Manastir* and *Resna*. But although it was a powerful flame burning for reform and Ottoman modernization, it did not burn for very long. The great hopes that were supported by liberal Europe in 1908, leading to withdrawal of the foreign officers attached to the Macedonian militias, were dashed by the end of 1909, when as Marriott observes, 'It soon became clear that the Young Turks, so far from turning their backs on the traditions of their race, were Osmanlis first and reformers afterwards. Abdul Hamid's brief triumph had been marked by fresh massacres of Armenians in Adana and in other parts of Anatolia.'[41] In most districts the imperial system had declined to such an extent that the army and the military became little more than a state within a failed and failing Empire. After the success of the uprising against the Empire in the highlands of northern Albania in the same year, and the mutiny of the *Manastir* garrison in June 1909, the entire Prespa and Ohrid regions descended into lawless chaos. The region, which for so long had been lost in obscurity, was plunged into the eye of the international storm.

The external powers were impotent to influence events in the localities, even *Manastir*/Bitola itself, which with its febrile political subcultures became a centre of Albanian nationalist ambitions, along with those of Serbia, Greece and Bulgaria. As early as 1880 an Albanian assembly in *Manastir* had projected a future Albanian state of *Arnautistan* to unify the Albanians of Macedonia, based upon the city, and entered into talks with the *Manastir* French Consul.[42] However, the smaller and weaker nationalities like the Albanians were no match for the ambitions of expanding Greece and the entrenched strength of the Bulgarians and IMRO in the Macedonian and parts of the northern Greek countryside. The Greek irredentists saw themselves as a force for modernization, but they were not alone in this respect. Many Albanians saw *Manastir* as a future Albanian city as numerous Albanophone inhabitants divested themselves of the Ottoman identity and espoused the Albanian national cause. As early as 1908 the Congress of Manastir had been held to codify a western Albanian alphabet which became an important nationalist symbol.[43] Few Turks knew anything of the new bourgeois world of commerce and business that was developing, dominated in many trades by Jews in *Manastir*/Bitola and *Salonika*, and by Greeks in the provincial localities. The Greek state in Athens was very aware of the wealth in agriculture and trade that would later pass to it through the division of Macedonia after the Balkan Wars and the 1913 Treaty of Bucharest. A detailed study of the economic opportunities was immediately published in Athens and a census was made by 1913. This census has proved to be highly controversial, its critics seeing it as a means to count anyone who could speak any Greek at all as 'Greek' in their identity and national consciousness, and as readily available raw material for integration in the expanding Greek state. The census enumeration mechanism was repeatedly used by nineteenth-century Greek governments to validate the military gains of national expansion. Thus, the first Greek national census was in 1834 but no new census followed until 1870, that mainly to validate the inclusion of the Ionian Islands in Greece after 1864. The next was in 1889, after Thessaly had become Greek in 1881. The population rose from 2.6 million in 1907 to 4.7 million after the Balkan Wars gains in 1912 to 1913.[44]

In the prefecture of Florina/*Lerin*, the 1913 census showed a population of 20,728 residents in the Prespa district, made up of 11,127 males and 9,644 females. The lower female number is probably due to the heavy toll of childbirth-associated deaths. *Nivica* is shown as having 674 people, a far greater number than have lived there at any time since, although as some nearby villages and small settlements are not explicitly mentioned in the census documents there may have been an aggregation of the data. Some of it may have been prepared as advocacy material for the international Boundary Commissioners after the Balkan Wars. Virtually every Prespa place name is recorded in its 'Bulgarian' form, thus in the census documents modern Agios Germanos is *German*, Antartiko is *Zhelevo* and Vrondero is *Grasdeno*. This modest Greek official recognition of the dominant ethnic patterns of settlement around the lakes was not to last long. Official thinking in Athens was permeated by an almost Marxist notion of the concept of 'false consciousness', where if a new citizen lived in part of Macedonia that was seen as fully Hellenic in antiquity it was seen as the duty of the state to 'rescue' them from what was seen as the mischief imparted by the Exarchist priests and schools for modern Greece and thus 'restore' their Hellenism.

The language used by Athens officialdom, the Church and the army officers itself reinforced this ideological struggle, with the *katherevousa* Greek used in official literature with its numerous borrowings from ancient Greek reflecting the preoccupations of the Royalist expansionist project and making it difficult even for local *demotic* Greek speakers to fully understand their new masters. Little time was to pass before the new government began to put forward policies to destroy all manifestations of Macedonian or Bulgarian culture, with forced imposition of a new identity through Athens government and clerical authorities absolute control over the belief systems and the entirety of intellectual and religious and cultural life. A new ideological state apparatus was in motion. Numerous schoolteachers were brought in, and where some sort of indigenous local leadership was required, Vlachs were often chosen in preference to those with a Macedonian consciousness/language use. It was a colonial operation. As Andrew Rossos has written: 'All statistics, except the Greek ones, are also in general agreement that these Macedonians represented the single largest group on the territory of Aegean Macedonia before 1913. The figures range from 329,371 or 45.3% to 382,084 or 68.9 % of the non-Turkish population, about 35% of the total population of approximately 1,052,227 inhabitants.'[45]

These regions in the coming years were to see massive movements of population in Greece, on a scale that had never been previously encountered. By the end of 1922 over 400,000 'Turks' had left Greece under the Treaty of Lausanne population exchange provisions, and 1,300,000 Greek and other Christians left Asia Minor for Greece. In the period up to 1928 about half a million of these people were settled in Macedonia, Epirus and Thrace and some other parts of the country, transforming the ethnic content of Macedonia. A tiny village like Agios Germanos and nearby Laimos on Prespa littoral absorbed about eighty Asia Minor families, but the great majority were settled elsewhere east of Prespa on deserted *ciflik* farms. But all this was to come. In the years immediately before the First World War a different future seemed to beckon, where the overriding Athens priority to develop and integrate newly gained Macedonia economically with the rest of Greece meant that a degree of de facto (if not de jure) tolerance of ex-Ottoman minorities was accepted particularly if like the Jews in many places in ex-Ottoman 'Turkey-in-Europe' towns they were making a major contribution to general prosperity through trade and professional skills. Few Jews have ever lived in the Macedonian countryside.

The narratives of social and anti-Ottoman revolution dominated Prespa region as it dominated all of Turkey-in-Europe in the years leading up to the First Balkan War in 1912. It was a dualistic narrative, of competing national ambitions of Greece and Bulgaria, and the numerous other citizens of different ethnic minorities were effectively excluded from political influence. The Albanian band of Sali Butka that Upward reports as existing around Prespa in 1907 seems to have disappeared as Albanian independence approached, only to reappear as an ally of the Austrians in the fighting around Korca in the First World War[46] The political struggle was becoming increasingly exclusively military, to the extent that what are nowadays often seen as 'Marxist' terms like 'the armed struggle' were then as commonly used to designate Orthodox Christian *cetas*. The position of the neighbouring kinship states changed in this period. Greek society moved solidly behind the irredentists, particularly with the growing link to the struggle for the liberation of Crete from the Empire and the emergence of Eleftherios Venizelos as an outstanding Greek political leader.[47] The position of Bulgaria was much more difficult, as Douglas Dakin points out the limited support that Sofia gave IMRO did not bring the political rewards from the Powers that the Sofia government hoped for, and many IMRO activists took different and competing political paths.[48]

The period of the years leading up to the Balkan Wars (1912–13) laid the foundation for the modern divisions of geographic Macedonia. The scale of the Greek victory is perhaps not widely realized today, over a hundred years later. In the later nineteenth century Greece and Bulgaria had in many senses been comparable to small emerging states, and Bulgaria with its innovative education and medical systems and well-ordered military had often been seen as the more advanced and progressive. But as a result of the Balkan Wars Greece had increased her lands by over two-thirds, and the population had risen from about 2.7 million people to over 4 million. The new territory acquired included some of the most fertile and productive agricultural land in the southern Balkans, although it did not include the plains of *Manastir*, much coveted by the Greeks, or the productive Pirin Macedonian lands around Melnik and Sandanski, now in modern south-west Bulgaria. Their importance of the new lands was not simply economic, although Greece was always in food deficit, but also in terms of the modern Greek identity. It seemed that the dreams of early *klephtic* Greek nationalist warlords such as 'General' Makriyannis in the mountains in the independence period had at last been fulfilled. The Rumeliot warriors had triumphed.[49]

The armed bands before the 1912 to 1913 wars and the Greek army during and after it were seen by the Greek masses as recovering the inheritance of Alexander the Great and his vast conquests, and the acquisition of the new lands, along with the recent acquisition of Crete, gave Greece a new standing on the international stage.[50] The Prespa communities with the majority of people speaking the Macedonian dialect of Bulgarian and a large Christian Orthodox majority had been rent by intense religious competition for two generations. Now they found themselves as Bulgarian/Macedonian-speaking minorities within the new borders of a Greek state with a faraway capital in Athens that used a language as incomprehensible to most of them as the Turkish of the Ottoman Empire in the preceding four centuries. The surviving Muslims were in a similar demoralized position. The vast theocratic empire in which they had a secure – if usually humble and impoverished – place was collapsing. Their standing and confidence never recovered from the terminal decline of the Ottoman Empire, particularly the Albanian speakers in rural settlements and the large numbers of displaced Turks fleeing from *Manastir* and surrounding areas. The 1913 Treaty of Bucharest which allocated the spoils of the Second Balkan War produced fault lines across the region in its division of Macedonia that have never been resolved by diplomacy. All sides in the conflicts coveted *Manastir*, particularly Athens, but it was an irony that the strength of IMRO and then the Balkan Wars and the First World War period and the activity of the Boundary Commissioners afterwards in setting the limits of the new states led to the venerable city being cast into Royalist Yugoslavia, although the Serbs had less population and cultural presence than any other of the contending parties.[51] This occurred ultimately as a result of the military dispositions in the Great War, and the victorious imperialist powers desire to reward Greece and Serbia and punish Bulgaria.

As always in history, the Prespa hills and forests offered refuge to the displaced and oppressed and with the always chronic Macedonian labour shortages accentuated by the wars; it was not difficult for the Turks and Albanian peasants to move to the lake villages and attempt to restore their previous standing that they had enjoyed before the Empire collapsed. Although there had been dreadful massacres of Turkish soldiers and civilians in and around *Manastir* many people had been able to escape to the Pelister Mountains and south to the Prespa forests.[52] Smallholding-sized parcels of land were readily available, although on the hills the Vlachs jealously guarded long possessed grazing rights. The last residents of *bey* and *aga* rank in lakeside Ottoman-origin places like *Bu'f*/Limnos departed voluntarily or were driven out by local people in a landgrab for the *ciflik* farms. Land was plentiful but able-bodied people were not and this situation was soon to be worsened the following year with the outbreak of the First World War followed by the devastation wrought by the international influenza epidemic. Women bore a particularly heavy burden both as the main farm workers and as childbearers/rearers and often also as semi-beasts of burden. The depredations endured by the ordinary citizens at the hands of Greek nationalist or pro-Bulgarian IMRO bands had been serious enough, but the arrival of modern mechanized armies and the development of the Macedonian Front where the Serbian front line ran right across the middle of Lake Great Prespa brought new problems which the long suffering people of Prespa were ill-equipped to face.

The issue of Macedonia had played only a minor part in the thinking of the Serbian elite prior to the war and when the creation of a Yugoslavia began to become a reality as the war progressed the energies of the Yugoslavist founders were focussed on Croatia, Bosnia, Slovenia and Montenegro.[53] Yugoslavism as an ideology and political project was a northern Balkan creation. The Bulgarian 'threat' was a matter created by the occupation and the possibility that a significant proportion of the people might prefer to retain an Exarchist or specifically Macedonian identity after the war was not a factor in their thinking. The Bulgarian challenge was seen as purely a security and military matter, and this resulted in a definition of the post-war and post-Versailles Treaty Yugoslav government modus operandi that was repressive in the extreme. [54]

5

New nations and new borders divide the Lakes, 1914–23

> It was a matter of common knowledge that they possessed a secret organisation extending over the whole of Macedonia, and that their agents were busily engaged in enrolling recruits for the coming struggle, and putting vigorous presence upon such Bulgarian devotees as still remained under the religious domination of the Greek Patriarchate to declare themselves for the Bulgarian Exarchate.
> – E.R. Wyndham Graves, *Storm Centres of the Near East, 1933*

The new international borders that crossed the Prespa Lakes in 1914 were determined by very recent Balkan Wars and those created later by the First World War continued to determine all the changing political, economic and social realities that developed. The local security mechanisms that had survived so long under the Ottoman Empire had collapsed, those the traveller Fredrick Moore had described in 1906 as 'big bird's nest built on stilts. The nestling wears a soldier's uniform and carries a gun. He is a field guard, an institution designed to protect "Christian" peasants from "brigands", Albanian and Bulgarian'.[1] But unlike this quaint, ineffective Ottoman army and its world, the new international borders were severe, functional, to an extent mechanized and it was dangerous to try to cross them illegally. The new borders also affected intellectual life and the possibilities of academic research and debate about the Prespa monuments. As a contemporary Macedonian art historian has observed: 'it is a paradoxical fact that the discovery and study of Prespa was less complicated when it was part of the Ottoman Empire up to the Balkan Wars of 1912-1913, than it was afterwards when the borders of the three separate states were drawn across Prespa.'[2]

At first the war was focussed elsewhere. The First World War hostilities on the Macedonian Front began in the Lake Dojran region on the borders of Greek Macedonia and Thrace and in the 'Monastir Gap' in the central salient.[3] In western Macedonia, neither the Allied nor the Triple Alliance armies were initially very active in the Ohrid and Prespa Lake region. The front dividing the British, French, Greek and Serbian Allied armies from the Germans and Bulgarian forces was over 170 miles long. This was over twice as long as the Western Front in France and Belgium, but little action was initially seen in the far western region around the Prespa, Ohrid and Korca. The length of the front was essentially a product of the railway, where it was possible to move soldiers and supplies much more quickly and over greater distances than in the days of the ox cart. It bore out the dictum of the Prussian military theorist Von Moltke that the railway and the modern rifle meant that high command could not plan a battle in advance. The official British historian of the conflict, Cyril Falls describes only an initial British 'skeleton' deployment of a small force in Koritsa/*Korca*.[4] For long periods the atmosphere along much of the long front stretching east across the central mountains to Dojran was tranquil, as British army officer Edward Stebbing described in his war memoir:

> Verbeni presented a wonderful sight under the rays of the setting sun this evening. The village and surrounding fields were packed with troops, horses, mules, donkeys, parked artillery caissons, ammunition and supply carts, and so on . . . As the sun dropped behind the mountains to the west those to the east turned a bright crimson, and the dust, rising in clouds from the main road close by, full of passing troops, put on a pale crimson hue in which trees, men and beasts loomed weird and fantastic.[5]

Verbeni was in the Monastir Gap to the east of Prespa and not far from the railway line linking *Salonika* with *Uskub*/Skopje and Serbia, and here the relative tranquillity was not to last very long as the battle for control of *Manastir* as a city became central to both Serbian and Greek ambitions.[6] The Albanian hopes there had been dashed after the Balkan Wars in 1912 to 1913 by the lack of modern organized Albanian military capacity. The relatively advanced, partly mechanized and well-organized armies of Bulgaria, Serbia and Greece dominated the urban regions. All three armies had accessed modern artillery and other heavy munitions, which the Albanians had not. In rural areas the comparative order associated with these mechanized forces was completely absent. Many Macedonian region villages were still recovering in 1914 from the destruction of the Ilinden period and then the Balkan Wars, when over three hundred settlements in the southern *kazas* of *Manastir vilayet* had been looted and burnt and the surviving inhabitants often suffered from serious diseases and food shortages. The transition from the horse and cart Balkan armies of the 1912 to 1913 period to the developing mechanization of many aspects of the Allied forces in the First World War had changed territorial priorities, so control of the relatively open and passable lands of the Gap were a central objective for both sides in the conflict as movement by mechanized vehicles was feasible there. It was always very difficult and often impossible to move let alone utilize even light artillery pieces in the wilds of the forests or to move them on primitive tracks in the mountains, but the road the Ottomans had constructed gradually along the east side of the Prespa Lakes was more functional – at least outside the winter months – and would become an important, if minor, channel of military movement in the conflict.

Infantry warfare on the open lands to try to control the passes and the railway lines with the exchange of artillery barrages remained the dominant military doctrine, and doctrine in the Balkans, as on the Western Front determined strategy and tactics. The Prespa hills, in comparison to today's heavily wooded Prespa landscape, were then often bare and treeless, a product of intensive overgrazing for centuries, forest fires and the demands of the Ottoman imperial system for Balkan timber. As such they did not lend themselves to guerrilla warfare, particularly as aircraft were now part of the more modern armies. *Manastir* remained up to the middle years of the World War very much a major Ottoman garrison town, far smaller than modern Bitola and dominated by an enormous central military parade ground surrounded by bare limestone hills. In August 1916 during the Bulgarians' advance the front had run west from *Manastir* to a point on Great Prespa Lake just north of modern Krani village and by the end of the war had only moved a few miles northwards to meet the lake near Pretor.

In essence the Prespa region was not involved significantly in the 'crushing of Serbia' demanded by the Hapsburgs three years earlier. There was nevertheless significant fighting over the struggle to secure *Manastir*, which culminated with its shelling by the Bulgarians on 17 November 1917, when over two thousand shells fell on the town and burnt out over a thousand dwellings, the day before the Great Fire which destroyed much of *Salonika* the following day.[7] The only action of significance in the winter of 1917 was the attempt of the Italians based in Epirus and southern Albania near modern Leskovic to form a new front stretching across the mountains west to the Adriatic at modern Saranda, on the Albanian coast opposite Corfu. This was a move strongly but ineffectually opposed by the two French battalions based at Koritsa/*Korca*. It was a development of very minor importance in the First World War but one which foreshadowed Italian military activity in southern Albania, Corfu and Epirus at later points in the twentieth century starting with the Corfu crisis in 1923,[8] when the newly empowered Mussolini in Rome sought to take over the island and culminated with the Italian invasion of Epirus in 1940.

Yet very major changes were in the making in the international boundaries across the lakes that were in essence militarily determined, and the decisions of the 1913 Boundary Commission had often been influenced by imperialist military criteria as well as chance and local factors.[9] In its ethos the Commission was a very British creation and was in origin formed by dignitaries in the Royal Geographical Society in London who had long imperial experience in producing suitable administrative divisions in British colonies and dominions. In essence it followed a 'winner takes all system' so the majority nationality or ethnic group was allowed to dominate all others in a region. The Commissioners were subject to intense local lobbying, the most notable by the Greeks in Epirus/*Chameria* when the Albanian border was being designated, memorably described by the French newspaper correspondent Henry Baerlein.[10]

The establishment and international recognition of Albanian independence in 1913 had also begun to open up some of these questions in ways that would fundamentally determine the national futures of the people living around Prespa. There is little doubt that in 1912 at the time of the outbreak of the First Balkan War there were a majority of Macedonian/Bulgarian speakers and Orthodox Exarchist Christians living around the wider region of the Prespa Lakes, but in the border settlement arrived at for Albania in 1913, seven villages around Pushtec on the west side of Lake Prespa were allocated to Albania, although mixed Muslim/Orthodox, as a result – according to contemporary anecdotal evidence – of the Commissioners' criteria of market usage, and as these villagers used Korca/*Koritsa* market for their commercial transactions and shopping, they were placed by the Commissioners in Albania.[11] A small coal mine had opened at Drenovo near Korca and coal was a very valuable commodity for the lake villagers living under the bare and treeless (to this day) Thate Mountains and so they used Korca/*Koritsa* market to buy fuel.[12] On random factors such as this, the process began of the first of a series of decisions between 1913 and 1924 that would bring the modern national boundaries for the lakeside communities into being and formalize the process of new national identity formation that has continued to the present day. Defined national borders were the key to stable population identity formation in the view of the Powers and the nascent League of Nations. The small probably trilingual community of *Nivica* was already on the path that was to lead to it becoming modern Greek Psarades, with its modest prosperity but major population decline, while other similar communities that had a secure if poverty-stricken existence in late Ottoman Prespa have been obliterated in the wars of the very violent long twentieth century.

In the background were the Bulgarian irredentist ambitions that sought to integrate much of Macedonia into a post-war 'Greater Bulgaria', on the back of the anticipated success of the Bulgarian army allied to Germany and the Hapsburgs. There is no doubt IMRO had a strong local presence remaining in the Prespa region, particularly given the nature of the quasi-religious 'freedom or death' oaths taken by new members which were sworn, for life, and taken over a Bible, a revolver and a dagger.[13] In 1916 in Switzerland the prominent Sofia historian A. Ischirkov had published his *Les Confins Occidentalaux des Terres Bulgares*, ostensibly a serious study of the history but clearly designed to influence a future post-World War peace conference and the prospect of border revisions, based on the recovery of the Bulgarians '*national patrimonie*'. The region of Prespa and Ohrid was central to his arguments, a further illustration of the inescapable heritage of late antiquity and Byzantium around Prespa and Ohrid in issues determining local identities in Macedonia in the twentieth century.[14] In reality, Bulgarian ambitions were to be crushed by the nation being on the losing side in the First World War, so that the official British Foreign Office Intelligence Handbook 'Macedonia', published in November 1918, could summarize the settlement as one where

> Lake Okhrida is divided between two sovereignties by the Serbo-Albanian frontier, which runs across the south-western part; Lakes Prespa and Dojran are similarly traversed by the Greco-Serbian frontier. The lakes are all noted for their fish.

The advent of the Autonomous Albanian Republic of Korca, 1916–20

By the second year of the war in 1916 the relative tranquillity along the front on the eastern side of the Prespa Lakes contrasted markedly with developing turmoil and military confrontation in the old Ottoman *kaza* of Korca. The Hapsburg forces had invaded northern Albania in the spring of 1916, as part of their wider *Drang nach Serbia*, the attempt to utterly crush the Serbian forces after the latter's initial success against the Hapsburg forces in 1914 to 1915.[15] The Bulgarians had occupied parts of eastern Albania, prompting the French army to move into Korca which they took over in November 1916. The crisis also precipitated the entry into the regional conflict of the Greek nationalists of the Pan-Epiriotic Federation which had established itself with an armed militia, the Sacred Army of Zographos, controlling *Agyrokastro*/Gjirokastra as early as February 1914 where an 'Autonomous Republic of Northern Epirus' had been declared. The Athens Royalist government that took over power in January 1915 formally incorporated the area of Northern Epirus into Greece in March 1916, with two administrative centres, Gjirokastra/*Agyrokastro* and Korca/*Koritsa*. Greek occupation only lasted a few months before the Bulgarians occupied the city of Korca and the Greek soldiers fled. The Allied commanders could not countenance a future division of Albania dominated by the Bulgarians and substantial French forces moved into Korca in November 1916, trying to link up with the wider Macedonian Front to the east.

As the war evolved the French army held Korca and much of the surrounding region, including most of Ohrid and Prespa regions, as the British and their Serbian allies held the central sector where the Bulgarian forces had collapsed and retreated. The political future of the Prespa and Ohrid regions was unclear. Korca had a significant Greek minority in the population and nearby majority Vlach communities like Voskopoje (once Byzantine *Moskopolis*) were clerical foci with historic Orthodox churches that looked to the Patriarchate in Constantinople rather than the Exarchate for religious leadership. Many Vlachs were trilingual with Greek, Albanian and Vlach but the liturgy in their churches was conducted in Greek. The Vlachs at that time in Voskopoje were the majority-ethnic group, as nowadays, and were bilingual in Vlach and Greek as primary languages, although many could also understand and use

Illustration 6 The First World War French fort opposite Psarades.

some Albanian, a product of their extensive trans-Balkan trading relationships.[16] The *Moskopolis*/Voskopoje monastery and churches had been attacked earlier in the war by Albanian militias led by nationalist poet Sali Butka who worked as a local ally for the Hapsburg army to the north. The area under French military control was soon to become a French political protectorate.

Earlier in the war, the struggle for Korca had become a critical objective for Greek irredentists and the English Albanologist and feminist author Mary Edith Durham, along with James Bourchier, the distinguished London *Times* Balkan correspondent, had played vital roles in stymieing Greek nationalist ambitions there. The French placed their man, Themistocli Germani, as local regent, and he followed relatively progressive pro-Albanian policies, establishing numerous Albanian language schools, including the first school for girls in Albania, and closing down all Greek language education.

A picture of this little studied period is to be found in the memoirs of Korca Republic official Nikollaq Zoi, an intelligent man originally from near Korca but who had grown up in an Albanian emigre community in what is now modern Romania.[17] In essence the French co-opted the *beys* and other prominent citizens of a nationalist bent, like Zoi, and allowed them to have control of a regional government that started quickly to build Albanian institutions, while the French soldiers guaranteed the external security. The French commanders were interested in the lakes, perhaps sensing their strategic and economic importance and began building some border fortifications most of which were in areas along or near the modern Albanian-Greek borderline, thus adding to the evolving new international 'hard' borders dividing the lake dwellers from each other. In September 1917 the area under French control increased when they captured the town of Pogradec on the southern tip of Lake Ohrid, and there they introduced the *Frange* as the currency of the Korca Republic in the same year. The Republic continued a shadowy economic existence until the Paris Peace Conference in 1919, where Greek claims on Northern Epirus were rejected by the Powers, and the territory became part of the main Albanian state. In the localities themselves, chronic instability continued, with local armed *ceta* bands and what remained of IMRO challenging the Greeks for local authority and all the mountains remained anarchic.

The Albanian Prespa lakeside villages were deeply exposed to these violent and chaotic exchanges for control of territory and the unstable foreign military control that replaced the Ottoman army. Road building was an imperialist military priority for the Allied armies. As a sign of future Italian ambitions in the Balkans, the cross-Albania highway running from Saranda in Albania to Florina via Erseka and Ohrid was constructed, where it met the route of the old Via Egnetia.[18] In the Prespa villages their proximity to the front line led to turmoil. Local oral tradition in the modern Albanian village of Pushtec suggests the church was taken over by the Bulgarians while the inhabitants fled to the hills and the lower slopes of the Thate Mountains to the west of the lake villages. The French occupation brought peace of a kind, and stability, but also prioritized Albanian language and culture in education, removing Bulgarian as well as Greek from the system. Thus Prespa in this key period can be seen as repeating in microcosm the division of the wider Macedonia that had begun after 1912 and the First Balkan War. The Korca Republic was a profoundly urban creation, exclusively focussed on Korca itself, and it must be an open question as to whether it had much real presence at all in very rural areas such as the Prespa shoreline. Nevertheless, some French Republic military buildings can still be seen today, such as the small fort with standing walls overlooking Great Prespa Lake lost in the juniper forest off the Psarades eastern coastal path and the low walls of the remote Mount Devas hilltop fort a kilometre north of Pili village. Here and in many other Korca-focussed districts, it was simply a French military occupation, and it is perhaps symbolic of the local Greek psychology that these monuments to what is seen as an 'Albanian' republic created by the French occupation are not signposted anywhere in the Greek part of the modern National Park and are hard to find.

There is little evidence for the existence of the French Republic in modern Korca city either and the French heritage in the city had generally received little attention from Albanian historians, despite later Albanian communist leader Enver Hoxha having attended and then taught at a French *lycee* there in his youth. In reality the Korca Republic provided a model for many institutional systems that were adopted by King Zog and his followers after 1924 as he sought to build a functional modern state. In Prespa a semi-derelict and neglected fort half overgrown by forest remains on a small hill facing Psarades. It is near a small track that runs eventually through the forests to the Albanian border with Greece. The crumbling fort is riddled with old bullet holes and in a poor state but nevertheless conveys well the atmosphere when it was built, probably in 1916, when the French army needed a watchtower to be able to survey the vast and empty sheet of water of Great Prespa Lake stretching north into what was soon to become the first, Royalist Yugoslavia. The 'invisible' frontiers of language and ethnicity that were always present were beginning to coalesce into modern 'hard' borders. New nationhood and new borders were indivisible and modern frontier posts and military control began to bring stability and many benefits to the region after so many years of late Ottoman and then wartime anarchy and violence.[19] The French also developed economic interests in Prespa and the wider Macedonian region. Exploiting the very rich fish supplies in the Prespa Lakes, a fish processing plant was set up in the Vlach village of Pili, two miles west of modern Psarades. Pili was once a tiny ancient Roman staging post on the road around Lesser Prespa that ran through the forests and mountains towards distant Korca/*Koritsa*, and some minor ancient Roman ruins can be seen nowadays on the lakeside in a bean plantation. The First World War French army saw itself as a Napoleonic force for economic progress and modernization, with an '*Oeuvre Civilisatrice*' and in the wartime years had set up a substantial manufacturing base in Florina/*Lerin*, including a soap factory, brush factory, a furniture workshop and tobacco curing sheds. In a development that was minor at the time but presaged very important developments later in the twentieth century, three small lignite mines were opened up, the first regional precursors of the giant contemporary opencast operations near Ptolemaida that are central to modern Greek electricity supply. In an equally revolutionary development in agriculture, metal ploughs were introduced and modern threshing and reaping machines in the almost quarter of a million acres controlled by the French military force.[20]

The background to these efforts was the uncertainty over landownership in Greek Macedonia after the First World War.[21] Virtually all material production in most of northern Macedonia was based upon the land. The large ex-Ottoman *ciflik* estates had in the different periods of expansion of northern Greece in the late nineteenth and early twentieth century become effectively nationalized and passed to the Greek state, and then mostly had been either given to or appropriated by small peasant landholders.[22] A family smallholding could be as small as two or three acres. In most cases the peasants had few or no legal titles or documentation to the land and held it by local tradition, *adet*, in Ottoman Turkish convention. Possession of land was nine-tenths of the de facto law. In Prespa both in the period after the Treaty of Versailles and the population exchanges, and during the 1930s, uncertainty over tenure produced a climate of endemic conflicts in the locality, and widespread distrust of the Athens government and its local agency, principally the Greek army and security apparatus. It was often difficult for families with a bad 'biography' to obtain land tenure documents, particularly those seen as 'Bulgarian'. Little was known in Athens about the general Prespa region until the geographer G. Athanasopoulos described the region in a paper for the Hellenic Geographical Society in 1922.[23] The chronic political instability in Greece in these years at national level increased local tensions in Macedonia. As Michael Llewellyn-Smith has written, in 1916 northern Greece had a parallel government to the ostensible government in Athens when Eleftherios Venizelos established his power in *Salonika*/Thessaloniki.[24]

Prespa was exceptional in Greek Macedonia in having ancestral productive resources that did not depend on cultivating the land and pastoralism. Fishing had sustained *Nivica* and nearby Prespa village life for centuries. As in other lakeside locations, the drop in water levels in the late twentieth century has revealed previously unknown Roman remains, as on Pili shoreline. Pili then and now had a majority population of Vlach pastoralists who nowadays have mostly abandoned sheep farming to work on bean production on the good stretch of arable land on the lake margins. The Prespa sardines used then to be dried and hung on strings to be sold as a delicacy in French markets, although it is probable they were first used after 1920 in the food supply for the still numerous French soldiers garrisoning the Korca Republic. The trade continued in different forms throughout the twentieth century until shortly after the end of the Cold War, with an annual visit of a large refrigerated French lorry to take away a load of plundered sardines to Paris. The original factory established by the French military lasted for a period after the integration of Lower Prespa into Greece after 1923, but closed at some time in the late 1920s with the collapse of the regional economy and the wider refugee crisis in Greece following the 1922 catastrophe of the Greeks in Asia Minor against the Turkish forces under Kemal Ataturk.

In the immediate aftermath of the end of the First World War the foreign military presence was soon reduced, and the wider political future of the entire Macedonian region came to be dominated by the conflicts to the east where the Greek and Allied armies were involved in dismembering the last remains of the Ottoman world in the crisis period following the Treaty of Sevres. The Greek claims on Northern Epirus had been rejected in the Paris Peace Conference in 1919, with Soviet Russia and the United States strongly defending the unity and survival of Albania, and the focus of Athens government activity shifted to the struggle for Constantinople and western Asian Minor. Village boys were still being conscripted into and dying within the Greek army, as the Psarades town square war memorial shows nowadays, and at the same time the international influenza epidemic was taking its toll on the general population. South of the Greek border at Agios Germanos, local anarchy prevailed until the arrival of Serbian soldiers from the north to guard the border. Demobilized Serbs were being settled in quite substantial numbers in nearby – newly Royalist Yugoslav – towns such as Struga, where the large Albanian population had been forcibly displaced.[25]

Only about eighty refugees from Asia Minor after the Catastrophe of 1923 were settled in the immediate Prespa vicinity, a decision resulting from the very limited quality of arable land around the lakes. They were settled at Lefkonas, Pili, Laimos/*Soufkotski* and Agios Germanos, mostly on the old *Saofkotftsi ciflik* land. The Athens' government resettlement policy for refugees in Macedonia focussed on the arable lands surrounding towns like Kilkis, Drama and Serres, where substantial tracts of *ciflik* land owned by Ottoman landlords and religious institutions before 1914 stood empty and uncultivated. This involved the inevitable Greek focus on the *polis*, urban constructions with a large local garrison and usually a massive new church built on a prominent high place. The 'refugee quarters' of these and other places throughout Greece can still be recognized nowadays with their rows of more or less identical box-like houses in orderly patterns with straight streets. Some refugees moved also to empty land near Florina, but in the poor agricultural conditions of the time a significant proportion did not remain there for very long but moved to the larger cities, particularly Thessaloniki, to try to find urban employment. Some of those who remained became the nucleus of the modern Florina satellite village of Proti, on the northern outskirts of Florina, always a stronghold of political radicalism that is still known colloquially as *Micri (little) Moscow*.

The imposition of the new Greek government rule did not bring harmony to the mountains and the lakes. Religion as always in the region was a key fault line. The Greek nationalist position had always been – and in many respects still is – that the Macedonian villagers were in essence Greek Christians who had been traduced by imported Bulgarian Exarchate priests and schoolteachers in the late nineteenth century. The explicit programme of the Patriarchist Bishops, in Florina, in particular was to restore what they saw as a true Byzantine-descended church, in harmony with ancient tradition. Recently built churches such as the very large Exarchate building outside the entirely Macedonian-speaking and later strongly pro-communist village of Vrondero west of *Nivica*/Psarades were closed and replaced by new churches/priests loyal to the Constantinople Patriarchate. Greek-speaking priests were under the direct control of the diocese of Florina. The Russian-financed church at *Nivica/Psarades* survived physically but was also placed under firm Florina Patriarchist diocesan control.[26]

The Vlach pastoralists in the nearby hills were often willing supporters of this process, as most Vlachs wanted cultural differentiation from the Macedonian-Slav majority and had never received the same intensity of Exarchate proselytism as the lake littoral dwellers. It is obviously only a matter of speculation and there are no sources outside oral tradition, reliable or not, but it is likely that the close commercial connections of the transhumant Vlachs with recently Hellenized Thessaly after the Ottoman collapse there in 1881 had imbued at least some of them with the new consciousness of nationhood in the expanding Greek state. The local people remaining were mostly without leadership with the few educated people having left for villages on the north side of the new Yugoslav border, where at least the liturgy was said in a language they could understand – if under new Serbian Orthodox church control – or gone as far as deciding to move to Bulgaria.

A central Greek government assault on the traditional economic freedoms of the lake dwellers began and the Athens government tried to impose taxes on the fish caught in the lakes which led to rioting and violent disorder in and around *Nivica*/Psarades in 1924. The Greek army established local checkpoints to seal the border, particularly with Albania, and the forests were allowed to grow over the old track roads and close them, while the military made demands on slender local cereal and other staple food supplies. Aspects of the modern heavily forested landscape in what is now the Prespa National Park began to develop then, as nature reclaimed land that had been grazing land that had fallen into disuse as a result of the war, the new borders interrupting centuries-old grazing routes and accentuating general depopulation. Similar processes were taking place all over mountainous northern Greece. Here and elsewhere goats were beginning to displace sheep as a dominant pastoral animal and doing serious damage to the forests to the extent that later, in the 1930s, the Metaxas government started to try to reduce the goat population of northern Greece as a whole. In Greek Prespa life was made more difficult in villages which were subjected to violent incursions by the army who claimed to be looking for weapons held by IMRO supporters. The church sought to Hellenize religion in Prespa and in a key construction in 1927 a new church was opened, St Nicholas, on the site of the old Ottoman garrison mosque at Kallithea.[27]

Underlying the intense local and regional ethnic tensions was the aftermath of the Paris Peace Conference in 1919 where under the ascendant Eleftherios Venizelos even the most ill-informed local people of all ethnicities knew ambitious further Greek claims with background French/British imperialist support would be made on their territory.[28] The Versailles decisions had legitimized the takeover of what had been regarded as most of 'Aegean Macedonia' by Greece and brought the Macedonian issue into Greece, however reluctant Greek political parties were to admit it at the time. The Paris conference also marked the arrival for the first time of the United States as a major factor in Balkan international relationships. The country had not been involved in the settlement after the Balkan Wars in 1913, but the Great War had changed everything. Within the United States the interests of particular national lobby groups, then as more recently in the ex-Yugoslav wars after 1990, were powerful. As Petsalis-Diomedis writes:

> 'Owing to considerable pro-Bulgarian feeling in the United States (the two countries had never broken off relations) they wanted direct negotiations with the Bulgarians in Paris. With regard to Macedonia, they rejected – as did the British – an autonomous state but favoured the partition of the uncontested zone, leaving Ishtib and Kocana to Bulgaria. As for the Greco-Serbian border, they were inclined to press for the secession of the Dojran-Gevgjeli border zone to Greece.'

The 'uncontested' zone referred to was a concept that had emerged in a secret annexe to the Serbian-Bulgarian Treaty of March 1912, prior to hostilities later in the year, and would have meant, if implemented, that swathes of Macedonian territory including

Ohrid, *Manastir*/Bitola, Prilep and other nearby towns, and all the Prespa Lake districts, would become Bulgarian. The 'contested' zone lay to the north and principally concerned the fate of *Uskub*, modern Skopje, and Kumanovo. In terms of the decisions in Paris affecting Prespa the key reality was the reoccupation of Korca/*Korytsa* by Greek troops in 1919. The Boundary Commission in 1913 had accepted an Austrian proposal that Korca and the surrounding ex-Ottoman *kaza* should be in Albania, and the boundary line concerned came to be known as the Florence demarcation, the Protocol of Florence. It represented a significant defeat for Greek nationalist ambitions, not only in *Koritsa*/Korca because it meant that the port of Saranda and the important border town of Gjirokastra/*Agyrokastro* was placed within Albania, and the Greek army advance on Korca in 1919 was designed to present the Paris conference with a fait accompli which Athens hoped it would accept. The Powers did not do so, and the Greeks have never recognized the Florence Protocol which remained the case throughout the twentieth century.

From the point of view of the Prespa Lake dwellers the future was very uncertain. Although under Greek control in the military sense the northern region like the country as a whole was rent by the National Schism between the Royalists and the Venizelos's Republicans. It was not long before the crisis entered the deliberations of the newly formed Greek Communist Party (KKE). In 1921 a KKE delegation to the Communist International (Comintern) arrived in Moscow after the party had agreed to take part in the Third Comintern Congress.[29] It has been an idée recu of modern western historiography exemplified by historians such as Richard Clogg that this placed the Macedonian issue in Greece under Soviet control. The publication of KKE internal and Comintern documentation shows that this was not always the case.[30] The reality was that the Comintern element internationalized the issue and forced the Greek communists to look at policy in a wider Balkan context.[31] There were major splits in the party over policy, and in the Comintern, and Moscow was often not in control of what the Greeks decided.[32] Part of Macedonia had only been taken by Serbia in the Balkan Wars but fell mostly under Bulgarian control in the World War. The Paris conference was distant and in the days before most of the modern apparatus of 'humanitarian intervention' had been created the Powers lacked levers to enforce their will upon the ground, particularly when quite a substantial part of the economic life of all the communities was outside a monetary economy. The Powers knew IMRO still existed, exemplified by the continuing prominence of local leaders like Done Kirkov from Drenoveni, a veteran of the Balkan Wars, and it remained the objective of IMRO to destroy the nascent Yugoslav state edifice and create an independent Macedonia.[33] But IMRO was divided and there was the new factor in all Balkan diplomatic calculations with the 1917 Russian Revolution and the establishment of the Bolshevik government in Moscow.

It did not take long before the long-standing controversies about the Macedonian Question found their way into the Comintern, the Communist International, augmented by the appointment of Vasil Kolarov, a Bulgarian, as General Secretary of the Comintern in Moscow in 1922. Some Macedonian nationalists had started to look towards the new Russia, not least because at the Paris conference the Serbs, with French backing, had successfully resisted Italian plans for an autonomous Macedonia within the new Royalist Yugoslav state. As Boskovska points out, in the localities the new Yugoslav state followed the most draconian policies against IMRO or suspected IMRO sympathizers that were then extended to the entire population, even to the extent of issuing detailed controls for the peasant's movement and forbidding them from grazing their animals in the forests.[34] Emigration was encouraged, so in the view of the authorities successfully ridding the land of pro-Bulgarian bandits, *Bulgarski bandita*, more land would become available for Serbian colonists.[35]

In practice, as in Kosovo to the north, this Serbian colonization policy was a failure in most districts, as after the enormous toll taken on the Serbian population by the losses in the World War there were never enough new settlers to follow the central government southern colonization plans written in Belgrade, whether for Kosovo or Macedonia. The church was also often a barrier to Serbification. Although the new higher clergy were loyal to and appointed by the Serbian Patriarch and approved by Belgrade, local priests who had survived the wartime period often retained elements of their Bulgarian Exarchist practical and theological culture, IMRO sympathies, and in private were a support for Macedonian villagers. The central governments, whether in Athens or Belgrade, also found the construction of functional local administrations very difficult, as civil servants in both countries, particularly in the new *banovina* of South Serbia, were unwilling to work in the deep south of Yugoslavia given the often unpleasant and dangerous conditions.[36] Health was a particular issue, just as it had been in late antiquity. Skopje still had endemic malaria problems, as did many other low-lying places throughout Macedonia, and tuberculosis was a scourge in the poorer parts of the towns.[37] There were also linguistic issues with Serbian officials from northern Yugoslavia who spoke the standard Ekkavian dialect of Serbo-Croat having considerable difficulty understanding local people in Macedonia, and vice versa. Village dialects were very difficult for them and very few of them spoke Albanian or Turkish, or other minority languages.

The poor social and economic conditions bore down heavily upon the peasants and very small working class in the towns, and this was reflected in growing support for the Yugoslav Communists. As E.H. Carr observed in his study of the post-Versailles settlement and its wider effects: 'the notion still entertained by the peacemakers of 1919 that any solution which seemed to them to be manifestly rational, and which commended itself to all independent "experts" would be voluntarily adopted by those concerned was a fruitful source of failure and confusion'.[38]

In the first Yugoslav Parliamentary elections in 1920, the Communists won fifty-nine seats, in third position behind the Democrats and the Radicals. It is unclear how much this was in support of Russian and Comintern policy that stood for an independent Macedonia or was merely a protest against the prevailing dire social conditions but what was certain was that in Yugoslav eyes in Belgrade, in Athens and in foreign capitals the old menace of IMRO was reviving in Bolshevik clothes. In Sofia a modernized IMRO was also developing under the leadership of Mikhailov and many *comitadjis* had integrated with the wider society, abandoning the forests for urban life. The organization was nonetheless rent by vicious feuds and involved in regular assassinations of which the most important was the street corner assassination of Bulgarian Prime Minister Stambouliski in Sofia in 1923.

The Bolshevik Revolution and its international ramifications had introduced a fundamentally new factor into Greek, Yugoslav and a wider regional polity that was to also accelerate the chronic political and economic instability of the region, whether in tiny communities like *Nivica*, towns like Resen and *Manastir*/Bitola or cities like Thessaloniki/*Solun*. Throughout the nineteenth century Tsarist Russia had been present as a regional influence and had a clear but limited regional role. After 1918 it was replaced by a Soviet state where in every Balkan nation there was a functional and developing communist movement tied to Moscow through the Communist International, the Comintern, that offered the vision of the liberation of the poor and – ostensibly – national independence within an international socialist commonwealth. The region was ruined by the years of war before 1918, with the German traveller and social-democrat politician Wendel noting in his book, *Von Marburg bis Monastir*, published in 1920, that the ruins of Thessaloniki were like 'a northern French town' after the war on the Western Front. A fertile climate for the revolutionary and the extreme nationalist had been created by the conflicts. The Versailles settlement was a product of the liberal internationalism of the time guided by the interests of the main imperialist powers. The generally weak and dependent middle-class elites in the Balkan towns and cities were in a poor position to maintain their ascendancy in the new states like Albania and Yugoslavia which had weak governmental and state structures without recourse to authoritarian and ultimately fascist methods of government. The powers had believed that the old Macedonian Question had been resolved by the imposition of the new Versailles-sanctioned international borders. In reality it had merely suppressed the old issue of the division of Macedonia that the post-Balkan Wars treaties had made after 1913, as it suppressed or avoided other conflicts and potential conflicts. The new framework of communist underground organizational capacity in the wider Balkan region and the junction of the policy of the Greek communist policy with the Macedonian cause in Greece were to haunt the region for the next generations and continues in a modified form to the present day.

6

Nivica becomes Psarades

The construction of Greek Macedonia, 1924–39

The post–First World War revolutionary tide subsided with the isolation of Bolshevik Russia, the fall of Soviet governments in Hungary and Bavaria and the imposition of the Versailles Treaty international order after 1923. The Versailles settlement was hailed at the time as bringing an end to war and international conflicts, and ushering in peace under the aegis of a benign League of Nations, but in reality many territorial and sovereignty problems remained unresolved. This was certainly the case in the Balkans, where the new central state of Yugoslavia had unstable and undetermined relationships with its neighbours, particularly in the south where, as the favoured state created by British and French imperialism, it had swallowed much of historic Macedonian *Turkey-in-Europe* into its new territory. The order arising from the Versailles Treaty in northern Greece started to consolidate, and the Belgrade and Athens governments worked to impose their national identities and cultural norms on divided Macedonia. Greece accelerated the process of Hellenization that had begun after 1913 within a year of the end of the Second Balkan War in the sprawling and mountainous but very depopulated new lands in the north, which were devastated by wartime losses, emigration, the international influenza epidemic and the exchange of populations with Turkey.[1] Moslems who had left the region for Turkey under the exchange of population provisions had in the main settled in and around Bursa, particularly those from in and near Florina/*Lerin*. Hellenization of the remaining population was seen openly as a colonization project, and as senior Athens diplomat Dimitri Pentzopoulos wrote in his 1962 memoir, it was seen as justifiable and was 'implemented with due consideration to national security'.[2] The army commanders wished to see a clear and defensible northern Greek border using natural features like mountains used to their strategic advantage, with no potentially dissident minorities or non-Hellenes living there, and they believed their exclusion was justified by the Versailles Treaty. It should be borne in mind that a massive system of new identity formation in Greece was already in existence after 1924, which had been created to deal with the 'decultureisation' of many of the Asia Minor refugees, which was paralleled by a similar scheme (in reverse) in Ataturk's new Turkey.[3] These imperatives were further accelerated with the Asia Minor refugee influx into Macedonia after 1922. It was easily extended to the so-called *Slavica* population who were seen in Athens as a very marginal group compared to the hundreds of thousands of Turkish-speaking Asia Minor refugees.

Population displacement had begun in many Prespa villages as long ago as 1903 to 1908 and accelerated through the Balkan Wars (1912–13) and then continued during the First World War and the influenza epidemic. Before the wartime displacements, the region throughout the nineteenth century had also been subject to major labour migration, as the impoverished mountain villagers were unable to find work on the *cifliks* and so tried to scrape a living as migrant traders and pedlars or began to emigrate far from their homes, first to the Hapsburg lands. A strong Macedonian-identity population remained in many places. In 1923 a Bulgarian travel and cultural author G. Tranov visited *Neverska*, modern Psarades, and noted it as 'one of the most beautiful villages of Prespa', with 'seventy four houses, many two storied houses, purely Bulgarian and inhabited by eighty families'. How reliable his observations are must be open to question, and his ethnic definition probably depends on ability to speak Bulgarian rather than local citizens' loyalty to the Exarchate. It nevertheless shows a functional and moderately prosperous community, with much of the same street layout and local institutions as contemporary Psarades. Some scientific interest in the lakes, mainly from local amateurs, was beginning to develop, and in 1925 an experiment using aniline-coloured water was able to conclusively demonstrate that water continually flowed from the *Zavir* sinkhole on the Albanian side of Lesser Prespa Lake through to Lake Ohrid near Sveti Naum monastery.[4]

Yet a new population was arriving in the region as long-standing residents died or left.[5] Greece had hundreds of thousands of Christian refugees from Asia Minor to settle under the Versailles Treaty exchange of population provisions. They settled wherever they could make a living and escape the squalor and unemployment of the government camps. According to Greek official statistics, 538,595 persons were moved into the northern nomarchies after 1922, the great majority Greeks from Asia Minor, and thus transformed the population composition of the region.[6] Macedonia had the most critical manpower problems of any part of Greece, with many ex-Ottoman *cifliks* in 1918 semi-deserted and the fields uncultivated and returning to scrub and forest. Some places like the hills near Lake Dojran in eastern Macedonia were still affected by large amounts of unexploded ordinance and agriculture was difficult or impossible there. Modern land drainage schemes had only touched a few parts of the lower Vardar/Axios river valley and the sea delta and much of the land south of Pella was marshland and swamp, the dreadful conditions British and other soldiers had endured during the war.[7] It was inevitable that many Asia Minor people would be settled in the uplands, happy to be removed from the overcrowded and disease-ridden slums of Thessaloniki and other coastal towns like Kavala where they had congregated. Many were still living there in tented camps where tuberculosis, diphtheria, syphilis and malnutrition were common, and infant mortality was very high.[8] They also often lived in cultural isolation from their long-established neighbours, with different outlooks and, above all, more relaxed marriage customs and conventions. In particular ex-Asia Minor urban women had enjoyed a degree of relative freedom that was absent in deeply patriarchal peasant families in the new village homes in Greece.

The isolation of the Prespa Lakes region from the main tides of the mechanized combat between 1914 and 1918 had left the villages in a relatively favourable position compared to those in the open plains of central and eastern Macedonia which had been completely devastated by the war. The Greek army nevertheless continued to be a major force in the western Macedonian landscape, in the absence of many aspects of a functional civilian state, and after 1922 and the National Schism, the ructions in the army between pro- and anti-monarchist factions impinged on the northern border regions. With the 'new lands' of Macedonia always seen as an index of national security, the crisis of authority there played into the hands of those officers who were resisting civilian control of the armed forces and saw their career prospects improved by stressing instability and the need for firm military repression of the people at local level.[9] Population exchange in some places continued after the Versailles Treaty period, particularly connected to the tensions between the new Yugoslav government and Athens, and the implications of the collapse of the Treaty of Sevres. At local level around the lakes there is strong oral memory of nationalist strong arm gangs forcing Slav-speakers to emigrate, particularly if they were occupying desirable fertile land.[10]

Muslim Cham Albanians were moving to Turkey from Epirus, accelerating labour shortages in north-west Greece, as were Albanians from Kosovo and other parts of the south Serb *banovina* who saw Turkey as a land of freedom where they could practice their religion without hindrance. Belgrade in turn wanted to secure official minority status for some Slav-speakers in northern Greece which it had designated as 'Serbs', and the Pangalos government in 1927 in Athens signed an agreement to allow this, and to allow Serbia a free trade zone in Thessaloniki port and control of the Thessaloniki-Belgrade rail line, but the agreement was never ratified and led indirectly to the fall of that Athens government.[11] The issue of minority rights was used cynically by both governments in Belgrade and in Athens as a sprat to catch the important mackerel of trade deals. This was the first and in many senses the last effort to introduce ethnic minority policies into modern Greece in the twentieth century but it failed. The stern dictates of the Treaty of Lausanne had legitimized mono-ethnic nations not merely as a necessity but as an ideal. It was a central strategic interest of both the Ankara and Athens governments to enforce the Lausanne provisions, as has remained the case to the present day.[12] Athens did not wish to see the special status of the Moslems with a Turkish cultural identity in Thrace repeated elsewhere in Greece.[13]

The last remnants of the Ottoman system had collapsed relatively peacefully, even in Ottoman military-dominated *Manastir*, leaving a military and security vacuum to the north of the new border between Greece and the Kingdom of the Serbs, Croats and Slovenes. The IMRO *cetas* still existed in informal networks in many districts and in the aftermath of the World War small arms and munitions were cheap and plentiful, but the position of IMRO sponsoring kinship state Bulgaria on the losing side with the Central Powers had reversed long-standing international relationships in the southern Balkans that had evolved since the Congress of Berlin. The question of Bulgaria as a kinship state was critical for IMRO. The main focus of IMRO guerrilla paramilitary activity against the Serbian army was in what is now eastern Macedonia, with a marked focus on towns like Berovo, Kratovo and Strumica. In his 1924 study of IMRO after the World War R.A. Reiss was using official Serbian gendarmerie records of local conflicts and these show that encounters between large IMRO armed militia groups and the Yugoslav security authorities were almost absent around Ohrid and Prespa, with only two incidents, both near Ohrid, out of the 293 clashes Reiss studied between 1918 and 1923. In eastern Macedonia IMRO was still very powerful and fighting between IMRO and the Serbian army reduced much of the region to violent chaos. Reasonable proximity to the neighbouring kinship state, Bulgaria, was essential for the remaining IMRO bands, as it was for the IRA in relation to Ulster and the Irish Republic throughout the twentieth century.[14]

The leadership of IMRO was seriously split and fragmented with even the most 'pure' revolutionary Yane Sandansky seemingly compromised by the events of the World War and the difficult international position of Bulgaria. Gotse Delchev was dead and his lieutenants Todor Alexandrov, Alexander Protogerov and Ivan Mihalov were to fight over his heritage to the point of near self-destruction. The move led by Protogerov towards an IMRO alliance with the Soviet Union and the Comintern to fight for a Balkan Communist Federation was the final divisive policy that emerged in 1924.[15] Bulgaria was no longer seen as a progressive new Christian state in the eyes of the Powers but had been seriously weakened by the Bolshevik Revolution in its traditional friend Russia and the bitter fighting between the Bulgarians and the retreating Ottoman forces in Thrace, which had involved savage human rights violations that had received wide international publicity and condemnation. Soon after, Mihalov was gunned down and then Protogerov was assassinated four years later in 1928. The old leadership was in ruins, and the dominant Belgrade and Athens states characterized remaining IMRO followers only as criminals and bandits.

IMRO also suffered from the bitter decline in relations between Greece and Bulgaria in these years, with the so-called War of the Stray Dog, a Greek-Bulgarian crisis in 1925, when the Greek army invaded the south-west Bulgarian border town of Petrich after two Greek soldiers were allegedly killed by Bulgarian border guards. Petrich was, and is, the main town in the IMRO stronghold of Pirin Macedonia, now south-west Bulgaria, where IMRO was in practice an independent local state within a state with a tax-raising capacity and a draconian judicial system. The assassination in 1923 of Bulgarian Prime Minster Stamboliyski in a classic IMRO 'hit' where he was gunned down opposite the old Sheraton Hotel in Sofia had been planned in the Pirin. The League of Nations played a positive role in damping down the crisis, stopping a major Greek army offensive on Petrich at the last minute, at a time when in the mid-1920s the League still had credibility and widespread international respect, unlike the time of the rise of fascism ten years later.

Over the northern Greek border in the new Yugoslav kingdom the Serbs started to settle colonies of demobilized soldiers in the new lands of the southern *banovina* but numbers were small and there was little or no state capacity there except the thin and stretched military command, and the developing influence of Serbian Orthodox church, particularly in clerical centres like Ohrid. The King's government in Belgrade had no modern concept of nation building and were attempting to impose a Yugoslav identity on a diverse and rebellious population by military means that became increasingly dictatorial as it met with less and less success. Most demobilized Serb soldiers went home as soon as they could to their families and home villages elsewhere northwards into 'Old Serbia' and it was not long before, as in other historical periods right up to the present day, there was a major population deficit in rural Macedonia, on both sides of the new border. Settlers with a secure Serbian identity tended to be concentrated in certain towns, like Kumanovo, Prilep and Ohrid, and had little or no hegemony or even collective presence in most of Macedonia. There was a chronic shortage of willing Serbian 'professional' colonists such as school teachers, lawyers, medical staff and civil servants generally, and the transition to a 'normal' state building problematic was never successfully made, as it also crippled Royalist Yugoslav Kosovo. Education was a central issue. In Greece the Venizelos government had begun to allow some primary education in *demotic* to try to fight almost universal illiteracy, and a *demotic* Greek primer was written. In *Nivica*/Psarades a school was built and opened in 1925, a sign of the prioritization of this key village in local processes of Prespa Hellenization.

Over the border the Yugoslav government was less successful in culturization. Even in a major centre like *Manastir*/Bitola, education in separate Jewish, Turkish and Serbian language schools continued well into the 1930s. In contrast, Greece had a developed and well drilled bureaucratic machine with considerable experience throughout the nineteenth century in integrating new territories and a church with extensive international contacts and support. *Nivica* as a key village on the southern shore of Great Prespa Lake was a long-standing centre of Greek attention and therefore had some real advantages for its material development – if an atmosphere of intense cultural repression – after it found itself in post-Versailles Greece. The more northern Prespa villages on the other side of the lake border in the new Yugoslavia languished in rural obscurity under often draconian military control, although with greater tolerance of Muslim religious minorities than in Greece. In terms of social relationships *Nivica* village also had the compelling advantage – in official Greek eyes – of the absence of an ex-Ottoman mosque or any Muslim-minority presence, unlike nearby Great Prespa villages like Lefkonas/Kallithea, in Greece east of *Nivica* and Krani, over the Yugoslav border or some of the villages on western Great Prespa Lake shores newly assigned to Albania, such as little *Tsernouska*, modern Zaroshe. The French military occupation and the Korca Republic period had brought one very significant new transport improvement here, the construction of a vehicle-usable road around the entire southern shore of the lakes, although it later became long redundant by post-1949 politics and Cold War borders. The road leading that way from Psarades towards the border is nowadays only used by hikers and birdwatchers, smugglers and illegal Albanian migrants but is still called 'the French Road' by older Psarades residents. It was nevertheless dangerous to travel near Ohrid and Prespa, as it remains in some places today. Some years after the Versailles Treaty the English traveller and Yugophile Grace Ellison noted in 1932 that it was against the law to travel around Ohrid at night and described the 'long dangerous unfinished roads' and travel with 'no maps'.[16]

The position of the Orthodox churches is important in considering this period; the IMRO as a clandestine revolutionary organization had been intimately linked with the Bulgarian Orthodox church through the ramifications of the post-Congress of Berlin agreement on the Exarchate with the Sultan. The end of the Ottoman Empire had left the existing religious dispensation in ruins, not merely in disarray, and in this vacuum the Serbian Orthodox church was given effective – if not exclusive – religious suzerainty by the Versailles Treaty and a privileged position in the new *banovina* of South Serbia which had been created. In this clerical expansionism the Serbian authorities were only continuing existing policies which had been in place in the conquered ex-Ottoman lands since the sweeping advances of the Serbian army southwards in the Nis region battles after 1875 and then elsewhere into Kosovo and Macedonia after 1912 in the First Balkan War. Serbian Orthodoxy grew in influence at the point of a sword. Intense pressure had been put on first the Bulgarian-oriented bishops and afterwards the parish priests to adopt a new ecclesiastical identity, demanding that the language of the liturgy was changed to either Serbian or Greek, the saints names amended and those who refused were accused of political propaganda and treason. The language of the Orthodox liturgy had a key role in establishing not only the temporality of the individual believer in relation to God and Salvation but in state formation itself. The language of time in the modern Greek state had changed after 1821, which in many ways was paralleled in the remaining Ottoman Balkan domains by the construction of urban clock towers in every sizeable town and city, so all the Sultan's subjects ran on uniform temporality, like the laws on Standard Time in the United States introduced after 1832. The language – Greek or Bulgarian – of the liturgy was also critically important because although for Orthodox Christians the liturgy is outside normal human temporality and although the Bible was freely available in both languages, very few people could actually read it.[17]

As long ago as January 1913 the Exarchist Bishop of the mining town of Veles in the Vardar valley north of Prespa region had been driven from his palace under arrest and his servants beaten up by Serbian soldiers. His palace was then requisitioned as the Serbian army headquarters in the city. In *Uskub*/Skopje the bishop Archimandrite Methodius was beaten unconscious by four soldiers and narrowly escaped with his life. The Exarchist clerics were the visible representatives of the old *millet* order and from the Serbian military point of view a substitute for attacking IMRO who were largely invisible and had gone underground and melted into armed anonymity in the localities.[18] All educated people, whether priests, schoolteachers or others, were seen as real or potential agitators by the Yugoslav authorities and in a legal climate inherited from the Ottomans where crime and political dissent were often directly equated many suffered human rights violations, and fled to exile in Bulgaria. The Macedonian/Bulgarian identity peasants around the Prespa Lakes were left leaderless. The Serbian soldiers had been told they would find 'Serbians' in the new lands and the Greek soldiers expected south of the border to find 'Greeks' but in reality found inhabitants whose language they had extreme difficulty in comprehending and with quite different traditions, identity and cultural values.

In Macedonian Greece around Prespa, saints' days were a particular difficulty for the Hellenizing Greek clergy. An important annual festival was held in Agios Germanos every July dedicated to *German*, the Slavonic-origin Bulgarian saint, associated with *German* the Slavonic pre-Christian deity of water and rain, and known locally as *San Germanos*. This festival was suppressed by the incoming Greek clergy after 1920 and replaced by a conventional mid-summer *Panagia* taking place in August and dedicated to the Virgin Mary. The Slavonic saint *German* embodied the villager's sense of identity through contact with a mediating holy figure reaching into the very distant past, ultimately reaching back to the arrival of the Slavs and Bulgarians in the region. Hellenization involved the destruction of this memory, of not only ethnic identity but also the mass of popular beliefs, superstitions and Macedonian folk tradition that has always been particularly strong in the wider ex-Bulgarian Second Empire world dating back to the Bogomils' heresy and before that to pagan survivals from late antiquity. The substitution of the significant days in the Greek national calendar showed where the Greek church has become the civic religion of the modern Greek national state.

The Greek Orthodox church bishops in the 'new lands' south of the border were in a similarly exclusive power to the Serbian bishops to the north of it, and their appointments were controlled directly by the Patriarchate in Constantinople after 1918, in contrast to those in the church in 'Old Greece'; the Serbian bishops faced, though, in the Althusserian sense, a major issue of 'survivals'. Their church had been placed by the Powers as the determining ideological state apparatus in the new country of Yugoslavia, but where the substantial numbers of the Slav-speaking population had a Macedonian or residual Bulgarian identity and spoke the different Macedonian dialects, in the days before the language had been modified by communist Belgrade and given official recognition post-1945 under Tito's language 'reforms'. There was little or nothing the Serbian priests could do about this, but this was not the case in Greece where the non-Greeks were seen as a small and undesirable minority suitable for either slow expulsion (the Cham Albanians) or more or less forced assimilation (the Macedonians and Bulgarians).[19]

Muslim-minority groups in the new South Serbia with a long-standing Turkish identity retreated to the hills and their traditional pastoral lands, but they did have certain limited legally embodied rights as a religious minority throughout the country which Muslims in Greece outside Thrace did not. The nearest significant groups were (and are to this day) in the River Radika valley north of Struga. The *yoruck* nomads centred on Radomir to the north-east remained in pastoral isolation.[20] Ironically, in view of later twentieth-century Balkan history, the Serbs were less worried about the remaining Muslims than their co-Orthodox religious rivals, the Bulgarians.

Most of the significant numbers of Albanians who remained in western Macedonia north of the border and further west in what had been Ottoman *Chameria* and was now Threspotia in modern Epirus were Muslims, and they were in a state of acute displacement and disorientation with the collapse of the theocratic empire in which they had held a secure position for hundreds of years. The local populations around Prespa and Ohrid Lakes faced particularly difficult dilemmas with these issues, as both were also centres of long-standing Christian culture and heritage dating back to the earliest days of the Byzantines in the southern Balkans and where there was also a strong 'Bulgarian' inheritance in popular culture, language and folk religion. Once again, the inheritance of late antiquity and Byzantium became a central driver in issues of national identity and twentieth-century politics in the region. The Serbian colonization project within the first Royalist Yugoslavia was heavily dependent on a view of history where modern Serbia, through the Church, was a direct inheritor of Byzantium and thus opponent, as the medieval Nemanja emperors had been, of Bulgarian ambitions in the region. But it was taking place in territory where there was a strong Bulgarophone popular cultural tradition of religious dissidence and folk beliefs outside conventional Orthodoxy, from pagan survivals, the distant empire of

Tsar Samuil and the strength of Bogomilism in the early medieval period and later local cults and shrines, some dating back to pagan origins in antiquity.[21]

The issues of temporality were left to the Church by the Athens government but this was not the case with issues of place. In a society where most people only travelled far if they were emigrating abroad local village identity was crucial, and in 1925 to 1926 under the dictatorial General Pangalos's military government in Athens legislation was passed so that hundreds of Macedonian villages with Bulgarian/Macedonian names had new spatial identities imposed, so in that year *Nivica* was officially renamed Psarades, nearby *Grazdeno* became Vrondero and so on throughout Macedonia.[22] The long slow process began of building up Agios Germanos as a small *urbs* and centre of Athens influence with the embankment of the small Agios Germanos river that flows into the lake, to prevent it flooding the lower village of Laimos. Prespa villages with Vlach names and majority populations fared better and were often left alone completely, in the Prespa region like lakeside Pili, with its etymological derivation from the Vlach word meaning 'gate'.[23] As in many later times in the twentieth century the agenda for Macedonia was set and implemented by the military in Athens and Thessaloniki and at all times, in all periods up to the present day, Greek Macedonia unlike anywhere else in the country remains under the direct authority of the Greek Interior Ministry. Pressure also began to be exerted for local people to change Macedonian/Bulgarian origin names. In Psarades a very common name was Popovski, which had to be changed to Papadopoulos, and this pressure intensified as the 1930s and the Metaxas dictatorship emerged.[24] All authorities agree that after 1928 and the onset of the World Economic Crisis, emigration from Greek Macedonia began to increase after a period of relative stability, but the overall population rose, according to one source, from 1.4 million inhabitants to about 1.7 million.[25]

As this enforced Hellenization was under way, in the remote Prespa region and elsewhere in Greek Macedonia, the struggle for power in Athens began to impinge on Macedonia. Although Eleftherios Venizelos was not a friend of the Macedonians, and saw them as material waiting to be assimilated into the 'higher' culture of Greece, he was not concerned to forcibly extinguish local identities as strongly as many army officers and the bishops, and there were some elements of genuine cultural liberalism in his outlook, which most of the local Greek state officials, the Church and the schoolteachers did not share.[26] In the 1928 Greek census data there was still a category for 'Macedonian Slavs' where 82,000 people were recorded, 1.3 per cent of the total Greek population, the last census in the twentieth century where this was so. But as the world crisis after the Wall Street crash and the rise of fascism began to affect the entire region, the atmosphere in Greek Macedonia began to change. Tensions were accentuated by the end of the United States' 'open door' immigration policy for Greeks in 1924, thus reducing émigré remittances to families and employment opportunities and cutting off an important economic safety valve that reduced internal social tensions.

In some respects this was linked to the consolidation of the Soviet Union on the international landscape and the slow transformation of the Greek Communist Party, the KKE, from a very small party resting mainly on support in a few regional centres such as Volos and among Asia Minor and Pontus exiles and the tobacco workers' union to becoming a genuinely national party, if still small, and very urban. The Communist Party was also growing rapidly north of the border within Yugoslavia with membership rising to nearly 4000 by 1921. In 1924 at the Third Congress of the KKE the party made a decision for a minority policy in Greece that seemed of minor importance at the time but was to have profound long-term consequences for all of Macedonia and for Greece for many years. The policy of self-determination involved an open option for an 'Independent Macedonia and Thrace' in a future socialist Greece. This was a policy approved by the directorate of the Comintern in Moscow, and it immediately led to the party being seen in a new dimension by the very numerous citizens in Greek Macedonia who still held a primary Macedonian identity. The communist cause in Greece was to become equated with the Macedonian cause, in the eyes of the governing establishment in Athens and probably the majority of mainstream Greek citizens.[27] Although this policy was abandoned in the mid-1930s it left an indelible image of national disloyalty with most Greeks. The change of Comintern and KKE line ended this situation, and Greek party membership increased tenfold between 1931 and 1936. Yet even in this difficult climate with the growth of fascism in Europe and the looming threat of another war, the eyes of scientists were beginning to focus on the future of the southern Balkan lakes. In 1934 an expedition of British hydrologists visited Prespa and other lakes, prompted by the drying up of Lake Maliqi near Korca in Albania.[28]

The early liberalism of Venizelos had in any case been rescinded in response to the intense social tensions in Greece as the Depression developed, and strong anti-labour movement legislation was passed in 1929, the *Idionym*, which established the principle of imprisonment and/or internal exile for political offences. Islands such as Anafi, near Santorini, were forced to construct prison camps, and by 1933 the system was fully functional, to be expanded later under the Metaxas dictatorship. The vast majority of inmates at Anafi and the other prison islands were communists, or alleged communists, and included a significant number from Macedonia, particularly Florina, and the always radical villages around the town. By the middle period of the Metaxas dictatorship in 1937 an archipelago of about fifty-nine political prisons stretched across Greece from Corfu to Samothrace and from Crete to Macedonia, with only the Peloponnese (Old Greece) relatively free of political incarceration.[29] Macedonian nationalism and Greek communism were becoming inextricably intertwined in these years, and Metaxas's gaols were to become universities of a new kind of Macedonian revolutionary, communist and non-communist, and quite different from the days of IMRO.[30] The use of any non-Greek language, whether Bulgarian, Albanian, Macedonian, Vlach or Turkish, had been banned throughout Greece in 1936 legislation, and the issue of language use was used as a tool by the police and the army for savage repression of opponents of the corporatist regime. The ostensibly 'progressive' aspects of Metaxas rural policy in setting up new agricultural cooperatives such as the 'Prespa' dairy unit set up in 1936 and developing existing cooperatives set up between 1930 and 1932 paled into insignificance against the background of dictatorial political repression.

The Metaxas period also brought other burdens to the people, apart from those associated with direct political repression, as graphically described by Australian journalist Bert Birtles who travelled widely in northern and island Greece in 1935 to 1937.[31] An understandable Athens initiative against deforestation and overgrazing brought limits on the size of flocks, particularly goats, which were a mainstay of the higher villages around the Prespa Lakes, at a time when there had been some increase in material development in villages like Psarades, with returning exiles from the United States and Australia building solid stone houses in the old local style that can still be seen today below the 'Africa' hillside, and the population of around 600 people recorded in the post-Balkan Wars census in 1913 remained stable. Some public health improvements were developing with modern medicine, which reduced infant mortality and improved women's lives somewhat. Taxes on fish were increased, and intense social tensions developed as a result. In return for the prospect of further development and light taxation on the fish trade, local residents were forced to accept the imposition of a Christian Greek identity, willingly or not.

Even in the difficult political climate in the early 1930s, opposition to the suppression of the Macedonian identity continued. The difficulties of the Athens government were increased by the 'return' of Macedonian language and culture in the Yugoslav education system over the northern border, after the demise of the rigid enforced use of Serbian in the 1920s in education and public life. As Troch points out: *'From the 1930's, publications, journals, and even the theatre in Skopje increasingly used Macedonian. In particular educated Macedonian students, precisely the target group the authorities had hoped would adopt Serbian, openly began to demand the recognition of the Macedonian language and the "language question" became the "crystallisation point of the autonomy movement".*[32]

Local inhabitants in Greek Macedonia were soon aware of this and the improvement in the language use situation north of the border provided both food for thought and an incentive for the Greek Left to take up the Macedonian issue again. In 1932 a correspondent of the communist *Rizospastis* newspaper from Athens wrote a report from the Kastoria and Prespa regions setting out what he saw as the 'Macedonian national minority', who were 'neither Greek, nor Serbian, nor Bulgarian', and noting that this language was spoken by more than 100,000 people as their mother tongue.[33] In the Diaspora, the growth of social and political radicalism in the 1930s brought a boom in publication in the language, based in many places on the continuing – if often illegal – publication of the IMRO newspaper *Makedonsko Delo*, particularly in the militant Macedonian stronghold city of Toronto, Canada. An important development, in view of later events in the Communist International under Stalin's Bulgarian henchman Georgi Dimitrov, was the greater interest in the possibility of an independent Macedonian state within a wider Balkan Communist Federation. In the post–Second World War period this was to become an issue in the Stalin-Tito split leading up to the final breach in 1948.

The right-wing parties based on the machinations of the Athens political elite had little local political strength in rural Greek Macedonia in these years. Offices in regional cities like Drama, Serres, Florina or Kastoria were little more than flag-waving operations to collect votes after handing out largess at election time. Local political designation, such as it was, depended much more on whether a family was with or against the King, or with the party of Eleftherios Venizelos, who always did spend some time in Macedonia at election time and had some knowledge of the districts.

Patronage networks stretched into the countryside from the city headquarters of the parties, usually promising much at election time but delivering very little afterwards. The military and security police was a significant economic factor and job creation machine and if a family was seen as having 'bad biography' by the military, nothing could be expected in terms of jobs, medical care or local favours in return. Civil society in the modern sense did not exist.

In the wider world of Macedonia the traditional health scourges of the past continued to take a regular toll. Malaria was endemic in the low-lying and marshland areas and other serious diseases persisted despite the efforts of the Macedonian government agencies and American public health advisers to control them. Although in terms of government functionality and efforts emanating from Athens and foreign agencies like the Rockefeller Foundation there was a real commitment to social and agricultural improvement, the familiar paradigm of progress being set back by disease and epidemics continued to assert itself, bringing depopulation, increasing emigration and low work capacity in the surviving local residents.[34] In 1935 a serious typhoid epidemic caused by bad sanitation broke out in Kilkis and spread elsewhere in the region. Tuberculosis was endemic in many places, particularly refugee-settled villages in lowland and eastern Macedonia. Although policy was to close down collective latrines and construct private house facilities, build freshwater supplies and remove manure heaps from villages and introduce garbage collection, in many areas little was achieved in practice. Study of mortality records for the Prespa villages would suggest that the public health situation was considerably better than in lowland Macedonia, with plentiful freshwater from mountain streams, fewer malarial mosquitos at least in the upper villages and the great scale of the Lakes able to absorb quantities of animal and human waste without difficulty. Tuberculosis was primarily a disease of Greek urbanization and the towns, as the Bishop of Salonica, Apamias, pointed out in his famous address 'The Problem of Urbanism in Greece' on rural and urban development in 1929.[35]

As the international clouds darkened and the Second World War approached, the people of the Prespa villages and the rest of northern Greece faced an uncertain future, without leaders in whom they could have any confidence. The region remained at the level of material life much as it had been before the Balkan Wars in 1912 but with a radically different population composition in many places. The structures of government and public authority had been radically transformed, so a man or woman born into the world of late Ottoman Greek Macedonia in *Nivica* would have lived through the end of the theocratic Ottoman Empire, the military authority of the 1914 to 1918 period and the National Schism before the arrival of the chaotic and instable governments of bourgeois democracy of the post-Versailles Treaty period, where King George himself observed on one occasion that the most valuable possession he had was his suitcase.

In this world, the apparent verities of the Greek communists and the Soviet system built more and more influence and adherents, until under the Nazi occupation the Macedonian national cause, the cause of the wider Greek nation, the cause of modernization and social justice seemed to merge into a single perspective for freedom and progress. Yet underlying economic realities were changing; the lands that had been empty and depopulated in 1918 were now experiencing rising population, despite the health issues, but land supply was not increasing. The Metaxas period had increased tensions between the Greek and Macedonian Slavic-identity communities, and as William Hardy McNeill wrote as long ago as 1947, at the height of the Greek Civil War 'Greek and Slavic peasants were driven to compete against each other for the very means of their livelihood, and the latent national antipathies rose as a result'.[36]

In Ohrid in 1936 a new Macedonian nationalist organization MANAPO, *Makedonski Naroden Pokret*, the Macedonian National Movement, had held a Congress and defined its objectives in much the same terms as Todor Alexandrov's pro-Soviet IMRO had seen them twenty years before.[37] However hard Athens government tried to kill the many-headed hydra of Macedonian nationalism before 1939, it survived and grew over the northern border, in a complex and uncertain relationship with Tito's Yugoslav League of Communists.

7

Prespa during war and Axis occupation

The interwar years around the Prespa Lakes had seen a continual and intermittently effective effort by the governments in Athens, Tirana and Belgrade to impose their will upon the inhabitants and bring them into the world of what the elites saw as modern and evolving Balkan states. But the concept of the state and government has often meant little to modern Greeks in their history, however strong their devotion to the ideal of the nation, the *ethnos*.[1] The same processes were at work in the neighbouring countries around the lakes, where the hopes of growing Yugoslav and Albanian democracy and development in the immediate post-Versailles years saw a slide backwards into Royalist semi-dictatorships at the centre and local disorder at the periphery. The Greek government was particularly unsuccessful, with banditry remaining common throughout the mountains, particularly in major ranges like the Grammos, Tayetos and Pindus. The Greek state in Macedonia as experienced by the villagers was almost exclusively a military/urban clerical and pedagogic entity, and the Church worked closely with the army to achieve such Hellenization as was possible mainly through the education system. The material life and agricultural practices of the peasantry were markedly conservative, even archaic, and the early foreign aid experts in Greek Macedonia sponsored by organizations such as the Rockefeller Foundation found extreme difficulty in bringing modernization, even in uncontroversial areas such as clean water supply and land drainage.[2]

The onset of the Second World War and the Axis occupation removed at a stroke the flimsy bourgeois-democratic state apparatus that had developed in Greece, many aspects of which had already been seriously weakened by the Metaxas dictatorship after 1937. It had disappeared long ago in Yugoslavia under the Royalist dictatorship. In Athens the Metaxas government had passed draconian laws forbidding any use of the Macedonian language, and numerous offenders were imprisoned for a variety of often trivial anti-state offences. Thus, the indigenous Macedonian/Bulgarian culture and language of the majority of the people of Psarades/*Nivica* became secret and 'closed' their experiences and culture a 'secret history', and the villages turned inward, as they always had in times of social tension and disorder.[3] Memories of the oldest inhabitants interviewed in the early 1990s recall a world where the men tended to learn some spoken Greek before the women while the minority languages, particularly Vlach, were kept alive in the female world of the family. All commerce was supposed to be conducted in Greek, a key weapon in the government's Hellenization programme, based on the role of Greek in that respect in the late Ottoman Balkans. In the law courts in Florina some use of Macedonian seems to have been accepted, if strongly discouraged, in the pre-Metaxas years. In the crisis in 1940, with the invasion of northwest Greece by Mussolini's Italian forces, the young men of Psarades nevertheless played their part, with four names of the dead on the small marble war memorial in the village square today.

The Germans and their allies had moved southwards through the Balkans in 1941, after the failure of the royalist government in Belgrade to prevent the military onslaught. Prespa and its surrounds fell into the Italian occupation zone, although its boundary to the north and the east was very near the region of Bulgarian and German suzerainty.[4] Agricultural and fish self-sufficiency was paramount. The Italian occupiers who had swept into the region from Albania in 1940 as part of Mussolini's invasion of Greece distrusted the relative freedom and independence of the fishing communities and as Paul Vouras has pointed out 'burned many of the inshore and lake fishing vessels'.[5] Bitola was bombed by Italian aircraft. Daily life was reduced to a struggle for survival, with the people delving deep into their long heritage of enduring a harsh and repressive fate, and again as in earlier periods, there was a significant withdrawal from the monetary economy, aggressive hyperinflation and barter determined trade, such as it was.[6] In late 1940 the Italians ordered all the inhabitants of Psarades to leave after they had taken every pastoral animal from the people and all their cheese, dried fish and stored provisions and left the villagers near starvation. Most of the people went on a forced march across the fields to Agios Germanos. As Roderick Beaton has pointed out: 'It was a sudden and brutal return to the subsistence economy that had been the inheritance of the Ottoman Empire and the Byzantine before it.'[7]

Katerina, an elderly villager, explained in an interview in 2014 that she only survived because her mother carried her as she led the family to walk from Psarades to Agios Germanos, narrowly escaping being killed by a bomb on the way. When they were there the men started to make nets in secret, although it took six months to make a net large enough to go down the necessary fifty metres into the lake to catch the sardine shoals. Fishing remained the only means of survival for the rest of the occupation period, most agriculture and pastoralism was impossible in the lowland areas. At this time Agios Germanos was still called *San Germanos* by many people something the Italian occupiers encouraged. As in urban Greece cereal crop shortages and malnutrition soon appeared, with flour and wheat disappearing from the markets after being requisitioned by the occupation forces.

The initial force of the Italian invasion of Greece in 1940 had resulted in a long front line north of the Greek-Albanian border that at its most easterly end passed through Korca/*Koritsa* to reach Prespa just north of the modern village of Pushtec in Albania. The events of this period are well known, with the heroic resistance of the Greeks in Epirus driving back the Italian fascist invaders and taking thousands of prisoners. A British military mission was deployed to try to aid the Greeks, with later prominent author Patrick Leigh Fermor posted to Korca and then to Pogradec, but as the German forces replaced the Italians the fall of Greece to the Axis began to quickly evolve.[8] Within the Prespa Albanian villages a secret resistance organization was established around the Ostreci family land near Sveti Naum monastery.[9] Later in the war, by the end of 1943, the rightist Balli Kombetar militia was firmly established in the hills above Krani led by local Albanian nationalist warlord Musa Krahjin. The German command poured fourteen Divisions into the conflict, with a total of over 600,000 military personnel. By the end of 1943 this rose to twenty Divisions and over 700,000 men.[10] British air power through the RAF was insufficient to slow the invaders, with only about a hundred aircraft against several hundred German planes. The air war came to Prespa in the form of a RAF disaster; a flight of six *Blenheim Mark I* bombers came over Lesser Prespa Lake on 6 April 1941 followed by three German aircraft and two were shot down and crash landed in the lake near Microlimni. Only the two pilots escaped with their lives.[11]

Psarades, Agios Germanos and the eastern lakeside villages were to some extent isolated from the original thrust of the invaders, as German armour poured southwards through the 'Monastir Gap' south towards Edessa and Thessaloniki, and followed the railway line down to Mediterranean. In doing so they were repeating the route taken by so many former invaders of Greece by following the river valleys. In an equally time-honoured response local people fled with their animals and what possessions they could carry to the hills or in the case of Prespa the largely trackless forests.

By the end of April 1941 the control of the Italian, Bulgarian and German forces was total, with Bitola under the Bulgarians and Germans, and the enormous force of the Bismarck Division at its height over 70,000 men installed in and around the ex-Ottoman barracks. A force of Allied mostly Australian soldiers had fought a short battle with the Germans near Pisoderi, but stood no chance against the far greater Axis force, and some fled west, to avoid being taken prisoner, across the Prespa Lakes. The British infantry force concentrated on the Adriatic side of the Pindus had retreated south to the Peloponnese and was evacuated from Kalamata.[12] A priority target for the Nazis was the large and influential Jewish community in Bitola and anti-Semitic laws were passed within days of the arrival of the foreign soldiers and signed off personally by Bulgarian King Boris III in Sofia.[13] Macedonia was divided into three zones by the occupiers, with Prespa then as always a place of borders where the Italian, German and Bulgarian occupation zones met across the Lakes.

Within the Prespa villages and the Resen and Bitola regions generally old political divisions quickly reopened after 1940, based on local ethnic and national divisions ultimately stemming from the outcomes of the Balkan and the First World War and the division of Macedonia. The Greek Communist Party in June 1941 had called for armed resistance against the occupation after Hitler had attacked the Soviet Union and had started forming armed groups but they lacked central coordination.[14] The Yugoslav League of Communists formed a Prespa Party Committee which held its first meeting on 2 August 1943, although the Great Prespa villages had been rent by intermittent violence since early 1942[15] Resistance had developed more quickly in mainland mountain Greece. In the north in July 1941 an armed band appeared near Kozani, and in August 1941 the Germans found a large arms cache near Florina.[16] Three Greeks were shot in a reprisal raid as a result, setting a pattern in the occupation that was to become normal, culminating in the Nazi massacre of civilians at Klisoura in April 1944 when 223 old people, women and children were murdered.

Elsewhere in the part of Macedonia and Thrace under Bulgarian control, a mass revolt of the population broke out in Drama in September. The Bulgarian troops were important to the Germans. Comprising about 40,000 men, their linguistic background was useful in some areas, and given some of the German troops were poor quality, quite old or battle convalescents, the Bulgarians were a useful if thuggish shock force in the villages. In the same month, Ethnikon Apeleftherotikon Metoron (EAM), the National Liberation Front, was formally created by the KKE on 27 September 1941. EAM organizers, mostly communists, were arriving in the villages by the beginning of the winter, although at first limited in impact by the weakness of KKE support in rural areas. On 10 April 1942, the decision was announced to form a formal army, Ethnikos Laikos Apeleftheritikon Stratos (ELAS), the National People's Liberation Army, and gradually lonely and often very isolated acts against the occupiers became better coordinated and organized. Near Prespa, the First Bitola Partisan Detachment was founded on Mount Pelister in late April 1942, and although suffering teething problems later became a key unit in western Macedonia against the occupation forces and their supporting Albanian Balli Kombetar pro-German militias.

As the autumn and winter of 1941 to 1942 drew on, the threat of major food shortages approaching the Athens famine conditions intensified in the northern Greek cities. The invasion gave the Communist Party an opportunity to re-establish itself as a major force, after the serious setbacks of the late Metaxas period when it had been infiltrated and disrupted by the government's secret police and the army. In response, the Bulgarian fascist occupation forces started to recruit a militia, the *Ohrana*, which in many cases drew on ex-IMRO personnel with a Bulgarian cultural identity, who saw collaboration as opening a route to uniting Macedonia with Bulgaria under a postwar settlement, to form a 'Greater Bulgaria'. This outlook was less pronounced in the Prespa villages than in the very pro-Bulgarian area north of Kastoria but for a period until the grim realities of the Bulgarian puppet administration began to be clear there was some support for the occupiers.[17] There was also significant, mostly communist-led, opposition through what would later become ELAS. Many Prespa village residents had a shared language with the Bulgarians, and a shared view of the Church, unlike the distant and formal relationships with the Germans.

The difficult and complex atmosphere of the time is conveyed by a senior female Yugoslav Partisan in Bitola, Jamila Andjela Kolonomos, who in her memoir of the occupation of her city by the Bulgarians shows how a middle-class Jewish girl from a prominent banking and trade family was drawn into the communist-led resistance and into the complexities and physical hardships of Partisan warfare.[18] The local guerrillas were all in the remote countryside and Prespa forests south of Bitola, or on Mount Pelister to the north, not in the towns, and there was a yawning cultural gulf between them and the mass of initially mostly Jewish recruits to the cause from the urban area.[19] Bitola Jews were nearly all from Sephardic families and used Ladino as their main language.[20] The cultural gap was overcome, in time, and recruitment was later accelerated from the towns' community after the rounding up of more than 7000 Macedonian Jews who were within reach of the occupiers and their deportation from Skopje to Treblinka extermination camp in 1943. For Bitola, Resen and Prespa *andartes* an early focus of the struggle was the Greek-Macedonian village of *Buf*, now renamed Akritias, with its large pastoral community and position on the fish trading route from Great Prespa towards Florina and ultimately Thessaloniki. Kolonomos escaped here from Bitola for military training and equipment, in relatively safe conditions. In the hills the forces of the Nazi occupation had many difficulties, particularly those of mechanized vehicles on tracks never designed to take them, and unlike the Macedonian shepherds who often formed the backbone of the nascent Partisan units had no detailed knowledge of the terrain. Detailed maps of the localities did not exist at all. In Balkan villages in the mountains, the shepherds have always been the local elite and their natural *elan* was easily transferred to the Partisan identity, and ELAS and its Yugoslav allies quickly adopted the traditional position in society of the revolutionary soldier. They remained nevertheless, in essence, armed civilians and if their duty was to kill occupation soldiers, it was not difficult. It became more difficult as the Civil War period replaced the Axis occupation, when killing fellow Greeks became the agenda.[21]

As the savage brutality of the occupation became a heavier and heavier burden on the Greeks and Macedonians, of all ethnicities and backgrounds, resistance grew.[22] Western Macedonia including Prespa went over very fully to EAM and ELAS, in contrast to the Bulgarian occupation army regions of eastern Macedonia where there was some genuine support for the occupation. In late 1942 the Regional Committee of the KKE, the Greek Communist Party, began to produce a Slav-language newspaper explicitly for the Prespa region, *Prespanski Glas*/Prespa Voice, an indication of the recognition by the Greek communists of the strategic importance of the area.[23] The Prespa Lakes region was ideal guerrilla country, and what had started as the small and isolated groups of fighters that Kolonomos and the Bitola Jews and communists founded in 1941 grew by 1943 and the foundation of ELAS in Karpenisi into a mass resistance movement supported by communist and non-communist alike. In a parallel development in Yugoslavia, the Yugoslav communists held a meeting in Prespa in Cervna Voda village in November 1943 of all the senior Partisan leadership that took over the leadership responsibilities for the guerrilla war and established the outline framework for a common Balkan campaign, with a common Balkan headquarters. The Italian occupation zone in Albania with its local headquarters in the Prespa region at Korca was less severe and less efficient than the German and Bulgarian zones in central and eastern Macedonia, and a small arms transfer and munitions route to supply ELAS was set up along the old 'French Road' route on the south side of Lesser Prespa Lake.

The winter of 1943 to 1944 saw the Albanian communist Partisans under Mehmet Shehu's local command sweep northwards from their original bases near Vithquq north of Korca and by the spring of 1944 they were in control of most of southern and parts of central Albania although pockets of opposition from Balli Kombetar nationalist and Greek Epirots remained in some places.[24] The Prespa Lake villages in and around Pushtec came under full Albanian Partisan control, by Shehu's 1st Brigade. The region became a secure and fruitful source of support to the Macedonian and Greek Partisans, although the political complexities of relationships between Hoxha and Shehu and the Greek and Macedonian units were never simple.[25] However, the development of a vast swathe of liberated and semi-liberated territory stretching from the Adriatic coast south of Vlora across to Ohrid and Prespa Lakes and into the heart of Macedonia immediately further increased the strategic importance of the Ohrid-Prespa region, and led to the creation of a de facto supply and logistics operation that was a precursor of the Greek communist Democratic Army (DA) headquarters at Prespa near Pili in the Civil War after 1946. The knowledge of what was happening was soon picked up by German military intelligence, and in Psarades and elsewhere along the lake littoral every boat and fishing net was again destroyed and burnt if it had not been hidden, although on the whole the village houses survived relatively intact, unlike many in the Pindus and south of Kastoria. The loss of boats devastated the only means the people had of securing any cash income, and families had to try to feed their children with improvised netted fish and from game and products of the forests. Beans were still grown and some rice in the old Ottoman-irrigated area on the lakeside south of modern Karies village. Women did most of this burdensome and heavy work as the men had either been conscripted into the Greek army or had joined the guerrillas in the hills. The plight of the children was very difficult, with virtually no dairy products available after the Germans and Bulgarians had commandered all pastoral animals. The threat to family life was in time to set the scene for the *paidomazoma* where the communists later in the Civil War period organized the evacuation of the vulnerable families to safety in the newly communist lands to the north of the border and then to security in exile in Eastern Europe after 1949.

The social world of the Partisans in the hills around the Prespa and Ohrid Lakes was very different from anything the *andartes* recruits had known in their villages. The Yugoslav Partisans and Greek *andartes* had brought social revolution, particularly for women. The time-honoured village family structures and local informal patriarchal traditions had disappeared, to be replaced by a rigid military command structure and with political commissars attached to units responsible for propagating political objectives. This was undertaken in response to the increasing skill and professionalism of German Anti-Partisan warfare.[26] The once all-powerful priests were marginalized, although many came to actively support ELAS as time went on, and some fought very bravely in both Yugoslavia and Greece in the popular resistance forces. Discipline was severe. Sexual relationship was forbidden in ELAS, to safeguard the increasing number of female recruits, and suspected pro-Bulgarian *Ohrana* agents and sympathizers were summarily executed.

It was fairly easy for the local ELAS leadership to isolate and eliminate *Ohrana*, outside the few very strongly pro-Bulgarian villages such as *Zhelevo*/Antartiko east of Prespa where they faded into local populations, as the people involved like Dono Kirkov in Karies had a long pre-war record of IMRO and pro-Bulgarian activism and were well known in their local communities, but the Vlachs were a more complex problem. Living alongside their Macedonian Slav neighbours in the same villages for centuries they had been targeted by the Italian fascist occupiers and at a later stage in the war a 'Roman Legion' Vlach militia was formed in Thessaly to work with the occupying forces against ELAS.[27] The Vlach-majority Pili village 4 miles from Psarades held a particular importance, as it controlled the route across to Albania.[28] There is no evidence to suggest any significant contact with, or support there for, the pro-occupation militia, and as always in Vlach history the communities came to an accommodation with the dominant force at the time, now the ELAS fighters and soon their nascent 'Mountain Greece' political and social structures and judicial processes, schools and other institutions that were later in the war to be the basis for the Mountain government.[29] The Vlachs respect for the established state borders was purely notional, as it has remained with their local knowledge of remote tracks and mountain paths around the lakes. The numerous caves that in peacetime had pastoralism uses were turned into munitions and supply dumps.[30] In Psarades itself, there were contradictory political currents among the families that remained in their houses and tried to survive the occupation there. As is the case today, KKE and radical commitment was much more common among those of recent Turkish or Albanian descent, ex-Asia Minor refugee families, and 'immigrants' from northern lake towns such as Resen who had moved south or to Ohrid during the period of Ottoman collapse and the World War. In the ideological structures of the villages, loyalty to the Orthodox church was much stronger with long-established resident families, whereas those with a degree of 'Ottoman' inheritance in their personal culture and memory often had only a more formal Christian identity.[31]

During 1944 the liberation of northern Greece proceeded apace, as it also did in Albania and Yugoslavia, and the guerrilla army of ELAS swept southwards to the Gulf of Corinth, dominating all before it, and no doubt rank-and-file members expected that Athens would soon fall into their hands and a new leftist government of Greece would be formed.[32] This was a miscalculation. The British imperialist forces held Athens and had no intention of surrendering the city or the government to what was seen by the military commander General Scobie and Churchill himself as a communist and pro-Soviet organization. The EDES militia of Epirot adventurer Napoleon Zervas engaged in a factional campaign with British help in the north-west in Epirus and weakened ELAS. Unknown to all local political and military actors, on all sides, on 9 October 1944 at Yalta in the Crimea, Stalin, Roosevelt and Churchill had agreed an informal and secret agreement for the division of the post-war Balkans, where most of the Balkans would become communist, if that was determined by local realities, while Greece was to remain within the British sphere of influence, in reality a dependency of the British Empire.[33]

Stalin had begun his sabotage of the nascent revolution in the Greek mountains. On the ground, what became known as the Second Round of the Greek Civil War commenced, with heavy fighting and widespread civilian casualties in Athens itself.[34] The atmosphere had been transformed between the late summer of 1944, when ELAS and British troops held joint parades in many towns and villages to celebrate the end of the occupation, and in the first week of December the British army fired on unarmed demonstrators and precipitated the so-called Battle of Athens. The British army under Scobie saw ELAS as entirely a Soviet Union-oriented organization that through EAM would bring a communist revolution in Greece and in the Battle of Athens in that year were able to halt the leftist advance.[35] In the far north, old nationalist issues were emerging within the fighting *andartes* and in their political leadership. Tito's emissary to ELAS, the senior Montenegrin Partisan Svetozar Vukmanovic (General Tempo), was a critic of many aspects of the policy of the Greek communist's leadership, focussing on KKE leader Nicos Zachariadis (1903–73), in particular the concentration on an 'urban' route to taking power.[36] Partly under Yugoslav tutelage, a new Macedonian Partisan force had been formed by the communists, the Narodno Osloboditelen Front (NOF), to draw people with a Macedonian identity into the Greek resistance, and the Macedonian Question reappeared yet again within the dilemmas of the Greek communists. But the political atmosphere was changing and at the Varkiza conference held at a village near Athens, under British direction, an armed truce was agreed between ELAS, the KKE and the British that involved the *andartes* laying down their arms and entering into an agreement where free elections would be held. There was an intended amnesty for military actors from ELAS and other groups, and various military reforms to develop a new Greek army would be enacted. It was an extraordinary volte-face for the ELAS and communist leadership and soon rank-and-file protests against the leadership's policy were heard. ELAS and its allies controlled well over half the mainland and had substantial influence on islands like Samos, Chios, Lesbos and Levkas, and in the mountains of the Peloponnese.

In rural and mountain western Macedonia generally, and particularly in and around Psarades and Prespa, most of the agreement was never implemented and Prespa escaped the worst of the so-called White Terror period. This was not the case in the Greek towns and from June to October 1945 there was a reign of terror in Florina, particularly directed against the Slav-identity population.[37] Although weapons collection points were opened in Kastoria and Florina, few guns were actually collected. The people remained armed, the ELAS mountain government revolution stayed intact and life carried on much as it had before the dramatic events in and around Athens. The semi-police state that was set up under the aegis of the British Embassy in Athens was only effective in the towns and cities, where the Greek internal security operatives, including many veterans of the Metaxas and Nazi collaborationist periods were given free rein to spy upon and if possible disrupt the activity of the Left.[38] As the new National Army moved into the north, or attempted to, it met immediate resistance and many of its troops were of low quality and poorly motivated, and in action as McNeill points out: 'Contained many disreputable characters who freely disregarded the civil liberties promised by the Varkiza Agreement.'[39]

Under these circumstances, control of the Prespa and western Macedonian border region became more and more important. This was recognized by the communists in KKE who in late 1942 had begun a new underground newspaper, *Prespanski Glas*, The Voice of Prespa, in the Slav-Macedonian language, while the Florina committee of NOF was publishing *Slavomakedonski Glas* there.[40] To the north of the border the communist movements in Albania and Yugoslavia were consolidating their control of Northern Prespa and the open border meant Greek fighters could easily be resupplied. The borders that had been laid down in the First World War period had collapsed and a simple pass was all that was needed for fighters and their families to travel anywhere in the liberated Balkans. In Psarades the immediate priority of the people once the armed peace was consolidated was to rebuild their fishing boats and their flocks. Agios Germanos village became the centre of power on the east side of Lake Great Prespa, with the establishment of a postal service, medical and educational facilities. A hospital was opened, partly in caves by Lesser Prespa Lake, near Pili village. Although the first National Army unit arrived and took over the police post at Microlimni on Lesser Prespa and set up a garrison at Kallithea using the old Ottoman military buildings, the few soldiers there had little purchase on the surrounding villages and mountains. The Prefect appointed from Athens arrived in Florina but after discovering the actual situation of dominant *andartes* power there returned to Athens and no functional relationship with the central state machinery existed. This was common over all the provinces of northern and central Greece.

The food situation had begun to improve with the arrival of the United Nations Relief Mission (UNRRA) and its 700 mostly American, Australian and British staff in late 1945. There were frequent strikes and gradually the KKE began to recover the ground lost among the people through the signing of the Varkiza deal, and unrest was increased by the yawning gulf between the living conditions of the urban poor and the better-off merchant and shop-owning and professional classes in the cities. In the background was the changing international situation. The victory of the Labour Party in elections in 1945 in Britain was imminent and the Soviet Union was consolidating its power over many East European states. Greeks across the political spectrum hoped the new government in London would herald a new Greek policy, above all to remove the forced return of the Greek king. In France and Italy the large communist parties seemed as though they could take power at some point. None of these hopes came to fruition. In Greece Stalin kept to the letter of the secret Yalta agreement and did not directly send aid into Greece. The burden of semi-colonial rule stayed in London and the arrival of the Labour government in the autumn of 1945 did not bring the changes of policy which most Greeks had been hoping would occur, and the economy lurched closer and closer to collapse, with the dollar-drachma exchange rate changing from 149 to the dollar in late 1944 to 5000 to the dollar by January 1946. The savings of the mass of lower middle-class people were wiped out, unless they could convert paper money into gold coins or some other physical store of value. Rent, an important source of middle-class income in a society where there was little capacity or trust in monetary instruments or the stock market and where government debt was very widely distrusted, could not be collected. In Prespa and many other rural areas, the predictable response of the people was to turn to barter and withdrawal from the monetary economy and central government tax-raising capacity collapsed.

In order to maintain Churchill's policies, which in most respects the Attlee government did, Britain would be required to pour money into Greece.[41] Whether this was to take place or not was then almost an irrelevance in the northern mountains where as C.M. (Monty) Woodhouse wrote – as an observer generally ideologically opposed to the communist-led political objectives of EAM:

> 'Having taken control of the whole country, except the principal communications used by the Germans – they had given it things they had never known before. Communications in the mountains, by wireless, courier and telephone had never been so good before or since; even motor roads were mended and used by EAM/ELAS. The benefits of civilisation and culture trickled into the mountains for the first time. Communal life was organised in place of the traditional individualism of the Greek peasant. EAM/ELAS set the pace in something the Governments of Greece had always neglected: an organised state in the Greek mountains.'[42]

It was in these mountains that the future of the country would be decided, in a tide of blood and suffering.

8

Freedom and civil conflict, 1945–9

The centrality of Prespa

The collapse of the Nazi occupation forces in 1944 and their retreat from Greece northwards into Yugoslavia had precipitated a new period in Greek and regional history. The popular forces controlled the non-urban northern landmass with its many mountains and remote areas, with the Prespa region already developing as a key military supply and logistics centre, yet ostensibly the future of the country was being decided in high-level diplomatic exchange in Athens. The international dialogue led by Great Britain between the parties in Athens meant little north of the Gulf of Corinth. The Florina/*Lerin* region, including Prespa, was by mid-1947 dominated by seven NOF units, Macedonian militias, allied to the communist Democratic Army (DA). According to Psarades oral tradition these were sufficient forces to completely dominate the area, unlike the very different world of the Bulgarian and many east Macedonian and Thracian Partisans where the limited numbers of active soldiers had been dwarfed by the scale of the surrounding mountain landscapes, and liberation was only achieved with the arrival of the Soviet Red Army in Bulgaria. News of this development was picked up by the British Consulate in Thessaloniki, which in these years functioned primarily as an intelligence centre, and according to G.M. Alexander: 'The Foreign Office had reason to suspect the Yugoslavs were already promoting disorder in northern Greece. As early as September 1945 the British Consulate in Thessaloniki had reported that armed bands of Slavs belonging to the Popular Front of Macedonia (NOF) were operating in the mountains directly along the Greek-Yugoslav border.'[1] In London the climate was made more difficult after the Yugoslav League of Communists' newspaper *Borba* in Belgrade published a leading article stating that 'The Greek Imperialists have no right at all to hold Macedonians under their yoke. Thessaloniki, isolated from Vardar Macedonia had lost her economic importance. If incorporated into a united Macedonian she would regain her former splendour'.[2]

The nature of these fragments of intelligence reinforced the view in London and supported by Ambassador Reginald Leeper in Athens, that the British had a unique understanding of the threat to Greece from the 'Slav-Macedonians' and an absolute right to protect Greece from it, by any means necessary. It would be a difficult struggle, the environment of Prespa was perfectly suited to the military task and the forces available to the DA and NOF were easily sufficient to achieve full military control of the area, although in the period immediately after the defeat of ELAS in 1945, thousands of Macedonian Greeks had fled over the lake from Prespa and elsewhere along the border as they feared the National Army would murder them as proto-Bulgarians.[3] In reality the Greek National Army was only able to deploy in the large towns and Florina was the main regional garrison, as it has been both before 1939 and remains up to the present day in western Macedonia. The central Athens priority was to prevent the town from falling into the hands of the communist *andartes*. In the wider region nearby communist governments were in fairly secure positions of power in Bulgaria, Romania, Albania and Yugoslavia, as the Yalta agreements between Stalin, Churchill and Roosevelt had made inevitable, and Greece remained isolated in the region. The northern Greek frontier did not exist as a meaningful national border along much of its length, with all road crossings in western Macedonia with Albania, Bulgaria and Yugoslavia controlled by local communist Partisan units or the military and police units of those new governments. General Scobie's British troops had succeeded in stopping ELAS from taking power in Athens, but the physical victory won by force of arms in the main urban area was not a reliable signpost for the peaceful political future of Greece.

Great Britain as the main external actor with significant numbers of troops on the ground had become the replacement occupying force of an essentially colonial nature after the Germans had left. The Varkiza agreement signed in February 1945 stipulated that the popular forces should lay down their arms, and in an extraordinary demonstration of the residual power of the British-Greek relationship, and the most serious of the many mistakes of the KKE leadership in the wartime period, the majority of the KKE leaders supported the Varkiza provisions and some ELAS units also did.[4] It was a decision taken by a leadership conditioned by Stalinism and mostly from the urban working class with little or no military experience. In reality, some KKE rank and file kept substantial quantities of arms, and individual militants and different *andartes* groups also kept munitions, but as events were to show, they were usually hidden in urban areas and were not easily available to the expanding DA and its sympathizers in the mountains. In the earlier years of its existence, the DA was very much a locally based military force. As Smothers and his colleagues working on a research report for the New York-based Twentieth Century Fund found in early 1947 in the Lower Prespa-region village of *Roulia*/Kotta: 'the great majority of the andartes whom we saw were natives of the general area in which they operated, some were encamped close to their home villages. This was much more rarely true of soldiers or gendarmes.'[5]

There was substantial internal opposition to the Varkiza decision, which many rank-and-file KKE members and fighters in the mountains saw as a capitulation.[6] Most significantly, Aris Velouchiotis (1905–45), the founder of ELAS in Karpenisi in 1943, did not agree with the policies of the KKE leadership and retreated with his men to the heights of the Pindus Mountains in the north. It was not a safe refuge, even for a man who had lived on the margins of society, in prison or as a revolutionary activist for twenty-five years, and he was gunned down in the early summer in obscure circumstances. Velouchiotis has remained a martyr to the Greek left ever since, a Che Guevara figure where posters depicting his bulky black-bearded figure on horseback are ubiquitous in many Greek university rooms. In his concept of the political struggle and its relationship to the military realities, he was close to the post-war analysis of Tito's emissary to the Greek resistance, the senior Montenegrin Partisan commander Svetozar Vukmanovic, usually known by his wartime nickname of 'General Tempo'. Tempo, Tito's emissary to the Greek armed resistance, saw the need for the primacy of the armed struggle in the mountains against a background of circumstances where the British army that had seemed liberators were turning into occupiers.

The weaknesses of the KKE strategy based on the urban workers and mass demonstrations and the mechanically applied Bolshevik model for seizing power were becoming more and more apparent.[7] But although a prominent leader like Velouchiotis could be lost, in the countryside much of the apparatus of popular power and social and judicial institutions established under the Mountain government by ELAS remained. Athens was seen by most of the Prespa population, as elsewhere in Greece outside 'Old Greece' in the Peloponnese, as a distant capital under what they hoped would be under only temporary foreign control. Even in the Peloponnese and the south, much of the central mountains and the Tayetos south of Sparta remained under ELAS control throughout late 1943 and in 1944.[8] British power was relatively efficient in the lowland Peloponnese, on most islands other than Samos, Chios, parts of Crete and Ikaria, and in the larger towns and cities, but the soldiers had little civilian backup and in practice ELAS activists and the KKE were able to continue political work even in Athens much as before. The party newspaper *Rizospastis* continued to appear, and the radio station *Eleftheri Ellada* continued to broadcast. Some fighters fled to Yugoslavia to regroup. The impoverished working class in the large cities remained generally loyal to the left, if politically impotent, while the mass of small traders, shopkeepers and local officials supported the nationalist parties of the Right.

The relatively united struggle for national freedom in the period from 1943 to 1945 with ELAS had fragmented largely on the basis of class and an urban/rural division.[9] The absence of a post-Ottoman landowning class around Greek Prespa encouraged support for the Left, but elsewhere in Greece the situation was more complex. Thus, in the distant Tayetos Mountains south of Sparta in the Peloponnese the lowland and coastal olive growers generally supported the Right, which in the occupation had led to pro-German sentiment, whereas the impoverished pastoralists in the mountains fed and supported the communist Democratic Army.[10] Churchill's policy and its later continuation by Foreign Minister Ernest Bevin in the post-1945 Labour government had succeeded in stopping a military victory for ELAS, but it was a total failure in limiting the popular base of the communist left and the allies of the KKE, and in many respects laid the basis for the subsequent civil conflict that lasted until 1949.

In the far north, particularly in central and western Macedonia, the writ of the British and Athens hardly ran at all. In this stage of the Civil War the later news blackout did not exist and as the Athens government reported, the *andartes* could move more or less at will over the northern border and across the Prespa and Ohrid Lakes. A 'White Book' published in Athens in late 1947 recorded: 'A small number of bandits which had entered Greece from Bulgaria attacked the village Psarades district of Prespa and took away various foodstuffs. On January 12th, 1947, they withdrew into Albanian territory.'[11] American historian William Hardy McNeill has attributed the hostility of the population to the new Athens government National Guard force as a product of the 'relatively good record ELAS and EAM had made in the north and the Right had committed more outrages in Macedonia than in other parts of Greece during the first days of its newly found power'.[12]

In much of Greece, even in the Peloponnese, there was often a seamless transition between ELAS and the DA, with the same local commanders in charge before 1945 as after 1947. The immediate problem for Athens and the British was to try to secure the northern border which had almost disappeared in western Macedonia.[13] With the forces at the disposal of General Scobie and the Regent Archbishop Damaskianos's government this was a pipedream. The guerrillas surveyed the advances of first the German occupiers and then the Greek National Army, looking down from the Byronic crags like gods on the mortals below. The communist army soldiers were often drawn from the mountain villages and were used to the terrain and its hardships and knew the localities well. Most of the National Army soldiers were conscripted town boys who had led easier lives and had little training or appetite for irregular mountain warfare. Around the Prespa Lakes the tracks and minor road running round Great Prespa Lake had been controlled by the Partisan forces of Albania and Yugoslavia since late 1944, and the border remained completely open after the Varkiza agreement was signed. In the Lesser Prespa area, the National Guard had occupied the ex-German base at Microlimni village and the old Ottoman strongpoint on the road at Kallithea on Great Prespa, but the small forces of the National Guard based there had little impact on the surrounding rural areas and forests in the absence of roads capable of taking heavy mechanized vehicles. In Epirus there was a different situation, where the EDES militiamen of Napoleon Zervas who had been evacuated to Corfu returned and began a reign of terror from late 1944 onwards against the Left, and the Albanophone Cham population of north-west Greece, driving thousands of them into exile in Albania and Turkey and elsewhere.[14]

In and around both Prespa Lakes, the DA began to grow into a state within a region which itself was a stronghold of popular power that was out of control of the Athens government. A specific social and cultural life was developed, with showings of Soviet films, concerts of Macedonian/Bulgarian language songs and popular poetry and dramatic performances. Women played a main part in organizing these events and participated in a significant way in the people's courts and schools. Other 'statelets' of popular power remained in the Pindus, other mountainous areas, some islands and the central Peloponnese mountains, and parts of Arcadia and the Tayetos. The issue of chronic Greek state absence outside Athens and absence of state legitimacy had transmuted into a new form, where the apparatus of popular power through ELAS and the Mountain government was replacing the power of Athens. The ELAS ideal was of a state of the people, rather than above the people, with local village and town assemblies loosely modelled on Soviets. Yet the vision of the popular leaders had one great and compelling weakness, in that its fullest development was based on a region, Prespa and western Macedonia and other mountains like the Pindus range and Mount Olympus which were largely without significant towns, let alone cities, whereas a *polis* was throughout the centuries the psychological focus of Greek life. The *zadruga* village structure inherited from the traditional Slavonic peasantry was still the basic unit in the northern mountains but however strong the local loyalties it aroused, in the end they remained only local. The state as a relation of production was very limited indeed.¹⁵

The Mountain government and its successor local institutions was based on the dominance of the people's army which was vulnerable not only to the tangible and present threat of the renewing Greek National Army but also to the airpower monopolized by the US Air Force and the British Royal Air Force, either directly or indirectly through the use of Greek pilots in their lent aircraft.¹⁶ Air power destroyed the British efforts to defend Greece in the north in 1940 to 1941 and foreign financed and trained airpower was to turn out to be the Achilles' heel of the popular forces during the Civil War period.¹⁷ The new communist states in the central and northern Balkans did not have modern anti-aircraft weapons to supply to either ELAS or the DA successor. Documents show that Tito and his government supplied machine guns, mortars, anti-tank mines, rifles and handguns, tents, clothing and food to the Greek forces.¹⁸ There was nothing from Yugoslavia that could restrict government air power, apart from a very few small anti-aircraft guns. Heavy machine guns were also in very limited supply, about two per DA battalion.¹⁹ Only the Soviet Union had anti-aircraft weapons in quantity, and Stalin's decision to keep to the letter of the Yalta agreements and keep out of the Greek struggle was unknown to the fighters in uniform on the ground or their local commanders on either side in the conflict.

Population displacement was a key weapon in the Athens government and American arsenal, with about 20,000 refugees from villages forced into government camps at the beginning of 1947, a figure which rose to 31,000 by the end of the year.²⁰ Army forced removals continued at a rate of about 15,000 people a month the following year, so no less than 200,000 people had left their homes by the end of the war, many never to return.²¹ In the villages in the new Socialist Yugoslavia and in the Mala Prespa region of Hoxha's Albania a very different situation evolved. In both countries the land was collectivized and collective farm units were constructed out of rough-cut local stone, and the people struggled to define their new identities. A researcher in Pushtec, the largest Albanian village on Great Prespa Lake, recorded this comment in 2002 from an elderly man which illustrates the many transformations in the lives of people in Albanian Prespa in the twentieth century: 'In 1920 when Greece came over, it was Greek rule here and we studied Greek. When Ahmet Zogu came in 1924, we studied Albanian. In 1945 teachers came from Macedonia and we began having classes in Macedonian. We started learning Albanian from the 4th Grade of the elementary school, until then we have classes in the Macedonian language.'²²

The locality was heavily militarized as the Civil War in Greece developed, and later on Enver Hoxha, ever nervous of the capacity of religion to divide the Albanians and knowing the Korca region well from his pre-war education there, was very aware of the traditional Bulgarian Orthodox church loyalties of the lakeside inhabitants in late Ottoman times. He decreed that the village church in Pushtec should be turned into an agricultural store and shop. Under communism the Prespa villages were relatively favoured as they had been strong centres of support for the Partisans and in Pushtec a small health centre, a new school and better roads were constructed. In the same way the de facto control by the UDBA Yugoslav secret police of the Prespa area south of Resen with a prison and other facilities at Otoshevo ensured a degree of investment in similar material improvements, particularly roads capable of taking military traffic. The old fruit growing industry north of Pretor and up towards Resen was expanded under collectivization and boosted by taking lake water for irrigation, something which has contributed to falling Prespa water levels over the years. Yugoslav Prespa, like the rest of the new society, rested on the basic concept of sharing all resources, something that the villagers had had to do to survive around the Lakes for centuries.[23] In Greek Prespa in contrast, life was in ruins, as the final tide of the Civil War swept over it, and virtually all the civilian population had left.

In Yugoslav Prespa the main objective of the UDBA was the elimination of the Albanian nationalist Balli Kombetar (National Front) militia from the entire region. Krani and the more northern mostly Albanophone and Muslim Great Prespa Lake village of Grncari had been important centres of Ballist activity under the Nazi occupation, where some Albanians had acted as a local militia for the fascist occupiers. Ballists were also active in the Mount Pelister Albanophone villages on the Bitola side of the mountains. They were ruthlessly repressed and many abandoned their weapons and went on the run to seek safety in Greece. In a difficult decision for the British military authorities, given they had been in many cases active Nazi collaborators, the Ballists were given de facto if not de jure political asylum, provided they went to British colonies. Some ended up in Albanian emigration centres in Australia, New Zealand and Canada.[24]

Within a year, the once fluid and open northern Greek border with transnational relationships based on Balkan Partisan control and Yugoslav and Albanian communism became a heavily militarized and closed frontier, with the establishment of a seven mile wide-security zone along the Greek border which in theory banned all normal economic activity and travel. All small roads and forest tracks were closed with thick barbed wire entanglements looking like the Western Front in the First World War, and larger and more important roads were mined. This completely isolated not only Psarades and Pili but all the lake villages, and a military control post was built at the end of the 'Great Field' to prevent all travel towards or away from the Albanian and Yugoslav borders that remained occupied until 1993. Grass and trees started to grow in the numerous ruined and empty houses in villages within the zone like Vrondero/*Grazdeno* and some, such as Agathoto/*Turnovo*, have remained in ruins until the present day.[25] The American-Greek-British campaign had triumphed in a military sense, the Greek Right and Royalists believed communism in Greece had been eliminated forever, but the military victory had been obtained only on the basis set out by the ancient Roman historian Tacitus of creating a desert and calling it peace.

The population control methods used were apparently effective but in reality showed that the only way Athens could control Prespa was by banning access to it, the authorities did not have the men or infrastructure to do anything else, and initially no effort was made to bring economic development and reconciliation after the war. The Prespa villages were left in ruins or near ruins on show forever as a warning of the costs of rebellion against the Athens state in Macedonia, much as the Sultan reminded his opponents of the costs of rebellion by impaling heads on spikes above the gates of Constantinople. The might of the American forces at the onset of the Cold War could end the conflict but they could not effectively control political developments, change the ideas of those involved or eliminate those who saw themselves as Macedonians/ Bulgarians within Greece and the brutal methods used reinforced the loyalty of many to communism and to the Soviet block for many years which had offered safe refuge to them and their children. A bitter harvest had been sown which has remained divisive in the Greek polity to the present day. The children of exile who carried little bags of soil hurriedly taken from the family garden in their paltry luggage out of Greece also carried historical memory however hard various national and international bodies have sought their forgetfulness.

The Greek National Army in reality had a long and difficult struggle before it finally achieved victory in April 1949, and it was only able to do so because of American military inputs, principally a flood of heavy weapons, mechanized vehicles and aircraft. As the winter ended the DA strongpoint in the central Peloponnese Mountains and the Tayetos south of Sparta were overrun, and 2,000 DA fighters were killed and about 5,000 taken prisoner. Remaining fighters moved north via Sparta to the Prespa and Grammos regions and joined existing DA units there. In the Tayetos mountains small remaining DA groups were often finally subdued by the placement of poisoned food near their hideouts.

Under the declaration of martial law, an early weapon against the DA was the mass incarceration of arrested communists or alleged communists and DA soldiers, on what became an internal archipelago of over fifty prison islands and mainland prisons of which Makronisos off the coast of Attica and Ikaria, near Chios, are only the best

Illustration 7 Andartes fighters in Prespa during the Civil War.

known.²⁶ Under the British-written martial law regulations, virtually all human rights, even those of a limited kind in laws dating from the Metaxas years were suspended.²⁷ A colonial legal framework that had originated in the suppression of the Indian Mutiny in the nineteenth century was imposed on Greece. Many Prespa fighters or alleged communist sympathizers were incarcerated. Urban prisons in Athens were crammed with hundreds more inmates than they were ever designed to take, often women, and tuberculosis and malnutrition were rife. The programme was accelerated in response to the military gains of the Left in late 1946 and early 1947 when in British and American eyes the country seemed on the way to becoming a People's Republic and joining the Soviet orbit, if not yet as a fully fledged communist state. A new factor in the situation which concerned Western powers was the rapprochement between Yugoslavia and Bulgaria over the future of Macedonia, embodied in the Bled Agreement, signed in August 1947, which involved Bulgarian recognition of the new Macedonian People's Republic within Yugoslavia. Western diplomats feared it could become the nucleus of an expanding Macedonian state-entity which could threaten to incorporate the Slav-influenced parts of northern Greece.²⁸ Another aid to the Right was the encouragement of local paramilitary gangs of Rightist militiamen, called by the Macedonian speaking villagers *Maiti*, who terrorized villages that were particularly close to the northern border such as those on the slopes of Mount Voras/*Kajmaktsalan* on the central border with Yugoslavia where they tried to drive the village inhabitants out of Greece and into Yugoslavia.²⁹

External factors were also beginning to have a determinant role in events. Decisions taken in Washington and London were eventually to lead to the defeat of the DA as a force in Prespa, as elsewhere in Greece, three years later. The severe economic crisis in post-war Great Britain after 1946 meant there was no prospect of the London Labour government being able to finance the counter-insurgency of the Greek government for any extended period.³⁰ The United States took over the British mantle of anti-communism, both militarily and politically. In an emergency appeal to Congress in March 1947 US President Harry Truman had asked for $400 million emergency military aid to Greece and what later became known as the Truman Doctrine, a determining foundation of the Cold War, took shape. The policy planners in Washington drew up plans for a major and unrestrained counter-insurgency operation against the DA. US policy planners had been looking at options of this type since 1945 throughout Eastern Europe but the presence of the recent World War ally Russia and the Red Army in many countries prevented any attempt to implement those ambitions. Greece was different, with the Yalta agreements firmly in place, no Soviet army presence in the country and a closely allied existing force controlling the ground in many cities in alliance with the new Greek National Army. It seemed in 1946 to 1947 that all that was required to secure a landmark counter-insurgency victory was an input of American know-how and munitions. The first officers of the American military mission arrived in Greece in May 1947, by which time the Democratic Army in the north had expanded its power to the point where it had driven the National Army out of most of Greece north of Larissa and Arta, leaving it only as garrison troops in some towns.

The Greek communists in the KKE leadership had begun serious military mobilization of its cadres in late spring 1947, and although this showed a realistic evaluation of the military situation that had been absent in the previous year, by June 1947 the government had begun a policy of mass arrests of real or alleged communists that deprived the DA of considerable manpower.³¹ The issue of munitions was particularly critical and very badly handled. As Stavridis points out:

> Instead of first securing a force and then bargaining from strength, the KKE succumbed to pressure from the Greek government and declared its policy while it was still awaiting supplies. Once the supplies did arrive, initiatives could be taken more quickly, but by then the Greek government had made significant headway in depriving the KKE of its source of recruits.³²

The Greek communist leadership with its overwhelmingly urban political culture and assumptions did not have the skills that the Yugoslav leadership had in integrating the military campaign based on Partisan unit warfare in the mountains and with the long-term strategic political objectives.

In this situation, the strategic importance of the Prespa base area and its remote location on the northern borders as a logistics and supply base increased considerably and an informal airstrip was constructed along the *Megali Campos* causeway between the two Lakes between Agios Germanos and Pili east of Psarades to allow small aircraft to deliver munitions supplies from the northern neighbours. Psarades itself was developed as a food supply centre, from both local fishing and importing supplies across the lakes from Albania and Yugoslavia. The semi-underground hospital in caves near modern Pili village on the Great Prespa lakeside was particularly important, at a time when the DA and NOF were very short of medical facilities to care for and try to rehabilitate wounded combatants. The DA was increasing in size and by mid-1946 comprised about 26,000 soldiers, and although there were some desertions there were few of the mass desertions that had repeatedly taken place with the Greek National Army.³³ Yet the DA popular force was still following an outdated and ineffective military doctrine, with an officer training school being established near Florina where the doctrinal emphasis was on preparing to fight large-scale pitched battles for the control of towns, rather than the type of strategy followed in Yugoslavia and Albania and most important of all in revolutionary China, where Mao's communist guerrillas sought to obtain total control of the countryside and then effectively strangle the food and munitions supplies going to the urban areas and to cut them off one from another.

As Constantine Tsoucaras has pointed out, in late 1945 and early 1946 the mass of the Greek peasantry were mostly ready to rebel and take over the countryside, and many of the smaller towns to establish popular power, but they were never given the signal to do so by the Athens-centric KKE leadership.³⁴ During 1947 the first failures of this strategy started to become apparent, where an attempt by the DA to take the town of Metsovo failed in October, as did the attempt to overrun and secure Konitsa at the end of the year. The latter was a serious setback to the leftist cause, as Konitsa was close to the border with communist-controlled southern Albania and had been designated as a projected future capital for Greece. The KKE ambition was to establish an alternative capital in northern Greece, much as had happened under Venizelos for a period in the First World War, which would then obtain recognition from the communist neighbours, within the new framework of the Cominform which had been established as successor to the Comintern in 1947. In the background was the plan developed by the Bulgarian Comintern secretary Gjorgi Dimitrov to develop a Communist Balkan Federation. The idea of a Balkan Federation was not of course new, or a Comintern or communist invention, it had been seriously considered as the right policy for the future of the Balkans in internal debates among senior officials in the British Foreign Office in the 1930s, when no communist states existed in the region.[35] The Yugoslav concept itself dated back to the nineteenth century and envisaged a federal solution to the competing national questions that were emerging as the Ottoman and Hapsburg empires collapsed.

In the meantime the military difficulties of the DA intensified on the ground. This would worsen for the DA in the following year, where however bravely the soldiers fought under the first capable and imaginative Greek guerrilla leader the war had produced, General Markos Vafeiades, they could never be resupplied or reinforced from Prespa and elsewhere along the northern mountain borders as efficiently and quickly as the National Army could by mechanized transport on roads from the south and also, increasingly, by air. Little Psarades became central to the wider struggle as Vafeiades military HQ and he stayed himself at a large house in the upper village below the 'Africa' slope that still stands today. DA mules and horses were pastured on the lakeside grasslands and in the marshes. The village that for centuries had existed in total obscurity had become the epicentre of the struggle for the future of Greece.

As 1948 dawned little had changed on the ground, and more and more of the practical control of the war passed from Greeks to the British and American mission's military commanders, and further American military supplies poured into the country. The National Army grew to over 150,000 men, doubling in size since early 1947, although many had little military training and suffered serious morale problems. Their pacification effort nevertheless was a failure. The DA was always able to regroup in the mountains above areas such as Thessaly and where remaining local populations on the whole were supportive particularly in areas where local commanders in the DA were often ex-ELAS veterans and generally seen as national heroes from the days of the fight against the Nazi occupation. They saw the National Army as a hostile and alien force. In summer 1947 the DA, as Close describes, 'thwarted a major offensive against the Grammos by attacking them from both sides of the Pindus Mountains'.[36] The scale of the American military aid programme dwarfed even the massive forces of the previous German occupation, but it was difficult for the National Army to utilize the flood of munitions and equipment effectively and the government force spent most of the winter of 1947 to 1948 attempting to fend off DA attacks on urban centres that it held. Most US equipment demanded literate users which was far from the case with the National Army recruits in their native Greek language, let alone in English. The National Army was also held back by problems among the callow lads who had been conscripted with no basic mechanical skills like being able to drive a vehicle. They were often instinctively unwilling to kill other Greeks, even if they were communists. The DA was effective and often devastating when taking over small towns and urban centres but had little or no purchase of larger cities which in the Prespa region meant only Florina and Kastoria.

Illustration 8 The house in Psarades where Democratic Army leader Markos Vafeiades stayed in 1948.

Under the Bled Agreement that was signed by the Albanian, Bulgarian and Yugoslav General Staff in August 1947 a comprehensive military aid and training programme for the DA had been laid down, but in the conditions of the time some provisions were never implemented or only partially implemented. Discussions in the 1990s in Prespa with surviving militants and their families suggest the hope of major and decisive military aid from the north was a key aspect of the generally high morale of the leftist soldiers in the rank and file, but such hopes were based on illusions and ignorance of Yalta and much of it was never forthcoming.

The overwhelming numerical and technical superiority of the American-controlled Greek National forces was bound to overwhelm the DA over time but the continuation of leadership conflicts with the KKE leadership clashing openly with Vafeiades and removing him from his post led to perhaps a quicker conclusion than some had thought likely. The last party congress of the KKE to be held on Greek soil for over forty years took place in January 1949 and had affirmed its support for Stalin in the split in the international communist movement denunciations of Tito. The borders with Yugoslavia were formally closed. This event has been seen in some historiography as a determining factor in the defeat of the DA, but this is an oversimplified view and not the case. The war had already almost been lost by this stage and there is no reason to believe the continuation of Yugoslav aid and kinship state refuge would have made much difference to the final outcome.[37] Borders with Albania and Bulgaria in any case remained open for some time. KKE leader Zachariades was a product of the narrowest Stalinist tradition in Greek communism, and a heroic figure in the eyes of the urban rank and file of the party, someone had endured four years forced labour under Metaxas before 1939 and then spend much of the occupation incarcerated in terrible conditions in Dachau concentration camp. He had little grasp of the military realities and opportunities in the northern and central mountains.[38] He abandoned Vafeiade's successful strategy and reorganized the DA units into orthodox brigades. The Prespa region and its adjacent territories were transformed from secure and productive rear base areas to insecure and threatened redoubts.

The difficulties in maintaining daily life for remaining civilians were acute. Psarades was reasonably well placed as it was a functioning food and supplies logistics centre taking goods from the northern Yugoslav shores of the lake by boat, but hunger and infant malnutrition was growing in the more remote hill villages. Military conscription to the DA was extended to include children as young as fourteen, which caused great local resentment and encouraged some families to send their children away over the northern border, although as Danforth and Van Boeschoten point out the regular conscription age for many European countries in the twentieth century was then only fifteen.[39] Whatever the moral issues, which still arouse very strong feelings in Greece, in the spring of 1948 long columns of children marched north through Psarades and along the lakeside to Laimos and then over the border to safety in Yugoslavia at modern Dolno Dupeni village. Here they were washed, clothed, fed, deloused and then allocated places in different refugee destinations in the socialist bloc countries. Many Prespa children were first sent to Bulkes, north of Belgrade, and then later transferred to what became long-term residence in orphanages in Czechoslovakia and Hungary. Almost all the most prominent citizens of the non-Vlach older generation in contemporary Psarades nowadays were refugee children, either in Hungary or in Czechoslovakia.

Meanwhile the Prespa Vlach pastoralists tended to retreat with what remained of their flocks over the northern borders, particularly on the easy traditional summer grazing route from *Grazdeno*/Vrondero into Vlach kinship villages over the border in Albania. Children continued to be evacuated into temporary camps in the neighbouring countries, many never to return to Greece. From being the flourishing hub of popular power in the immediate post-war period, Prespa, colloquially known as 'Frontier Corner' by US and UK air force leaders began to collapse into beleaguered defeat and was increasingly empty of non-military population. Individual Prespa villages paid a very heavy price in lives for their activity in the DA. Little Laimos, then named *Robi* by the Great Prespa lakeside below Agios Germanos, is thought to have had about 700 inhabitants in 1945, about 150 of whom were recent immigrants from Asia Minor. About 110 men and women fought in uniform and thirty-seven were killed.[40] An estimated 90,000 people eventually crossed the northern border as refugees by early 1950, but already by October 1949 the DA has declared a cease fire after the devastating

Illustration 9 Refugee children in Hungary after 1949.

bombing and National Army assault on the remaining DA strongholds of Mount Vitsi and Mount Grammos.

The limited successes of the winter campaign where towns like Karpenisi were attacked and held in December 1948 for a time against the National Army turned to ashes as spring approached. The 'Operation Pyralvos' of the National Army forced its way northwards and broke the control of the DA on the passes leading north to the border, and by the end of August 1949 over two-thirds of the National Army was deployed facing the remaining DA strongholds on Mount Vitsi near Florina and across the Grammos Mountains above Konitsa. 'Pylavos' destroyed the 6000 guerrillas – often fighting in near-suicidal conditions against a now mechanized force – who were facing the 48,000 NA troops, north of Thessaly, an event which caused junta-period historian Tossizza-Averoff to write: 'For those who maintained at that time that the war in Greece was being carried on by bands of brigands, the number and nature of the sacrifices should offer much food for thought'.[41] An assault by the DA on Florina mobilized over 4000 rebels but the National Army withstood what BBC reporter Kennneth Matthews later described as 'wave after wave' of attacks, and foreign supplied airpower destroyed the DA with massive casualties, perhaps 1100 killed or injured against only about fifty National Army dead.[42] The Battle of Florina in February 1949 marked the beginning of the end and the few remaining civilians began to retreat from Prespa villages over the borders into Albania and Yugoslavia.

In the spring of 1949 the soldiers of the DA mixed with many civilians had retreated over the *Megali Kampos* open field making up the causeway running between Lesser Prespa and Great Prespa Lakes, and the region was effectively abandoned. By this time the composition of the forces in and around Psarades and Prespa had changed significantly. In the final attempts to defend the Grammos Mountain redoubt and the Prespa/Vitsi HQ, DA soldiers still capable of fighting had been ordered to come north from all over mainland Greece, some from as far away as the southern part of the Mani region in Messenia and Laconia, and from some islands.[43] The Cold War narrative of some historians who argue that the final demise of the DA came when it was a predominantly 'Macedonian' force is inaccurate and misguided.[44] Greek army aircraft, some with American pilots and kept in the air by USAF and RAF technicians, bombed the retreating columns, with gross human rights and laws of war violations against unarmed civilian refugees, even as far as villages over the border in Albania.[45] The aeroplanes of the newly formed Royal Hellenic Air Force were in essence under British training and control.[46] The crisis in Greek communism that had opened in the 1920s over Macedonian policy seemed to have run its course with the Greek Right in unchallenged control of the country and tens of thousands of leftists and people with a Slavonic identity forced into exile. The KKE has always been throughout its history a political party of martyrs and martyrdom, and the events of the Third Round of the Civil War seemed to be the last phase of a doomed and tragic history. Prespa, once a throbbing hub of cross-border activity, had become a depopulated forest and scrubland with the Greek army reducing to ruins the houses of those who had fled. The Lakes were silent except for the rich avian life. The caves that had once protected the DA leadership were empty and gradually brown bears and wolves returned to reoccupy them from the higher mountains, as they still do today. The beautiful and aristocratic Balkan lynx stalked the forest floor in silent nightly patrols under the juniper pines, a predator seeking prey. The Psarades people had gone, leaving houses with strings of red peppers drying and much of the bean harvest in sacks abandoned to rats and mice. But the exodus was not universal everywhere. Prespa experienced the most intense repression but elsewhere in northern Greece there were still villages that maintained their Slavonic Macedonian language and cultural identity. The exodus was complete in Prespa because of its military centrality in the later stages of the Civil War. Elsewhere, even quite nearby as, for instance, in the Vevi area to the east of the Manastir Gap far more people with a Slav-Macedonian identity and language use remained in their villages. They were subject to a fierce post-war campaign against their culture and property by the Athens government, when after January 1948 the law of 'M' was passed, enabling the Athens government to confiscate their property and withdraw their citizenship, a law that remained in full force until 1985.[47]

The children of the Prespa village families were on their way to find new homes in the austere but caring orphanages in the safety of distant cities such as Prague, Warsaw and Budapest.[48] The Dalmatian pelicans and pygmy cormorants flourished in their traditional fastnesses on the lakes, but with nobody to watch them float slowly over the moving clear waters except the Greek army conscripts in their new border observation posts. The hamlet of Kulla, at the west end of the Great Field, became the main road checkpoint, its Albanian-origin name meaning 'fort' redolent of the time when no doubt it performed the same function for the Ottoman road control system. It might seem as though a world and a society by the ancient lakes had been destroyed forever but this was not to be the case. Prespa seemed empty but it was not empty for long.

In the Prespa Albanian lakeside villages like Pushtec there was a stable if poverty stricken and heavily controlled surviving lakeside society, with quite widespread support for communism. The village was designated a 'Hero Village' as a result and was visited on several occasions by Enver Hoxha and Mehmet Shehu, and given priority in school and road construction. In Yugoslavia a specific version of the Macedonian identity was embodied in the Macedonian republic in the Yugoslav federal state that excluded the Bulgarian identity but did institutionalize the language and general culture and within a few years bring into being a new Macedonian Orthodox church. The inner resilience of Greek mountain society in Macedonia would guarantee that a Prespa society would be reborn, however difficult it might be. But that occurred in a new world of competing empires, those of the Soviet Union and its allies in the Warsaw Pact alliance, and America and the North Atlantic Treaty Organization and between them dissident communist Yugoslavia where the northern Greek border and the border of NATO crossed the Lakes. The villagers had escaped the menace of Nazi enslavement, in many ways through their own efforts and military bravery in the resistance, only to find themselves in what was becoming the new American *imperium*, a political dispensation that failed to bring the economic development promised by the Marshall Plan so that in the years 1955 to 1971 nearly a million people left Greece to avoid political persecution or to find work, and over 600,000 peasants migrated to the cities. Athens doubled in size in the decade after the Civil War ended. Mountain pastoral society in its old form had been destroyed in many places by the Occupation and Civil War, with the total number of sheep in Greece dropping from about nine million in 1939 to six million by 1949.[49] It also occurred in a world where very quickly the Greek government sought to elide the events involving the defeat of the DA on the Grammos Mountains, in Prespa and elsewhere, from the national memory and consciousness.[50] The recent history of Prespa was to be destroyed as comprehensively in the minds of Greeks as the patterns of centuries-old human settlement there.

9

Exile and return

The Cold War years, 1950–90

Golem merak imam mamo,
Partizan da odam
Partizan da odam, mamo
Na Vicho Planina
My hearts strongest wish, mother
Is to be a Partisan
To be a Partisan, mother
On Mount Vicho.

– Macedonian song¹

The Partisans in the Macedonian mountains had lost a war but were already passing into legend. In his study of a Languedoc village during the Albigensian persecution, *Montaillou Cathars and Catholics in a French Village 1294-1324*, Emmanuel La Roy Ladurie notes the fate of those on the losing side of the religious persecution in the Inquisition conducted by the Roman Catholic hierarchy. Those who had recanted the Cathar heresy and had been allowed to live were forced for the rest of their lives to wear badges of a yellow cross, the sign of a confessed heretic. Few veterans of the Democratic Army (DA) in western Macedonia had the same opportunity of recantation and survival offered to them. In the Prespa villages the only choice for the great majority of the *andartes* and their families with a Greek-Macedonian identity after 1949 was death or exile. The psychological torture imposed through the 'recantation and forgiveness' process in island prison camps like Makronisos and Ikaria was primarily directed at mainstream Greeks who could have their 'national consciousness' rescued and then be moved to easier prisons or released after their 'confessions'. Those with a primary Slav identity were seen as beyond redemption in most cases.

The government in Athens was happy to see them leave and live in exile, particularly those described as Bulgarians or Macedonians, and it assisted them to leave, often forcibly through right-wing gangs who attacked those seeking to remain in their villages, the same structural role that the Zervas EDES militia in Epirus/*Chameria* had played in expelling the Cham Albanian population. In the same way, in London the Foreign Office reflection on events was complacent and happy that the long-standing problem of the future of Macedonia had been 'solved', but officials still felt it needed close British scrutiny, with a FO minute of March 1949 having noted that 'The creation of an autonomous Macedonian state would solve Soviet problems. Salonika would be offered to Tito's successor and Bulgaria would get E. Macedonia and W. Thrace. It is clear, therefore, we must do all possible to prevent Macedonian autonomy'.[2]

Yet resistance continued in western Macedonia. In the conventional narrative of the Greek Civil War, the autumn of 1949 saw the final end of hostilities and peace came to northern Greece under the undisputed control of the Greek army and their American and British military advisers. The border north of Psarades became a main front line marking the boundaries of the Warsaw Pact and North Atlantic Treaty Organization military alliances when they were formed and the border with the Yugoslav Communists after the Tito-Stalin split in 1948. The Communist military headquarters at Prespa and on Mount Vitsi[3] had been destroyed by US and Greek airpower and tens of thousands of people had left as refugees during the war and perhaps as many as 80,000 more moved on in the years after the war when the region became a very depopulated economic desert.[4] Yet what the British military in Athens nicknamed as 'Frontier Corner' remained a very 'Balkan' frontier, and as the Cold War froze into immobility, efforts at sporadic civil and military resistance continued.

Although the Yugoslav-Greek border had been officially closed, the border with Albania was not (although heavily militarized) and refugees from Greece coming to Albania were welcomed and provided with basic human needs. At a local level contacts were maintained in defiance of the changes in international politics, so in early 1946 a group of Macedonian teachers from Bitola went to live and work in Pushtec for two years, remaining in practice until 1948 when with the Tito-Stalin split all education in Macedonian was closed down in Albanian schools.[5] The calculations of Great Powers and elevated geostrategic planning from NATO and the Soviet Union did not translate well into the complex reality of mountain and upland Macedonia. Sabotage of Greek army vehicles was common, along with theft of military stores and food supplies, although attacks on soldiers were rare. The army suffered from frequent fuel shortages as supplies were stolen by (or sold to) remaining inhabitants. Nevertheless, violence continued for a time after the official end of the war in 1949, with the National Army losing fourteen officers and 177 soldiers dead in northern Greece the following year[6] and lesser numbers in succeeding years.

Some people remained, although the great majority had left Greek Macedonia; in the other Prespa Lake littoral countries normal life of a kind developed in communist Albanian and Yugoslav villages on the west side of Great Prespa, which had not been so severely damaged in the war, while to the north in Yugoslavia much of the land between the Greek border and the town of Resen and Bitola itself was placed under the direct control of the feared Yugoslav internal security police, UDBA. This repression was primarily directed against anti-communist ethnic Albanians. Desultory Albanian resistance to the Yugoslav communists had continued for a short time after autumn 1944 from diehards in the Balli Kombetar (National Front) militia, but as the power of Belgrade was consolidated the last pockets of fighting died down in villages like Grncari and Ballists fled into exile. The UDBA secret police under the command of Tito's security chief Alexander Rankovic became the dominant presence in Yugoslav

Prespa and established a secret police headquarters that in later Titoist years was turned into an UDBA vacation centre at little Krani village.

On the other side of the Yugoslav lake littoral near the dismal modern village of Oteshevo, a police interrogation centre with underground torture rooms saw the end of many Ballist prisoners and other oppositionists. Marshall Tito visited the place on some occasions, as part of his reviews of the southern border defences of Yugoslavia, and stayed at a grand-scale party house nearby. A telephone surveillance unit had been built on a nearby hill facing into Greece by Russian technicians after the war and was kept in use by the Yugoslav army after 1948. International relations were very poor around the lakes for many years, all three nations used heavily armed motor patrol boats to secure their waters, and islands in the lakes like Golem Grad became overgrown and empty wildernesses. As the technology became available, first the Yugoslav military and then the Greeks obtained more sophisticated listening equipment which was installed on hills near the borders to monitor military and other telephone communications.[7]

Refugees from the conflict were given a warm welcome in Yugoslavia. Substantial numbers of people were involved, with an estimated 20,000 of the 30,000 DA soldiers, and Macedonian and Greek civilians abroad in exile in Yugoslavia.[8] An emergency programme of housing construction was started for them, which has led to small 'Greek exile' districts in larger towns like Tito Veles, Stip, Bitola and Skopje. A newspaper was published, *Voice of the Aegean's*, and in early 1950 the Union of Refugees from Aegean Macedonia was formed, primarily to lobby on social and education issues for the refugees and to form an intelligentsia among the refugees.[9] Many had serious health problems as a result of war wounds and were unable to work. Other exiles quickly became prominent in Titoist Macedonia, like Naum Pejov, from the famously 'Macedonian' village of Gavros, near Kastoria. In the main these people were those who had taken the Tito side in the 1948 split with Moscow in the international communist movement. The cultural offensive continued from Yugoslavia until 1954, when with improving relations with Greece, *Voice of the Aegean's* was closed down and replaced by a more anodyne magazine, *Makedonija*, and an annual book was published for many years recording exile community events and activity.

In Greece the complex networks of local tracks and very minor unpaved dirt roads that had crossed the border in many different places and had been used by shepherds, fugitives and local travellers for hundreds of years were closed, generally by army bulldozers causing small landslides sufficient to block the way, but this did not prevent the leakage of this banned literature into Greece via the Prespa villages. One of these old derelict roads can easily be seen today on the north side of Laimos and Agios Germanos villages running up the hill past sheepfolds to the RM border. The more substantial road running into modern RM from Agios Germanos to Dolno Dupeni was closed, mined and enclosed by barbed wire entanglements. The Albanians did not have the same level of technology as their neighbours, but relied on a draconian 'shoot on sight' policy by the numerous border guards placed at regular intervals along the border and on lake patrol boats. Fishing in most of the central part of the Lake Great Prespa where the borders met was impossible and very dangerous. This benefitted the carp and sardine stocks, and also the pelicans and other wildlife. With the disappearance of the congregation, the Psarades church of *Koimisis tis Theotokou*, the Dormition of the Virgin Mary, on the hill overlooking the lake stood lonely in a grove of ancient juniper trees that had surrounded it for so long and through so much political turmoil.¹⁰

These border changes caused major problems for the Vlach pastoralists who had been a substantial presence in the Prespa Lake region. Transhumance links with Albania that had existed since Ottoman times were broken and government pressure was imposed on the Greek Vlachs to give up pastoralism and settle in the largely empty Prespa villages. As elsewhere in Greece, mountain pastoralists were much more likely to have collectivist/communist sympathies than settled cultivators. Olive cultivation needs a settled pattern of land inheritance and ownership given the long gestation period of the trees before maturity and fruit. New settlers were also brought in if they were thought to have a 'sound national consciousness' to build up villages like Pili with an existing Vlach identity. A key objective for the central government was the stabilization of the 'wild North' through modern land tenure documents. The Vlachs were described in official publications (and often still are) as 'landless', and the whole process deprived them of ancestral but unwritten (*agrapha*) grazing rights. It turned them from free independent pastoralists into proletarianized bean field workers as part of the US-led 'modernization' of Greek farming. The development of commercial bean cultivation was nevertheless a lifeline for Greece as with food shortages in many Greek cities persisting and the running down of UNRRA relief efforts the government in Athens prioritized extending bean cultivation as part of developing indigenous food production.

In many localities, although not Prespa, American reconstruction operatives were moved in to impose a market-driven agriculture where there was sufficient fertile land and workers to make this possible.¹¹ This happily coincided with the economic interests of the Vlach pastoralists who were unable to use many of their old transhumance routes owing to new Cold War borders, and they did eventually began to settle in houses abandoned by families who had fled into exile. This did not affect all the Prespa villages, some that were very close to the new borders and in ruins like *Turnovo*/Agathoto on Lake Lesser Prespa were kept empty by the military, and remain ruined today, but there was a degree of repopulation in others a little further away from Albania and Yugoslavia borders, like Laimos and Kallithea on Great Prespa lakeside. These were also villages with historic agrarian traditions and a reasonable amount of fertile land on the lake margin that was ideal for bean growing. In American and UNRRA agricultural advisers' eyes, beans were the economic future and the solution to all western Macedonian problems.

Set against these positive aspects, there was continual emigration pressure and accelerated depopulation. A generally accepted estimate for the depopulation in and around Psarades is a drop from about 650 inhabitants in 1935 to about 150 in 1949. The radical population changes brought by the Civil War had to all intents and purposes severely damaged the dowry system in most places, as the few available single women of marriage age often had no money or property inheritance at all. If an individual or family could return, it was to a climate of extreme economic uncertainty, and very few families pre-1939 had ever had cadastral register documents to show legal title to their property, such as it was. Yet a wider world was opening to them, reproducing the old conditions for mass emigration from Macedonia in the pre-1914 period. By about 1952, fairly normal postal and open (if heavily controlled and monitored) telephone communication had begun to centres of previous Diaspora emigration, going back in some cases to the late Ottoman and First World War period, such as Toronto in Canada, and Australian cities, particularly Melbourne. This facilitated greater emigration from the jobless regions, along with the growth of civilian air travel. As Greek citizens, and seen as white-skinned people, some western Macedonians were eligible for assisted passage schemes financed by the Australian government. Perth became a popular destination for Prespa region emigrants.

In many villages, although not Psarades, the number of children in school dropped below thirteen, the Greek government's legal minimum, and the schools were closed and in many places deaths exceeded births for the entire post–Civil War period.[12] By the early 1950s the substantial amount of mostly American-origin food aid channelled through UNRRA and the Marshall Plan apparatus, meat in particular, was tailing off and in response small herds of cows began to develop along the lake margins and on the growing marshy grasslands nearby. There was also the issue of electric power. In the wartime period and after there was no mains electricity at all in any Prespa village but by the 1960s and early 1970s in both Albania and Yugoslavia electrification came, and in Greek Prespa there was a similar development. Electricity could and soon did power refrigeration, something that eventually made the first very early tourism gradually possible and also assisted the fish trade. A kind of halting and limping modernity was coming to the lakes, in both communist Albania and Yugoslavia and capitalist Greece, although with many inefficiencies. Animals remained the main method of transport, of both people and goods, given the expense of motor vehicles and the lack of reliable petrol supplies outside the cities.

The Greek state was anxious to try to establish a 'normal' population in the region, and in 1951 about 7000 Vlach settlers were brought in, from Epirus, Yannitsa region and Thessaly, with the two largest groups placed in Agios Germanos and Kallithea, and the remainder in Vrondero and Pili. Population levels had remained much more stable under Yugoslav socialism on the north side of the lakes, with 17,467 inhabitants being recorded in Resen municipality in the last census in the old Yugoslavia.[13] In a separate population movement, Greek ex-refugees from Pontus, twenty-eight families who had been made to live in Pili left the village and established their own community in modern Karies/*Orovnik* village, with its largely vacant agricultural land.[14] Any normal pattern of economic reconstruction was profoundly hindered by the general lack of population, lack of electricity supply until 1964 and the awareness among many Vlachs that with improving – if still uncertain – Greek international relations with Yugoslavia the tenure of houses they had taken over from Slavophone exiles in the Prespa villages might not ultimately be very secure. Macedonian Greek exiles in Skopje, Bitola and elsewhere still monitored very closely what was happening in their old villages, and while many never wished to return to the land that had destroyed their way of life and killed or wounded many member of their families, they certainly did want property compensation for what they had lost. The KKE in exile had an efficient and close to the ground intelligence network in Greece which most exiles used whether they were communist families or not, aided by Yugoslav and Romanian intelligence. The

Association of Greek Civil War veterans had been formed by the Yugoslav League of Communists in Skopje which acted as a lobby for veterans within Yugoslavia, a welfare organization, and a clearing house for information from Greece for exiles.

Awareness of this in Athens caused an accentuation of Greek nationalist pressures. An intense propaganda effort was mounted to characterize the Civil War, *emfilios*, the war of brothers as most Greeks had come to call it, as *Symmoritopolemos*, bandit war, and to characterize those who had taken part and ended up on the losing side as merely criminals. Nevertheless returns to the villages were already starting to take place by about 1953, usually those who had not taken an active part in the Civil War, but also sometimes those who had cracked under torture in prisons or on prison islands and signed the *Dilosi Metanoias*, the 'declaration of repentance', and in the case of the numerous women who had been in the DA, 'become women again'. They were allowed to return to their homes. In the case of Psarades a senior male member of a returning family was co-opted into local government structures supervised by the Greek Ministry of the Interior, under continuing border region martial law, and his descendants have remained prominent in village life in the region ever since. This also meant in practice that early returning exiles could take over empty land and grazing rights in abandoned areas, and 'good biography' families were encouraged to do so. A new local elite was beginning to form, at the economic expense of the exiles.

Legal changes in respect of exiles property and civil rights continued. After the Law M/48 had been passed, 'On confiscating the properties of the bandits who participated in the war' in January 1948, on 23 August 1953 the Greek parliament passed a law No. 2536 'On resettlement of the bordering regions and assistance to the population' where those who had left Greece for more than three years could lose rights to any property they owned in Greece. In practice this meant over one and half million acres of land was confiscated, including forest, grazing land, pasture and arable land, and the buildings standing on it. In the main this was land which had been distributed in the interwar period after the collapse of Ottoman estates. This was linked to a major initiative to get those with a Macedonian linguistic identity to leave their homes and settle elsewhere in Greece, often on the islands, where the developing tourist industry was often short of labourers. A sixty kilometre wide 'cultural security zone' was to be created south of the northern border where only 'the faithful sons of the Greek nation', those who were *Ethnikophrones* 'nationally minded' could settle.[15] This plan was condemned in Yugoslavia, as a plot to separate Macedonians from their homelands and was dropped and never implemented, in perhaps the first successful intervention by any external country on the Civil War exiles behalf. Nevertheless the Greek government machine continued to grind on against the human rights of the Civil War refugees. In 1959 a new law was passed, depriving exiles of all property rights if they had been out of Greece for more than five years.[16] In 1962 an additional law was passed, No 4234, where those who had been stripped of Greek citizenship were banned from ever returning to Greece, legislation which also covered their wives and children. In April 1985 the right to recover lost property was limited to those who were 'Greeks by birth only'. Little improved for the exiles over the years until August 1989 when a law officially rehabilitating those who had taken part in the Civil War was passed, but the pension rights given specifically excluded those with Yugoslav-Macedonian or another citizenship.

It is a sign of the indifference of the main European Union powers to the Greek Civil War legacy that none of these issues were ever raised or discussed with Athens during either the EU accession negotiations or the early years of Greece as a full EU member after 1982. International attention throughout the 1950s involving Greece had been almost exclusively focussed on its international relations and was dominated by the long drawn-out Cyprus crisis and its ramifications. Internal issues involving economic development and the possibility of improving the people's lives was not on any international agenda, with the country left to the mercy of free trade and open markets. In the region, the Papandreou PASOK government in the 1980s followed a bifocal policy towards the Civil War refugee issue, with some relaxation on travel and property recovery restrictions for those of Greek *genos* (of Greek 'stock') but maintaining the old laws that prevented the development of any education or religious practice in the Slavic root language.[17]

In the villages there was trade, with Prespa fish always in demand in Thessaloniki and other cities, but transport difficulties made trade very limited until the asphalt road from Psarades to Florina was completed in 1976. New communities were being formed, and with that a new local political consciousness. The Vlachs had always been much less likely to support communism than the Macedonian Slavs, and as often economic beneficiaries of the victory of the Right and usually devout Orthodox Christians brought a new political culture with their growing economic dominance in many villages. A different situation prevailed in the numerous Vlach villages in Albania between the Greek border and Korca and Voskopje, where the communities were tolerated by the Enverist one-party state but as southerners were generally spared the persecution meted out to independent pastoralists in northern Albania.[18] But it was a contradictory world. A Psarades Vlach family that had been involved in the DA and ended up taking the path of exile to Romania in 1950 only returned to Psarades after 1990. The more positive aspects of life in the socialist block were causing problems for Athens. News from Yugoslavia portrayed a picture of a growing presence of the nation in the international arena, the development of the Non-Aligned Movement, and some relaxation in the political system as the key year of 1956 approached in the international communist movement. Schools and hospitals were of a much higher general (if basic) standard in Yugoslav towns than in rural Macedonian Greece in the 1950s. Education in the Prespa villages was very limited with many like a now prominent Psarades taverna owner having left school aged twelve to become a fisherman and his sister having emigrated to the Czech republic when she was seventeen, mainly to try to get married to a suitable Greek-Macedonian exile community member. Given the Vlach dominance in many villages nearby, there was an acute shortage of marriage partners.

In Yugoslav Macedonia, towns near Prespa like Bitola had been favourably regarded by Tito's leadership group in Belgrade, mainly as a result of the local Partisan support and were receiving investment as part of the around 800 million dollar a year US subsidy of Tito. The early movement towards full collectivization of agriculture was halting and uncertain north of the lakes. It was the policy of the government, finalized in 1952, to bring uncultivated wasteland into cultivation, of which there was a great deal of land in the nascent People's Republic, but Prespa was a long way from Belgrade, and the government's focus near the southern Yugoslav border was, understandably, almost exclusively on military and security issues, and getting existing small farmers integrated into the socialist market system to improve the chronic meat shortages that persisted after 1945 in many parts of the country. In practice, the only significant development was the industrialization of the fruit growing areas south of Resen, which involved substantial extraction of Great Prespa Lake water into irrigation projects. The priority, as Tito's close henchman and ex-senior Macedonian Partisan leader Lazar Kolisevski wrote in later years, was for small producers to 'seek ways and means of association with the cooperatives and socialist economic organisations'[19] In practice, as many other external authorities from antiquity onwards have found, interference in Macedonian peasant traditional practices in agriculture was a thankless and unfruitful task.

In the sphere of ideology and education, communism could accomplish much more and much more quickly. Macedonian culture was actively promoted in Yugoslav education and began to achieve widespread recognition in foreign higher education institutions.[20] Thus, although in one sense indigenous Greek communist activity at the political level through the KKE had been almost extinguished, outside the political underground in the large Greek cities, and the party was illegal, there was quite widespread knowledge in northern Greece of the more positive aspects of the Titoist version of the system and strong family affiliations with childhood exile countries in the Soviet bloc. Developments in Yugoslavia based on social ownership and workers' self-management, however imperfect in operation, also caused considerable propaganda problems for the Greek Right and the Americans, who for years had sought to control the population through fear of Soviet-model Stalinist communism.

As economic reform gained momentum in Yugoslavia, the workers' 'self-management' system as it developed after 1952 had particular resonance in Prespa and western Macedonia given the long-established traditions of rural syndicalism, self-sufficiency and distrust of central government authority. Greek capitalism had brought an over-mighty and arbitrary state to the region, but very little in terms of material life, health care or education. The legalization and secure position of the new Macedonian Orthodox church in the Yugoslav Macedonian Republic after 1953 was also seen in a very positive light in the Prespa villages, where even in a 'favoured' village like Psarades the church had been closed down since 1949 and the cemetery bulldozed. Burials had to take place in a wood on the upper '*Africa*' eastern hillside above the village for many years. It was also possible for Greek-Macedonian political or economic exiles in large centres such as Toronto to mix socially with Yugoslav Macedonians who were beginning to take advantage of Tito's relaxation of restrictions on travel to work or live abroad as *gastarbeiters*. A transborder marriage of a now prominent citizen in contemporary Psarades took place as a result of this new situation. Thus, in a way that would have been impossible to foresee in the time of bitter defeat in 1949, a new Greek-Macedonian consciousness was emerging on an international basis.

The pattern of increasing local mobility and personal freedoms for Greek Macedonians that had developed during the 1960s ceased for a short time after the military coup in 1967, although some Prespariots still look back on the junta period until 1974 with some very limited approval as a time of better roads and more reliable electricity supply. Remittances from the overseas Diaspora were improving. The first organized tourists appeared in about 1970, in the mid-junta period, and the first attempt at developing Psarades. An upper road along the south end of the lake inlet was asphalted, and some street lighting put in, now looking odd, and stranded, far from the water near the people's allotments. In the developing local economy, Vlach families, moving one or two at a time, began to take over empty and derelict property in Psarades itself, in some cases paying a small rent to owners now resident in exile.

In the background were international issues that had emerged in the early 1950s and affected the situation of all Greek Macedonians. As a result of the 1948 split between Tito and Stalin, the position of Bulgaria became more important in the region over Macedonian matters. The strongly Stalinist Bulgarian communists had dropped their support for the 1947 Bled Agreement, which had provided for a degree of autonomy for the Macedonian Pirin region of south-west Bulgaria and Sofia readopted its 1924 policy dating from the Comintern calling for a united federal socialist Macedonian state.[21] In Greece, this was seen by many in the governing elite with alarm, and as reopening old Bulgarian ambitions to recover in 'Aegean Macedonia' what the Bulgaria had 'lost' as a result of treaties signed after the Congress of Berlin. In Balkan terms, Athens saw Yugoslavia as beginning to be encircled by the Soviet Union, Albania, Bulgaria and Romania, and this produced a slight thaw in relations.

In Prespa there was a noticeable relaxation in border policing and local cross-border contacts using unofficial tracks became more possible and in the case of Psarades led to a now quite prominent figure in the village finding his wife in a Yugoslav village on the lake just north of the border. The high tide of this improvement had been between 1956 and 1961, until 1962, when the Skopje regional government came under the influence of more nationalist figures and growing cross-border trade was restricted, and a 1959 border control agreement was revoked in Athens.[22] This affected fish sales from Psarades to buyers across the lake from Resen. Increasing freedoms were also linked to the growth of tourism in Yugoslavia where with improving highways, motoring holidays were developing and foreign and Yugoslav elite travellers with cars were able to easily visit Bitola, Ohrid and Resen and the northern fringe of Lake Great Prespa although close access nearer the border was discouraged.[23] Prespa Albanian exiles in Australia tended to be centred in Perth and Melbourne, and were in practice unable to revisit home villages in Yugoslavia until near the end of the Cold War. The occasional officially sponsored tourist from the West was allowed as early as 1953, if they were thought to be politically reliable by Belgrade. The British Yugophile writer and archaeologist Alec Brown described in his 1954 book *Yugoslavia Life and Landscape* an accompanied tour in the Macedonian Republic seeing villages on Lake Great Prespa 'that are built facing away from the lake waters because of the cold north winds'. In his eyes, then, Prespa was – when seen from some distance – still a harsh traditional Balkan wilderness. It was nevertheless a wilderness that was beginning to attract more and more scientific interest, and in a seminal decision in 1965 a Greek study of the watercourse and irrigation flows in the entire Prespa Lakes basin began, prompted in part by the sudden rapid declines in the lake levels that were taking place, which culminated in the drought years of 1987 to 1990. It was a time of change, of opening of the hitherto closed Prespa village society. The same processes were taking place in the political sphere. The 1960s was a period of rapid change in Greek rural life. In terms of the Albanian Prespa villages little had changed in their enforced isolation for many years but with the CIA-sponsored Greek army coup of April 1967 change was to come from an unexpected direction.

The junta cast a dark shadow over Greek life everywhere.[24] Even in little Psarades its effects were felt with a renewal of military and Interior Ministry pressures on the population. One Psarades citizen who was then a very young man just starting his military service abandoned his army uniform and as the son of a fisherman knew how to find his way safely across the lake border and claimed political asylum in Albania, where he worked in the Patos oilfield for a period.[25] The mood of rebellion was fired by fear of a return to the times of gross human rights violations that had characterized the Civil War period. But in the odd atmosphere of what Evangelos Kofos has called the junta's 'Balkan Flirtations' under maverick Athens Foreign Minister Panayiotis Pipinelis, after the initial military clampdown, border and wider diplomatic tensions eased, and some institutional contacts were developed further with Belgrade on trade and tourism.[26] In Prespa, the road crossing at the border between Agios Germanos and the northern Great Prespa Lake road to Resen was opened, if intermittently, and the atmosphere of claustrophobic military isolation of the early Cold War years eased somewhat.[27] Then, in a move that local people in Prespa could hardly believe, the junta reopened diplomatic relations with Albania in 1971 after a thirty-year gap, and appeared to drop the cause of the Greek minority in south-west Albania that had been a totem of Greek diplomacy ever since the First World War period and in the Paris Peace Conference after the Second World War. It was not a break with previous relationships and was presented to the wider Greek public as a product of 'detente' in the Cold War at the time. In the slight relaxation in the Albanian one-party state during these years, a school in Macedonian was opened in Pushtec, although a visitor from Skopje in 1980 found virtually no books in it. Many citizens with a 'Macedonian' identity had been forced to change their names (as all Albanians had) in 1975 as a result of government dictates about correct names in an Albanian communist state.[28] In 1976 an inter-government agreement was signed that permitted, among other things, a carefully controlled opening of contacts, so that Greek minority patients from Albania needing specialized medical treatment could go to Ioannina to receive it, a deal that also made it easier for Prespa people with relatives in exile in Albania to have a modicum of contact, at least through the mail.

In terms of tourism, little changed on the ground over the years. British writers John Crossland and Diana Constance visited the area in 1981 and found access to much of the new 'wild and lonely' National Park restricted by the military, which prevented visitors from going beyond Agios Achilleos village unless they had a special pass from the garrison in Kastoria.[29] Tourism in these years was primarily Greek and clerical and based on occasional religious pilgrimages to remote Prespa churches and monasteries which were becoming more accessible to coach tours of Orthodox activists from Greek cities as road conditions improved. Nevertheless society was beginning to change elsewhere. International ornithological concern at the critically endangered Dalmatian pelican caused by the destruction of wetlands for tourist development on the Adriatic coast led to scientists focussing on the importance of the Prespa Lakes breeding grounds. A French expedition in 1972 had made a documentary film on Prespa about the birdlife that was shown on French TV in the last year of the Athens junta government.[30] In the landmark 1976 semi-official publication, *Churches of the Prefecture of Florina*,[31] some Prespa Christian buildings are described, and photographed, although not all. The photographs give a revealing picture of the poverty and misery of the deserted countryside, with significant Byzantine and Post-Byzantine churches often ruined windowless shells, with small trees growing inside them, and no road access to them. The military did, however, allow access by boat from Psarades to the rock icons near the village, which had survived the years of conflict but in many cases, like the Virgin below Roti hill needed urgent restoration. On Achilleos Island the Byzantine basilica was a roofless ruin and at Karies the Church of the Assumption a shell with no windows, surrounded by blackened timbers and piles of rubbish. In a significant omission, there was no mention of the important church at *Grazdeno*/Vrondero and other buildings in villages to the west of Psarades, or Psarades church itself, presumably because the art historians had not been allowed access to them. The victory of the Greek Christian-nationalist cause in 1949 did not result in responsible custody of national heritage monuments within the closed military border areas. In contrast, in Yugoslav Macedonia, the important Byzantine church of St George at Kurbinovo in the eastern hillside village above Lake Great Prespa with its outstanding frescos was fully restored and was visited by artist Pablo Picasso in 1966 when attending a peace conference in Ohrid.

The traditional Greek security apparatus was much less efficient at preventing change from another unexpected direction. An international impetus in the specialized world of ornithology had seen the opportunities to try to tap research funding from the European Union and well-funded bird conservation organizations such as the Audubon Society in the United States into the measures that would be needed to protect the Dalmatian pelican and other rare wildlife that lived on the Prespa and Ohrid Lakes. In the natural world after 1985 substantial water loss in both lakes began, coinciding with a period of drought throughout the southern Balkans but not exclusively caused by it. A level seven metres below normal had been reached, causing ecological changes which put the pelican colonies under extreme stress, particularly in the breeding season. Yet in human society, daily life in Psarades in the 1980s was a good time and the region seemed to be settling down to a kind of normality as the memories of the Civil War years and exile faded, and the tide of Civil War blood that had killed all seven children of the uncle of a Psarades tavern owner receded into history. The end of the Cold War after 1989 should have been a time of further optimism, but it was also a time of illusion given the nature of the developing crisis in Yugoslavia so near to the villages over the northern Greek border.

In Athens as the Berlin Wall fell and the Cold War ended in 1989 the PASOK project of Andreas Papandreou and Kostas Simitis was running towards its end and the optimism that has swept Greece after full European Union membership in 1982 and associated rural investment was also fading. But few would have anticipated the scale of the crisis in the southern Balkans that was to soon transform the atmosphere everywhere, from major cities like Zagreb, Belgrade, Thessaloniki, Tirana and Skopje to tiny Prespa villages like Vrondero and Pili. Nationalist perspectives from the past were reviving. In Skopje and the countryside in the Socialist Republic of Macedonia, the party was taking a renewed interest in the promotion of what it saw as legitimate 'Macedonian' nationalism and in 1986 interwar historian D. Dimov republished his landmark biographical study of the last days of the IMRO in the post-Versailles Treaty period, *The Macedonian National Question 1875-1924*. In it IMRO militants were seen as legitimate and honourable political martyrs for a good cause rather than murderous terrorists, and news of its reappearance caused very critical reactions in Thessaloniki intellectual and political circles. But no one concerned could have dreamed that within five years IMRO, in a new form, would have been refounded in RM/FYROM and in September 1991 the people would vote to become an independent Republic of Macedonia. A dream was being fulfilled in Skopje, while in Athens it was seen as a returning nightmare. The New Macedonian Question was opening, with the Greek political establishment aghast at the existence of a new Macedonian state-entity, and they were soon doing everything they could to stifle its existence and the prospect of a successful future. The long-forgotten difficult issue of Greece's northern border and its relationship with its neighbours was to soon renew itself, as it had so often done before at times of crisis in the twentieth century, and the Prespa villages and in particular Psarades were nodal points on that border.

10

The Lake world

Conflict in Albania and Yugoslavia, 1991–2001

> We scrambled by a stony mountain track to Nivica, a wretched little fishing village on the other side of the lake. The people here had fled to the island of Grad during the insurrection, so had escape, but the village had been robbed, their fishing tackle destroyed, they had an outbreak of smallpox, and were in great distress.
>
> Mary Edith Durham, 'The Burden of the Balkans', 1905[1]

The momentous events in Eastern Europe at the end of the Cold War, which culminated in the fall of the Berlin Wall in 1989 and the end of communism in the region, had no immediate effect upon the isolated communities of the Prespa Lakes. In 1990 Edith Durham would easily have recognized many aspects of contemporary subsistence life in Psarades, against a more prosperous social and economic background. Carp were caught and dispatched with a heavy hammer on the head while still in the fishing boat, beans were harvested and dried, workers in the fields tied up the long sticks ready for use next year. Red peppers, reputedly the best in the Balkans, were roasted ready for winter supplies. The prices Prespa beans were fetching was watched against inferior products grown elsewhere, but at the same time everyone was also watching the television and reading the newspaper, amazed by the fall of the Berlin Wall, and thinking of relatives living in the old Soviet countries. It suddenly seemed that communication and travel would be easy. Then gradually the looming Yugoslav crisis moved closer to Prespa. At first the key events were in the northern Balkans. The disintegration of Yugoslavia had begun in 1990 when Slovenia was allowed to slip relatively unscathed from the Yugoslav Federation. The following year, the war between Serbia and Croatia began in earnest, eventually spreading to Bosnia and then south to Kosovo and finally to Macedonia, within 30 miles of Prespa. Simultaneously, the hard-line communist regime in Albania ended with the country's first multi-party elections held in March 1991, which far from providing stability, led to the complete collapse of power and authority.[2] There followed a time of intense political crisis and social chaos throughout Albania and ex-Yugoslavia, which inevitably began to impact upon the Prespa region initially through population movement issues.

After the virtual disintegration of all organized social and economic life in Albania and with foodstuffs about to be exhausted, tens of thousands of Albanians attempted to flee to Italy and Greece. Albania's relations with Greece had deteriorated due to the exodus of more than 5,000 members of Albania's Greek minority who, since late December 1990, had been crossing the border into northern Greece. Although the majority had Greek passports, the Greek embassy in Tirana was reluctant to issue more than a minimum of visas, fearing that Greece might be overwhelmed by large numbers of ethnic Greek Albanians. The Albanian government estimated the officially recognized minority in southern Albania to number 50,000, but Greece had long claimed a figure of 100,000 or more (all of whom would be eligible for Greek citizenship if they crossed the border), while the extreme nationalist Vorio (northern) Epirus Organization in Greece claimed up to 250,000.

To diffuse a potential refugee crisis, the then Greek Prime Minister, Konstantin Mitsotakis, was invited to Tirana where he sought to discourage a further exodus by urging ethnic Greeks to remain in Albania and keep faith in the reform process. However, most of the potential refugees, knowing their political elite perhaps better than Mitsotakis, appeared to have little confidence in the dramatic changes under way in Albania or the capacity – or even the will – of a distant government in Athens to protect their interests. Instead, not knowing when they would get another chance to leave the country, hundreds of young Albanians, initially mostly men, clutching little parcels containing meagre food supplies continued to trek southward over the formidable border mountains into Greece. Thousands more, who gathered in border villages preparing to cross, found little resistance from the once-feared Albanian border guards now that the penalties for attempting to leave the country, which had been up to twenty-year prison sentences, were no longer in force. These included non-ethnic Greek Albanians who had hastily often faked Hellenized names and converted to Orthodoxy in order to get into Greece.

As well as crossing over the Grammos Mountains, Albanians trekked across the Thate Mountains above Korca on the Albania-RM border and then through the dense forests dividing Albania and Greek Prespa to avoid detection by Greek border police, eventually reaching the shore of Great Prespa Lake and its surrounding villages. Their arrival caused alarm among the inhabitants of Prespa. In September 1992 at a wedding feast in Pili, a purely Vlach village south-west of Psarades, which was attended by the authors, a group of men were angrily discussing how to protect their livestock from being stolen by hungry Albanian migrants hiding in the dense juniper forest. 'We have lost over twenty sheep this winter', said a burly young man. He then described in matter of fact tones how he had killed an Albanian refugee while out wild boar hunting that spring. He had stumbled across the unfortunate Albanian asleep in a clearing, and after slitting his throat with his hunting knife had left the body as a reminder to other Albanians not to kill Vlach sheep. The local Greek police apparently ignored the incident, as overall sentiment in Greece was strongly anti-Albanian at the time. The murder of an immigrant had entered the world of the wedding.

The first dance begins, a line of carefully elegant young women, arms moving rhythmically like reedbeds in the lakeside cool north wind. The young men and old women do the work and clear the tables. Other wedding guests described the alienation of the Vlach community in general from the Athens government and the better conditions for Vlachs in Skopje, where a Vlach political party had been formed. Looking down on all the Greek state does provide in Pili, the schoolrooms, Christos spoke in Vlach 'Est Romani', meaning 'I am a Vlach', and then pointing at the school. 'It is a crime but we are poor. What can we do? They do not allow Vlach books in the school, nothing.' A woman opines: 'When the EU money is handed out this remote corner of northern Greece gets nothing, even towns like Florina and Kastoria miss out. And people from Athens and Crete and Holland. They come to watch the birds, but they are strangers in their own country. No idea that anyone speaks Slav or Vlach.' And then cherry jam is provided on little dishes as allegations of cultural repression echo around the wedding. The proliferation of 'Macedonia is Greek' flags hanging everywhere in the villages conceals disturbing tensions. Across the lakes in Ohrid, an IMRO 'Protection Committee' has been formed, as fear of a Greek military incursion spreads through the communities.[3]

Meanwhile, the hitherto tranquil life in Psarades was gradually changing in the wake of the conflicts in Yugoslavia and civil turmoil in Albania. Whereas the majority of Prespa's inhabitants during the 1990s relied upon beans and other agricultural crops for their livelihoods, Psarades still depended almost exclusively upon fishing, and in the case of older inhabitants, particularly widows, a single cow. Little bent old ladies with walking sticks who had seen so many years often used to follow the animal round the village as their daily round and to meet and talk to friends and acquaintances. Cow dung was carefully collected in buckets and used on the vegetable patches by the lake. Fishing started very early in the morning before first light and by lunchtime the men were having a restorative beer and chatting by the boat jetty. Yet outside events were impinging on them. With the borders of Yugoslavia and Albania visible across the Lake, the tiny village felt itself vulnerable and isolated. Insecurity now dominated Psarades life.

People began to buy large dogs, particularly Alsatians to protect their boats and fishing equipment, but some wandered into the forests and were never seen again. Long-standing gripes and petty rivalries (often of family/political origin) between different Psarades families sometimes flared up in allegations about the fate of a loved dog. Sheep and chickens were being stolen by itinerant Albanians, and valuable Japanese fishing nets had also begun to disappear during the night allegedly, stolen by Albanians. The village acquired its first police presence as security had now become a serious issue all along the Yugoslav and Albanian border, with an old military observation post at the north end of the village that had been built by the French military in the First World War becoming a police station. A dark night in the winter on the lakeside with a frosty north wind was a very different place from the idealized summer world of the ecologists and birdwatchers. The Utopian beauty had transmuted, as Arcadias do, into a threatening and sinister lawless wilderness. Above all, local people associated the Albanians with guns, and this reputation grew with the crash of post-1991 Albania into poverty and state collapse and then later on the looting of the military magazines in the uprising linked to the pyramid bank crisis in 1997 where Albania was flooded with weapons. The RM village of Velishte, on Quaf e Thanes border pass road, became notorious as a centre of arms dealing, only a short drive from Resen, Bitola and Struga.

Prespa shepherds had always owned shotguns, but Kalashnikov AK-47s were a very different matter. In this climate of fear, the very limited post-1989 cross-lake contacts between the different national and ethnic groups came to a standstill.

In the wider region, the effects of the disastrous environmental policies of the Cold War years were still taking their toll on the lakes. French ecologist Jean Gardin has noted that in Albania, the totalitarian state of Enver Hoxha was characterized by its Promethean vision of human supremacy over nature.[4] But the processes of society were turning against the natural environment. In RM the market for apples from the south of Resen Prespa industrial scale orchards rapidly declined as most of them had hitherto been sold to war-torn northern republics. Agricultural and sewage discharges into the lake became an issue and conflict over the limited water supplies intensified. Locally, Tirana government policy had led to the diversion of the Devoll River into Lesser Prespa and the digging of a canal from this lake to irrigate the arable Korca plain, continuing a trend of wetland reclamation that began before the Second World War with the draining of Maliqi Lake on Korca plain, which was completed by cruel forced labour in the early communist period. This put further strain on the water resources remaining in Lesser Prespa Lake for many years. On a more positive note, it led to the planting of millions of trees on mountainsides. This stopped quickly after the fall of the communist regime in 1991. Collective irrigation and draining canals were put out of use, resulting in the formation of a new Maliqi Lake, an ecological benefit, and forests were destroyed by both locals and city-dwellers from Korca (or even Tirana) in a race for private appropriation of the best part of the existing collective property, an ecological setback. This resulted in an increasing amount of sediment deposit in Lesser Prespa.[5]

In the meantime, there were some positive developments in the field of government activity regarding the environment around the Prespa Lakes. As long ago as 1959 a joint Commission of the Yugoslav and Greek governments had been established to study and manage hydro-economic questions, including the hydro-economic problems of Lake Prespa, although it rarely seems to have met, and issues of water quality and integrated water management were not part of its remit. In the locality work focussed on practical matters. In the spring of 1991, a spectacularly successful re-establishment of the carp was recorded following the crash of the stock of this species in the 1970s and 1980s. A conservation review by the Prespa-Ohrid Nature Trust found that during the period 1950 to 1990 vast areas of pasture and forests in communist Albania were converted to arable land, 54 per cent of which was irrigated from both lakes. By 1990, however, about two-thirds of these areas had been abandoned and converted back to pastures and meadows. This assisted water retention in the Lakes. Tourism on the Yugoslav side of Prespa developed in this part of the basin until the late 1980s, but a significant reduction occurred thereafter, when a decrease in the water level of the Lakes changed the previously sandy beaches to muddy, shallow coastal areas, sometimes with reedbeds. This also occurred in Greece. The number of tourists dropped by almost a half from 45,000 to about 27,000, leaving the tourism industry in the Prespa region as small scale, seasonal and based on a few small hotels, private accommodation and restaurants.[6] The decline in tourism and general work prospects, together with the continuing environmental degradation, led to a Prespa-wide population decrease. Many hill villages around the Lakes never saw inhabitants return from exile due to their Macedonian identity, and remained, as many do today, sad and deserted, if often picturesque, reminders of the Civil War conflict. The census in Greece in 1991 had recorded just 144 residents in Psarades.

In 1990, in the new international context and reflecting the worldwide growth of environmentalism, an attempt was made to protect the Prespa region with the foundation of the Society for the Protection of Prespa (SPP) with the participation of ten environmental organizations such as the Greek Ornithological Society, Arcturus, the World Wildlife Fund, the Friends of Prespa and others. The SPP, whose headquarters was, and still is, based in Agios Germanos and Laimos aimed to manage the area's natural resources, protect its endangered species and promote sustainable forms of development and public awareness of Prespa's environmental importance. This was the first coordinated effort to protect the area and since its inauguration the SPP has gained international recognition for its valuable work. One of the main conservation priorities at this time was to protect the Dalmatian pelican and, by extension, the wetlands of Lesser Prespa Lake, which in the early 1990s had the EU's only breeding colony of the species with less than 200 pairs.

Nevertheless, the protection and viable development of Prespa required the participation and harmonious cooperation of the three states that share the area – Greece, FYROM and Albania. Consequently, environmental, social and developmental projects required development at a trans-boundary level. The same also applies to Lake Ohrid, where the fact that the town and vicinity has been for many years a UNESCO protected site has not prevented many environmental problems that remain focussed on overfishing the unique lake species of trout and raw sewage discharge, mainly from the Albanian town of Pogradec. By the end of the decade, this pressing need for trans-boundary cooperation had become formalized in February 2000, when the prime ministers of the three countries sharing the Prespa Lakes catchment basin triggered a major trans-boundary cooperation programme with their declaration of the formal creation of the Prespa Park. Although tensions remained, and later in spring 2001 RM was rent by armed conflict between the ethnic Albanian National Liberation Army and the Skopje-based state, with serious damage and loss of life in Bitola only an hour away, a better future for the Prespa region seemed possible. Despite past turbulent relations and prevailing political uncertainty in the region, Prespa became the first trans-boundary protected area in South Eastern Europe on the 29th anniversary of the World Wetlands Day. The creation of the Prespa Park appeared as a possibility to both test re-drawn neighbours' relationships and bring modern rural and environmental management in a remote and problematic border zone of northern Greece.[7]

The concept of a shared National Park was central and seen uncritically as good by all involved at the time, with its Utopian assumptions of EU-funded fast-track economic development that had become an ideology akin to theology among the modernizing PASOK Greek government elite who at that time still dominated Athens politics. There was very little consultation at all with local people around the Lakes, and existing local democracy was being undermined by the loss of the school and the local Mayor in Psarades and the centralization of all activity around the centre of Agios Germanos. Tourism was seen as a panacea, and the effect of tourism of the kind the three governments envisaged on the identity and traditions of Psarades was never considered. The decultureisation process continued with the ending of the last restrictions on non-Greeks and non-residents on buying property in the new Park, enabling some fallen houses to be bought by middle-class outsiders from Thessaloniki and elsewhere, and eventually, after about 2012, one or two rich foreigners. The Swiss critic of the National Park concept, Michael Keller has shown in his projects in the Ticino region of Switzerland that centrally imposed parks often do little to either produce viable economic development or protect local traditional lifestyles and identity.[8]

The very first meeting of the Prespa Park Coordination Committee (PPCC) was held in Skopje in January 2001, at the invitation of the Macedonian Ministry of Environment and Physical Planning. The Committee was composed of three representatives from Albania, Greece and the Republic of Macedonia (representing the environment ministries, local authorities and NGOs). Observers from the Convention on Wetlands, from donor organizations and from NGOs also participated. Jean Gardin notes that the Prespa Park presented a strategic opportunity for cooperation: in 2000 the Kosovo war had just finished and very sharp tensions resulted further south dividing Albanian-speaking and Macedonian-speaking citizens of Macedonia. In addition, the presence in Greece of some 700,000 immigrants (primarily Albanians) caused a debate often turning to racism in spite of a first campaign of regularization. Lastly, the consolidation of the name of Macedonia by the ex-Yugoslav Republic opened up a period of troubled relations with Greece.[9] However, well before the declaration of the Prespa Park the three neighbouring countries had already protected sections, or all, of their sides of the catchment basin of Prespa. In the Macedonian Republic, two National Parks were created during the Yugoslav period – Galiciça (1949) and Pelister (1960) – and from that time any new construction has been forbidden and pastures and logging have been under state regulation. Albania and Greece had also proclaimed national parks covering the whole catchment basin of the Prespa Lakes in their respective territories.[10]

The PPCC adopted an ambitious work plan, including the preparation of a project on integrated ecosystem and natural resources management for the entire Prespa Lakes region. A trilateral secretariat was established, with an NGO member from each country to develop a Strategic Action Plan for the sustainable development of the Prespa Park, thanks to initial financial support from the Greek Ministry of Environment, Physical Planning and Public Works. Two project proposals were of primary importance: that of coordinated water management and support for cross-border cooperation activities. But in a worrying development the programme implementation unit of the European Union's Phare programme in Skopje proposed to construct a road right through the marshes in the centre of Macedonia's only Ramsar Site.[11]

The second meeting of the PPCC was held in the Women's Cooperative Hotel in Psarades the following November and was hosted by the Municipality of Prespa and the Society for the Protection of Prespa. The acting chairman, Mr Michalis Modinos, president of the National Centre for Environment and Sustainable Development of Greece, conveyed the full support of the Greek government to this innovative form of international co-operation for a region suffering from a spiral of environmental degradation accompanied by depopulation and social problems.[12] During this year, the Committee noted that major hydrological interventions had in the past been undertaken in the Lesser Prespa area and that the old canals diverting the Devoll River into the lake stopped operating at the end of 2000. Recently, however, a new canal had been built to take water out of the lake for irrigation purposes. The Secretariat suggested that the problem should be addressed in a holistic way in the context of the hydrological programme. The Albanian delegates presented an irrigation programme of the area for which the new work was carried out, while reiterating the firm commitment that the Devoll waters would not be directed into the Lake again in the future.

The meeting was held in Psarades' Women's Cooperative Hotel, due to the village's close proximity to the borders of the neighbouring countries. During the 1990s, there was a significant increase in the number of women's cooperatives founded in Greece. They were specifically located in less developed, mountainous areas and faraway from big urban centers, such as Thessaloniki. The cooperative's primary aim was the improvement of women's position in small communities, offering them the opportunity for a supplementary income apart from their household engagements and activities in family farms. The region of Florina, due to its specific climate conditions and natural and cultural resources was considered as a pole for winter tourism as well as an emerging agro-tourism destination.[13] Two villages chosen for the establishment of women's cooperatives were in the traditional mountainous villages of Nymfeo and Ano Kalliniki, both near Florina. There two micro cottage cooperatives were set up, the first one producing traditional food stuff and beverages and the second one with the trade-name 'Pelagonia', producing traditional costumes. Both villages were chosen, in part, because of their important architectural tradition.

The other women's cooperatives were founded in the villages of Psarades and Agios Germanos where they operated two agro-tourism guesthouses. The cooperative of Agios Germanos, which started its operation in 1985, is the oldest. The women from the surrounding villages created this cooperative, aiming to provide tourism services, to promote traditional cuisine and the natural and cultural environment of the area. Their guest house, with a capacity of twenty-five beds, initially belonged to the Prefecture of Florina, which offered it to the cooperative and later it was bought by the women's cooperative. The women's cooperative of 'Psarades' was opened in 1994 and was built by the Prefecture of Florina. This architecturally stark and unattractive hotel has a capacity of thirty-one beds and is unfortunately located in a very prominent position facing the village on the opposite side of the Lake. The operation and management of the hotel was offered free of charge to the women's cooperative.[14] While the cooperative guest house in Agios Germanos has been a very successful enterprise, the same cannot be said of the women's hotel in Psarades. This large, unsightly construction has been a distinct failure. It was only occupied for a few years and remains today isolated, empty and increasingly dilapidated.

Throughout the 1990s, tourism was still mostly restricted to hikers, birdwatchers and the occasional journalists covering the region as the Yugoslav conflict and Albania's political turmoil continued to rage.[15] During the first half of the decade the Albanian border had virtually ceased to exist, even though the Prespa region has been a military security zone ever since the borders of Greece, Albania and Yugoslavia were drawn up after the First World War. The border area around the Prespa Lakes is so wild and porous that it enabled a steady stream of Albanian migrants to continue to slip unnoticed into Greece, creeping under the trees like ghosts in the extraordinary bright moonlight for which Prespa has always been celebrated. Although most of them made their way down to Athens and other large cities in search of work, a few remained in the Lake area where they provided cheap labour, especially in the local bean industry, in all the villages surrounding the Greek side of the border. Where a family wanted to repair or expand their house, even those from the Diaspora, Albanian stonemasons began to be employed and soon integrated well into village life, as they were skilled, and filled a local labour market gap, and generally did not try to settle in the village permanently. This situation remains largely the same today.

Prespa-region agriculture relies directly on the cheap labour of Albanian migrants. The bean monoculture that has developed since the 1960s is particularly endangered, manual work is irreplaceable, arable lands are rare and consumption centres are far away. Albanian workers therefore represent the only chance of business survival. Hundreds of workers cross the frontier for spring and autumn work. While they do not stay permanently (in seasonal work, mostly looking after cattle, mechanical and building works, etc.), they inhabit ruins and abandoned houses for some periods or commute daily from Albania.[16] The economic crisis linked to the Yugoslav wars affected the entire region, with once bustling Ohrid becoming a ghost town in winter and businesses closing down. Spirilling diesel prices and supply shortages caused by the Yugoslav hyperinflation meant that the once famously reliable Yugoslav bus services began to break down and long queues of hundreds of people at the Struga and Resen bus stations were a common sight. Alarm over migration flows spread to Greece, with semi-wild and often hungry Alsatians and Rottweilers allowed to run wild around the Niki border post north of Florina to discourage illegal migrants. But from the same semi-sealed borders between RM and Greece vast profits were being made by Greek business people, some close to the Athens government from smuggling diesel fuel across it.

At the beginning of February 2001, the Yugoslav wars finally reached the previously peaceful Republic of Macedonia. There, an armed insurgency began when an ethnic Albanian militant group, the Albanian National Liberation Army (NLA), which sought the secession of Albanian-majority areas, attacked the Republic's security forces. In a short conflict, violence was serious in Bitola and minor in Resen but did not spread to outlying Prespa and Ohrid villages where Muslims and Christians had coexisted – if not always happily – for a long time. The conflict ended with the Ohrid Agreement, signed on 13 August of that same year.[17] Although the war lasted just six months and overall casualties remained limited, seething ethnic tensions continue in both the Republic of Macedonia and Kosovo. Also, the political climate in Albania still remained highly volatile, which renewed visitors concerns about safety in the region and reduced tourism, particularly in Ohrid. But times were changing. The Albanian insurgency in the Preshevo valley in Serbia on the western Kosovo border failed due to lack of active NATO support, and the hated Milosevic regime in Serbia fell quite soon afterwards in 2000. Despite the political fragility in the southern Balkans, international attention in the region began to wane following the 9/11 attacks in America and has continued to decline to the present day.

Gradually foreign tourists began to trickle back to the Prespa region, primarily in Greek Prespa. In Psarades new tavernas opened and a few village homes began to let rooms to occasional visitors, who were still, in the main, hikers and birdwatchers. The qualified success of the international operation to save the Dalmatian pelican was beginning to attract widespread attention in the conservation world, and in April and May 'tweeters', expert birdwatchers, drawn from many countries became quite numerous together with serious environmentalists who had come to Prespa to observe and photograph the reviving rare species. Life in Psarades, however, continued in its time-honoured manner with women daily visiting the various vegetable patches and collecting eggs from the vast number of chickens roaming the village, while the men busied themselves mending fishing nets and chopping wood to store for the harsh winter. In the evening elderly women dressed in black gathered in little groups outside houses to gossip while their men-folk had nightcaps in the tavernas. But institutional life was weak and in some eyes weakening fast. The Psarades school had already closed and was turned for a time into an ecology centre, and the one shop was always teetering on the edge of closure, finally opting to open only in the summer tourist months. Rooms around the main square that had been modernized to accommodate foreign tourists opened only for a short time around the August *Panaghia*. The church had a steady quiet life, with the restored graveyard on the hillside at last providing a dignified resting place for the village dead after so many years without a cemetery gradually filling as the elderly passed away with their white gravestones bearing the familiar Psarades names of Papadapoulos and Dimonopoulos and Vlach names like Tzepis.

Illustration 10 Pushtec village and Maligrad Island in Albanian Prespa.

Meanwhile, in Albanian Prespa life also continued much as it had done for centuries with the lakeside villages largely cut off from developments in the rest of Albania as they always had been, although there was some population movement from Albania towards Macedonia as well as Greece. In March 1991 forty people had fled from the Albanian Prespa villages to Bitola, claiming that they could live better there than in Albania. They also said it was impossible for Macedonian-identity people to flee Albania to Greece, as everyone with Slavonic sounding names was sent back at the border.[18] The roads remained largely muddy tracks and few houses were fully occupied as the young and able-bodied had crossed over into Macedonia to find work. As with other minorities, Albania's ethnic Macedonian population, known as 'Bulgareci', had no independent organization under communism and suffered cultural discrimination. Although Albania did not then officially recognize its neighbour's constitutional name of 'The Republic of Macedonia', after Albania's first multi-party elections in the summer of 1991 the new government relaxed restrictions on the minorities' rights and allowed the provincial Radio Korca to begin broadcasting in Macedonian for several hours a day and in September, the then Minister of Justice approved the creation of a political association for the Macedonian community at first called Bratska (Brotherhood) and later renamed Prespa. The Association campaigned for more educational provision in the Macedonian language and more local control over their affairs. In July 1991 the then RM/FYROM Prime Minister Nikola Kljushev visited *Liqenas*/Pushtec and met members of the Macedonian minority there.

Throughout the 1990s further measures ensured Albania's 'Bulgareci' received education in their own language. This followed an intervention by Albanian leader Dr Sali Berisha, who had speculated in a speech whether the minority group in Albania was Macedonian or Bulgarian, which caused uproar in Skopje.[19] In March 1998 the Macedonian Education Ministry, in co-operation with its Albanian equivalent, compiled various textbooks, printed in Macedonian, for pupils of Macedonian ethnicity. At the time there were approximately 600 ethnic Macedonian children attending instruction in Macedonian, from grades 1–4. Later, in grades 5–8 around 60 per cent of all instruction was in Macedonian.[20] Throughout the 1990s Albania remained in a constant state of political turmoil, culminating in a virtual civil war during 1997 to 1998 leaving over 4,000 people dead.[21] This led to a stagnated economy which further exacerbated the extreme poverty of Albania's citizens and propelled thousands more Albanians to flee the country. Such poverty was most extreme in the country's furthermost border regions including the Prespa villages, but due to their remoteness were not affected by the serious violence in 1997 to 1998.

Throughout Albania in the 1990s, foreign humanitarian aid was flooding into the country and the rivalry between Macedonia and Bulgaria to deliver aid to the 'Bulgareci' villages around Prespa, and so further their respective influence, became acute. For example, in August 1997 the Bulgarian government sent a shipment of aid addressed to 'all Bulgarians in Albania'. The shipment, however, was detained at the Macedonia border. The then Macedonian President, Kiro Gligorov, argued: 'The people of Albania need help but humanitarian ventures should not be used for political purposes.'[22] Gligorov objected to the fact that the aid shipment had been addressed to 'all Bulgarians in Albania'. The 'Prespa' organization also objected by issuing the following strongly worded statement:

> If you think the Macedonians from Prespa are Bulgarians, you are very wrong. As you have earmarked the aid to 'Bulgarians' in Albania, which do not exist, you will have to withdraw it back. We are Macedonians, speak Macedonian, feel Macedonian and have our Macedonian schools. Regarding your concern for the 'Bulgarians' in Albania, keep it for the citizens of the Republic of Bulgaria.[23]

Despite a long history of marginalization, the people of Albanian Prespa appeared on the surface to have retained a sense of 'Macedonian' rather than 'Bulgarian' identity. This was, however, a highly debatable and controversial issue. Ever since the Comintern in Moscow supported the notion that the Macedonian Slavs were a separate nationality in 1934, the post-war Balkan communist regimes gave their backing to the development of a distinct Macedonian identity and as a result, Albania's Slav minority was recognized by the Tirana government as 'Macedonian'. In the aftermath of communism, Albania's political class still felt unable to re-evaluate the status of the country's minorities. Indeed, in an interview discussing the Slav minority in 1998, the then Albanian Foreign Minister, Paskal Milo, encapsulated the sensitivity of the issue when he stated: 'After World War II, we know this minority as Macedonian. I'd rather not elaborate on why we chose this way, but the communist regime made this decision and it's difficult for us now to change that.'[24] In recent years the Bulgarian Orthodox church has taken a very active policy towards this minority in Albania, with major investments such as the restoration of the main church in Pushtec and visits by leading clerics to the area. Many of the minority now study for higher education in Bulgaria, and Bulgarian number plates are a common sight on village cars.

The situation regarding the minority in Greek Prespa during the 1990s was far more controversial. It was often highlighted by the growth in the early 1990s of new visitors from the numerous Macedonian, Australian and Canadian Diaspora families, even including priests of the Macedonian Orthodox church, banned in Greece itself, who could not be obstructed from arriving at Greek airports as they held Australian or similar foreign passports. But Athens government policies, reflecting the vast majority of Greek public opinion, remained unchanged. The Greek authorities, from the outset of the modern Greek state under its current post-1923 borders, have consistently denied the existence of the Macedonians, with all their multiple ethnicities, Slav, Albanian, Turkish, Torbesh and Roma as a separate people from the Greeks, or as national minorities and instead officially referred to them as Slavophone Greeks, while the Bulgarians consistently claimed them to be Bulgarians.[25] Although a majority of Macedonian-speaking people in northern Greece have a Greek national identity (i.e. they identify themselves as Greeks and as Macedonians or as Greek Macedonians), a significant number of them have a Macedonian national identity (i.e. they identify themselves as Macedonians and not as Greeks). Since the mid-1980s, a small number of these Macedonians, many of whose families experienced severe persecution during the Greek Civil War, became politically active and began to demand human rights for the Macedonian minority in Greece.[26]

As early as 1984 the Central Organizing Committee for Macedonian Human Rights was established in semi-underground circumstances in northern Greece.[27] In the next few years similar organizations were formed by Macedonians in Diaspora communities in Canada and Australia. Among the goals of these groups was the repeal of several specific laws which discriminate against Macedonians. Two laws (passed in 1982 and 1985) explicitly exclude Macedonians from the general amnesty under which political refugees who left Greece after the Civil War were allowed to return to Greece and reclaim their property (which had been confiscated by the Greek government) only if they were 'Greek by birth'. Another law (passed in 1982) ceased to recognize university degrees obtained in the Republic of Macedonia on the grounds that Macedonian was not an internationally recognized language.[28] In Australia where the Greek and Macedonian émigrés are on very poor terms, there were violent reprisals against community buildings and churches, on both sides of the ethnic divide.[29]

The Greek authorities attempted to quell this embryonic Macedonian national assertion and on 20 July 1990 local authorities reportedly forcibly disrupted a Macedonian 'national day' in the village of Meliti in Florina district, and émigrés alleged that similar incidents took place that week and some Greek Macedonians in government employment were forced to transfer to distant regions of the country on pain of dismissal.[30] A series of other rallies followed on the Greek-Yugoslav border in protest against Greece's refusal to grant visas to the Macedonian minority. Despite the rise in nationalist tensions, the Prespa population remained relatively distant from the growing Macedonian assertiveness in Florina and Thessaloniki. Although most people spoke Macedonian in their homes, they spoke Greek in the street and at work and were generally reserved when questioned about events outside their community.

In Psarades during the 1990s, the most pressing concern was not the question of national identity but to keep out of regional conflicts and to modify their village life to find a way to live with the dramatic decrease in the water level of Great Prespa Lake. Many Psarades citizens were also angry that the remaining restrictions on Macedonian exiles in the ex-socialist countries were still in force and preventing free travel to their ancestral villages in Greece. From 1985 to 1995 the water level in Great Prespa Lake dropped by more than 5 metres.[31] In Psarades, given the recent very violent history of the region and generally reasonable local inter-ethnic relations, the priority in most minds was to avoid any involvement in the growing regional uncertainties and disorder. At the same time the problems of the exiles and the wider issue of the Macedonian identity were coming to the centre of international attention, with huge rallies in Thessaloniki organized by nationalists under the slogan 'Macedonia is Greek'. Also, as has sometimes happened before in twentieth-century regional history, the publication of works of academic study proved to be a catalyst for intense political controversy. The contrarian views on Macedonia of American anthropologist Loring Danforth has meant that he needed police protection when speaking at Princeton University and elsewhere. Later, analysed with great skill in her book *Fields of Wheat, Hills of Blood*, Anastasia Karakatsidou shows that despite recent migration and a strong private Macedonian identity, most citizens she studied in her field work village

Illustration 11 The old fishing house in Psarades in 1960.

of Assiros in the Langadhas Basin were in the end happy to be Greek citizens and to conform to the external norms of life in the modern Greek nation state.[32]

In Psarades and the Prespa villages in the 1990s, life was not ideal but the internal conflicts in Albania and RM were not an incentive for Prespa villagers to look for border changes or an autonomous Macedonian area based on western and northern Greek Macedonia.[33] Yugoslav Macedonia no longer looked a promising model of a Macedonian society but was divided, tense, threatened by Albanian nationalism where many protagonists were serious Muslims with a Turkified culture (seen from Greece) and as the Kosovo war approached, under increasing de facto international supervision. The minority of Psarades people who voted for the KKE Greek Communist Party were influenced by the KKE's rejection of the Macedonian issue in its current policies, and as in many cases the village 'intellectuals' (as KKE adherents are in so many Greek villages) gave the KKE a wider influence than its modest electoral vote might suggest. There is also the issue of the power of the past over the present, and the ever-present acculturation mechanisms of the Greek state and church, now reinforced by the mass media.

During the mid-1990s, in Psarades there was a conscious programme to increase the Hellenic character of the village, with the construction in 1996 of an Orthodox shrine dedicated to the Virgin on the lakeside, in its way an echo of Byzantium, a reflection of God on the moving waters, so that pilgrims in church bus parties could light a candle

Illustration 12 The old fishing house in Psarades in 2013 showing the dramatic fall in water level.

and pray after visiting the rock icons and cave churches on their lake boat trip. This was part of a wider programme, to extend and reinforce, as the Athens government saw it, Hellenization into places long contested between Greece and Albania throughout the twentieth century. Rural areas did not receive anything. In practice – although seen as a threat by many Albanians – it only involved aid donations such as paying for a new bus service in Korca/*Koritsa* and donating ten buses to the city. Locally, the Athens based state was ever active, with European Union funds being used to distract from concerns about the deepening ecological crisis. Much of the main village street had been gradually pedestrianized, producing a strange suburban effect, with new trees planted and although the latter work is useful this endless quest for 'modernity' is destroying the nature of the *zadruga*-descended little settlement with so much attractive Macedonian folk identity that existed twenty or thirty years ago.

The rapid disappearance of water from the Lakes not only had a negative impact on the region's ecology but also threatened the livelihoods of the Psarades fishermen, as well as the families who had opened restaurants alongside the Lake where visitors came specifically to enjoy their meals at the water's edge. Every Sunday from spring until autumn coach-loads of mostly elderly visitors from Thessaloniki and other urban centres in northern Greece would arrive in Psarades for a preamble along the lakeside and then enjoy a long leisurely fish lunch by the water at the first couple of tavernas at the entrance of the village. These lunches are important to fisherman's incomes, as large whole carp can be sold in Psarades tavernas for these lunches, and very profitably, compared to the prices offered by fish wholesale buyers. Traditional cultural symbolism is powerful. The fisherman has a long heritage in Christianity, from the fisherman companions and Disciples of Jesus to the present day. In most of the clerical commentary that is given to the visitors, there is a very strong emphasis on the Greek nationalist interpretation of the Byzantine heritage and probably few visitors ever learn that many of the major Prespa monuments, particularly Agios Achilleos church on the island in Lesser Prespa Lake, were constructed by Bulgarian-speaking Christians. A past Golden Age of universal Greek Orthodoxy in the Byzantine Empire is postulated, in a mist of lost greatness and uplifting sentiment. The reality, a few miles away north of the border, was of poverty caused by the Athens economic blockade and the gasoline ration being cut from forty to twenty litres per family. As one of the authors wrote in a notebook at the time, in 1993 'the people in the Macedonian Republic founded by Tito feel their peaceful course of leaving Yugoslavia without war was being ill-rewarded.' A day's drive away then Prishtina was covered with the election posters of key Milosevic henchman Arkan.

In Psarades, by contrast, in response to the threat of spreading disorder from the north, and the rapid growth of VMRO-DPMNE in Bitola, Resen and the villages, government and church money was suddenly appearing in Psarades, for the first time since before the Second World War. Various infrastructure works were initiated, but the ecological crisis that was developing could not be arrested by these futile EU-financed plans. By the end of the 1990s, with the accelerating drop in the Lake's water level, Psarades's tourist cafes and taverna establishments were no longer at the water's edge and were therefore gradually abandoned in favour of those few tavernas clustered at the end of the village where guests could still have a glimpse of the Lake. A new jetty had been built to accommodate the fishing boats and the unfortunate intrusion of other motor boats into the village. Foreigners are allowed to buy and use motorboats that travel at far higher speed than the permitted limits and disturb the pelicans. There have been good investments from the government and National Park authority but how long it will continue to be functional if water levels continue to fall remains to be seen. In an irony, the new jetty has become popular with the pelicans and cormorants performing their mating rituals in the early spring, some resident all year round but most of the pelicans make their arduous, long journey back to the Lake from their winter homes in the southern Mediterranean and North Africa.

There have been innumerable studies researching the causes of the decrease in water levels in Great Prespa, which include climate change, earthquake effects on the lakebed, less rainfall and water extraction for agriculture, north and south of the border. All the Balkan lakes are under stress, and so far the Prespa Lakes have not encountered the more acute crisis on Lake Doiran in central Macedonia, where over-extraction of underground water by Greek farmers south of the international border is draining the lake to the point of possible extinction. Of great concern is the impact this could have on the wider region. According to one study, a further drop in the Prespa Lakes level may have serious regional consequences. The Prespa Lakes still contribute 25 per cent of the total inflow into Lake Ohrid through underground karst channels; falling lake levels decrease this discharge. Lake Ohrid, in turn, feeds the Drin River in

Albania. Here reduced water levels have caused timber water restraint boards to be placed across the mouth from the lake to the River Drin, effectively partially damming Lake Ohrid to maintain its water level. This entire catchment may therefore be affected by falling lake levels as its water resources are of great importance for Greece, Albania, RM, for tourism, agriculture, hydro-energy, urban and industrial use.[34]

11

The Prespa Lakes

Peace and environmental crisis, 2001–18

We know so much about the lake dwellers we would fain know more. We know that in prehistoric times the shallow waters of these and other lakes were all dotted over with their picturesque habitations. Here in his wattled hut rising from a platform, erected upon piles, primitive man led a toilsome life. He grew wheat upon the shore, which he crushed between stones, and from the fibre of hemp he skilfully wove nets with which to obtain an ample supply of fish from the water below and around him.
— S.J. *Capper,* The Shores and Cities of the Boden See, *London, 1881*

Lakes often mirror what the onlooker wishes to see, whether in idyllic nineteenth-century Switzerland around the Boden See, Henry Thoreau's nineteenth-century America where he wrote that a lake is 'the earth's eye' or twenty-first-century Macedonia. In and around the year 2002 the peace and beauty of the Prespa Lakes and mountains seemed to be a symbol of the calming of the wider Balkan region. The tripartite National Parks agreement between the three governments of Albania, Greece and Republic of Macedonia/Former Yugoslav Macedonia had been signed the previous year. The ex-Yugoslav wars had also concluded with the signature of the August 2001 Ohrid Accords bringing armed peace to RM after the conflict between the ethnic Albanian National Liberation Army (NLA) and the Macedonian armed forces.[1]

The wars brought by the conflicting powers of Russia, through its proxy Serbia, and the imperial United States with its de facto dependencies of Croatia and Albania and newly freed Kosovo seemed to have concluded. The vision was a coherent policy from the international community, principally the European Union and the United States which would bring the fissiparous new nations in the region together, under a benign international dispensation, and integrate them into the globalized world. Greek governments saw this – as always – as taking place under Greek regional leadership, with Greece the dominant regional power as a long-standing EU and NATO member. As the only EU member in the early days, and with Bulgaria after membership inactive on Macedonian issues, Greece was in practice able to determine EU policy and funding priorities towards the National Parks, often to its own financial advantage.

A new period of stability and progress appeared to be developing in the vision of the political elites. The establishment of the National Parks around the Prespa Lakes had led to the gradually improving relationships between the three littoral countries, some small-scale economic development was taking place and the future of the region seemed more secure. Ecotourism was growing gradually from a low base, and with better marketing the market for Prespa fish was growing in the region. It seemed a long and devastating period of dislocation and violence was over.[2] Only the name issue was outstanding as a bilateral issue between the Athens and Skopje governments. Entrenched positions remained between Athens and Skopje on all the major issues, with Skopje Prime Minister Nicola Gruevski in 2009 calling for the recognition of a Macedonian minority in Greece, a proposal that was firmly rejected by the then Athens Prime Minister Costas Karamanlis.[3] An amnesty for exiles in 2004 had been billed as a 'general amnesty' but in fact visitors from Eastern Europe with a Macedonian 'bad biography' were only allowed to stay in Greece for nine days.[4]

The world of the Prespa Lakes and forests since the end of the Greek Civil War in 1949 had, in the previous two generations, changed more fundamentally than in any period of history. Most of the visual landscape around the lake villages had previously changed little since early Ottoman times and the mode of production was much older, based on small-scale fishing and pastoralism. Village locations and land use patterns derive from decisions taken in late antiquity and then the early medieval period, those based on a long previous history. For the people of Prespa the end of the Civil War in 1949 took place in a context reminiscent of the Highland Clearances in eighteenth-century Scotland, where a dissident population was forced into exile from their historic lands. Only the natural world benefitted from the relative absence of the shepherd, his dogs and his gun. Militarized Cold War borders benefitted the wildlife. The empty and depopulated lands in the post–Civil War years saw the reforestation of many areas that had been bare grazing land for hundreds of years, and the green tendrils of plant growth crept around ruined and burnt-out houses, Byzantine churches and Ottoman forts alike. The unique Prespa cyclamen flowered in the autumn under the dwarf oak, and the occasional visiting British tourist collected juniper berries from ancient trees to enhance their gin cocktails. Fish stocks and bird life had flourished in the general absence of much human population to disturb them outside the very short summer season.

Yet the vision of the leaders who signed the National Park agreements was a Utopian vision, as the problem of chronic absence of respected states in the southern Balkans remained unchanged, and the multiple interconnections of the regional communities with different foreign countries have multiplied. New patterns of trade exchange dependent on Eurasian links are important. Russian tourists crowd Kastoria to buy furs, and shop signs there in Russian have become as common as those in French or English. The first Chinese visitors have begun to appear in Ohrid, Thessaloniki, Bitola and elsewhere, and China is financing new highways in Serbia and Macedonia, a sign of the opening of the southern Balkans to wider Eurasian influences. American visitors are very rare. Yet in a globalizing world, many local democratic rights for those with a Macedonian identity remain absent. In Bulgaria in the Pirin region independent Macedonian campaigning organizations are banned.[5] Travel restrictions have in practice remained on many Greek-origin families with a Macedonian identity who have been living in exile. Turkish influence in towns just north of the Prespa Lakes like Resen and Bitola has rapidly increased, with the opening of a large *Gulenist* school outside Struga, and a renewal of serious Islamic commitment in the wider region after the languor of the Yugoslav years. The Vatican and Italy remain a powerful influence in the Albanian communities and background politics along the Adriatic coast, and the Albanian minority are a lever for Italy and the Roman Catholic Church in Skopje politics.

After the relaxation of Greek-Yugoslav relations in the period from about mid-1976 until the late 1980s, when some closed road crossings were reopened, and then later closed, the first modern tourist visitors had come to Prespa, in almost all cases from Greece to see the historic Christian cave churches and shrines around the lakes and to venerate the icons. Traditional Macedonian family Diaspora links, mainly with communities in cities and towns in Canada and Australia, were strengthened with the onset of affordable passenger air travel. Although always a long way from the mainstream of Greek life, Psarades and the wider Prespa region benefitted from the growing trickle of summer visitors, and long abandoned houses were fitted up to become small tavernas and rooms to let. More recently, the first western European visitors were mostly scientists and then organized groups of birdwatchers, who began to arrive in small numbers, mostly in the spring to see the Dalmatian pelican breeding season on the lake waters. The quality of the lake water was already beginning to cause some concern, with marked declines in some species such as water snakes, which had been very common when the authors began their researches in the 1990s. But the central ecological issues were not taken very seriously by the international community in this period, with its long-held positions on the problem of Macedonia excluding concerns about climate changes and the ecological crisis. The inheritance of the Civil War and the crisis of Greek communism has always remained in the background in Prespa, and with it the inheritance of British and then US policy in the 1944 to 1949 periods. As Geoffrey Chandler, a British diplomatic ex-participant with a generally conservative outlook, has since written: 'There had seemed little doubt that the Greek Communist Party would once more attempt to resort to force to gain power. But British influence could have been used to see that the rebellion which could not have been prevented did not become Civil War.'[6]

Yet by 2000, for the first time for two generations, the dilemmas and convoluted history of Greek communism and the British and American roles as a catalyst for the Greek Civil War leading to the ultimate emptying of Prespa after 1949 seemed for a time to be increasingly irrelevant. The improving narrative of daily life conflicted with the still unrecognized nature of the RM/FYROM state to the north, but Greek public opinion remained unreconciled to the new reality of an independent Macedonian state recognized by over a hundred countries in the United Nations under its chosen name of Republic of Macedonia. But the region was less enclosed than it had used to be. International concern over the environment was developing.[7] Some tourists were starting to return to old haunts on the Macedonian side of the lake once the war in western RM concluded by August 2001.[8] Although the days of 1993 to 1994 with huge mass demonstrations in Athens and Thessaloniki under the banner of MACEDONIA

IS GREEK were past, all students of public opinion agreed that the overwhelming majority of Greeks were adamantly opposed to recognizing the chosen name of the Skopje-based state. Human rights issues for the long-exiled Civil War generation were beginning to be faced, and in January 2004 the Athens government announced some limited time visits for previously blacklisted people would be allowed.

In this sense the heritage of the Civil War was still alive, if now mainly in the political subconscious. Yet after the 'small package agreement' brokered by American Balkan negotiator Richard Holbrook in summer 1995 relations between Skopje and Athens had improved and business between cities like Bitola and Florina was increasing, while growing number of RM citizens went shopping in Kastoria and visited northern Greek resorts on Halkidiki for their summer holidays. RM was increasingly chained into a strange political limbo. EU membership has been continually promised but has not taken place. Key elements in the Skopje government leadership remain under effective American control. International agreements on energy supply meant that RM was excluded from the developing pipeline supply of Russian gas to the region that has benefitted Bulgaria and Greece, and all gas came via Greece, with the nation increasingly falling under the economic grip of Greece. Local initiatives and business were closing the gap between the states, even in the absence of international agreements on the name dispute.[9]

Yet in the background, particularly in the clandestine dialogues within the North Atlantic Treaty Organization, a new development was coming from an unexpected direction. NATO as the hard power arm of the American *imperium* was still expanding its membership, and although RM had been a good friend of NATO ever since the Kosovo war in 1999 and had afterwards contributed soldiers to US-led international coalitions, it was not a NATO member owing to the name dispute.[10] These positive contributions only brought US betrayal on the key issue of the name and the state identity as Macedonia, and so in all probability will increase Russian influence in the region in the medium and long term.[11] Many sectional and vested interests were at work behind the scenes.[12] Defence professionals in Greece were anxious that Turkey had access to RM airspace and in the climate of deteriorating relations between Greece and Turkey, military pressure grew in Athens for a solution to the name dispute to be found. Athens demanded within NATO to be given control of the RM airspace as a price for the very limited concession of a name involving the use of the word 'Macedonia' in the proposed new state name of '*North Macedonia*'. Greece itself was vulnerable to US and international pressures after the banking crisis when the aftermath of the 2015 referendum on financial reform and debt had left the Tsipras government at the mercy of its international creditors and the European Union. In imperial eyes, Greece could be seen as losing effective sovereignty over its territory or in the common parlance of the US administration it was becoming, in international terms, a 'loser'.

The choice of Prespa as the site for the 2018 name deal signing between the two governments of Skopje and Athens was very significant.[13] Secret negotiations based on the long-standing UN negotiations had started in 2016 between the interested parties, and at the end of that summer sleepy little Psarades village was shocked by an extraordinary development. In an unannounced visit to the far north – usually only visited by Greek Prime Ministers at election time or for the annual set piece economic outlook speech in Thessaloniki every September – the Greek Prime Minister Alexis Tsipras appeared on a quiet weekday when most tourists had gone home, with a very small official entourage. He sat and drank a coffee and made an inspection of the village. After he had drunk his coffee, he went for a short walk and surveyed the view of the lake from the fishing boat jetty, watched from a respectful distance by his security men and a few grooming pelicans and the nonplussed inhabitants. It was as if a Homeric god had suddenly descended in a cloud to the lakeside. He then drove away, without explanation. Villagers thought perhaps a new development of the National Park was being considered, and with their deep cynicism about Athens politicians, thought little more of it, and carried on with the bean harvest; but it was a harbinger of the fact that yet again, tiny Psarades and the surrounding Prespa region would become the setting for international events reflecting the competition of foreign powers.

The diplomatic wheels between the two government capitals were also turning. In December 2015 Greek Foreign Minister Nikos Kotzias had met his opposite number Nikola Popovski from Skopje in Athens to discuss a new framework for the solution of the name issue.[14] Although there had been United Nations negotiations in progress for many years under ex-State Department official Matthew Nimetz they had always foundered over the simple issue that in the last analysis a country can only have one name. But the ex-communist Kotzias was very well aware of the Civil War inheritance and his boss as Prime Minister Alexis Tsipras was an idealist with little personal knowledge of the southern Balkans or knowledge of the New Macedonian Question who was prepared, under intense US pressure, to sacrifice what had always been a Greek 'red line' on the RM/FYROM name. In doing so, he hoped to improve his country's poor international image. Much of Tsipras's career had been built on very astute opportunism and adaptability, in a long-standing tradition of Athens political leader's modus operandi but these qualities did not serve him well in Prespa. In the background was also the international refugee crisis, where both countries were bedevilled by the consequences of German Chancellor Angela Merkel's controversial 'open door' policy.

The issue of regional stability and long-standing national identities was not clearly understood by the London lawyers in the generally Blairite ambience involved in the Prespa preparation process. Many had been involved in the Irish peace processes and sought to impose that model in the Balkans. With Greece now the largest foreign investor in RM/FYROM Greek investors in the political Right had seized upon the traditionalist irredentist agenda in a new modern guise, and they were keen to secure an EU legal framework in RM/FYROM where they could take over large tracks of RM land and also the rumoured rich mineral resources still unexploited underground. In the deep background was traditional Italian-Greek regional rivalry, with Italy a growing presence in Skopje through the influence of the iconic Mother Theresa movement and her Skopje museum shrine among the ethnic Albanians, and significant Italian investment in shoe and clothes manufacturing, particularly in eastern towns like Stip. Although only about 5 per cent of the Macedonian people there are Roman Catholic, most of them ethnic Albanians, the Vatican has been a significant if quiet and unobtrusive backer of the Skopje state, not only since independence in 1991 but since the foundation of the schismatic Macedonian Orthodox church in the early 1950s under Titoist communism.

In a statement issued on 17 December 2017, Skopje Foreign Minister Nikola Popovski was cast as the more dogmatic of the two parties and stressed the obstacles and difficulties. But his government under VMRO-DPMNE leader Nikola Gruevski was disliked by the United States, the President Georgi Ivanov was seen as sympathetic to Russia and it was apparent to journalists and observers present that Washington was considering removing them from power to replace Gruevski with their young protégée from the Social Democratic Party in Strumica, the inexperienced and malleable Zoran Zaev. The most powerful country in the world was facing a resurgent Russia, a difficult inconclusive war in Afghanistan, a failed attempt to replace the Syrian government in Damascus, a failure to obtain regime change in Venezuela and overarching issues in Turkey. Senior personnel changes in the State Department under the Trump administration included influential officials in new posts who were prepared to think of some kind of new Yugoslavia uniting the Balkan economies as an answer to the problems of the region. The problems of empire were once again reaching the southern Balkan Mountains on the borderland of south-east Europe, and improving internal relations between the Balkan states were again at the mercy of the clash of Great Powers on the Balkan periphery, as had so often happened in the Prespa region in the late nineteenth and early twentieth centuries.[15]

NATO badly needed a diplomatic success if of a modest kind given the general difficult background after Russian leader Vladimir Putin's successful initiative in the Crimea and against a background of declining respect for, and interest in, NATO in many European countries. Newly elected US President Donald Trump expressed his doubts about the value of NATO on occasion, prompted by the failure of many rich NATO members to pay an appropriate financial contribution to the organization. In the winter of 2015 to 2016 it was agreed in Brussels, London and Washington to destabilize and remove Gruevski's VMRO-DPMNE government in Skopje in the looming spring 2016 elections in RM and then force a name change through both Parliaments.[16] In addition to the changes in the Trump State Department, there was still an influential group of generally pro-Greek and liberal ex-Clinton and Obama era officials in Washington and elsewhere in the United States who saw the opportunity to push through a deal on the name that would 'throw a bone to Greece' and show the Greeks that they were not without friends in Washington at a time of reviving Turkish power in the eastern Mediterranean.

Thus, there was – in terms of the conflicts between the administration and the Democrats in Washington on most issues – a temporary identity of interest over the policy on Macedonia. Most Greek Americans vote Republican outside the north-east of the country and were much divided over the issue, but key opinion groups saw the deal as an opportunity to effectively destroy the independence of the Skopje government and gradually colonize economically the country. But most Greek people saw the proposals as an attack on their traditional national identity, and were suspicious of growing Turkish and Russian influence, particularly within fragmenting NATO, and strongly disagreed with what was happening. In terms of Greek opinion, the name change deal rested upon chronically unstable foundations, as recent political developments have demonstrated.

Regional tensions with Turkey cannot be ignored. In recent years Turkey has been flexing its muscles in the eastern Mediterranean. Greece is pushing back against Turkish demands that it demilitarize 16 Aegean islands. The Turkish government maintains it is defending Turkey's rights and remains committed to negotiation, but there are warnings that Turkey's increasingly robust diplomacy threatens to isolate Ankara and escalate regional tensions. Turkey has accused Greece of keeping troops on the islands in violation of the 1923 Treaty of Lausanne, which governs the Aegean Sea between Turkey and Greece. The dispute dates to 1974 when Athens started to militarize the islands off the Turkish coast in response to Turkey's invasion of the Mediterranean island of Cyprus. Turkey is now asking for the islands' demilitarization following an increase of Turkish jets violating Greek airspace. In January 2020, Turkish President Rexip Erdogan further ratcheted up tensions, announcing that Turkish research ships would be deployed in contested Cypriot waters to search for hydrocarbons. The discovery of large natural gas fields in the eastern Mediterranean by Israel and Cyprus has unleashed a scramble by regional countries for fossil fuels. Ankara accuses Greece and other regional countries of seeking to shut it out of the forecast bounty of vast energy reserves. The Prespa deal was to become a rare card in the Greek hand which could be played against Ankara particularly the rights it gave the Greek military over Macedonian airspace.

A key issue in the Prespa proposal was to be the public presentation with methods of media control meant for war used by NATO in peacetime, particularly exclusion of real debate in the largely government-controlled Skopje media. The document setting out the Agreement was lengthy and was opposed by almost all international experts on the region.[17] The Republic of Macedonia Constitution of 1991 contains no provision to change the name of the country, nor did the Holbrooke 'small package' agreement of 1995. NATO soft power operated through numerous NGOs in Skopje which were pressing for ratification, many of which were partly or wholly financed by the Soros Foundation.[18] Opposition in both countries to the proposed new name of *'North Macedonia'* was intense, and it had only been possible for the US Embassy in Skopje to force the deal through the Skopje parliament by a combination of threats and pressure against some elected members, and above all illegal disregard of the results of a referendum held on the Prespa deal.[19] Skopje President Georgi Ivanov had already refused to sign off the deal document.[20] It was an abnegation of democracy. In Greece Tsipras faced a confidence vote in Parliament that was the first sign of the growing destabilization of his SYRIZA government caused primarily by the Prespa process that led to his loss of power the following year.[21]

In Prespa the arrival of the numerous signatories to sign the agreement was looming but unexpected, as in Psarades and neighbouring villages, it was believed, correctly at the time, that the little village of Otoshevo on the opposite side of Great Prespa Lake had been chosen. In fact this was indeed the case at first, in itself a sign of the ignorance of Prespa history of the NATO staff, as Otoshevo had been a notorious

Yugoslav secret police gaol and torture house after the Second World War, and so was hardly an ideal image to sign an international agreement that was due to bring peace and harmony to the region. When this was realized within NATO and the EU, the site of the signing ceremony was hurriedly moved to Psarades and the villagers were instructed to clear away all cafe tables, sweep up, tidy their winter woodpiles and chain up their sheepdogs, in case the place looked untidy or backward looking on television. The locality was then flooded with police and security personnel.[22] The Greek Orthodox church locally was a fierce opponent of what was happening, seeing the Prespa proposals as a threat to the country and a possible boost for the schismatic Macedonian Orthodox church. The Psarades church bell was draped in the Greek and Byzantine flags and rung regularly until the Athens Minister of the Interior officials in the Prime Minister's entourage told the priest to desist. On 17 June 2018, the day before the signing ceremony thousands of patriotic Greeks tried to converge on Psarades after the news of the plans had leaked out, and as London *Times* correspondent Anthee Carassava wrote the following day:

> Riot police fired tear gas to disperse protestors who hurled sticks and stones and shouted 'traitors' in an attempt to break through the first of about 20 cordons ringing the area. Acrid plumes of smoke smothered the lush forest, forcing some protestors to flee. Dozens climbed trees, while some wearing motorcycle helmets and black clothes fought with police for more than three hours. At least 5000 demonstrators including monks and nuns flooded the Prespes region from daybreak, waving giant flags and unfurling banners in the latest protest against a deal that they claim humiliates Greece.[23]

Suddenly Prespa was no longer an ecological Utopia, an environment carefully managed by outsiders and a model for coexistence. A pitched battle was fought along the roads in Pisoderi village on the road to Florina, injuring among others a policeman son of one of the main taverna owners in Psarades. On the following day the Athens newspaper *Kathermerini* recorded that smoke hung over Psarades, but commentator Athenios Grammenos revealingly observed in the same newspaper that 'It was time for Greece to lead the Western Balkans, paving the Euro-Atlantic way for its neighbouring state', in a restatement in modern political cliché of the nature of the local hegemonic role Greece had sought in the southern Balkans since the end of the Cold War and long before. More realistically, on the same day, a Greek member of the European Parliament Georgios Kyrtsos pronounced: 'That after an eight year long financial crisis in which the country was effectively run by international creditors, the last things Greeks need is a deal relinquishing their national identity.'

An opinion poll taken the same day showed nearly 70 per cent of Greeks opposed the signing of the agreement and name change. Skopje leader Zoran Zaev appeared in Psarades in a boat which tied up at the fishermen's jetty and scattered the pelicans and pygmy cormorants. The Foreign ministers signed the Agreement and then quickly disappeared for lunch. It was a strange event, a throwback to the 'spin' dominated world of the Blair-Clinton era, perhaps conditioned by the fact that the PR agency charged with spinning the deal had worked extensively in Northern Ireland and was partly based there. The signing was exclusively designed to flood the international media with photographs showing mutual harmony, as if a war had just ended, rather than the disruption of a period of relative economic and social progress that had actually been taking place in the last fifteen years before the interests of competing empires intruded.[24] Even long-standing United Nations negotiator Matthew Nimetz had refused to utter the illegal new 'North Macedonia' name in his speech at the Psarades event and during the surrounding third-rate political circus.

It was an omen of the uncertain future, as the motorcades sped away from Psarades in clouds of dust along the mountain road towards Florina, on the exact route laid down by the ancient Roman engineers who built the *Via Egnetia*. As Royal United Services Institute Director Jonathan Eyal observed many years ago during the Yugoslav wars, the Macedonian Question is ultimately insoluble, and it seems extremely unlikely that with the growing competition for power and influence in the southern Balkans by Turkey, NATO, Russia, Bulgaria and Greece, the Prespa Agreement will fulfil the hopes of its progenitors. After Prespa Macedonia is struggling for survival, with increasing focus on the role of the ethnic Albanians there without whom the Prespa deal could never have obtained a majority in the Assembly. In his history of the region journalist Misha Glenny wrote that the ex-Yugoslav wars had brought in the era of the '*parastate*' and that 'Macedonia was the most fragile of the new states to emerge from former Yugoslavia, less secure even than Bosnia-Hercegovina'.[25]

The central case against the Prespa name-changing process is that it has not made the state less fragile, but on the contrary, although it was undertaken to improve regional stability, against a much exaggerated threat of Russification, the reality has been a marked weakening of the legitimacy of the government institutions in Skopje, alienation of the political class and the educated from the old notion of the international community (apart from now extraordinarily privileged Albanian minority) and worsening ethnic relations. The Prespa agreement was a key factor in the collapse of the Tsipras government in Greece in the period after it was signed. NATO has brought instability. Critically, given considerable increase in emigration and capital flight, and general internal instability, new elections in Skopje were held in spring 2020 against the background of the coronavirus pandemic, with the Zaev government barely surviving. By 2021 it had lost a secure coalition majority. In the background, Prespa remains what it always has been, in the words of the author of *Blue Guide Yugoslavia* written many years ago, 'a wild lonely place, girt by trackless forests and lonely peaks'.[26] The sensible advice given to the foreign powers by the greatest living Greek, the composer Mikis Theodorakis, that both traditions of Macedonianism, the Greek and the Slavonic, should deserve equal respect in any settlement has not been followed.[27] In 1998 the most influential Greek author on the current Macedonian issues Evangelos Kofos wrote: 'The Greeks of the Diaspora, however, were in no mood to humour or to tolerate incursions into the "sacrosanct" tenets of their identity and heritage.'[28] In essence, given the massive concessions awarded to Greece in the Prespa process, NATO and the United States have become hostages to the outlook of hard-line Greek nationalism, particularly the Greek lobby in the United States, and as a result, the future of 'North Macedonia' is seen with deepening pessimism by a growing proportion of the citizens, of all ethnic groups.[29] Or as the travel writer Kapka Kassabova has written recently of the Prespa name change and the difficulties between the two countries, 'healing the surface of it; underneath a chasm of discord and denial still gaped, maintained by both sides'.[30] The verdant Utopia of Prespa has turned in on itself and become something different, as Utopias do in human history.

Appendix A

Place-name usage in late Ottoman and twentieth-century Prespa[1]

Towns

Bulgarian/ Macedonian	Greek	Albanian	Turkish
Bitola	Monastir	Manastir	Toli
Tsarigrad	Constantinopoli	Constantinopolis	Istanbul
Solun	Thessaloniki	Salonika	Selanik
Resen	Resen	Resnja	Resna
Skopia	Skopje	Skupi	Uskub
Lerin	Florina	Florina/Follorine	Filorina
Goritsa	Koritsa	Korca	Gorice[2]
Akrida	Ohrid	Oher	Ohri
Kostur	Kastoria	Kosture	Kesriye
Vodena	Edessa	Edessa	Vodine
Ovcharani/Vosterani	Meliti	Turbeli	

Prespa-region village name district

Macedonian	Greek	Albanian
Nivica	Psarades	
German	Agios Germanos	
Zhelevo	Antartiko	
Starkouvo	Plati	
Orovnik	Karies	
Rembi	Laimos/Milonas	
Roudari	Kallithea	
Grasdeno	Vrondero	
Koula	Kulla	
Rouli	Kotta	
Levkonas	Levkonas	Popli
Lanik	Microlimni	
Binovo	Pili	
Turnovo	Agathoto	
Opodo	Pixos	
Turnovo	Agathoto	

Outside Prespa district

Macedonian	Greek
Drenoveni	Kranonias
Biglishta	Bilishte (also Albanian)
Kapshtica	Krystalopigi

Appendix B

Religious and ethnic identities in Prespa villages in RM

The data given below is based on field research in the Great and Lesser Prespa Lake villages in 2017 and is only intended to give a general impression of current ethnic identities and religious affiliations. It is not based on census material and in some villages where there has been significant emigration may not convey more than an approximate picture of population/settlement. Data on the Muslim category covers the Torbesh ethnic identity and may also include a few Roma in the villages nearest to Resen. In the summer season Orthodox numbers are generally augmented by visitors from Macedonian towns, from Bulgaria and also from northern ex-Yugoslavia, mostly Serbs, using holiday properties. All Prespa villages in Albania are, or were, nominally majority Muslim but in some, particularly Pushtec, the Orthodox church is reviving. Tren village, east of Lesser Prespa in Albania, is mixed Orthodox/Bektashi Muslim. Bilisht town is majority Bektashi/Muslim.

Arvati – 70 per cent Albanian-Muslim, 30 per cent Orthodox
Asamati – 50 per cent Orthodox, 50 per cent Muslim
Bela Crkva – 100 per cent Orthodox
Brachno – 100 per cent Orthodox
Carev Dvor – 30 per cent Turkish-Muslim, 30 per cent Albanian-Muslim, 50 per cent Orthodox
Drmeni – 50 per cent Orthodox, 50 per cent Muslim
Dolno Dupeni –100 per cent Orthodox
Ezerani – 100 per cent Orthodox
Gorna Bela Crkva – 50 per cent Orthodox, 50 per cent Muslim
Grncari – 70 per cent Albanian-Muslim, 30 per cent Orthodox[1]
Krani – 70 per cent Albanian-Muslim, 30 per cent Orthodox
Kojnsko – 100 per cent Orthodox
Kozjak – 100 per cent Turkish-Muslim
Kurbinovo – 100 per cent Orthodox
Leskoec – 100 per cent Orthodox
Ljubojno – 100 per cent Orthodox
Nakolec – 50 per cent Albanian-Muslim, 50 per cent Turkish-Muslim
Oteshevo – 100 per cent Orthodox
Podmodcani – 100 per cent Orthodox

Portrevnik – 100 per cent Orthodox
Prelubje – 100 per cent Orthodox
Pretor – 100 per cent Orthodox
Rajca – 100 per cent Orthodox
Renovo – 100 per cent Orthodox
Slivnica – 100 per cent Orthodox
Stenje – 100 per cent Orthodox
Surlenci – 100 per cent Orthodox

Appendix C

Some non-Greek terms in Prespa and Ohrid region

Ban	Governor
Boyar	Member of the aristocracy
Ciflik, chiflik	Farm, rural estate
Bekim	Doctor
Berga	Mountain, hill
Bria	Town
Cogognes	Storks (also Coll. Pelicans)
Crkva	Church
Dava	Town
Diza	Fortress
Firman	Ottoman imperial decree
Gora	Mountain
Hadji	Pilgrim who has visited the Muslim holy sites
Hajdut	Brigand, bandit (modern Coll. 'Mafiosi')
Kamini	Ancestral free land
Kaza	Administrative district
Kirdzhalis	Brigands, bandits
Millet	Officially recognized non-Muslim religious community
Pan	Swamp, marsh
Para	Ottoman silver coin, now (Coll.) money, 'dosh/wad' (also 'marketplace')
Raya	Tax-paying Ottoman subjects
Reka	River, stream
Stolnic	High official
Stur	Place, settlement
Vali	Governor of a *vilayet*
Vilayet	Ottoman province
Voyvoda	Governor (often military)
Waaf (vakuf)	Muslim religious endowment
Zura/zara	Water

Appendix D

The Macedonian toponym

The term 'Macedonia' originated in antiquity and is associated with the Kingdom of Macedonia as it developed under Philip II and Alexander the Great. The nature of the Macedonian kingdom has become a subject of intense political controversy, particularly since the emergence of a new Macedonian state in 1991 that existed until 2018 and was recognized by over a hundred United Nations members as the Republic of Macedonia. The country was renamed '*North Macedonia*' in 2018, in a highly controversial action that was enforced to open membership of NATO. It remains to be seen what the future usage of this name will be outside Western international official circles. In this book it is used only when writing about very recent events. In Greece the country was called FYROM for many years, standing for former Yugoslav Republic of Macedonia, and this acronym remains in both official and popular usage in many places in northern Greece. The term 'Macedonia' as a geographical term in antiquity is not, however, controversial and is used in this book to denote the lands which now include parts of modern Greece, the renamed Skopje-based Macedonian state, parts of south-west Bulgaria and a very small part of Albania.

The term largely disappeared from political usage under Byzantium and the Ottoman Empires, to reappear in discourse in many aspects as a product of nineteenth-century nationalism. In the Ottoman Empire most of modern Macedonia was seen as *Turkey-in-Europe* and a small part within Ottoman *Roumeli*. With the disintegration and final collapse of the Ottoman Empire most of what is now in the Macedonian state was taken under the First World War period Treaties by Greece and Serbia, the more northern part incorporated into the administrative division (*banovina*) of South Serbia, a situation that prevailed until the Yugoslav communists took power in 1944–5, after which Macedonia became a constituent republic of the new federal Yugoslavia. It was first called the People's Republic of Macedonia, which was later amended to the Socialist Republic of Macedonia. This was based on the decision made in August 1944, at the first session of the communist led Antifascist Assembly of the National Liberation of Macedonia (ASNOM). In Greece, Macedonia is an administrative region of northern Greece.

Throughout this book we have used the terms appropriate to the period of history we are discussing, without taking a view on the nature of the Macedonian identity, other than to recognize both the Hellenic and Slavonic identities exist.

Notes

Preface

1 Horden, P. and Purcell, N. *The Boundless Sea: Writing Mediterranean History* (Abingdon, 2020). The concepts in this book are developed in relation to the author's earlier *The Corrupting Sea* (Oxford, 2000).
2 This etymology is not accepted by some scholars in Skopje, who believe the origin is from the Serbian word *presip*, meaning a sandbank. This seems unlikely, and possibly politically determined, as the Prespa lakeshores in Greece are rocky. There are only sandy shores on Great Prespa Lake north of the Greek border.
3 The term 'Macedonian language' is used in this book to denote the Slavonic language spoken by many inhabitants in the region. Other languages are also spoken – for example Vlach, Greek and Albanian – and our use of the linguistic terms as descriptive does not endorse any particular ethnic or national identity designation the citizens concerned may or may not consider themselves to have.
4 Bryer, A., 'The Means of Agricultural Production: Muscles and Tools', in Laiou, A. (Ed.), *The Economic History of Byzantium from the Seventh through the Fifteenth Century*, Dumbarton Oaks Studies XXXIX (Washington, DC, 2002), pp. 101–13.
5 Overton, T., *Landscapes: John Berger on Art*, Ch. 29 'Historical Afterword to the *Into Their Labours Trilogy*', p. 186.
6 For example in the work of Michael Hertzfelt in Crete, Loring Danforth in FYROM/RM and John Campbell in the Pindus Mountains in northern Greece.
7 See Horden, P. and Purcell, N., *The Boundless Sea*, p. 22 ff, and Brent Shaw's detailed critical analysis of their views, 'Challenging Braudel: A New Vision of the Mediterranean', *Journal of Roman Archaeology*, 14 (2000): 419 ff. These complex debates are relevant to this book as some scholars would regard the Ohrid/Prespa region as outside the Mediterranean zone of the region.
8 For a linguist's view on the nature of the current spoken language in western Greek Macedonia by those who see themselves with an independent and Slavonic Macedonian identity, see Hill, P., *The Dialect of Gorno Kalenik* (Columbus, OH, 1991), and the extensive writings of Victor Friedman, in particular, 'Observing the Observers: Language, Ethnicity and Power in the 1994 Macedonian Census and Beyond', in 'New Balkan Politics', *Journal of Politics* 1 (2001/2002): 123 ff. Skopje, 2002. For a Bulgarian view, see Mangalakova, T., *Ethnic Bulgarians in Mala Prespa and Golo Brdo*, http://www.imir-bg.org, Sofia, 2004, and 'Memorandum regarding the Language Dispute', Macedonian Scientific Institute (Sofia, 1997). Also, Friedman, V. Janev, G. Vlahov, G. (Eds), *Macedonia and Its Questions: Origins, Margins, Ruptures and Continuity*, Vol. 38, Studies on Language and Culture in Central and Eastern Europe (Berlin, 2020), particularly Friedman's 'Macedonian at the Margins: The Dialects of Kostur/Kastoria', p. 61ff.
9 Todorova, M., *Balkan Identities: Nation and Memory* (London, 2004), p. 62ff.

10 See Memusaj, R., *The Albanian Legislation on the Linguistic Rights of Minorities* (Tirana, 2002).
11 For an interesting picture of Athens' central government cultural and social pressures in forming a homogenous national identity in the Cold War period, see Friedl, E., *Vasilika: A Village in Modern Greece* (New York, 1962). Vasilika is near Mount Parnassus, not far from Athens, and very distant from Macedonia, without significant minorities and was not much affected by the Civil War. Yet it was seen by the Athens government in the same way as dissident identity Macedonian villages in the far north of the country in the enforcement of the approved national culture.

Chapter 1

1 prespaNet_Review-of-Conservation-Efforts-April-2017.
2 Prespa Cattle: Evaluation of a research tour in May 2006 Hans-Peter Grunenfelder, MSc. Monitoring Institute for Rare Breeds and Seeds in Europe in collaboration with SAVE Foundation. www.save-foundation.net.
3 Yonovski, C., *Prespa* (Skopje, 2000), p. 170. In socialist Yugoslavia tourist development was much more advanced than in northern Greece. There was none in the Albanian lakeside villages. Tourist hotels existed in Resen before the Second World War, and a few inns at Prespa villages such as Nakolets could accommodate visitors. In the early communist period, Jewish youth summer camps were held in and around Pretor village. The tourist hotels at Otoshevo and Carina came later and were exclusively used by staff of the Ministry of the Interior. Between 1961 and 1985 there were tourist ferry voyages on the lake until falling water levels stopped the use of the piers and routes were abandoned. Nudism began in the 1960s at Vakuf beach near Steyne village on the western lakeside. The resorts at Asamati and Krani were developed in the 1980s, primarily for campers. For a modern guide, see Tanevska (and others), *Region Prespa* (Skopje, 2004).
4 Late nineteenth-century maps, for example those of the German ethnographer and philologist Weigand, suggest Zarosch was then the most important village.
5 For a picture of the situation in the Korca region at the end of the Cold War, with an emphasis on the Vlach communities, see Balamaci, N., 'Albania in the 1990s: A Travel Memoir and Oral History', *Journal of the Hellenic Diaspora* 19, no. 2 (1993): 121–48.
6 *Albania Daily News*, 18 September 2006.
7 The iconography of the ruins has been subject to recent academic debate. See *Journal of Modern Greek Studies* 38, no. 2 (October 2020), N. Papadopoulos, 'Ruins of the Borderland: Ruin Affect, Aesthetics, and Otherness in the Prespa Lake Region', pp. 399–423.
8 *Macedonian Minorities: The Slav Macedonians of Northern Greece and the Treatment of Minorities in the Republic of Macedonia* (The British Helsinki Human Rights Group, Oxford, 1994), pp. 3–4. On the more recent position in Albania, covering both Vlachs and Macedonians, see K. Giakoumis, 'The Policy of Non-Discrimination and the Protection of Ethnic Minority Cultural Heritage in Albania', *International Journal of Cultural Policy*, New York, 26, no. 4 (February 2019).
9 Interview with BBC correspondent, Maria Margaronis, BBC News: www.bbc.co.uk, 24 February 2019.

10 Budimovski, 'Makedontsite vo Albanija', NIP Studenski Zbor (Skopje, 1983). Quoted in Hugh Poulton, *The Balkans – Minorities and States in Conflict*, Minority Rights Publications, 1994, p. 201.
11 Recent Tirana government data claims there are about 5,200 people who claim an explicit Macedonian identity in Albania. See Giakoumis, Op. cit note 8.
12 For debates within the Vlach communities on the future, see the journal *Farsarotul*, published in Connecticut, United States, by the Farsarotul Society: www.farsarotul.com.
13 For Romanian government policy in the late nineteenth century, see Minov, 'The Romanian Question and the Romanian Propaganda in Macedonia 1860-1903', *Journal of History* LIV P. 6.1 (Skopje, 2019).
14 For a discussion of the wider issues, see Balamaci, N., 'Can the Vlachs Write Their Own History?', *Journal of the Hellenic Diaspora* 17, no. 1 (1991): 9–36.
15 Author's discussion with Tom Winnifrith, London, 2007. Also in Winnifrith, *The Vlachs: The History of a Balkan People* (London, 1987), and the publications of the Uninea Cultura Aromana in Germany and Fundatsia Gramostea in the United States.

Chapter 2

1 For the general setting, see Cary, M., *The Geographical Background to Greek and Roman History* (Oxford, 1949).
2 For a wider discussion, see Schama, S., *Landscape and Memory* (London, 1996).
3 See Harris, D. and Hillman, G. (Ed.), *Foraging and Farming* (London, 1989). The introduction of different cereal plants, particularly barley-family grains and rye, was the basis for the Roman agrarian society in the wide plains to the north and east of *Heraclea Lyncestis*. In earlier history, studies of the Danube region indicate the appearance of a Bronze Age elite based on pastoralism, and the wealth accruing from it, displacing the relatively egalitarian and sedentary agrarian societies with an emphasis on matriarchy and a lack of 'feudal' land tenure practices. See also Gimbutas, M., *Bronze Age Cultures in Central and Eastern Europe* (The Hague, 1965). The categorizations are controversial, particularly in connection with 'feudalism', but the general picture is relevant to the history of the Prespa and Ohrid regions as an indicator of the extreme nature of agricultural regionalization in the early historical periods in the southern Balkans. Advanced Roman field agriculture existed only a few miles from forest society based on foraging and gathering. The evidence from detailed studies made of agriculture on Neolithic Italy shows that wild vetch, peas and beans and other legumes were in common food use as early as the fifth millennium BC, and no doubt similar developments occurred in Macedonia. The bean known as the Common Bean was the ancestor of the renowned modern Prespa crops.
4 See Thompson, G., *Aeschylus and Athens* (London, 1941), p. 31 ff.
5 Lynk as a name is probably derived from the proto-Illyrian word for 'wolf'. See Mikulcic, I., *Heraclea Ancient City in Macedonia* (Skopje, 2007), p. 27. It was a centre of Illyrian tribal settlement. Archaeological work is currently in progress on hilltop forts in the area. The *Lynkai* tribe is mentioned by Thucydides (II 9.2) and Strabo (VII, 323).

6   For a discussion of the general issues, see Halstead, P. and Jones, G., 'Agrarian Ecology in the Greek Lands – Time, Stress, Scale and Risk', *Journal of Hellenic Studies* 109 (1989): 25–40.
7   For background on the use of animal bones, especially from deer horn, to make tools and the transition from dependence on wild animals to domesticated animals, see publications of the International Council for Archaeozoology.
8   See Manuwald, G. (Ed.), *Cicero Agrarian Speeches* (Oxford, 2018), 'De Lege Agraria 2 101-102', p. 99. The themes Cicero explores concerning the right to appropriate common land, a process which he sees as bringing 'peace, tranquillity and quiet', are an interesting illustration of the fear of wilderness among the Roman elite, something carried on as far as Ohrid and Prespa are concerned up to much later periods. The ban on land sales Cicero envisaged to prevent the formation of large estates was never enforced in 'colonial' regions like the Balkans.
9   Op. cit., Mikulcic, I., *Heraclea Lyncestis Ancient City in Macedonia* (Skopje, 2007), p. 31 ff.
10 For an overview of recent archaeology around the Prespa Lakes, see Grozdanova, V.B., *Golem Grad Prespa I* (Skopje, 2011), and *Golen Grad Prespa II* (Skopje, 2015), the publication of a research programme that started in the 1960s under the staff of the National Museum in Ohrid. The research originally focussed on excavations on Golem Grad Island. The drought between the years 1987 and 1989 exposed Roman material underwater at the site of Pretor and the remains of a drowned Roman road that led to later investigations of changing lake levels.
11 For a study based on and around the island in Lake Great Prespa, see Grozdanova-Bitrakova, V., *Golem Grad in Prespa from Orestians to Romans* (Macedonian Affairs, Macedonian Information Centre, December 2006–January 2007), p. 49.
12 See Grazdanova-Bitrakova, V., *Golem Grad Prespa I* (Skopje, 2011), p. 20 ff. Prespa is not mentioned or discussed as separate from Ohrid in the ancient sources, thus Strabo (7,7,8) writes of 'salting fish on the Lychnis lakes'. Strabo also writes of a tribal people called the 'Bryges', who inhabited an area north and east of Lyncestis (modern Lake Ohrid) as neighbours of the Lyncestai and the Pelagonians. These recondite issues are important in the political debates about the origins of contemporary settlements as Albanian authors designate Illyrian tribes there as the autochonous ancestors of the modern Albanians.
13 This has been confirmed by recent archaeology in the site of Kremenica, in the Baba mountains foothills above the lakeside village of Dolna Bela Crkva and also in the early Neolithic site of Ramniste above the modern village of Stenje, on the lower Galiciça mountain slopes. Both are hundreds of meters above the modern lake level.
14 See 'Golem Grad Prespa II', p. 37 ff. The salient point for contemporary settlement origins is the demonstration of the rapid drop in lake level in the Late Iron Age period, and the evidence here and elsewhere of the growth of the first intensive settlement on the lake littoral between the fourth and the first centuries BC. A substantial number of lakeside villages like Nakolets and Krani probably owe their first origins to this period, although evidence for Psarades/*Nivica* is so far lacking.
15 Bitrakova-Grozdanova, V., *Golem Grad Prespa II* (Skopje, 2015), p. 56. Various small Illyrian hill forts have been recently discovered around the northern fringes of the Prespa and Ohrid Lakes, the most comprehensively excavated at Selishte, near the modern village of Bolno.
16 See Pettifer, J., *Blue Guide to Albania* (London, 1996), p. 31 ff.

17 See Dervishi, N., '*Ethnokultura e Fushegropes se Ohrit* (Ohrid, 1991) for an account of the important Trebenishte site and the division of the artefacts found there between Serbia and Bulgaria. Dervishi uses a definition of the Illyrian period which is controversial.
18 Hammond, N.G.L., 'Alexander's Campaign in Illyria', *Journal of Hellenic Studies* 94 (1974): 66-77.
19 Mythical creatures known to students of early Illyrian religion were called 'hours' by the German researcher Lamberiz. Female deities dominate this mythology who lived in remote caves or on mountains with wild goats with golden horns. See Progni, A., *Ne Tropoja* (Llugaj, 2016), p. 36, for data on the folk traditions of these cave and mountain cults in northern Albania and region. The main early cult of the Slav settlers around Prespa and Ohrid seems to have been around a water deity, known as *Bedi*.
20 See Hammond, 'Alexander's Campaign in Illyria'.
21 For the fate of the towns in later centuries, see Rizos, E., 'Citizens, architecture and society in the eastern and central Balkans during Late Antiquity (250 AD to 600 AD)', unpublished PhD thesis, Oxford University, 2010.
22 First excavated by Russian archaeologist Paul Nichaelovitch Milyukov in 1898-99. He later became the last Tsarist Foreign Minister in Moscow until the Bolshevik Revolution in 1917 and then an active collaborator with Winston Churchill in London trying to overthrow the Bolshevik government. Milyukov's work as an author heavily influenced by Panslavism played an important part in helping to construct later Balkan Slavonic cultural identities. See Bohn, T., *Russische Geschichtewissenschaft von 1880 bis 1905: Pavel Miljukov und die Moscow Schule* (Koln, 1998).
23 For the general approach of the Romans to road construction and use, see Walbank, F., 'The Via Egnetia: Its Role in Roman Strategy', *Rivista di Topograpfia Antica*, XII, 2002 (Galantina, 2003). The Via Egnetia is believed to have been about 6 metres wide over most of its extent.
24 Herodotus, 'Histories', 8, p. 584 ff (translation by Tom Holland), London, 2013.
25 For the relationship of a classical city like Heraclea to its rural surroundings in a Greek context, see Osborne, R., *Classical Landscape with Figures* (London, 1987).
26 For detail, see Shaw, B., *Bringing in the Sheaves Economy and Metaphor in the Roman World* (Toronto, 2013).
27 See Abeliotis, K. and Detsis, V., 'Life Cycle Assessment of Bean Production in the Prespa National Park, Greece', *Journal of Clean Production* 41 (February 2013): 89-96.
28 See Curta, F., *The Edinburgh History of the Greeks, C 500 to 1050: The Early Middle Ages* (Edinburgh, 2011), p. 48 ff.
29 See Mitrevski, D., *Skopje Fortress Kale* (Skopje, 2016). He writes (P. 117): 'After the gradual and long lasting warming of the climate in the 6th and 5th millennia, or more exactly, after the period of optimum warm and wet climate, during the Middle Neolithic period, the maximum temperature was reached in the Late Neolithic period, the level of the waters was dramatically increased which seriously affected the old lowland settlements and their economies.'
30 As set out in Wilkes, J., *The Illyrians* (London, 1998).
31 Mommsen, T., *A History of Rome under the Emperors* (London, 1996), P. 110. Also, Dzino, D., *A History of Illyricum in Roman Politics, 229BC-AD 68* (Cambridge, 2010).
32 Cf. Cvetkovic-Tomasovic, G., *Corpus des Mosaiques Paleobyzantines de Pavement* (Belgrade, 2002).
33 See, for instance, Theophylact's letter (No. 57) to his friend the Bishop of Vidin, written from Ohrid in 1093 or 1094, referring to the Bulgarian 'savages' he lived

among in his district of Ohrid ('Theophylacti Achridensis Epistulae') Ed. Gautier, P. (Thessaloniki, 1986), p. 322 ff. The letters have some interest for economic and social historians, particularly showing how the fish harvest of the lakes appears to have been under Theophylact's personal control and often used as gifts to his local underlings.

34 Ward-Perkins, B., *The Fall of Rome and the End of Civilisation* (Oxford, 2005), p. 38 ff.
35 Cameron, A., 'Albania between Antiquity and the Ottoman Empire', unpublished paper. In a sign of the vulnerability of the western inland region, there is no sign *Deabolis* (modern Korca) was refortified at all.
36 See Brown, P., *The Making of Late Antiquity* (Harvard, 1978), p. 22 ff. In its later very Christian and monastic identity by the eighth century, Prespa was a land of saints and monasteries, but as Brown points out, the sorcerer and the saint could be in many ways opposite sides of the same coin and even coexist in the same places.
37 Ward-Perkins, B., *The Fall of Rome and the End of Civilisation*, p. 84 ff.
38 For a discussion of this issue in the wider Mediterranean region, see Cameron, A., *The Mediterranean World in Late Antiquity* (Abingdon, 2012), p. 73 ff.
39 For a contemporary discussion, see Eisenberg, M. and Mordechai, L., 'The Justinianic Plague and Global Pandemics: The Making of the Plague Concept', *American Historical Review* (December 2020): 1632–67.
40 See Harper, K., *The Fate of Rome* (Princeton, 2017), p. 250 ff.
41 Brown. P. 'Salvian of Marseilles Theology and Social Criticism in the Last Century of the Western Empire', Dacre Lecture 2010, Oxford, 2012, p. 19.
42 There is an extensive literature on Italy in this context, particularly on the origins of the Mafia in late antique and medieval Sicily.
43 For the origins of the Vlachs as a people speaking a language closely derived from Latin, and their projected origin linked to the demise of the Roman road garrisons, see Winnifrith, T., *The Vlachs: A History of a Balkan People* (London, 1987).
44 This etymology is disputed by some Greeks, who claim the name derives from the Greek word meaning 'invisible', presumably referring to the little harbour on the lake. This seems very implausible.
45 See Browning, R., *Byzantium and Bulgaria* (London, 1975).
46 For their world, see the section on St Clement in Obolensky, D., *Six Byzantine Portraits* (Oxford, 1987).
47 The traditional account of these relationships is to be found in Browning, R., *Byzantium and Bulgaria*, which remains a seminal scholarly work, although modern scholarship has cast doubt on his notion of 'borders' as they then existed.
48 For a general discussion of the period which unlike much writing about the early Bulgarians brings their society to life in an easily comprehensible way, see Runciman, S., *A History of the First Bulgarian Empire* (London, 1930). Also Obolensky, D., *Pastoral Nomadism and the Origins of Bulgaria*, Ed. Pettifer, J. (Bulgaria; London, 1998), p. 53 ff.
49 See Runciman, S., *A History of the First Bulgarian Empire*, p. 99 ff.
50 There are numerous works published in Skopje in the period of communist Yugoslavia which sought to incorporate Samuil and his activity against the Byzantines into a conventional Marxist 'revolutionary' narrative, where Samuil is seen as a proto-Macedonian rebel against oppressive Byzantine cultural and political hegemony. They contain interesting research but it is hard not to feel the general approach is mainly conditioned by then current Yugoslav-Greek relations seen as replicating Byzantine-Bulgarian relations. For a contemporary view, see Shukarova, A. (and others), '*History of*

the Macedonian People (Skopje, 2008), paper by Panov, M., *The Creation of the Medieval State in Macedonia*, p. 95 ff and Antoljak. S. *Samuil and his State*, Skopje 1985.

51 Fine, J., *The Early Medieval Balkans: A Critical Survey from the Sixth to the Late Twelfth Century* (Ann Arbour, 1983), p. 192 ff. There has been extensive scholarly debate on Fine's view of Macedonia then as only a geographical identity.

52 For a general narrative, see Curta, F., *The Edinburgh History of the Greeks. C 500 to 1050* (Edinburgh, 2011).

53 For comparison with the lakes of eastern Macedonia in the modern period, see Ogilvie, A., 'A Contribution to the Geography of Macedonia', *Royal Geographical Society Journal*, London, January 1920. Ogilvie only describes the region north and east of Thessaloniki and does not mention Ohrid or Prespa at all in his writing, a sign of his almost total dependence on British army data collection during the First World War period occupation administration. It gives a remarkable description of the seriousness of the malaria crisis in the region at that time, other public health issues and the crisis in agriculture.

54 Runciman places the final collapse at Prespa of Tsar Samuil's family power in August 1018. See Op. Cit. p. 245 ff.

55 Apart from being a prominent Byzantine cleric, Theophylact is an important figure in later Macedonian identity formation debates. See Mullett, M., 'Theophylact of Ohrid Reading the Letters of a Byzantine Archbishop', *Birmingham Byzantine and Ottoman Monographs*, Vol., 2 (Birmingham, 1997). His letters give a graphic depiction of the harsh social and economic conditions in his time and insight into popular beliefs and medical practices.

56 See Brown, P., *Treasure in Heaven: The Holy Poor in Early Christianity* (Virginia, 2018), p. 36 ff. The very early Christians living around the lake caves after 300 AD may well have been exemplar of the 'holy poor' supported from the growing urban Christian communities in centres such as *Lynchnidos* (Ohrid) and *Heraclea Lyncestis* (Manastir/Bitola). At the same time, the hermits were spared much of the burden of agricultural drudgery, *ponos*, as they could live largely from the rich fish and game harvest of the lakes, apart from support from local Christian communities.

57 Quoted in Ohler, N., *The Medieval Traveller* (Koln, 1989), p. 50. English translation by Hillier, C. (Woodbridge, 1989).

58 Ohler, *The Medieval Traveller*, p. 101.

59 Fine, *The Early Medieval Balkans*, p. 271. In a generation earlier the lake region had become involved in the struggle to protect Orthodoxy against the Latin crusaders and the claims of the Latin church to unify Christendom under Papal leadership, when 'a special papal legate, Benedict whose assignment was to affect Church Union, arrived in nearby Thessaloniki in the summer of 1206. In response to this the Greek Church clerics held a synod at Ohrid, presided over by Demetrius Chomatianos'. Op. cit., p. 79. Chomatianos was the Archbishop of Ohrid's Chancellor, the Chartophylax, who later became Archbishop of Ohrid himself.

60 From Kravari, *Villes et Villages de Macedoine Occidentale* (Paris, 1989), entry on Nivica, p. 369. The evidence for the claim that the fishery was given directly by the Byzantine emperor to the Serbian king seems rather unclear.

61 See Fine, J., *The Early Medieval Balkans*.

62 Cvijic, J., *La Peninsular Balkanique* (Paris, 1918), p. 416 ff. The Serbian geographer considered the Vlachs belonged to 'ancienne civilisation Balkanique'. The earliest specific mention of Vlach pastoral migrations from the Macedonian region seems to date from about 1350 in Thessaly, as early as 1285 in Thrace.

63 Prespa 1, Op. cit., p. 32 ff.
64 There was an extensive and highly speculative literature in the Republic of Macedonia/FYROM claiming that Bogomilism originated in south-west Macedonia, among followers of the deceased Clement of Ohrid, which is beyond the scope of this book. It is claimed that Bogomilism played a major part in the creation of what writers see as the creation of a Macedonian proto-state in the second half of the tenth century.
65 See Kemp, *Healing Ritual Studies in the Technique and Tradition of the South Slavs* (London, 1935).
66 Bogomilism caused as many problems for the historians of communist Macedonia as later Western historians. In the standard party history textbook, published in Skopje in 1979, Alexandar Stoyanovski writes, 'The Bogomil heresy was a new phenomenon but it contained many elements adapted from the Paulician and Marsalian teachings which had been spread throughout Macedonia by colonists resettled from Asia Minor by the Byzantine Emperors with a view to destroying the compactness of the Macedonian Slavs.' ('A History of the Macedonian People'), p. 39.
67 See Skrivanic, G., *'The Roads in Medieval Serbia'* (Belgrade, 1974), p. 139 ff.
68 Discussed in Zachariadou, E. (Ed.), *The Via Egnetia under Ottoman Rule 1380–1699* (Rethymnon, 1996).
69 See paper by Whitby, M., 'The Late Roman Army and the Defence of the Balkans', in A. G. Poulter (Ed.), *The Transition to Late Antiquity on the Danube and Beyond* (London, 2007).
70 This was also the case in much of western Macedonia south of Prespa stretching over to modern Florina/*Lerin*, unlike Kastoria, where there were substantial Byzantine monasteries in the town and nearby.

Chapter 3

1 *Virgil, First Georgic*, David Ferry translation (New York, 2005).
2 For a good discussion of the issues affecting contemporary understanding of the conquest, see Adanir, F. and Faroqhi, S., *The Ottomans and the Balkans: A Discussion of Historiography* (Leiden, 2002) in the series 'The Ottoman Empire and Its Heritage Politics, Economy and Society' Volume 25. The discussion has wide implications in terms of different national Balkan historiographies, as recent research suggests the post-conquest end of functioning urban centres in many Balkan locations, for example Larissa in Thessaly, whereas Greek historiography always focuses on the continuing *polis* as a locus for transmission of Hellenism. For the general economic background, see Inalcik, H., *An Economic History of the Ottoman Empire 1300–1600* (Cambridge, 1997).
3 Nexhepi, R., *Prespa dhe Manastir*, p. 24 ff. The Albanian narrative does not clarify many issues of national and linguistic identity in the Bitola region Albanophone villages prior to Albanian independence in 1913.
4 For background, see Inaz, O. and Kose, Y. (Ed.), *Seeds of Power: Explorations in Ottoman Environmental History* (Warwick, 2019). For a comparative view of a later period in Italy, Bonan, G., *The State in the Forest. Contested Commons in the Nineteenth Century Alps* (Warwick, 2018).
5 For a study of a village in central Macedonia, see Lowry, H.W., 'Changes in Fifteenth Century Ottoman Peasant Taxation: The Case Study of Radofilo', in Bryer, A. and

Lowry, H.W. (Eds), *Continuity and Change in Early Ottoman Society* (Birmingham, 1986), pp. 23–37.

6. For a controversial view of the economic world of the Empire in its later period, see Palairet, M., *The Balkan Economies C 1800-1914: Evolution without Development* (Cambridge, 1997).
7. See the discussion of this issue in Alexander Prigarin's 'The Biopolitics of the Danube Delta: Nature, History, Policies' Op. cit.
8. Walker, M.A., *Through Macedonia to the Albanian Lakes* (London, 1867), p. 212 ff.
9. Ibid., p. 217. She also notes the *Han* function of Sveti Naum, where 'pilgrims, merchants and travellers pass in considerable numbers throughout the year' and the burden of Ottoman army detachments who billeted themselves there for long periods.
10. Fine, J., *The Late Medieval Balkans* (Ann Arbour, 1987), p. 415.
11. See Lowry, H.W., 'Changes in Fifteenth Century Ottoman Peasant Taxation: The Case Study of Radofilo', Op.Cit Note 5.
12. For Svac, see Cameron, A. and Pettifer, J., 'The Enigma of Montenegrin History: The Example of Svac', *South Slav Journal* 28, no. 1–2 (107–108), London, July 2008, p. v41 ff.
13. For the general narrative of events after the consolidation of the conquest, see Murphey, R., *Ottoman Warfare 1500-1700* (New Brunswick, NJ, 1999). Murphey's view that the conquest and Ottoman military demands after it did not cause the destabilization of southern Balkan rural society is unconvincing. For the general outlines of the early years of the imposition of the Ottoman imperial system, see Lowry, H.W., *The Shaping of the Ottoman Balkans 1350-1550: The Conquest, Settlement and Infrastructure Development of Northern Greece* (Istanbul, 2008).
14. See Papademetriou, T., *Render unto the Sultan Power, Authority and the Greek Orthodox Church in the early Ottoman Centuries* (Oxford, 2015).
15. Greene, M., *A Shared World: Christians and Muslims in the Early Modern Mediterranean* (Princeton, 2000).
16. Dankoff, R. and Elsie, R., *Albania and Adjacent Regions (Kosovo, Montenegro, Ohrid): The Relevant Sections of the Seyahatname* (Leiden, 2000), p. 223. Celebi's interest in sheep and pastoralism is both noteworthy, on his visit to the highland pastures north of Ohrid, and less attractive, his note that *Starova* was a 'mine for devshirme boys' to be carried off into the janissaries service where 'the most handsome' might achieve high office in the Empire. Celebi saw Struga almost entirely as a fishing and fish market centre, and notes the rich and diverse foods available in Resen. He did not visit the Prespa lakes, as far as his narrative shows.
17. For this transition, and how it has been seen by modern historians, see Bryer, A. and Lowry, H.W. (Eds.), *Continuity and Change in Late Byzantine and Early Ottoman Society* (Birmingham-Washington DC, 1980) and Matschke, K.-P., 'Research Problems Concerning the Transition to Tourkokratia: The Byzantinist Standpoint', in Adanir, F. and Faroqui, S. (Eds), *The Ottomans and the Balkans A Discussion of Historiography* (Leiden, 2002).
18. Information on this subject can be found in the Slivnica monastery church land registers, although only dating from the early sixteenth century onwards.
19. Lowry, H.W., *The Shaping of the Ottoman Balkans, 1350-1550: The Conquest, Settlement and Infrastructural Development of Northern Greece* (Istanbul, 2008), p. v44 ff.
20. See Salmon, T., *The Unwritten Places* (London, 1979).

21 For discussion of the wider issues in the social structure and rural-urban relations, see Parvava, S., 'Analect Isisiana', *Village, Town and People in the Ottoman Balkans, 16th to mid-19th Centuries* (Istanbul, 2010).
22 The generally accepted date of foundation of the little town is 993 AD, by the Bulgarian Czar Samuil, under the name *Sveti German*. For most of the Ottoman period its population was about 700 people.
23 For a comparison with Ottoman Bulgaria, see Lyberatos, A., 'Men of the Sultan: The Beglik Sheep Tax Collection System and the Rise of a Bulgarian National Bourgeoisie in Nineteenth Century Plovdiv', *Turkish Historical Review* I, no. 1 (2010): 55–85.
24 See Carrier, E., *Water and Grass: A Study in the Pastoral Economy of Southern Europe* (Glasgow, 1932), p. 138 ff. For antiquity and after, see Rider, M.L., *Sheep and Men* (London, 1983).
25 This can be seen from the writings of the English traveller, spy and Hellenist W.M. Leake in his journey in 1805 that he recorded in *Travels in Northern Greece* (London, 1835). Leake followed this route, which seems to have become a standard late Ottoman method of travelling from Epirus to *Fiuerina* (modern Florina/Lerin).
26 There is little evidence to suggest in Struga, or elsewhere in the southern Balkans, any Byzantine antecedent of *Ustruga* as a 'fair town'. Pre-Ottoman local trade was completely dominated by Ohrid, with much of the revenue going directly or indirectly to the Church. Early Ottoman fairs were always new creations, although specific evidence from Ottoman tax registers is largely absent as craft production, the backbone of the fairs, was not directly taxed under the Ottoman system. For a general discussion of urbanization and trade in the region in the late medieval and modern period, see Todorov, N., *The Balkan City 1400-1900* (Seattle, 1983).
27 No TT167, 1530, State Archives, Istanbul. The village is mentioned as an imperial allotment, a *humayun*. For background on the settlement of western Macedonia in the late medieval and early modern period, see Tsotsos, G., *Istoriki geographia tis dutikis Makedonias, To Oikistiko diktuo, 14-17 Aionas* (Thessaloniki, 2011).
28 For a comprehensive account of this process in modern Bitola, see Lory, B., *La Ville Balkanissime Bitola 1800-1918* (Istanbul, 2018).
29 See N.G.A. Hammond. Op. Cit. for a view on the relationship of ancient *Pisodendron* to the modern village of Pisoderi. Hammond seems unaware of the role of the Vlach pastoralists in the history of the revival of the village in the late Ottoman period.
30 For the world of nineteenth-century Korca/*Koritsa*, see Ismirlaidou, A., *Koritsa 1850-1908* (Thessaloniki, 1997).
31 Cousinery, M., *Voyage dans la Macedoine contenant des Recherches sur L'Histoire,La Geographie et les Antiquities de ce Pays* (Paris, 1831), p. 5. Cousinery was the first French Consul General in Salonika after the Greek War of Independence and an enthusiastic antiquarian explorer of classical monuments in Macedonia, particularly Pella and Philippi, where before modern archaeology, there were significant remains that could be seen. His book has some scattered perceptive observations on late Ottoman society in the region, particularly the large Bulgarian-speaking population and religious issues but is marred by much amateurish speculation about ancient history and society. His approach is firmly neoclassical, and there is virtually no mention of Byzantium in the entire text, in any context, and analysis of it shows the ideological reinforcement always provided by official France for the essentially Greek identity of the region. In this he was heavily influenced by the pioneering writing in France of Pouqueville, also a diplomat-spy-antiquarian on the W.M. Leake model.
32 Fine, *The Late Medieval Balkans*, p. 415 ff.

33 The most influential British map of Macedonia at the time of the Greek War of Independence, by John Thompson of Edinburgh (1827), does show Prespa and Ohrid but in absurdly misplaced locations.
34 Hyman, S. (Ed.), *Edward Lear in the Levant Travels in Albania, Greece and Turkey in Europe, 1848-1849* (London, 1988), p. 78 ff.
35 See Gounaris, Op. Cit., for an analysis of this subject, although his study is comprehensive and authoritative only for Salonika, much less so for *Manastir*.
36 American interest in the fate of Macedonia predated some of the European Powers. See Mitrev, T., *The United States of America and Macedonia 1834-1945* (Sofia, 1999). For many years Americans were almost exclusively involved with religious proselytism.
37 See Frazee, C., *The Orthodox Church and Independent Greece 1821-1852* (Cambridge, 1969), although the author perhaps overestimates the influence of Tsarist Russia on developments and exaggerates the decline in influence of the church after about 1840. For Russian policy, Jelavich, B., *Russia's Balkan Entanglements 1806-1914* (Cambridge, 1991).
38 Walsh, R., *Narrative of a Journey from Constantinople to England* (London, 1829), p. 63 ff.
39 See Jonovski, Op. Cit. At this time, IMRO was founded on the gorna prespa villages.
40 See Carrier, E., *Water and Grass: A Study in the Pastoral Economy of Southern Europe*, p. 372 ff. The central point affecting *Nivica* in the late Ottoman period after 1880 was that as a village with little fertile land and living in cereal crop deficit it was obliged to buy in grains for its inhabitants, and the advent of the railway made this much easier and cheaper to do and meant a larger village population could be sustained. The 1930s, when Carrier was researching and writing, was a period of widespread international concern about rural life in eastern and south-east Europe where many unresolved issues had carried over from the time of the Ottomans long after the Empire had ended. The League of Nations held a conference in 1939 in Geneva on the subject, which resulted in a voluminous four-volume publication of 'National Economic Monographs' in that year. The statistical data was provided by individual governments to the League and needs to be used with caution, if at all, but the texts of the Yugoslav section, No. 23, and Bulgaria, No. 28, are informative and provide a good (if often rosy-tinted) portrait of a phase in the evolution of the twentieth-century East European peasantry. The general political background to the event was clearly that of concern that rural economic and social crisis brought support for fascist dictators, and there was no participation or data input into the books from existing fascist governments in Rome and Berlin or Metaxas's Greek government.
41 For modern contexts on this issue, see Poulton, H., *Who Are the Macedonians?* (London, 1995).

Chapter 4

1 Gibbon, *Decline and Fall of the Roman Empire* (1), p. 23, London, 1966 ed. Gibbon's dismissal of the Balkan peoples as wild and violent barbarians in the early part of his history of declining Rome changes in the later chapters of his monumental work, so that when writing about the reigns of Valerian and Gallienus he sees the entire imperial edifice saved by the '*great princes who derived their obscure origins from*

the martial provinces of Illyricum'. In this Gibbon sets up a central dichotomy in perceptions of the region that has continued up to the present day, particularly when applied to Serbia, the Violent Savage- Masterly Soldier contradictory discourse. See Judah, T., *The Serbs* (Yale, 1997), for a discussion of the issue in modern political narratives. For an analysis of this rhetoric as it emerged in the controversies over international intervention in the ex-Yugoslav wars after 1991, see Simms, B., *Unfinest Hour Britain and the Destruction of Bosnia* (London, 2002).

2 Published in London in 1864, it is interesting that the Lakes are seen as 'Albanian', an indicator of the widespread regional use of the language at that time.

3 In Greene, M. (Ed.), *Minorities in the Ottoman Empire* (Princeton, 2005), paper by Petmezas, S., *Christian Communities in Eighteenth and Early Nineteenth Century Ottoman Greece: Their Fiscal Functions'*, p. 71 ff.

4 *Neverska* is the Bulgarian form of what in this period became known as *Nivica*, before that name was superseded in 1926 by Psarades. The fact that *Neverska* was used by the Constantinople Patriarchate in its 1900 census data is possibly an indicator of the Macedonian-Bulgarian ethnic majority population composition before the Ilinden Rising period in 1903. See note 2 of the chapter. For a Bulgarian nationalist view of the situation in the villages in a slightly later period, see Trangev, G., *Prespa* (Sofia, 1923). The population data Trangev quotes for *Neverska* would suggest a resident population in the village post–First World War considerably smaller than Greek-origin data.

5 See 'Statistique des Ecoles de Turquie d'Europe' 'Publications du Patriarchate Oecumenique', *Constantinople* (1902): 176 ff. *Neverska* is shown then as having a Greek school with eighty pupils and a Romanian school with 160 pupils. The quality of this data is probably not very high but does indicate the heavy Vlach presence in the hills to the south of the lakes and the importance of Romanian nationalist education projects targeted at the Vlachs. The Vlachs were also a priority target for Hellenizing education in the *Manastir vilayet* by the Ecumenical Patriarchate and the Greek government in Athens, in competition with the Romanian government and church in Bucharest. For an advocacy document published by an anonymous group of British philhellenes in Oxford, *The Population of Macedonia: Evidence of the Christian Schools* (London, 1905). The views put forward on the origins of Greek schools and accompanying data are controversial and unreliable.

6 Muller, E., *Albanien, Rumelien und die Osterrisch Montenegrinische Grenze* (Prague, 1844). He also records the *Manastir* garrison in 1838 comprised 16,200 Muslim troops, 2400 Turks, 5000 Bulgarian Muslims, 8000 Albanian Muslims and two other battalions of Muslim irregulars (also probably Albanians), all under the command of the General Commander of Roumelia (P. 188). Van Hahn comments also that in his own travel, the road from *Manastir*/Bitola to *Vodena*/Edessa was *'nicht nur schwerig, sondern gefahrlich'*. Florina/Lerin he records as half Albanian and Turkish Muslim, half Bulgarian Christians. *Manastir* in this period was recovering from its late seventeenth-century decline, where after the Austro-Ottoman wars the population had fallen to around 20,000 people, to recover to maybe forty thousand by 1835.

7 See Weigand, G., *Vlacho-Meglen Eine Ethnographisch-Philologische Untersuchen* (Leipzig, 1892).

8 Jelavitch, B., *Russia's Balkan Entanglements 1806–1914* (Cambridge, 1991), p. 228 ff.

9 Cvijic, j Op.cit Map 2 'Geographie Humaine'.

10 Durham, M.E., *The Burden of the Balkans* (London, 1905), p. 126. This was Durham's first book and contains some fine reportage of social conditions in the Prespa and

Resna regions in 1904, particularly the accounts of the crippling burdens of Ottoman taxation imposed on the people, the terrible roads and the dire conditions endured by women and infants. In her observations on agriculture, she notes the amount of corn growing on land near the lake, something very rarely seen after 1918, and also the place of rice in the diet, an Ottoman inheritance. Nakolets had a strong Albanian political consciousness, extending into the post-Ottoman years when in the 1920s the village was a stronghold of the *kacak* anti-Yugoslav rebellion, under Asllan Nakoleci, Mane Kapedani and Shemo Isai from Krani and other local nationalist leaders. See Nexhipi, R., *Prespa dhe Manastiri neper Shekuj* (Kercove, 2003), p. 167 ff. The village, like nearby Krani, was a centre of Balli Kombetar Albanian nationalist support in the Second World War and subject to heavy attack from Tito's communist Partisan forces. After 1945 many inhabitants went into exile in Australia, mostly to Melbourne.

11 For technical background, Kurz, O., *Empire, Clocks and Watches in the Near East* (Publications of the Warburg Institute, London and Leiden, 1975).

12 Papacosma, S., *The Military in Greek Politics: The 1909 Coup d'Etat* (Kent, OH, 1977), p. 102 ff.

13 FCO 371/677. Note by Sir Edward Grey on report from Elliot, British Embassy Athens, 3 December 1909.

14 There is a large literature in several languages on the IMRO, but much of it is of indifferent quality. The reality of IMRO changed considerably over the years from its foundation as an anti-Ottoman underground revolutionary organization with a multiethnic basis in Salonika in 1893 to its later evolution into what its critics, such as Duncan Perry, have seen as the first modern terrorist organization with an exclusively pro-Bulgarian orientation. Historiography has been retrospectively based on the assassination of the King of Yugoslavia in 1934. Most recent writing has been heavily influenced by Greek assumptions and an over-focus on one city, *Salonika*, as when, for instance, Mark Mazower writes in *Salonika City of Ghosts* (London, 2004), p. 265 ff. arguing that IMRO achieved little or nothing in the years before the First World War. It is arguable, for instance, that although IMRO was a failure in *Salonika*, its hold on the northern Macedonian countryside played an important part in frustrating Greek nationalist ambitions to take *Manastir*. British elite public opinion post–First World War was largely based on Joseph Swire's vehemently anti-IMRO book *Bulgarian Conspiracy* (London, 1939).

15 Yonovski, C., *Prespa* (Skopje, 2000), p. 43. Podmocani and its monastery became a place of refuge for IMRO fighters and activists trying to escape the Yugoslav police, and in the 1920s a prominent Prespa figure and former IMRO 'comitadji' Pande Yonov-Sudzov from Pretor became mayor there before he was killed in an ambush by Bitola police in 1927.

16 For a survey, see Bracewell, W., 'Opinion Makers: The Balkans in British Popular Literature, 1856-1876', www.ess.uwe.ac.uk/genocide/review, p. 91 ff. Bracewell makes some valuable points on the connections drawn between Victorian values such as honesty and cleanliness, and the alleged deficiencies caused by Ottoman culture and decline.

17 See Bridge, F. (Ed.), *Austro-Hungarian Documents Relating to the Macedonian Struggle, 1896-1912* (Institute of Balkan Studies, Thessaloniki, 1976). The documents are of considerable interest in illuminating the violence and disorder in and around *Manastir* and in the Prespa region at that time, but the Introduction is frequently inaccurate and includes much unscholarly and tendentious speculation. Also see Destani, B. and Elsie, R. (Ed.), *The Balkan Wars: British Consular Reports from*

Macedonia in the Final Years of the Ottoman Empire (London, 2014), although this collection is chosen to concentrate more or less exclusively on Albanian-Serb issues. More representative is Gounaris, B., *The Events of 1903 in Macedonia as Presented in European Diplomatic Correspondence* (Thessaloniki, 1993), particularly on IMRO and Bulgarian-Greek relations as seen from Greece. For a Bulgarian collection, reflecting the assumptions of the late Cold War period, see Bozhinov, V. and Panayotov, L., *Macedonia Documents and Material* (Bulgarian Academy of Sciences and Macedonian Scientific Institute, Sofia, 1979), and for a more contemporary view, Germanov, S., *Macedonianism as a Political Trend on the Balkans* (Macedonian Scientific Institute, Sofia, 2000).

18 For detail on the history of Krushevo/*Kicevo* (Albanian), see Brown, K., *The Past in Question: Modern Macedonia and the Uncertainties of Nation* (Princeton, 2003), p. 79 ff.

19 See Kunchov, V., *Makedonija: Ethographia i Statistika* (Sofia, 1900). See also Gingeras, R, *The Fall of the Sultanate: The Great War and the End of the Ottoman Empire* (Oxford, 2016), for a perceptive survey of the crisis on the Balkan fringe of the Empire at that time and the role of people from Nakolets in supporting the Young Turk Revolution in 1908, pp. 53-4. The village and the east side of Upper Prespa was calmed by the revolution, only to return to violence in 1911 when the Nakolets police post was dynamited by IMRO *comitajis*. The French literature is heavily influenced by philhellenist assumptions, for example Gandolphe, M., *La Crise Macedonienne: Enquete dans les Vilayets Insurges (Sept-Dec 1903)* (Paris, 1904), and Routier, G., *La Macedoine et les Puissances* (Paris, 1904).

20 The village name Nakolets is generally accepted to be of early Slavonic origin, from the word for *timber beam*, suggesting an original *palafites* lakeside settlement of houses raised above the marshland.

21 See Bridges, Op. Cit. Consular reports No. 179, and 224, although as early as 1897 (Report No. 7) a Greek band is reported as existing in the Ohrid and Prespa vicinity.

22 There was nothing new about this process throughout the nineteenth century and into the twentieth century. Earlier bands are generally described as simply criminal, as for instance in an article 'Outrages in Macedonia', in the 'Newcastle Morning Herald and Miners Advocate', Sydney NSW, 17 February 1891, where 250 Albanian outlaws are described attacking villages near *Manastir* and carrying off women and cattle to the mountains.

23 See article in *South Slav Journal* (London, Spring, 1997), Vol. 18, no. 1-2, p. 54, Pettifer, J., 'The Last Village in Greece': 'Nivica', 'Psarades', and Miss Edith Durham – a Note'. The authors have found no evidence in their field research to connect any contemporary Prespa village families with Crete or known descent in oral tradition from Cretans. Study of names of the dead in Prespa village graveyards and church cemeteries does not show up any family names particularly associated with Crete. In all probability members of the original armed band would have been absorbed into the Greek armed forces and armed volunteer structures by the time of the First Balkan War in 1912. See Cassavetti, Op. cit. on this topic.

24 The development of the mining industry was a central preoccupation of the imperialist Western powers and intimately linked to railway construction. For generally reliable data, see Petkovic, K. (Ed.), *Annales Geologiques de la Peninsule Balkanique* (Belgrade, 1924-1939).

25 See Sugarman, J., *Engendering Song Singing and Subjectivity at Prespa Albanian Weddings* (Chicago, 1997), p. 180 ff.

26 For a view of the role of the Vlachs in *Manastir* vilayet in the anti-Ottoman struggle, see 'The Newsletter of the Society of Farsarotul' Vol. XXXVIII Issues 1 and 2 2017 and 2018, Turnbull CT, study by Nikola Minov, 'The Aroumanions and IMRO'. The author provides valuable insights on the way some Vlachs were co-opted into the Greek nationalist project of the Great Idea, while others were involved with IMRO and Bulgarian revolutionary organizations, to the extent of holding leadership positions in some districts.
27 Gounaris, B., *Steam over Macedonia, 1870-1912* (Boulder, 1993), also Wolmar, C., *Blood, Iron and Gold: How Railways Transformed the World* (London, 2009). Gounaris's book also contains various statistical and economic history data which is relevant to understanding the appeal of IMRO to the Macedonian peasantry, particularly in the way Ottoman agricultural taxes on the peasants were used to help finance railway construction.
28 For a view of this process as seen from modern Macedonia within ex-Yugoslavia, see Trajanovski, A., 'L'Activite Politico-Educatrice de L'Exarchat en Macedoine dans les premieres annees avant et après la foundation de l'Organisation Revolutionaire Macedono-Odrinienne Secrete', in Apolstolski, M. (Ed.), *Macedoine* (Skopje, 1978).
29 From Upward, A., *The East End of Europe* (London, 1908), p. 221.
30 From Sonnichsen, A., *Confessions of a Macedonian Bandit: A Californian in the Balkan Wars* (New York, 1909), p. 122 ff. Sonnichsen was one of the few contemporary observers to see that the openness of the Bulgarians to revolutionary ideas compared to the clerical conservatism of the Greek military nationalists would become a handicap to the Bulgarians' ambitions with the Powers.
31 First translated from Greek into French as *La Flute du Roi* (Athens, 1910). A modern edition is edited by Diehl, E., Athens, 1982. The poem was composed, in *demotic*, between 1904 and 1908 at the height of the struggle for Macedonia. The hero of the story told is Emperor Basil II, the 'Bulgarslayer'. Basil II is depicted as stopping on his epic journey across northern Greece in Canto III as 'at Preslav by the Prespa way, that wonderous landscape painted like an isle, Upon the haunting lake with its lush fields, And its wooded mountains all around'. Modern Greek literary critic C.A. Trypanis noted in his volume *Greek Poetry from Homer to Seferis* (London, 1981) that 'the heroic example of Basil II remains valid, for men always seek a leader, and law and force are the powers that sustain or destroy a state'. For wider background, see also Leontis, A., *Topographies of Hellenism: Mapping the Homeland* (Ithaca, 1995), on the role of poetry, maps, myths and cultural artefacts in depicting for Greeks a 'lost' psychological homeland to which they needed to 'return', by conquest, if necessary. The confusion of the old Bulgarian capital of Preslav with the Lesser Prespa Bulgarian Second Empire site reinforces the views of some critics that the poet had never actually been to the region.
32 For a French military intelligence officer's record of the war, see Douchy, C., *La Guerre Turko-Grecque de 1897* (Paris, 1898). The maps are of more than local interest and show the Greek army irredentist objectives in the wider struggle for Macedonia, where as Douchy points out, the aim is a new 'Frontiere Reclamee, en Macedonie, s'etendrait de Gortscha (modern Korca in Albania) a Manastir, pour rejoinder le Vardar por Vodena', which would extend the Greek nation state to include Ohrid, Prespa, Struga, Kicevo and Veles to join with the then contemporary Ottoman frontier of 'Roumelie' (Turkey-in-Europe).
33 See section from the 'Correspondence of Pavlos Melas to His wife Natalia', edited by Douglas Dakin, in 'The Greek Gazette' Nos. 303-304, Vol. 26, London, November 1992.

34 Austro-Hungarian Reports of the Macedonian Struggle Op.cit Report No 165 dated 12 October 1905.
35 See Catsadorakis, G., Op. Cit., p. 49.
36 See Brailsford, H., *Macedonia: Its Races and Their Future* (London, 1906), p. 208 ff. Brailsford is often seen as a critic of Greek ambitions in Macedonia and a journalist open to the Bulgarian cause, and certainly this is true compared to the almost fanatical philhellenism of many British journalists in late Ottoman Macedonia, for example Trapman in the Balkan Wars period and Ward Price in the First World War. His most famous phrase which has become proverbial, even in modern Bulgaria, is 'It is not in Macedonia that the Greeks are seen to their best advantage'. The succeeding sentence is less often quoted: 'They have degenerated into a race of townsmen, who form an ignoble aristocracy of talent, half clerical, half commercial, which exploits an alien peasantry which it despises', p. 218 ff.
37 This dilemma was already starting to be reflected in Greek popular literature, such as Penelope Delta's children's book *Gia tin Patrida*, depicting life in the late Byzantine period in the Greek/Bulgarian world of Prespa and Ohrid. It was published in 1913, and the 'recovery' of Byzantium in her writings was a symbol of the Greek irredentist project in juvenile literature.
38 From Upward, A., Op. Cit., p. 322 ff. Upward was an intelligent man who had absorbed British philhellenism, and his John Murray published book contains a rare account of life in *Manastir* just before the Young Turk revolutionaries 1908 uprising. He is unreliable on ethnic issues and prone to racial slurs against Bulgarians. He gives a good picture of the band of Cretan fighters in the reform period of Hilmi Pasha, and the often neglected role of the Austrian and Russian political agents, there because in his view 'the recognition by the Powers that the Turkish government had failed in its duty'. In view of the later significance of *Zhelevo*/Antartiko as a key village for both the Greeks and Bulgarians in a succession of later twentieth-century conflicts around Prespa, particularly the 'Third Round' of the Greek Civil War (1947–9) it is interesting Vardas based his band there. There is also an amusing account of the efforts of the international commissioners to make the Ottoman tax system work properly, a doomed enterprise that only caused the peasants to hide their flocks in the hills. His estimate of the size of the Ottoman forces in Macedonia as 150,000 troops is surely an exaggeration.
39 For a scholarly study of the history of this key village from a pro-Bulgarian viewpoint, see Koroloff, L., *Drenoveni: The Life and Demise of a Macedonian Village* (Pickering, ON, 2014).
40 For detail, see Koroloff, L., Op. cit, p. 51 ff. Greek historiography does not dispute the circumstances of his death but casts doubt on the Bishop's responsibility. Whatever the truth of the allegations, there is no doubt that post-Ilinden the Greek hierarchy and the Greek Christian *beys* in Kastoria were active accomplices in the Ottoman repression of IMRO. Henry Brailsford had met Bishop Karavangelis after Ilinden and was impressed by his education and command of German but noted the large photograph of Traikov's severed head in his office and described him as one who 'persecuted Bulgarian peasants to drive them into his church', Op. Cit., p. 198.
41 See Marriott, J.A.R., *The Eastern Question: A Study in European Diplomacy* (Oxford, 1917), p. 435.
42 For a study of the position of the Albanians under the Ottoman system in western Macedonia after the Tanzimat reforms, see Xhemallli, V., *Shqiptaret e Maqedomise se*

Sotme Nga Kryengritija e Dervish Cares 1843 deri te Kryengritja e Dibres 1913 (Tetovo, 2012).
43 See Rexhep Nexhepi, *Prespa dhe Manastiri neper Shekuj* (Kercove, 2003). It is clear that at this point in the decline of the Ottoman power, *Manastir* occupied the role of 'city of culture and education' for Albanians that nearby Korca subsequently assumed under Albanian communism after *Manastir* had been irrevocably lost in Albanian nationalist terms to the new Royalist Yugoslavia under the Versailles Treaty boundaries. For the key event of the 1908 *Manastir* conference, see Demiraj, S. and Prifti, K., *Kongresi i Manastirit* (Tirana, 2008).
44 *The Enumeration of the New Provinces of Greek Inhabitants of the Year 1913* (Ministry of National Economy, Athens, 1913).
45 See 'The Macedonians of Aegean Macedonia: A British Officer's Report, 1944' by Andrew Rossos, http://www.gate.net/mango/britrep.html, p. 2. ff.
46 See Gurakuqi, R., *Principata e Shqiperise dhe Mbreteria e Greqise 1913-1914* (Tirana, 2011), and Kocaqi, E., *Administrimi i Shqiperise nom Austro-Hungaria 1916-1918* (Tirana, 2016).
47 For the British dimension, see Markovich, S., 'Eleftherios Venizelos, British Public Opinion and the Climax of Anglo-Hellenism (1915-1920)', in 'Balcanica', Institute of Balkan Studies, Belgrade, XLIX, 2018, http://www.balcanica.rs.
48 See Dakin, D., *The Greek Struggle in Macedonia 1897-1913* (Thessaloniki, 1966), for general background although Dakin's general approach rests on almost exclusively Greek official sources and the data used and his general analytic framework endorsing the Greek nationalist project needs critical evaluation.
49 'Memoirs of General Makriyannis 1797-1864', Ed. Lidderdale, H. (Oxford, 1966), and for a critical analysis, Veremis, T., 'Ioannis Makriyannis From History to Anthropology', in *La Revue Historique*, Institute of NeoHellenic Research VIII (2011): 85.
50 Significantly, archaeological exploration of the site of Pella began in 1914 within a year of the end of the Balkan Wars, a sign of the urgency of the appropriation of the ancient past of the Hellenistic kings of Macedon into the Greek national project. Ancient Pella has always been visible above ground, in parts, and was described by the Roman historian Livy and then by various nineteenth-century travellers, such as von Hahn. See Livy, *History of Rome*, VI. For an analysis of the role of archaeology in relation to Greek nationalism when the Greek military agenda shaped projects, see Davis, J., 'Warriors for the Fatherland: National Consciousness and Archaeology in "Barbarian" Epirus and "Verdant" Ionia, 1912-1922', *Journal of Mediterranean Archaeology* 13, no. 1 (2000): 76-98. There can be no doubt that the Vergina discoveries made by Manolis Andronicos and his team were of great (if unintentional) assistance to Greek propaganda in the period of intense controversy about Macedonian identity in the mid-1990s. See Andronicos, M., *To Kroniko tis Verginas* (Athens, 1997).
51 For the factors that led to the decline of Manastir/Bitola, see Jovanovski, D., 'Redrawing State Borders: Prosperity to Poverty in Ottoman and Post-Ottoman Bitola', in Davidova, E. (Ed.), *Wealth in the Ottoman and Post-Ottoman Balkans: A Socio-economic History* (London, 1998).
52 See Le Comite de publication DACB, *Come over into Macedonia and Help Us* (Constantinople, 1913), for contemporary eye witness evidence of atrocities committed on all sides but particularly against the Muslim population of *Manastir* and *Salonika* where the authors considered about 60,000 people perished in the 1912 to 1913 war years in western Macedonia.

53 Identities in Macedonia created through the use of religion played an important part in the redefinition of Serbia to include the territory of what became after the Versailles Treaty the *banovina* of 'South Serbia' and after 1945 the People's Socialist Republic of Macedonia in Titoist Yugoslavia. For the religious influences from the United Kingdom, see Pettifer, J., *Anglican Christianity and Nationalism in the First World War*, publication forthcoming.

54 Modern Yugoslav and Serbian historiography has yet to explore this issue. See, for instance, a mainstream standard work such as Andrej Mitrovic's *Serbia's Great War 1914-1918* (London, 2007), where Macedonia under occupation and its future is hardly mentioned, or IMRO as a political force, but only 'Bulgarian guerrillas'.

Chapter 5

1 Moore, F., *The Balkan Trail* (London, 1906), p. 165.
2 Grazdanova, C., *Kubinovo and Other Studies of Prespa Frescoes*, 'Matica' (Skopje, 2013), p. 8 ff.
3 This can be most clearly seen in accounts of the air warfare, such as H. Heydemarck's book on his time as a German air ace pilot *War Flying in Macedonia* (London, 1924). The map is particularly revealing, showing there was no German air activity at all in Macedonia west of Lake Dojran. For the war in the central salient, Palmer, A., *The Gardeners of Salonika* (New York, 1965).
4 *History of the Great War Military Operations: Macedonia* (London, 1933), p. 230 ff.
5 Stebbing, Edward Percy, *At the Serbian Front in Macedonia* (London, 1918), p. 201 ff. *Verbeni* village was renamed Itea by the Greek government in 1926, although the area nearby remains a centre of Macedonian-Slav language speech and culture to the present day, nearby Meliti in particular.
6 For the history of a nearby Manastir Gap village, Kleidi, with its dependence on the railway and the vulnerabilities of an open site on the plain, see Ioannou, S. and Ioannou, E.M., *200 Chronia Kleidi Florina* (Thessaloniki, 2017). This study elucidates a typical pattern of emigration from the small village with a far scattered emigration throughout the world. All names and places are printed in Greek forms and it is not an objective guide to some aspects of the ethnicity/history of the locality.
7 *The Balkan News*, Salonika, 22 August 1917, p. 1.
8 See Barros, J., *The Corfu Incident of 1923* (Princeton, 1965).
9 For detail on how the Commission saw individual border issues, see *Proces-verbaux de la Commission Internationale pour la delineation de la Frontiere Meriodionale Albanaise* (Florence, 1913). From the evidence of the documents it appears the Commissioners were far more concerned with limiting the expansion of Greece into 'Northern Epirus' and deciding what was to happen on the Grammos and Kolonia mountains than any issues connected with Macedonia or the Prespa region.
10 For a gripping account of the way the lobbying of the Boundary Commission took place by the Greeks to secure as much territory as possible, see *Under the Acroceraunian Mountains* (London, 1922). The author Henry Baerlein was an experienced French war correspondent with a background in ancient classics who had espoused the philhellenic project, and although an important eye witness source his work should not be regarded as an accurate account of local ethnic identities

in Macedonia and Epirus. His case rests heavily on the ancient Roman historian Polybius, in his statement that *'To the South of the Acroceraunian Mountains begins Greece'*. Baerlein's book was written partly to help the Greek cause and to counter the views of the nineteenth-century German geographer and antiquarian Heinrich Kiepert who in his *Manual of Ancient Geography* had claimed that Epirus was originally not Hellenic but had adopted Greek language and customs after the Peloponnesian Wars. These seemingly arcane controversies are relevant to modern debates about the influence of ancient historical and classical studies in ethnic identity definitions in the region, most obviously the nature of Macedonian society in the time of Alexander the Great.

11 Settlement patterns based on ethnicity remained essentially unchanged through the first two decades of the twentieth century, despite the political and military turmoil, thus the 'Ethnographic Map of Greek Macedonia' that was made by League of Nations Rural Settlement Commission in Geneva in 1924 shows the Florina/*Lerin* district as having in 1912 32 per cent Greek residents, 32 per cent Muslims and 35 per cent Bulgarians. The Muslims were in all probability mostly Albanophone. The major changes brought by the Asia Minor crisis changed the proportions, according to this source, to 61 per cent Greeks in 1926, 37 per cent Bulgarians and only 2 per cent Muslims. The data would suggest that many ethnic Albanian Muslims declared themselves as 'Greeks' to the League of Nations enumerators, probably on the basis of wishing to hold onto 'squatted' post-Ottoman land seizures. It should be borne in mind that the League was almost exclusively dependent on Greek government data sources in their assessments, and the number of Bulgarians is likely to be significantly underestimated.

12 For the recent history of Korca/*Koritsa*, see Ismirlaidou, A., *Koritsa 1850-1908* (IMHA Thessaloniki, 1997).

13 For an analysis of their role in identity formation, see Brown, K., *The Past in Question: Modern Macedonia and the Uncertainties of Nation* (Princeton, 2003), p. 79 ff.

14 In the earlier chapters, in particular, in Ischirkov, A., *Les Confins Occidentaux des Terres Bulgares Notes and Documents* (Lausanne, 1916).

15 For an authoritative account of this period and associated events, see Stone, N., *The Eastern Front 1914-1917* (London, 1998).

16 The Vlach pastoralists had complex economic interrelations with the Albanians in the more urban parts of the region, particularly in and around the villages north of Bitola/*Manastir* where a primitive textile industry had developed in some Vlach villages, and also the town of Debar, where Albanian banditry was so bad in the later Ottoman period some productive capacity was more or less destroyed. See Palairet, M., *The Balkan Economies C 1800-1914 Evolution without Development*, p. 343 ff. For the nineteenth-century background to these conflicts, see Lazarou, A., *L'Aroumain et ses Rapports avec le Grec* (Athens, 1976).

17 See Zoi, N., *Nje Faqe Historie*, published privately by Zoi's descendants in Korca in 2000. The most interesting parts of the autobiographical book are those that describe the émigré world of the educated Albanian nationalists in Romania before the First World War and the origins of the Korca Republic in the wartime period. Zoi's administrative career after his role in the Korca republic administration continued into the Zogist period, after he became Prefect of Korca in 1921. We are indebted to Xhevdet Shehu in Tirana for drawing our attention to this rare work. For the wider issues of Albanian developments, and the relationship of the Korca republic to the

later Zogist state, see Austin, R., *Founding a Balkan State Albania's Experiment with Democracy 1920-1925* (Toronto, 2012).
18 Discussed in Wood and Mann, *The Salonika Front* (London, 1920), p. 94.ff. There is a very large secondary literature on the Salonika front in English, mostly by ex-military participants, much of it not of a very high quality. For a good picture of the Macedonian Front in the World War, see Casson, S., *Steady Drummer* (London, 1935).
19 For a popular account of daily life, see Sindanowki, Op cit.
20 See Wood and Mann, *The Salonika Front*.
21 For the complex issues concerning land reform and its results in the 'New Greece' in the north, see Carabott, P. (Ed.), *Greek Society in the Making 1863-1913: Realities, Symbols and Visions* (London, 1997), paper by Hadziiossif, C., 'Class Structure and Class Antagonism in Late-Nineteenth Century Greece', and other discussion, as in W. McGrew's analysis of land tenure in modern Greece. The salient point from this literature as far as the Prespa region and most of western Macedonia was concerned was that it was very difficult for large landowners to form estates there and operate substantial agricultural operations in Macedonia outside the ex-Ottoman lowland ex *cifliks*, and while the new peasant landowners certainly related to capitalism, they did so largely through local market access, not production on any scale. In this sense little had changed since the days of the Boundary Commissioners and in reality, for centuries before.
22 This was often a very slow process. Land quite near Thessaloniki on abandoned ex-Ottoman *cifliks* was not distributed to landless peasants until as late as 1928.
23 This paper seems to have been used by the Greek poet Palamas in his works.
24 Llewellyn-Smith, M., *Ionian Vision Greece in Asia Minor 1919-1922* (London, 1973).
25 See Qira, Z., *Cell Number 31* (New York, 1976). Qira (1928-2002) was a an Albanian communist Partisan soldier in Albania and elsewhere in the Second World War who was later imprisoned in Titoist Yugoslavia. His autobiography sets out the fate of Struga where he grew up in the last stages of the First World War in the outskirts village of Velishte. After the Serbian forces occupied Struga, they drove out most of the Albanophone inhabitants and settled many demobilized Serbian soldiers there. Qira's long revolutionary career as an Enverist militant culminated in his work for the nascent Kosova Liberation Army in the United States in the 1990s. See Pettifer, J., *The Kosova Liberation Army from Underground War to Balkan Insurgency 1948-2001* (London and New York, 2012).
26 The modern church in Psarades can be seen today much as it was in late Ottoman times. It is not the first building on the site. Byzantine or early Ottoman-period church ruins can be seen a little higher up the hill where it stands and suggests a lost 'upper track' running from *Nivica* towards the village of Dolno Dupeni. It is surrounded by ancient juniper forest of ecological importance. It is a lonely and empty area, with Christopher Deliso describing Dolno Dupeni on the other side of the border as 'wildness, its sense of finality, of being the end of the way Borges had intended in his favourite story. The South rather than just another village in a line of villages running along the lake' (*Hidden Macedonia: The Mystic Lakes of Ohrid and Prespa* (London, 2007), p. 196.)
27 As a nod to the past, by far the largest number of church dedications in Florina district, thirty-two, are to St Nicholas, as the saint most closely associated with Russia, the Russians and the Russian Orthodox church.
28 For a summary of Greek irredentist claims, see Petsalis-Diomidis, N., *Greece at the Paris Peace Conference 1919* (Thessaloniki, 1978). These claims have formed the basis for the views of the modern 'Northern Epirus' lobby in Greek politics; for other relevant background, see Ruches, P., *Albania's Captives* (Chicago, 1965), and the immediate late Cold War polemical work *Northern Epirus Crucified* by Metropolitan

Sevastianos of Dryinoupolis, Athens, April 1986. For a pro-Greek foreign view, see Puaux, R., *La Malheureuse Epire* (Paris, 1922).
29. See Kousoulas, G., *Revolution and Defeat: The Story of the Greek Communist Party* (Oxford, 1965). Also Kiselinovski, S., *KPG i Makedonskoto nacionalno prasanje godina 1918–1940* (Skopje, 1985). For some wider issues, see Dagkas, A. and Leontiadis, G., *Les archives du Parti communiste de Grece* (Thessaloniki, 2009) (text in Greek), although the material reproduced for the 1918 to 1924 period is thin on the Macedonian issue.
30. For the relevant documents, in Russian and Macedonian, see Popovski, B., and Zila, P., *Makedonskoto prasanje vo Sobetckata nadevorezna politika (1922–1940)* (Moscow and Skopje, 2008).
31. For general background on this period, see the text of Yugoslav Comintern official Jules Imber-Droz, *Memoari Secretara Kominterne*, 2 Vols (Belgrade, 1982).
32. See Slupkov, I., *The Macedonian National Question in Greece in the Documents of the Communist Party of Greece* (Szczecin, 2006). Slupkov is very perceptive in her commentary on the post-Versailles period but does not fully reflect the importance of ancient and late antiquity history in the Macedonian debate.
33. For a fanciful account of IMRO in Bulgaria in this period but one which was very influential in Western Europe in those years, see Londres, A., *Terror in the Balkans* (London, 1935). Londres had been a prominent Paris journalist, and although not a serious historical work his book shows the close links between Yugoslav and French perceptions of the Balkans at that time. Also Swire, J., *Bulgarian Conspiracy*.
34. See Boskovska, N., *Yugoslavia and Macedonia before Tito between Repression and Integration* (London, 2015), p. 25 ff. Although Boskovska makes a very convincing case on the severity of the Serbian repression over most of Macedonia, around Prespa and Ohrid, given the terrain, it is perhaps open to debate how far the new Belgrade state actually had the security capacity to enforce the law very effectively.
35. The most useful study of Macedonian migration in this period is that of Lillian Petroff, in her book on the growth of the community in the key Diaspora centre of Toronto in Canada. She considers that the rate of emigration accelerated most rapidly after 1920, with hundreds of families arriving between 1918 and 1930. See Petroff, L., *Sojurners and Settlers: The Macedonian Community in Toronto until 1940* (Toronto, 1995).
36. See Boskovska, *Yugoslavia and Macedonia before Tito between Repression and Integration*, p. 31 ff.
37. As a sign of the extent of the problem in the British army in Macedonia in the war, Stanley Casson estimates in his autobiographical memoir of the period (*Steady Drummer*, London, 1935) that about 60,000 soldiers out of the near 100,000 in the British forces had malaria.
38. Carr, E.H., *Conditions of Peace* (London, 1942), p. 250 ff. Carr is now often seen a rather discredited pro-Soviet historian but this book written when he had left academic life in Cambridge to be chief leader writer on the London *Times* during the Second World War has many perceptive insights relevant to the Balkans.

Chapter 6

1. Official Greek data, which is reliable only as a general guide to developments, claims that after the population exchange in 1924 there were 1,279,000 Greeks in

Macedonia, 77,000 Bulgarians, 200 Moslems and 91,000 other minorities, made up of Roma, Turks, Albanians, Vlachs and others. This compared to 515,000 Greeks, 119,000 Bulgarians, 3000 Muslims and 98,000 'others' in 1912 just before the Balkans Wars.
2   Pentzopoulos, D., *The Balkan Exchange of Minorities and the Impact on Greece* (London, 2002). In terms of the Prespa region, the Versailles processes brought a setback for Greek irredentism, in 1923, with the return of the village of Zvezde to Albania and the exit of occupying Greek soldiers, as well as the loss of the fourteen lakeside villages now in Albania. This was confirmed by the 1925 Florence conference. See Winnifrith, T., 'Badlands-Borderlands', (London, 2002) p. 146 ff.
3   See Bedlek, E., *Imagined Communities in Greece and Turkey: Trauma and Population Exchange under Ataturk* (London, 2016). Bedlek shows that the destruction of the old cultural identities was to be achieved by the destruction of memory in education and religion.
4   Yonkovski, C., *Prespa* (Skopje, 2000), p. 28.
5   For a general appraisal of Athens' government policy in this period, see Carabott, P., *Aspects of the Hellenisation of Greek Macedonia 1912-1959*, KAMBOS 13, Cambridge Papers in Modern Greek (Cambridge, 2005).
6   *Digest of Official Statistics* (Athens, 1935).
7   For a graphic account written by a British private soldier William Mather, see '*Muckydonia 1917–1919*', Ilfracombe, 1979.
8   A good picture of the dire conditions facing the people can be found in American writer and humanitarian activist Harold Allen's book *Come over into Macedonia: The Story of a Ten Year Adventure in Uplifting a War Torn People* (New Brunswick, NJ, 1943). The pre–Second World War American Near East Foundation was a pioneer in what has become the conventional modern model of NGO relief work, and Allen provides a candid and objective account of their difficulties in trying to improve the lives of the people in the interwar years. It is also interesting in its historical assumptions about the identity of Macedonia, where the traditional 'classical' past of Greece is idealized, in contrast to the difficult Macedonian present, and the Slavophone Macedonian identity is completely elided. Agriculture was a very difficult area for modernizing Americans, who had little grasp of how Macedonian peasant society worked, but Allen was an honest observer and in the end came round to supporting many traditional practices. In the Cold War period he modified some of his earlier views to fit into US conventional wisdom on rural development based on anti-communism and anti-collective practice. See the Macedonian chapter 'Rural Reconstruction in Action', Cornell, 1953. Cornell has always been the most prominent US college with close links to agri-business philosophy and practice.
9   In *The Military in Greek Politics* (London, 1997), Thanos Veremis also puts forward the view that the changes in military-civilian relations after 1922 set the scene for the 1935 military coup. The security of northern Greece was of course central to military developments.
10 'Cahiers de Droits de l'homme', Geneva, No 24/25, 1927.
11 See Roudometoff, Op. Cit., p. 115 ff. on the instability in this period.
12 The current Turkish leader Rexhep Erdogan has recently (2019) on the instability in this period called for Lausanne Treaty revision, but it is unclear what he has in mind or how serious his intentions may be.
13 For a comprehensive study of the Muslim minority in Thrace with a 'Turkish' identity, see Featherstone, K., Papadimitriou, D., Mamarelis, A. and Niarchos, G., 'The Last Ottomans:

The Muslim Minority of Greece, 1940-1949', (Basingstoke, 2014) although written in parts with a rather uncritical view of Athens' government policies and the dimension of Muslim Roma and others outside the Komontini 'Turkish' mainstream is downplayed.
14 R.A. Reiss's book on this topic, *La Question des Comitadjis en Serbie du Sud* (Belgrade, 1924), was never translated or published in English or German and remains less known than it should be. Reiss's earlier book on Austro-Hungarian atrocities against Serbia in the First World War caused him to be seen in a poor light in German central Europe. It has some wider significance outside the history of the Balkans as an early example of the way those seeking revolutionary social change were characterized as terrorists by allegations about inhumane and violent treatment of civilian victims. Reiss does not explore the equally draconian measures of the Serbian gendarmerie against arrested Macedonian civilians alleged to be IMRO activists or supporters.
15 See the works of Popovski and Zila Op. Cit published in Skopje in Macedonian and Russian for a comprehensive scholarly collection of material from the Comintern archives on the Macedonian Question and policy towards the Greek Communist Party (KKE).
16 See Ellison, G., *Yugoslavia* (London, 1933), p. 121 ff.
17 Western churches missionary work was beginning to affect some Balkan countries, particularly the British and Foreign Bible Society in southern Albania, but until the twentieth century the organization had little visibility in most of Macedonia. The kidnapping of the American missionary Miss Ellen Stone by IMRO had been a traumatic event for the evangelical missionaries and had played a major part in conditioning Western public opinion against IMRO.
18 Carnegie Endowment for International Peace, 'Report of the International Commission to Enquire into the Causes and Conduct of the Balkan Wars', Washington DC, 1914, p. 53. The Carnegie reports had an ex cathedra unquestioned status at the time of the Paris conference in 1919 and affected many attitudes and decisions but now needs to be read critically. The high-minded liberal authors did not really understand IMRO very well and underestimated the evolution of the 'internal organization' and its complex relationship first with the government in Sofia and then revolutionary Russia.
19 Many did not wish to assimilate and left for Bulgaria, according to Sofia scholars about 40,000 people in the years after the Versailles treaty period.
20 Paper, 'Nomads in Macedonia: The Jurucks, A Community of a Time Past', in 'Makedonium',Winter 2004-5, no. 6, Skopje www.macedonium.com
21 There is a large literature in many languages on this subject, much of it outside the scope of this book. The ideological inheritance of the Russian-born Serbian historian Ostrogorski is important, as his view of the nature of the state of the Nemanjic medieval emperors is inscribed in many later Serbian expansionist projects, where the imposition of Orthodoxy is seen as the central element in nation building, a perspective that survives in some thinking right up to the present day, as, for instance, in the period of the 'Karic' church building in early Milosevic period Kosovo. See Cameron, A and Pettifer, J., 'The Enigma of Montenegrin History: The Example of Svac', *South Slav Journal* 28, no. 1-2 (107-8), London, 2008.

For survivals in popular belief and tradition in Macedonia outside Orthodoxy, see Kemp, P., *Healing Ritual Studies in the Technique and Tradition of the South Slavs* (London, 1935), where the author is able to demonstrate the relationship between modern popular beliefs and medieval and Bogomilist antecedents. Given the cultural conservatism of the Prespa lakes region, survivals of this kind were particularly strong, in the sphere of medical beliefs particularly, where most villages would not have encountered a modern science-based medicine until the 1930s. See also Ivanov, I., *Bogomilski Knigi iLegendi* (Sofia, 1925), p. 336. The development of the contemporary cult around the mystic 'Granny Vanga' at Rupnik in Pirin Bulgaria is particularly significant, in terms of both the strength of popular traditions and the difficulties the Bulgarian Orthodox church has in dealing with aspects of the national folk traditions.

22 For detail, see Simovski, T., *The Inhabited Places of Aegean Macedonia* (Skopje, 1998). Some village histories given are speculative. The legislation was Law 21st October 1926 n. 332. 'On the Obligatory Changes in the Names of All Settled Places in Macedonia', Official Gazette of Greece, 1926. By 1928, 1497 place names had been changed. In the same year the Pangalos government gave 14 million drachmas to build Greek schools in the Florina region with a Slavophone Macedonian population.

23 For detail on many derivations, see Vrabic, E., 'An English-Aroumanian (Macedo-Roumanian) Dictionary', Foreword by Donald, L. Dyer, University of Mississippi Romance Monographs, 2000. Vlach etymology is often controversial and this dictionary although a major scholarly work needs to be used with care. Some etymologies are often local modifications of Vlach root words, thus although Prespa Vlachs believe Pili means 'gate' the formally 'correct' term would be *poarta* in modern Romanian Vlach. Vlach, like modern Greek, has a *katherevousa* dimension in that many derivations that are seen as 'correct' are those closest to modern Romanian, and many colloquial and dialectal variants exist. Other colloquial Vlach parlance around Prespa takes some words directly from Albanian, for example fidelity, loyalty – Besa. English language Vlach historiography has little data on the Vlachs around the Prespa lakes, the pioneering Edwardian scholars Wace and Thompson do not seem to have visited Prespa and the region is hardly mentioned in their seminal work *The Nomads of the Balkans* (London, 1914). Greek scholars point to the obviously Greek-derived word used around Prespa lakes by Vlachs, that is the word for boat 'caiche', as a sign of long-standing autochthonous Greek settlement in Lower Prespa villages, Psarades particularly.

24 Popovski is still used in the Psarades Diaspora families, so that, for instance, in Perth, Australia, the name is still widely present.

25 As often occurs after periods of major war/social dislocation, families tend to have more children for a period afterwards, in Balkan societies as elsewhere. See Simovski, T., *The Inhabited Places of Aegean Macedonia*, p. 36 ff.

26 For a Greek study of the forced assimilation process in primary education, a key area of ideological struggle, see Kostopoulos, T., 'Heteroglossia and Assimilation Planning: The Case of Greek Macedonia Following Liberation (1913-1925), in *Language, Society and History: The Balkans*, pp. 457–67, Centre for the Greek Language (Thessaloniki, 2007). Kostopoulos considers the extreme measures adopted were a result of the sense of national insecurity after the First World War and Asia Minor disaster period.

27 See Slupkov, I.A., *The Communist Party of Greece and the Macedonian National Question* (Szczecin, 2006). For a major collection of the documents, in Macedonian, see Popovski, B. and Ziga, D., *Makodonskoto prazane bo dokumenthte na Koninternata*, 2 volumes (Skopje, 1999), and 'Soviet Foreign Policy and the Macedonian Question' (2 vols) by the same authors, Skopje, 2007. The material from the Moscow archives has yet to be considered or assimilated into non-Russian historiography, and it is likely to expose the oversimplified and schematic view of

the Macedonian/IMRO/Moscow relationship expressed by many authors writing on modern Greece.
28 Quoted in Catsadorakis, G., *Prespa au Coeur des Balkans*, p. 107. The expedition was led by London Royal Geographical Society members Holmes, Thorpe and Cotton. Their report is considered by modern ornithologists to contain many scientific errors, even on basic issues such as the migration patterns and nesting sites of the pelicans.
29 For a picture of prison life on Anafi, see Margaret, E. Kenna, *The Organisation of Exile: Greek Political Detainees in the 1930's* (Abingdon, 2013), a very well-illustrated and researched anthropological study.
30 For a cogent but selective account of the Metaxas period, see Vatikiotis, P., *Popular Autocracy in Greece 1936-41* (London, 1998).
31 Birtles, B., *Exiles in the Aegean* (London, 1938). This volume published by Victor Gollancz and the Left Book Club was widely influential in the anti-fascist climate in Britain, and his account of the return of the King through the 1935 coup d'état helped prepare public opinion for the struggles to assist Greek democracy in the following fifteen years.
32 Troch, P., *Nationalism and Yugoslavia Education, Yugoslavism and the Balkans before World War II* (London, 2015), p. 65.
33 See *The Macedonian Question in the Pages of 'Rizospastis' between the two World Wars* (Athens, 1982), p. 134 ff.
34 For a picture of the situation focussed on villages around Veroia, and elsewhere, see Eden, Op. cit. p. 111 ff.
35 Quoted in Allen, Op. Cit., p. 104.
36 McNeill, W.H., *The Greek Dilemma* (London, 1947).
37 Shukarova, A. (and others), *History of the Macedonian People* (Skopje, 2008), p. 243. In origin it was a radical students' organization focussed on reviving traditional Macedonian culture. It later became a founding part of the Communist Party of Macedonia within the YLC. See April 1939 document of the YLC 'The Communist Party of Yugoslavia and the Macedonian National Issue', which in turn was incorporated in most respects into the founding policies of ASNOM after 1943.

Chapter 7

1 This dichotomy goes back to the times of Greek independence in the 1820s and before, as Roderick Beaton has pointed out.
2 As described by H.B. Allen, in his memoir *Come over into Macedonia*, New Brunswick NJ, 1943. The account was controversial when it appeared, and remains so, with its emphasis on the intractable nature of many Greek-Macedonian rural dwellers problems and their basic lack of interest in the adoption of many US agricultural recommendations. It nevertheless contains valuable data on social conditions in the late 1920s and early 1930s, particularly on health reforms and malaria control.
3 For a discussion of the role of 'secret histories' in Balkan revolutionary movements, see Pettifer, J., *The Kosova Liberation Army from Underground War to Balkan Insurgency 1948-2001* (London and New York, 2012).

4 For the basis of the Nazi occupation, see 'Note der Reichsregierung an Jugoslawien, beigebunden: Memorandum zur Note an die Jugoslawische Regierung' (Berlin), March 1941. Hitler claimed the invasion was designed to protect Yugoslavia and the Balkans from British imperialism and to protect the human rights of the German minorities in the Banat, Voivodina and elsewhere in the Kingdom.
5 See Vouras, P., *The Changing Economy of Northern Greece since World War II* (Thessaloniki, 1976), p. 140 ff.
6 Ref. Palairet, M., *The Four Ends of the Greek Hyperinflation of 1941–1946* (Copenhagen, 2000).
7 Beaton, R., *Greece: Biography of a Modern Nation* (London, 2019), p. 274.
8 For a coherent if narrowly focussed account, see Carr, J., *The Defence and Fall of Greece 1940–41* (Barnsley, 2013). His account is strong on the technical aspects of the war, the role of the Royal Air Force in particular, less reliable on the political background, and omits the British military intelligence factor through ex–First World War operatives like classicist Stanley Casson, a major influence on the young Leigh Fermor.
9 Nexhipi, R., *Prespa dhe Manastiri neper Sheku* (Kercove, 2003), p. 284. It is unclear from Nexhipi's account of events how far this group was linked either to the Albanian Communists or to Balli Kombetar.
10 Data from Condit, D., *The Greek Civil War: A Case Study in Guerrilla War* (US Army Special Warfare Research Division, Washington DC, 1961).
11 Catsadorakis, G., *Prespa au Coeur des Balkans* (Paris, 2009), p. 38.
12 For political background, see Morewood, S., 'Failure of a Mission – Antony Eden's Balkan Odyssey to Save Greece, 12 February–7 April 1941', *Global War Studies* 10, no. 1 (2013): 6. For a highly critical account of Churchill's military policy, see Hastings, M., *All Hell Let Loose the World at War 1939–1945* (London, 2011).
13 A full account of this period west of Great Prespa Lake can be found in Jamila Andjela Kolonomos's book *Monastir without Jews: Recollections of a Jewish Partisan in Macedonia*, Centre for the Advancement of Sephardic Studies and Culture, New York City, 2008. Kolonomos became a prominent female communist Partisan, 'Tsveta' and Deputy Commissar of the First Macedonian Brigade, attaining the rank of Colonel. In later life she was prominent in political roles in Titoist Yugoslavia, and as an academic in Skopje university published various scholarly work on the Ladino dialect spoken by the *Manastir*/Bitola Jews. In an earlier generation, Jews from Manastir had taken important roles in the 1903 Ilinden Uprising. One prominent figure was Rafael Kamhi (1870–1969), a friend and associate of IMRO leader Damen Gruev, who eventually died in extreme old age in Israel.

For comparison with the situation in Greece, where the struggle to save Jews was linked much more directly to wider Zionist priorities and evacuating people to Palestine, see Bowman, S., *The Jewish Resistance in Wartime Greece* (London, 2006). This study bears out the background of Kolonomos's book, where it is argued virtually all Jewish Partisan recruits had been urban dwellers before the war. For a Yugoslav-period view, see Matowski, A., *A History of the Jews in Macedonia* (Skopje, 1982). Matowski shows the existence of Jews in the Ohrid-Prespa region long before Ottoman times, with a Rabbi Meir Koturski, noted in Byzantine chronicles in Ohrid as the author of a commentary on the Torah in 1107.
14 For a reliable account of the origins of the resistance movement and the role of the Greek communists, see Fleischer, H., 'The National Liberation Front (EAM), 1941-1947: A Reassessment', in Iatrides, J. and Wrigley, L. (Ed.) (Philadelphia, 1995). Hagen

Fleischer focuses rather exclusively on organization issues, rather than improvised popular action, and also depends heavily on C.M. Woodhouse's account of the politics of the time. His account of the internal 'policing' and law enforcement capacity of EAM/ELAS in the mountain villages is probably exaggerated.

15 Yonovski, C., *Prespa* (Skopje, 2000), p. 61.
16 See Iatries, J. (Ed.), *Greece in the 1940's: A Nation in Crisis*' (Hanover, NH, 1981), p. 38 ff.
17 For an account of events from a strongly pro-Bulgarian but anti-fascist point of view, see Koroloff, *Drenoveni The Life and Demise of a Macedonian Village*.
18 Several Bitola Jewish ex-Partisans rose to high positions in the Yugoslav People's Army after 1945, like General Beno 'Koki' Ruso.
19 The village where Kolonomos joined the Partisans was in Greece, over the southern Yugoslav-Greek border, then called in Macedonian *Buf*, now renamed Akritas. It had long-standing links to the Prespa villages through the fish trade.
20 For background, see Benbasa, E. and Rodrigue, A., *Juifs des Balkans* (Paris, 1993). In terms of the radicalization and poverty of most Bitola Jews at the end of the Ottoman period and after, it is claimed the population in Manastir dropped from about 6,000 Jews to about 3,000 between 1907 and 1927. Emigration to America played an important part, here as elsewhere. In Salonika no less than 8000 tobacco workers left for New York City in the years after the Young Turk Revolution in 1908. A substantial minority of these people were Jews. Benbasa and Rodrigue consider the decision of the Sultan to introduce military service for non-Moslems after the failure of the revolution played a main part in encouraging emigration.
21 For a discussion of the wider issues as they first emerged in the popular forces in the French Revolution and their many subsequent mutations in later European history, see Cobb, R., *The People's Armies* (Yale, 1988). As Cobb points out, it is usually the 'celebrities' of revolutionary armies who attract the most interest, both at the time and in later historical writing. But celebrity and success on the battlefield attracts much jealousy, as, for instance, Trotsky found in the Russian Revolution and in Greece Aris Velouchiotis in ELAS.
22 Accounts by a variety of participants have been published in the last generation. For a representative collection, see Scarfe, A. and Scarfe, W., '*All That Grief*' *Migrant Recollections of Greek Resistance to Fascism, 1941-1949* (Sydney, NSW, 1994).
23 See Chepreganov, T. (Ed.), *History of the Macedonian People* (Skope, 2008), p. 302 ff.
24 For an English language account by an ex-SOE officer sympathetic to the Albanian Partisans, see Hibbert, R., *Albania's National Liberation Struggle: The Bitter Victory* (London, 1991). For a contrarian view, see '*Sons of the Eagle*' by later Conservative politician Julian Amery, also works by Antony Quayle and David Smiley. The official Hoxhaist view of military events is to be found in numerous publications from the Albanian communist years.
25 The anti-fascist Partisan period still has a great hold on the imagination of the people on the western side of Lake Great Prespa in Albania, and there is a small museum dedicated to the history of the village in this period in modern Pushtec.
26 See Corkerry, S. (Ed.), *Anti-Partisan Warfare in the Balkans 1941-1945* (Mobile AL, 1999).
27 The Ottoman *vilayet* of Manastir extended south to northern Thessaly and Vlach transhumance agriculture continued across this territory until the late twentieth century. See Salmon, T., *The Unwritten Places* (Athens, 1995).

28 Field research in Pili in different periods, and in Psarades itself, has yielded very contradictory evidence in Vlachs oral memory of the wartime period. Some older Pili residents remember a united struggle against the occupation, while others are unwilling to discuss their memories or oral family memory. It is difficult to establish how many Vlach families in modern Pili have always been there, at least since Ottoman times, and how many newcomers were settled on empty land from Thessaly and elsewhere in the aftermath of the Greek Civil War.

29 For a convincing picture of the difficulties of the guerrilla war in eastern Macedonia, see Turner, D., *Kiriakos A British Partisan in Wartime Greece* (London, 1982). The book tells the story of Ernie Chapman, a Yorkshire miner in the British forces who was stranded in the retreat to Kalamata and escaped German custody to join a communist-led Partisan group in Macedonia operating near Pili village west of Dojran. There is a gripping picture of the *andartes* on Mount Paikon and the British SOE HQ at Pendalofon village in the northern Pindus in 'Free Greece' which should be much more widely known in the historiography. For a mainstream anti-communist SOE officers view, see Hammond, N., *The Allied Military Mission and the Resistance in West Macedonia* (Thessaloniki, 1993).

There is a very large and complex historiography on the British policy towards ELAS and EAM at that time, in the writings of Myers, Woodhouse and other SOE luminaries who published books after the Greek Civil War, most of them beyond the scope of this book. It is important, though, to note that throughout the emergency period from 1943 that SOE Greece only had a very limited presence north-west of Mount Vitsi towards Prespa and Ohrid, and SOE influence over *andartes* forces on the ground was much less than in the Pindus mountains and the Dojran region. The only SOE man exclusively based in the Vitsi-Prespa region was Sergeant Pat Evans, a junior NCO under Hammond, a very intelligent young man who had been a journalist before war broke out and spoke good Greek. SOE influence in the north was further reduced by the military crisis in Athens in December 1944 when ELAS troops refused to lay down their arms after a British-inspired directive to do so and when fighting between ELAS and the British forces developed. Some British personnel were withdrawn from rural northern Greece to reinforce garrisons in Thessaloniki and in Athens itself. Hammond became a distinguished classicist and ancient historian after the war, and his scholarly work has always reinforced the perspectives of Greek nationalism, particularly in the post-1990 controversies over Macedonian identity. Evans papers archived in King's College London provide a different perspective and much valuable information on ELAS and its operations around Mount Vitsi, and record that the vast majority of people living in the Vitsi area in 1943 to 1944 were of a Macedonian/Bulgarian linguistic and social identity. (Evans papers, Lidell Hart archives, King's College London, Secret Report on Sub Area Vitsi, 7 August 1944.)

Nicholas Hammond's account of the later period needs to be read very critically, and his use of Evans reports is partial and unscrupulous, but he is accurate and perceptive in showing how the British relied increasingly on the RAF to try to bomb German targets, particularly bridges, east of Prespa along the Florina-Pisoderi main road, but without infantry support, a modus operandi that continued later when the war was directed at the DA in 1947 to 1949. Although ultimately effective, the strategy was crude and indiscriminate and involved serious human rights violations against civilians and their property.

30 For a picture of the Vlach trans-border practice in later years after the Cold War, see Nitsakios, V., *On the Border Transnational Mobility, Ethnic Groups and Boundaries on*

the Albanian-Greek Frontier (Berlin, 2010). The study concentrates on the border just west of Prespa, in the main, particularly the Korca plain villages like Bobostica.

31 For analysis of how these divisions still influence Psarades and other Prespa village life and social and political loyalties, see Chapter 10.
32 There are many memoirs of this period by EAM and ELAS activists. For a representative account, Athanasiou, G., *Olopsixa* (Athens, 2002). The author was an early resistance guerrilla from 1941 with ELAS and then until the end of the DA campaign in 1949, going into exile first in Albania and then the Soviet Union from 1950 to 1975.
33 See Xydis, S., 'Greece and the Yalta Declaration', *American Slavic and East European Review* xx (February 1961): 6 Ff.
34 For a standard account that is reasonably objective, see Iatrides, J., *Revolt in Athens: The Greek Communist 'Second Round' 1944–1945* (Princeton, 1972).
35 For a very detailed analysis of the dilemmas in London about Greek policy, see Richter, H., *British Intervention in Greece from Varkiza to Civil War February 1945 to August 1946* (London, 1986), and his earlier text in German *Griechenland Zwischen Revolution und Konterrevolution 1936–1946* (Frankfurt, 1973). It is significant that at this stage in the conflict West Macedonia hardly figures in the narrative, compared to the position two years later.
36 For a discussion of the issues as they emerged in internal debates among Greek communists and leftists in the late 1970s and afterwards, see Eudes, D., *The Kapetianos Partisans and Civil War in Greece 1943–1949* (London, 1972). It is perhaps significant that this very influential book contains no mention of the Macedonian issue at all. Vukmanovic- Tempo's book *Struggle for the Balkans* (London, 1990) was important in promoting the Titoist case and implicitly that of DA leader General Markos Vafeiades against his detractors, and his political/military opponents in the Greek Communist Party. Vukmanovic's initial military analysis was written in 1949 and published in English in Hull in 1950 as *How and Why the People's Liberation Struggle of Greece Met with Defeat* (republished in London in 1985).
37 For a well-researched account of this period in the village of *Patele*, now Agios Pantelimon, near Lake Ostrovo, see Pevjovska, K., *Testimonies to Greek Terror in the Lerin Area* (Skopje, 1998). Also, Naumovski, A., *Lerin in Mourning* (Melbourne, 2009). Pevjovska's account shows how as early as mid-1946 forced relocation of villagers to Greek National Army held areas was a key element in the Athens government and British Military Mission strategy. In terms of British strategy in later decolonization wars, the technique became common in Malaya, Kenya and elsewhere. The US army model was derived from experience in conflicts in Latin and Central America. By mid-1946 almost every large building in Florina had been turned into a prison for forcibly displaced civilians and *andartes* before the latter were moved to Greek island prison camps. Her account describes very serious tortures and human rights violations, even by the standards of the time, including beatings, gender-based torture of women and random executions including a small number of inmates allegedly being buried alive.
38 This MI5 surveillance extended even to official British visitors to Greece, such as the Labour Member of Parliament George Thomas. Writing the Foreword of a League for Democracy pamphlet published in London in 1948, 'Britain in Greece: A Study in International Interference' by A.W. Sheppard, Thomas notes, 'As all my movements were being shadowed by MI5 (British Espionage), I had to take measures to prevent bringing trouble to anyone seeking to bring me information. At that time I thought it

was Greeks who were shadowing me. I was to learn later it was the British all the time.' P .4 ff.
39 McNeill, W.H., *The Greek Dilemma*, p. 163 ff.
40 The Partisan authorities in Greek Macedonia started education in the Macedonian-Slav language in schools in late 1944, and the Partisan song *Netram* became the anthem of the liberated areas until it was banned in Greece in 1946.
41 For detail, and a comprehensive analysis of the crisis Greece caused for the Attlee government, see Sfikas, T., *The British Labour Government and the Greek Civil War 1939-1945: The Imperialism of Non-Intervention* (Keele, 1994). Sfikas also puts forward a balanced and convincing account of the effect of loyalty to Moscow on the Greek communists.
42 Woodhouse, C.M., *Apple of Discord* (London, 1948), p. 146 ff. For the wider picture, see Fleischer, H., *In Kreutzschatten der Machte: Greichenland, 1941-1944* (Frankfurt, 1986).

Chapter 8

1 Alexander, G.M., *The Prelude to the Truman Doctrine: British Policy in Greece 1944-1947* (Oxford, 1982), p. 197 ff.
2 Quoted in FCO papers 27th August 1946 FCO 371/58615.
3 Leonard Scopes, the British Vice Consul in Thessaloniki, had visited a refugee camp for Greek Macedonians in Yugoslavia in September 1945 and reported that he thought 'most were willing to return to Greece and live as Greek citizens if the Rightwing terrorism against them ceased'. Alexander, G.M., *The Prelude to the Truman Doctrine*, p. 198.
4 There have been allegations over the years that KKE leader Georgios Siantos, nicknamed 'the Old Man', was a British agent and played a key role in the Varkiza decision to surrender weapons. As in many intelligence matters, exact verification of this claim is currently impossible. In defence of some of the KKE decisions, it is worth recalling how many of the leadership, particularly in Athens, came from Asia Minor refugee backgrounds and they often had in their political psychology an instinctive distrust of armies, military adventurism and a pacifist streak. Memories of Royalist-led military irredentist policies that led to the Asia Minor catastrophe in 1923 and the loss of their homes and lands were very strong a generation later in their minds.
5 From Smothers, T. (and others), *Report on the Greeks* (New York, 1948), p. 168. The later distinguished American historian of twentieth-century Greece William H. McNeill was a young member of this Twentieth Century Fund team.
6 There is a very extensive literature on this period, see Stavrakis, P., *Moscow and Greek Communism 1944-1949* (Cornell, 1989), and many works published in Greek by contemporary participants, in particular Bartziotis, V., *O Agonas tou Dimokratikou Stratou Elladas* (Athens, 1982). These have been augmented over the years by various local studies, often in the form of university PhD theses, on the story as it evolved in particular small localities. Although as in debates after many wars local participants have very strong and divergent views on particular issues and personalities, in the main the general narrative is confirmed of a KKE leadership that was insufficiently focussed and ruthless, and incapable of understanding many basic aspects of informal warfare, and in thrall to the currents of international pressures.

7   There is a very extensive literature on the regional crisis and the war in Macedonia. See for documents, Institute of National History, Skopje, 6 Volumes, 1968–1979 'Izvori na Osloboditelnata Vojna I Revolucijata vo Makedonija, 1941–1945' (Sources of the Liberation War and the Revolution in Macedonia 'on the basic orientation of the Yugoslav communist party'. For the Greek side, Chatzis, T., *I Nikifora Epanastasi pou Chathike (The Victorious Revolution That Was Lost)*, 3 Volumes (Athens, 1977–1979).
8   There is a collection of rare ELAS Peloponnese publications in the archives of Christ Church, Oxford, in the papers of College Classics tutor Eric W. Gray, Lecturer in Ancient History in the university (1939–77), who spent time with ELAS in Arcadia in 1943 to 1944.
9   For a discussion of the background issues, from a political science perspective, see Kalyvas, S., *The Logic of Violence in Civil War* (Cambridge, 2006).
10 For detail, Antonakaki, X., *To Antartiko ston Taygeto 1941–1944* (Athens, 1994). The title dates are inaccurate; the book covers the period up to 1949. Many DA *andartes* from the Kalamata, Sparta and Kardamyli regions were captured and imprisoned in mid-1948, mostly on the prison island of Makronisos, before they could move north.
11 'The Conspiracy against Greece' Greek Under Secretariat for Press and Information (Athens, 1947), p. 61.
12 McNeill, W., *The Greek Dilemma* (London, 1947), p. 166 ff. The American historiography on this period is more objective than the British, where British SOE officers who were Classicist university academics, principally Nicholas Hammond in the case of western Macedonia, succeeded in establishing a narrative that prefigured many apologia for the Greek Right and the Royalists in the post–Civil War and Cold War years. See Hammond's *Venture into Greece* (London, 1983), and *The Allied Military Mission and the Resistance in Western Macedonia* (Thesaloniki, 1993). The later volume draws heavily on the intelligence reports of SOE officer on Mount Vitsi, ex-journalist Patrick Evans, who near the end of his life had been planning to publish on his experiences but was too ill to do so, and Hammond used his material, with Evans's agreement. The narrative constructed is designed to reinforce Hammond's general views and in practice omits much of Evans fairly objective descriptions of what ELAS had achieved. For the role of later historical writing by a senior participant in the wartime period who later became the *doyen* of British Hellenism and a Conservative MP, see the writings of C.M. Woodhouse and analysis of them in Pettifer, J., *Woodhouse, Zervas and the Chams* (Tirana, 2010).
13 The actual status and practical functionality of the northern border varied considerably throughout the twentieth century. The geography of the border ruled out full control by the Greek military for large parts of its length, but parts were important in later conflicts, that is the occupation by the Greek army of mountains west of Prespa in 1940 (see Mackenzie, C., *The Wind of Freedom* (London, 1944), p. 73). When part of Macedonia became Greek as a result of the Balkan Wars (1912–13) and the 1923 Versailles Treaty settlement, it is arguable whether the majority of the Greek population even knew where the northern border was in any detail. The proliferation of maps produced by the Greek army in the interwar period indicates this. The same applied to many members of the foreign community in Athens. For example, Mrs R.S. Bosanquet, the wife of the prominent archaeologist of Knossos, wrote a well-informed and valuable book, *Days in Attica*, which was published in London in 1914 and describes contemporary Greek society after years of travel and residence but she makes no mention of most of northern Greece or Greek Macedonia at all.

14 See Meta, B., *Greek-Albanian Tensions 1939–1949* (Tirana, 2012), and Pettifer, J., *Woodhouse, Zervas and the Chams* (Tirana, 2008), Op. cit.
15 See Corrigan, P. (Ed.), *Capitalism, State Formation and Marxist Theory* (London, 1980). Also Anderson, P., *Passages from Antiquity to Feudalism* (London, 1974), for a discussion of the issue of survivals of earlier state formations in modern European societies and the writings of the French philosopher Althusser on survivals in ideology.
16 For a useful picture of the approach of the American military advisers to the Greek National Army in this period, see Harris, W., *Installing Aggressiveness: Advisors and Greek Combat Leadership in the Greek Civil War 1947–1949* (Pittsburgh, 2013). For a view sympathetic to the DA and critical of British and American military assistance to the Athens government, see Sheppard, A.W., *An Australian Officer in Greece*, published by the League for Democracy in Greece, London, in 1947. Colonel 'Rufus' Sheppard was originally involved in Greece as a soldier in the Australian Imperial Forces in 1941 and returned with the Australian refugee relief team in 1945, when he transferred to the UNRRA and headed up operations in Florina and Kozani. He resigned from his last position as Director of the Northern Greek office of the British Economic Mission in March 1947. His cogent radical views were systematically patronized and marginalized by most British ex-SOE officers in the historiography they created in memoirs and historical writing after the Civil War.
17 Memoirs of DA soldiers show that the Prespa DA officer training school was moved from Laimos, near Agios Germanos, first to Pyxos above Lake Lesser Prespa – an incompetent decision as it was very exposed to air attack – then to the village of Aetomelitsa in the northern Pindus, in mid-1948. See Scarfe, A. and Scarfe, W., *All That Grief Migrant Recollections of Greek Resistance to Fascism 1941–1949* (Melbourne, 1994).
18 See Rossides, E. (Ed.), *The Truman Doctrine of Aid to Greece: A Fifty Year Retrospective* (New York, 1998).
19 According to the data in the Myrovleto archives. This data needs careful evaluation and analysis, as in many places there were weapons left from the Occupation and some DA units seemed to have been well supplied locally. On the north side of the Prespa lakes small arms were plentiful given the scale of the munitions stores abandoned by the German occupiers from the Bismarck Division based in Bitola after they retreated north in late 1944. Demobilized Yugoslav and Albanian Partisans after 1945 were also an easy source of weapons and ammunition.
20 For a revealing guide to the thinking behind US policy, see Roucek, J., *The Politics of the Balkans* (New York, 1939), and *Balkan Politics International Relations in No Man's Land*, Stanford, 1948. As Roucek points out, 'A small mission of American experts, led by Dwight P. Griswold, was to be the real masters of Greece' after August 1947.
21 Kofas, G., *Intervention and Underdevelopment Greece during the Cold War* (Philadelphia, 1989), p. 95 ff.
22 Mangalakova, T., *Ethnic Bulgarians in Mala Prespa and Golo Brdo* (IMTR, Sofia, 2004), p. 2.
23 For a little known picture of the first year of Communist power in Yugoslavia after 1945, see the memoir of ex-UNRRA official and foreign correspondent journalist Anne Dacie, *Instead of the Brier Concerning Yugoslavs* (London, 1949). The section on land reform where a 35-acre ownership limit was imposed is particularly relevant to the analysis of the social structure nowadays in Yugoslav Macedonia and Serbia. Around Prespa it was and is irrelevant in the main, as most farms were always much smaller.

24 See Aliu, A., *Prespa ne Australie*, Op. cit., although in this book the collaborationist role of most Ballists is not explored. For the general background on the role of the Balli Kombetar in Macedonia in the Second World War, see paper by Hibbert, R., 'Albania, Macedonia and the British Military Missions, 1943 and 1944', in Pettifer, J. (Ed.), *The New Macedonian Question* (London and New York, 1999), p. 184 ff.
25 Vrondero, nicknamed 'the cold village', saw perhaps the most extreme population change, from 100 per cent Slav Macedonian before 1939 to 100 per cent Vlach after 1955.
26 See Voglis, P., *Becoming a Subject Political Prisoners during the Greek Civil War* (New York, 2002). At the end of 1944, about 12,000 leftists had been imprisoned for political reasons. The great majority of these were people detained during or after the Battle of Athens in December 1944 and were in origin British army detainees. By mid-1947 there were about 19,600 detainees in prison, mostly on islands, although many urban prisons were also used, with dreadful conditions. The number rose to about 25,000 by late 1948 and continued at about 17,000 to 20,000 until 1951. Research over the years in and around Prespa does not indicate any Prespariots we have met were gaoled on the main prison islands, although obviously there may have been individuals whose families did not return to Prespa in later years. Oral memory would suggest death in conflict or later political exile was almost universal for local DA soldiers, capture and imprisonment was much less common. About 300,000 people were forcibly relocated from their villages during the 1946 to 1949 periods, many never to return. A comprehensive study of this process as it affected rural mountain Greece based on archival data is lacking, although there are many worthwhile local studies.
27 See Sheppard, A., *An Australian Officer in Greece*. Anecdotal evidence suggests some British army officers involved were unhappy with the draconian martial law situation and tried to prevent the use of the death penalty and execution of DA prisoners and real or alleged KKE communists.
28 See Kalajdziev, H., *The Bulgarian-Yugoslav Rapprochement and the Macedonian Question* (Sofia, 1947), p. 5. From the point of view of Greek Macedonia and the Prespa villages, the main issue was that the agreement dramatically improved the standing of Tito with the political left, if not with the KKE leadership. The agreement also covered the Pirin issue, to the disadvantage of the Yugoslavs. See Mitrev, D., *Pirinska Makedonija u Borba za Nacionalno Oslobodenje* (Skopje, 1950), and by the same author *Pirin Macedonia*, Skopje, 1962. For current issues, see the programme of the illegal IMO-Ilinden, published in Petrich in Bulgaria in 2000.
29 In Greek, called Mount Kaimaktsalan.
30 Ref. Sfikas, T., *The British Labour Government and the Greek Civil War* (Keele, 1998).
31 See Stavridis, P., *Moscow and Greek Communism 1944-1949* (Cornell, 1989), p. 152 ff.
32 Stavridis, Op. cit., p. 153.
33 Close, D. (Ed.), *The Greek Civil War 1943-1950 Studies of Polarisation* (London, 1993), p. 210 ff. Close rightly stresses the importance of the Prespa and other nearby hospitals, as most others were in Albania, Yugoslavia and Bulgaria.
34 Tsoucaras, C., *The Greek Tragedy* (London, 1969), p. 104 ff. Tsoucaras points out: '*It seems that dogmatic insistence on pure Leninist theories led to open disregard to the potentialities of the peasant movement. Markos's deputy Kititzas told the French writer D. Eudes (in an unpublished series of interviews) that Zachariadis expressly forebade the broadening of guerrilla warfare on the basis of peasant conscription and set the maximum number of guerrillas as 10,000.*' This is a very complex and highly controversial subject where accurate data is lacking as whatever the views of the DA

and KKE leaders, more or less forced conscription into the DA was common around Prespa and elsewhere in mainland mountain Greece after early 1948. The fact that a man or woman had been conscripted did not prevent forced exile (interview with citizen with family from Pisoderi village, immediately east of Prespa, 2019.). DA soldiers who were Vlachs from this part of Prespa wider region generally went into political exile in Romania after 1949, as did a recently deceased citizen of Psarades who had been a DA soldier in his youth.

35 See Livianos, D. in 'Balkan Studies', 39.1, Thessaloniki, 1998 article, 'A Loveless Entanglement: Britain and Bulgar-Yugoslav relations 1924-1943'. The British diplomats generally preferred the term 'Balkan Union' to 'Balkan Federation'.
36 Close, *The Greek Civil War 1943–1950 Studies of Polarisation*, p. 217.
37 The *mythos* in this historiography is obviously to produce a sympathetic reaction to Tito's decisions in line with his new image as a potential Western 'asset' after the split in the world communist movement in 1948 involving Yugoslavia. There is an extensive literature on the subject although final judgement on some issues, that is direct British and/or US pressure on Tito to close the border must await the opening of several hitherto closed government archives.
38 See Eudes, D., The *Kapetanios Partisans and Civil War in Greece 1943–1949* (London, 1972) for a cogent analysis. The controversies over Nikos Zachariadis and his leadership continue to the present day, with his 'rehabilitation' in the official narrative of the KKE finally taking place quite recently. See statement of the KKE 'Event concerning the Rehabilitation of Nikos Zachariadis', http://inter.kke.gr/News/news2011/2011-10-03-zachariadis
39 For a comprehensive picture of the movement and resettlement of children from the Civil War in 1948, see Danforth, L. and Van Boeschoten, R., *Children of the Greek Civil War Refugees and the Politics of Memory* (Chicago, 2012), a book that has been very controversial both in Greece and particularly in United States. It is very strong on the refugee humanitarian issues but weak on aspects of the background history and politics, on both the Communist and Royalist sides. For good contemporary fictional evocations, see the novel of Zei, A., *Achilles Fiancée* (Athens, 1991), on the conflicts within the Greek communist exiles in Tashkent, and Victoria Hislop's novel *Those Who Are Loved* (London, 2019), on divisions in an Athens working-class family involved with the KKE.
40 Interview with Nikola Risto Mundushev, DA veteran from the village, 'Politiceon', Melbourne, Australia, 1999. The Greek census of 1991 records 250 residents.
41 'Le Feu et la Hache Grece '46-'49' (Paris, 1973), p. 338.
42 Matthews, Op. cit., p. 268. He estimated that by this point in the war about 36,000 rebel soldiers and people in associated civilian roles had died.
43 Interview with ELAS and DA veteran in village east of Karadmyli, Messenia, August 2019.
44 For a balanced general introduction, see Beaton, R., *Greece The Biography* (London, 2019).
45 The most fully verified bombing and strafing of civilians in Albania was in the little town of Bilisht, north of the Krystallopigi Greek-Albanian border crossing.
46 There are complex issues regarding the actual command and control mechanisms of this force. Greek pilots who were thought to be politically reliable were trained and organized within the RAF in the Middle East before the end of the Second World War. The Royal Hellenic Air Force was formed from Greek units within the RAF in 1946 and in theory had taken over full deployment from the RAF by December

1946. How far this was actually the case has been open to debate and a subject of controversy in Greece for many years. The aircraft were completely dependent on British-sourced spares and technology until 1948 when US-sourced aircraft such as the Curtiss SB2C-5 Helldiver entered RHAF service. The Helldiver played an important part in the attacks on the DA in the mountains in the final phase of the Civil War where napalm chemicals were first used for military purposes. For an objective discussion, see Flintham, V., *Air Wars and Aircraft: A Detailed Record of Air Combat, 1945 to the Present Day* (London, 1990).

47 See Skaric, S. (Ed.), *The Name Issue Greece and Macedonia* (Skopje, 2009), p. 92 ff.

48 For a very well-researched study of the *paidomazoma* that is both comprehensive and objective, particularly on later lives in Eastern Europe, see Op Cit Danforth, L. and Van Boschoten, R., *Children of the Greek Civil War Refugees and the Politics of Memory* (Chicago, 2012). The overwhelming majority of Greeks would not agree with its assumptions about the Macedonian identity.

49 Before the Second World War sheep meat made up about half of Greek meat consumption, and 60 per cent of dairy, the latter mostly in the form of *feta* cheese. Rider, M., *Sheep and Men*, p. 310. The influx of Asia Minor people, although not around Prespa, had elsewhere considerably reduced the supply of lowland winter grazing as a result of new urban development.

50 This media propaganda narrative was already being established by the Greek and British authorities while the Civil War was in progress. See BBC correspondent Kenneth Matthews book *Memories of a Mountain War Greece 1944–1949* (London, 1972), for a detailed account of the way censorship and access closure worked, even for a very non-political senior BBC correspondent who had good relations with British diplomats in Athens. Matthews foray into the rebel-held central Peloponnese was undertaken in defiance of government press controls and led to his expulsion from Greece. In the final stage around Prespa and Florina, only war artists and photographers like Bert Hardy sympathetic to the Right were allowed access, not journalists. One artist involved there was the young Nicholas Egon who in later life became a prominent philanthropist and supporter of Hellenic Studies in King's College, London. Matthews's journalism deserves systematic scholarly study which has yet to take place.

It depicts the extreme lengths the Foreign Office in London at the time went to determine the coverage of the war and Matthews's contrarian attempts to preserve BBC traditions of unbiased objective reporting. It is perhaps significant that his book was only eventually published twenty-five years later in the Greek junta years when the struggle to restore democracy in Greece caused the breakdown of the traditional Rightist and Cold War narrative about what had happened between 1947 and 1949. Matthews's claim that over five thousand Greek civilians had been murdered by the National Army in DA rebel-held areas – which included people he knew personally – was particularly difficult for the Right to refute. A rational analysis by an ex-MI6 officer who was active in Athens at the time and heavily involved in press/propaganda work can be found in Clive, N., *A Greek Experience 1943–1948* (Norwich, 1985). In later life Clive was to a degree self-critical of his early activities and felt that Ernest Bevin had been mistaken in continuing Churchill's Greek policy after the election of the Labour government in 1945 and that this contributed to the eventual Civil War (discussions with J. Pettifer/M. Vickers, 1992–2000). Irrespective of politics, his book contains a remarkable depiction of his heroic work in the Secret Intelligence Service/Special Operations Executive underground intelligence network in the Nazi occupied Souli Mountains and Ioannina in Epirus.

Chapter 9

1. This is a well-known traditional Macedonian song, translated by James Pettifer.
2. FO 371/78396/18 7 March 1949.
3. Mount Vernon is a name which has grown in use in 'official' Greece and by some foreign writers, particularly US scholars and mapmakers, but in this book the traditional regional colloquial term *Vicho* is used and also the traditional name from Slavonic etymology, Mount Vitsi, which is also often used in demotic Greek. Vitsi was generally used with Special Operations UK military staff in the wartime period in their reports.
4. Generally accepted (but estimated) data for the number and location of Greek-Macedonian political refugees who had settled in the socialist countries by the end of 1950 is 9,100 in Romania, 11,941 in Czechoslovakia, 11,450 in Poland, 7,250 in Hungary, 3,071 in Bulgaria and 11,980 in the USSR, the great majority of the latter in Tashkent (*Australian Macedonian Weekly*, 2 March 1996). In the later Soviet period substantial numbers of these people moved to the Crimea and other Black Sea regions of Russia, and a few to the German Democratic Republic. After the end of the Cold War the latter were often early returnees to Greece and some have latterly become prominent and wealthy in Greek business. Some from Tashkent moved after 1990 to Moscow where they have influential networks.
5. The Macedonian Times Skopje November 1997, article by Andonovski, H., 'Distinguished Macedonians in Albania', p. 33. It shows the polemic at that time.
6. See Woodhouse, C., *The Struggle for Greece 1941–1949* (London, 1976), p. 286. Woodhouse played a key role in Britain and the United States in the Cold War years in establishing an accepted narrative of events and excluding many controversial issues from academic discussion, as far as it was possible to do so. For a more objective account of the development of British policy, see Alexander, *The Prelude to the Truman Doctrine British Policy in Greece 1944-1947*, as discussed.
7. See Carabott, P., 'Aspects of the Hellenisation of Greek Macedonia 1908-1959' for some broader issues, KAMBOS, Cambridge Papers in Modern Greek, 2001, No. 14.
8. See Michailidis, I., 'Searching for a Motherland: Slav-Macedonian Political Refugees in the People's Republic of Macedonia (1944-2003)', in Tzovias, D. (Ed.), *Greek Diaspora and Migration since 1700* (Farnham, 2009), p. 73 ff.
9. A priority was the collection for oral history testimony about wartime experiences and the production of history books and school textbooks based on the memories. See 'Archives of Macedonia', Skopje, folio 946. Ex 'Greek' exiles were later on important in forming the Institute of History in Skopje. By the next generation a quite disproportionate proportion of RM historians were of Greek family origin or had some Greek-origin component in their families. Also, 'Osloboditelnata vojna vo Zapadna Makedonija 1941–1944', Ivanovski, V., *Institute of History* (Skopje, 1973), and 'Hronologija na nastinate vo Prespa 1912–1944', Ivanovski, V., *Chronology of the Events in Prespa (1912–1944)* (Bitola, 1995).
10. For the history of the ancient juniper trees (*Juniperetum excelsae*) around Prespa, see http//www.LIFE12NAT/GR/539-JUN EX project.
11. Many of the American staff were ex-New Deal development experts with experience of fighting the Depression in areas such as the western US dustbowl states.
12. For a rosy-tinted discussion of the demographic and social situation in the western Macedonian village of Kotta/*Roulia*, just south-east of Lesser Prespa lake, as it

appeared in the immediate post-junta period, see McNeill, W., *The Metamorphosis of Greece since World War II* (Chicago, 1978), p. 196 ff. McNeill notes, significantly, that although a visiting and non-domiciled American functionary and academic, he had been prevented from returning to visit the village by the Greek army in 1966, although he had been able to do so ten years before. The section of the text about Kotta/*Roulia* in the Civil War years when O'Neill was a relief worker is in essence an apologia for contemporary US policy and probably overestimates the role of foreign remittances in the local economy. He states, that 'instead of speaking Slavic, the men of the village preferred Greek', when in reality the Macedonian and Bulgarian languages had been outlawed as a result of US-leveraged Greek government policy and speaking either language was a criminal offence.

13 Yonovski, C., *Prespa* (Skopje, 2000), p. 15.
14 Catsadorakis, G., *Prespa au Coeur des Balkans* (Paris, 2009), p. 49.
15 Report by the Association of Macedonians in Poland, *What Europe Has Forgotten: The Struggle of the Aegean Macedonians* (Five Dock, NSW, 1995).
16 It was amended in 1985 under the then PASOK government to allow 'Greeks' to return and in theory recover property but excluded those with a Macedonian identity. Although PASOK genuinely sought to solve the problems by new liberal legislation in practice little often changed as officials in northern Greece continued to work within the old legal framework.
17 For a partial but well-researched and generally accurate picture of the situation by the end of the 1980s, as far as Macedonian exiles are concerned, which is highly critical of Greek policy, see Oxford Helsinki Human Rights group report 'Macedonian Minorities: The Slav Macedonians of Northern Greece and the Treatment of Minorities in the Republic of Macedonia', Oxford, 1994, written by Noel Malcolm, Jonathan Sunley and Mark Almond. For conventional narrative, Mackridge, P. and Yannakis, E. (Ed.), *Ourselves and Others: The Development of a Greek Macedonian Cultural Identity since 1913* (Oxford, 1997), which contains interesting papers most of which in essence reinforce traditional Greek nationalist thinking on the Macedonian Question, and Brown, K., *The Past in Question: Modern Macedonia and the Uncertainties of Nation* (Princeton, 2003), focussed on the history of Krushevo in RM/FYROM, and Brown, K. and Hamilakis, Y. (Ed.), *The Usable Past Greek Metahistories* (Lanham and Oxford, 2003).
18 For an interesting Korca/Prespa region Vlach family history, see Balamaci, N., 'Albania in the 1990's: A Travel Memoir and Oral History', *Journal of the Hellenic Diaspora* 19, no. 2 (1993): 121 ff.
19 Kolisevski, L., *Social and Political Development in the People's Republic of Macedonia* (Belgrade, 1959), 25 ff.
20 British scholars played a central part in this process, particularly Oxford Professor of Slavonic Philology Anne Pennington who was an avid collector of Macedonian songs and folklore, and also the independent scholars and translators Peggy and Graham Reid.
21 See Veremis, T. and Koliopoulos, J., *Greece the Modern Sequel* (London, 2002), p. 305, and Kofos, E., *Communism and Nationalism in Macedonia* (Thessaloniki, 1964).
22 Veremis and Koliopoulos, *Greece the Modern Sequel*, p. 306. After the coup in 1967, Athens initially curtailed most border crossings by Yugoslavs and cross-border Macedonian contacts, although there was little they could do about foreign-based people using their Australian, Canadian or American passports on summer vacation family visits.

23 For the development and political meaning of tourism within socialist Yugoslavia, see Grandits, H. and Taylor, K. (Ed.), *Yugoslavia's Sunny Side: A History of Tourism in Socialism (1950-1980)* (Budapest, 2010).
24 For background and the relationships between British policy towards Greece in the junta period and in the previous generation, see Maragkou, K., *'Britain, Greece and the Colonels, 1967-74: Between Pragmatism and Human Rights* (London, 2019).
25 Conscripts from a 'bad biography' background in Greek Macedonia were not generally allowed direct access to weapons or any weapons training when conscripts in the Greek army but were confined to activity such as truck driving, canteen work and other similar occupations (interview with ex-National Service recruit, Psarades, 1998).
26 Kofos, E., *Greece and the Balkans in the 70's and 80's* (ELIAMEP, Athens, 1991), p. 3ff.
27 For the wider background, see Nikolakakis, M., 'The Colonels on the Beach: Tourism Policy during the Greek Military Dictatorship (1967-1974)', *Journal of Modern Greek Studies* 35, no. 2 (October 2017): 425-50.
28 Enver Hoxha seems to have taken an interest in the Macedonian minority at this time, stating in his speech to the 7th Congress of the Albanian Party of Labour (communist party) in 1975 that he accepted there were between '3000 to 4000 inhabitants of the nine villages of Prespa'. These numbers are disputed by Skopje academics and writers and governments. See Budimovski, D., *Makedontsite vo AlbanijaNIP* (Skopje, 1993). For the wider area, see Ivanovski, V., *Hronologija na Nastanite vo Prespa 1912-1944* (Bitola, 1995).
29 In *Macedonian Greece* (London, 1982), p. 87.
30 Ref Catsadorakis, *Prespa au Coeur des Balkans*, p. 23.
31 Thessaloniki, IMHA, 1976.

Chapter 10

1 *South Slav Journal* 18, no 1-2: 67-8, Spring-Summer 1997, p. 54.
2 For a detailed account of the end of communist rule in Albania see: 'The Albanians-A modem History, Miranda Vickers, London, 2014' and: '*Albania from Anarchy to a Balkan Identity*, Miranda Vickers and James Rettifer, London, 1997.'
3 Interview, author with Lambe Arnaudov, president of VMRO-DPMNE in Ohrid, 28 July 1992. Arnaudov was at pains to point out that VMRO was split into different factions over what to do about they saw as Greek aggression towards their state and that he personally did not believe military capacity in Ohrid was necessary. He stated, 'When the federal (Yugoslav) army left Macedonia, there was a period without border protection. We have no real army yet, only a few young people, with few guns. We are not dangerous for Greece.' Local IMRO protection committees looked for support to Bulgaria at that time but the internal crisis there at the end of communism precluded much active interest at non-governmental level. For a traditional viewpoint, see Gotsev, D., *New National Liberation Struggle in Vardar Macedonia 1944-1991*, Macedonian Scientific Institute, Sofia, 1999.
4 Jean GARDIN University of Paris X – Nanterre, France. *The Tri-National Prespa Park in Albania, Greece and Macedonia (FYROM): Using Environment to Define the New Boundaries of the European Union*, 1 July 2015. The current situation is based on European Union Water management Directive 2000, 'Revolutionising Water

Management in the European Union', Brussels, 2000, also https://halshs.archives-overtes.fr/halshs-01170554, p. 8.

For more general issues involving the development of international law: Louka, E., *Water Law and Policy Governance without Frontiers* (New York, 2018). Louka is a cogent critic of the role of Athens government in Prespa developments. On p. 202 he notes, 'Greece is typified by a legislative culture and many rules and procedures are prevalent in the public sector when sometimes one gets the impression that bureaucracy exists for the sake of bureaucracy ... seen in terms of its approach to the EU Greece could be characterized as a reluctant follower. Reluctant followers are states that do not have the capacity to implement European policies.' If this is the case with Greece, how much more it is the situation with neighbouring states involved in the Prespa project such as Albania and FYROM/RM.

5 Ibid.
6 PrespaNet_Review-of-Conservation-Efforts-April-2017.
7 Jean GARDIN University of Paris X – Nanterre, France. The Tri-National Prespa Park in Albania, Greece and Macedonia (FYROM): Using Environment to Define the New Boundaries of the European Union. 1 July 2015. https://halshs.archives-overtes.fr/halshs-01170554, p. 1.
8 See *The Guardian*, London, 24 August 2019. Keller's thinking, and that of other Swiss environmentalists and new development thinkers, focusses strongly on local control, where, of course, the Swiss system of local cantonal decision making and referendums provides a framework for democracy that is often absent in all three riparian Prespa nations
9 Ibid., p. 10.
10 Ibid.
11 The Ramsar Convention on Wetlands of International Importance especially as Waterfowl Habitat is an international treaty for the conservation and sustainable use of wetlands. It is also known as the Convention on Wetlands. It is named after the city of Ramsar in Iran, where the Convention was signed in 1971.
12 Report of the Second Regular Meeting of the Prespa Park Coordinating Committee, Psarades, 19–20 November 2001, p. 3.
13 www.eng.auth.gr/mattas/17_1_5pdf. *Small Women's Cooperatives in Less Favoured and Mountainous Areas under Economic Instability*. F. Chatzitheodoridis, 2016.
14 www.eng.auth.gr/mattas/17_1_5pdf. *Small Women's Cooperatives in Less Favoured and Mountainous Areas under Economic Instability*. F. Chatzitheodoridis, 2016.
15 EU-funded cultural activity took off for a while in the mid-1990s, the time of highest EU regional influence, as in a poetry festival at Kallithea, 'Balkan Poets in the Land of Prespes', publication, Thessaloniki, 1997. Attendance was very small. Also '1997-1998', 'Eurobalkan Asylum for Poetry', Kallithea, Prespa, Thessaloniki, 1997.
16 Jean Gardin. The Tri-National Prespa Park in Albania, Greece and Macedonia (FYROM): Using Environment to Define the New Boundaries of the European Union. Borders of the European Union: Strategies of Crossing and Resistance, July 2015, p. 16.
17 See documents and analysis published by the UK Ministry of Defence Conflict Studies Research Centre (www.mod.csrc), the International Crisis Group (www.crisisgroup.org) and for the immediate post-conflict period 'Ohrid and Beyond', Institute of War and Peace Reporting', London, 2002, Brown, K. (Ed.) (and others), paper Pettifer, J., 'Macedonia at a Crossroads', p. 7 ff, and the publications of Blerim Reka at the South East European University in Tetovo.
18 Poulton, H., *Who Are the Macedonians?* (Indiana, 1995), p. 147.
19 *Nova Makedonija*, Skopje, 5 March 1995.
20 *Australian Macedonian Weekly*, Melbourne, 24 March 1998.

21 See James Pettifer and Miranda Vickers, *The Albanian Question – Reshaping the Balkans* (I.B. Tauris, 2009), for a description of the 1997 to 1998 armed uprising that brought Albania to the brink of civil war, pitting northerners against southerners, left wing versus right wing.
22 *Australian Macedonian Weekly*, Melbourne, 26 August 1997.
23 Ibid.
24 Paskal Milo: 'The Balkans' magazine, 18 ed., 2001, pp. 5–7.
25 Hugh Poulton: The Balkans – Minorities and States in Conflict, London, 1994, p. 175.
26 Danforth, Loring M., The Macedonian Minority of Northern Greece, www.culturalsurvival.org, June 1995. For a Greek view, Kofos, E. *National Heritage and National Identity in Twentieth Century Macedonia* (ELIAMEP, Athens, 1991). After the Macedonian independence referendum in September 1991, the language issue quickly became a divisive issue between Skopje and Sofia, see Kocev, I., Kronsteiner, O. and Alexandrov, I., *The Fathering of What Is Known as the Macedonian Literary Language* (Sofia, 1994), and Stammler, H., *What Is the National Character of the Macedonian Slavs?* (IMRO-Union of the Macedonian Brotherhoods in Bulgaria: Sofia, 1991).
27 For background, see 'Macedonian Minorities: The Slav Macedonians of Northern Greece and the Treatment of Minorities in the Republic of Macedonia'. A report issued by the British Helsinki Human Rights Group, Oxford, 1994 (author Malcolm, N., with additional material from Sunley J. and Almond M.), Op. Cit., and 'Testimonies', Macedonian Cultural Association, Florina, 1991. This organization was established in Florina on 18 April 1990.
28 Ibid.
29 See *Australian Macedonian Herald* newspaper, Melbourne, particularly for the years 1993 to 1995.
30 Hugh Poulton: The Balkans – Minorities and States in Conflict, 1994, p. 179.
31 Basic Data on the Hydrology of Lakes Ohrid and Prespa, www.researchgate.net, February 2007.
32 For a discussion of this seminal book and the bitter conflicts it caused when it was published, see review by Australian anthropologist Roger Just in the Times Literary Supplement, 13 February 1998.
33 Karakatsidou, A., *Fields of Wheat, Hills of Blood Passages to Nationhood in Greek Macedonia 1870–1990* (Chicago, 1997). The publication of the book and associated controversies caused a furore in most Modern Greek Studies departments in academia and widespread criticism of Cambridge University Press in the UK who had withdrawn it from publication, allegedly under government pressure. Although an outstanding scholarly work, particularly on the late Ottoman period in and around her chosen area of study in Langadhas Basin, the village of *Guvezna*/Assiros 30 miles north of Thessaloniki, the population composition of this region does not resemble most of northern Greek Macedonia, or Prespa and Ohrid regions, and the author does not convey fully the force of traditional national identities on the popular identity and imagination. It is also the work of an anthropologist and some views expressed on recent regional history depending on a limited range of secondary sources can be seen as inaccurate. She also underestimates the efficiency of the Greek school system and the Church in producing 'Greeks' from recent immigrants, at least in those days although it is questionable if that is still the case now.
34 The Water Level Fall of Lake Megali Prespa (N Greece): An Indicator of Regional Water Stress Driven by Climate Change and Amplified by Water Extraction? http://http//adsabs.harvard.edu/abs/2014EGUGA.16.3878V

Chapter 11

1. See 'Ohrid and Beyond', Institute of War and Peace Reporting (London, 2002), papers by Pettifer, J., 'Macedonia at a Crossroads', p. 7, and Popetrevski, V. and Latifi, V., 'The Ohrid Framework Agreement Negotiations', p. 53.
2. For background, see Danforth, L., 'Claims to Macedonian Identity: The Macedonian Question and the Break-up of Yugoslavia', *Anthropology Today* 9, no. 4(1993): 3–10. For a US view prioritizing security analysis, Liotta, P. and Jebb, C., *Mapping Macedonia Idea and Identity* (Westport, CN, 2003).
3. Commenting on the letter Greek government spokesman Theodoros Roussopoulos said Gruevski 'only repeated the well known and unacceptable statements regarding non-existent minorities', quoted in *Kosovo Daily News*, Prishtina, 18 January 2009.
4. Kassabova, K., *To the Lake: A Balkan Journey of War and Peace* (London, 2020), p. 337.
5. For background, from a Skopje point of view, Mitrev, D., *Pirin Macedonia* (Skopje, 1973). Also Ivanovski, O. and Korobar, P. (Ed.), *The Historical Truth The Progressive Social Circles in Pirin Macedonia in the Macedonian National Question 1896–1956* (Skopje, 1983). The main organization, IMRO-Ilinden, was banned in Sofia in 1992.
6. Chandler, G., *The Divided Land: An Anglo-Greek Tragedy* (London, 1959), p. 46.
7. See UNEP publication, 'Climate Change in the Western Balkans', Geneva, 2012, which stressed the influence of declining rainfall and more frequent droughts on the southern Balkan lakes and Kuusisto. K The Influence of Climate Change on European Lakes, with a special emphasis on the Balkan region, 'Balvois' Ohrid, May 2004 Also Van Gelder, L, World Bank publication 'Its time for action on climate risk in the Balkans', worldbank.org/en/news/opinion 2018/09/17, and Centre for Climate Adaption, Athens 'Climate Change Greece' 17/9/2020, and Encol, A. and Randhir, T., 'Climatic Change Inputs on the Ecohydrology of Mediterranean Watersheds', *Climate Change* 114: 319–41.
8. The history of tourism in Yugoslavia has been a barometer of external relations with the country and social change within Titoist Yugoslavia itself. See Grandits, H. and Taylor, K., *Yugoslavia's Sunny Side: A History of Tourism in Socialism (1950s–1980s)* (Budapest, 2010). As early as 1949 workers were showing a resistance to going to Ohrid and other state tourist centres in Macedonia, and insisted on going to seaside resorts on the Adriatic coast.
9. For a mainstream Greek view on the need for a new vocabulary to try to move the Macedonian Question forward in this period, see Gounaris, B., 'Macedonian Questions', *South East European and Black Sea Studies* 2, no. 3 (September 2002): 63–94.
10. There is an extensive literature on the dialogue between NATO and the then President of FYROM/RM Kiro Gligorov (1917–2012) on refugee issues prior to the 1999 Kosovo war and then during it. Gligorov's 'Der Spiegel' interview (4/4/1994) is revealing on his thinking. Stokenovac army camp north of Skopje was made over the NATO in early 1998 and free passage granted to NATO vehicles on the Skopje-Thessaloniki highway. For the late president's own views in his memoirs, including details of alleged Greek government bribery and corruption attempts to persuade him to agree to change the name of the country, see Gligorov, K., *Makedonia* (Skopje, 2002). For the conventional wisdom of the time on the internal situation, see Paintin, K., 'States of Conflict: A Case Study on Conflict Prevention in Macedonia', Institute of Public Policy Research (London, 2008). For a mainstream Yugoslav view of the

situation of Macedonia in this period, see Dobrokovic, N., 'Yugoslavia and Macedonia as New Neighbours in the Balkans: Experiences and Perspectives', CSS Survey, Belgrade, Centre for Strategic Studies, No. 16 April 1997, p. 3.

11 For the role played within NATO operations by FYROM/RM troops long before the current membership controversy, see Rogers, A. and Hill, J., 'Operations in Iraq Point the Way for Macedonian Military Reform', *Jane's Intelligence Review*, 17 March 2004, p. 14. The authors comment, 'In practice, Macedonian troops are receiving training from US, UK, Greek and Turkish special forces, and individuals have trained with US special forces at Fort Bragg.'

12 For a view of the situation in 2008, Pettifer, J. 'Macedonia – Names, Nomenclaturas and NATO', ARAG, 08/04, Balkan Series, Defence Academy of the United Kingdom, Shrivenham, February 2008, http://www.defac.ac.uk/colleges/arag. The view put forward then that a forced name change would produce instability between Athens and Skopje and be destabilizing internally in both countries has been borne out by recent events over a decade later.

13 For a comprehensive analysis of the failings of the Prespa Agreement from the point of view of the United Nations special envoy in the fifteen-year long dialogue on the name between Athens and Skopje, see Nimetz, M. 'The Macedonian Name Dispute: The Macedonian Question Resolved?', in *Nationalities Papers* 48, no. 2 (2020): 205–14, Cambridge, 2020. NATO planners fears also seem to have focussed on possible terrorism within Greece, see 'Kathermerini', Athens 27/09/20 story 'Weapons and ammunition found buried near Kastoria', near the village of Dispilio.

14 Ref http://www.mfa.gr/index2=id 17247.

15 For the nature of the opening in Eastern Europe to Eurasia, see Frankopan, P., 'The Silk Roads: A New History of the World, London, 2016' and Di Cosmo, N. and Maas, M. (Ed.), *Empires and Exchanges in Eurasian Late Antiquity Rome, China, Iran and the Steppe ca. 250–750* (Cambridge, 2018).

16 A concerted NATO-financed press campaign in Western Europe was organized to exclude, as far as possible, critical views of the Prespa deal in the media and to present a highly exaggerated view of the role of Russia in opposing it. Considerable effort was put into obscuring the identity of the London lawyer from 'Matrix' legal chambers who had drafted much of the document, along with American opposite numbers. This background indicates the assumptions of the world of the Bosnian and Kosovo wars transference into the quite different situation of the identity of Macedonia and Macedonians. The 4 to 5 per cent Roman Catholic lobby in Skopje and their foreign associates elsewhere were influential, as a small minority in a majority Orthodox and Islamic society. See Tisdall, S., 'Moscow Out-thinks, Outspends and Outmanoeuvres the West over Vote on Macedonia's Name', *The Guardian*, London, 2 October, 2018. Also 'Russia will exploit Macedonian name row in the Balkans', Oxford Analytica Daily Brief, 6 August 2018 for a balanced view. The Oxford publication rightly points out that the deal asks much more from the Skopje state than Athens, although it does not explore how much of the Prespa document is unenforceable.

17 'Final Agreement for the Settlement of the Differences as Described in the United Nations Security Council Resolutions B17 (1993) and B45 (1993), The termination of the Interim Accord of 1995, also the Establishment of a Strategic Partnership between the Parties', United Nations, New York, 12 June 2018. From the point of view of historians and students of regional history, perhaps the grossest distortion of history is to be found in Section 7 of the UN document, where there is no mention of the

medieval Bulgarian imperial origin and identity of many of the historic monuments in RM/FYROM or of the relationship of the Macedonian language to Bulgarian. The ancient and medieval heritages are depicted as exclusively Hellenic and there is no mention whatsoever in the document of the large Albanian minority in western FYROM/RM or the Christian or Islamic religions.

18 For a cogent analysis of the damage to the internal political life of the RM state and long-term Western interests caused by the Prespa process, see paper by Vankovska, B., 'A Critical Perspective on the Prespa Agreement: The Collateral Damages', Papers of the ECPR Conference, Wroclaw, Poland, 4th–8th September 2019 https//www.academia.edu/41407451/A_Critical_Perspective_on_the_Prespa_Agreement_on_the_Collateral_Damages. The case made reflects the similar criticisms of the processes by Princeton international law academic Richard Falk, where the human rights of the majority community in RM have been violated by NATO. For Falk's general approach, see Falk, R., *Human Rights and State Sovereignty* (New York, 1984).

19 For detail, see Vankovska, 'A Critical Perspective on the Prespa Agreement: The Collateral Damages'. Op. cit.

20 'The Independent', London, June 13th 2018 'Macedonian President refuses to sign deal with Greece'.

21 See London Times newspaper, 16 June 2018, report by Anthee Carassava, 'Greek PM faces confidence vote over deal to rename Macedonia'.

22 See 'The Greek Observer', 16 June 2018. For a general discussion of the Greek crisis and how society has been affected by it, see Sotiris, P., *Crisis, Movement, Strategy the Greek Experience* (Chicago, 2018), and Pettifer, J., *The Making of the Greek Crisis* (London, 2012).

23 London Times, 18 June 2019 'Sticks and Stones fly as Macedonia's name is too much for Greeks to bear'.

24 For a sometimes controversial discussion of the long history of competing empires and Great Powers in the Balkans, see Glenny, M., *The Balkans 1804–1999 Nationalism, War and the Great Powers* (London, 1999), in the following note, and more objective on some key issues, Mazower, M., *The Balkans* (London and New York, 2012).

25 Glenny, M., *The Balkans 1804–1999 Nationalism, War and the Great Powers*, p. 655.

26 Blanchard, P., *Blue Guide Yugoslavia* (London and New York, 1989), p. 399.

27 Speech to Athens demonstration, 21 January 2018. According to a report in the *New York Times*, 8 February 2018, Theodorakis stated in his speech 'The only solution, in my opinion, is to leave the people of Skopje believing in their own national myth while we remain faithful and unyielding with regard to the Greek nature of Macedonia'.

28 Kofos, E., 'Greek Policy Considerations over FYROM Independence and Recognition', in Pettifer, J. (Ed.), *The New Macedonian Question* (London and New York, 1998), p. 232. Also, Kofos, E., *Resurgent Irredentism Documents on Skopje Macedonian Nationalist Aspirations (1934–1992)* (Thessaloniki, 1993).

29 The official data indicates rapidly growing emigration of skilled and qualified people from Skope and the cities since the Prespa process began. This is also likely to underestimate the scale of the population movement given the number of citizens who hold foreign passports, usually either Swiss or German documents for many young people in the ethnic Albanian community, Bulgarian, Canadian or Australian passports among the majority community. The process is likely to have slowed considerably in 2020 as a result of the virus pandemic.

30 Kassabova, K., *To the Lake: A Balkan Journey of War and Peace* (London, 2020), p. 350.

Appendix A

1 A summary of generally accepted usage. Local traditions and official/colloquial usage varied widely.
2 In Vlach, Curceaua.
3 In Ottoman times, also known as Golem Pazar.

Appendix B

1 Also known as *Grintzaroi* (medieval Albanian origin).

Select bibliography

Aarbakke, V. *Ethnic Rivalries and the Quest for Macedonia 1870-1913*, Boulder, 2003.
Abbott, G. *Macedonian Folklore*, Cambridge, 1903.
Abbott, G. *The Tale of a Tour in Macedonia*, London, 1903.
Allen, H. *Come Over into Macedonia*, New Brunswick, NJ, 1943.
Alexander, G.M. *The Prelude to the Truman Doctrine British Policy in Greece 1944-1947*, Oxford, 1982.
Aliu, A. *Prespa ne Australi*, Skopje, 2004.
Anastasakis, P. *The Church in Greece under Axis Occupation*, New York, 2015.
Ancel, J. *La Macedoine: Son Evolution Contemporaire*, Paris, 1930.
Angelou, D. *Bogomilstvoto*, Sofia, 1993.
Anon. *Byzantine Sources for the History of the Peoples of Yugoslavia*, Belgrade, 1966.
Anon. *Macedonia Handbook Prepared under the Direction of the Historical Section of the Foreign Office*, London, 1918.
Anon. *Les Femmes Grecque au Combat*. Athens, 1975.
Anon. *Statisques des Ecoles de Turquie d'Europe'Publications du Patriarchate Oecumenique'*, Constantinople, 1902.
Anon. *KE tou KKE Demokratikos Stratos Ellades*. Athens, 2016.
Antoljak, S. *Samuel and hit State*, Skopje, 1985.
Apostolski, M. (Ed.), *From the Past of the Macedonian People*, Skopje, 1969.
Apostolski, M. (and others), *1000 Ans de L'Insurrection des Comitopoules et de La Creation de L'Etat de Samuel*, Skopje, 1971.
Apostolski, M. and Jovanovic, M., *Historioraphie de Macedonia 1945-1970*, Skopje, 1972.
Austin, R. *Founding a Balkan State Albania's Experiment with Democracy 1920-1925*, Toronto, 2012.
Baerentzen, L. (Ed.), *British Reports on Greece 1943-44*, Copenhagen, 1982.
Bakalopoulos, K. *O Bopeioe Elleniemos (1878-1894)*, Thessaloniki, 1983.
Balabanov, A. *Ohrid*, Zagreb, 1987.
Balakovska, K. (and others), *Crisis in Macedonia Minority Politics in Southeast Europe*, Rome, 2002.
Balamaci, N. *Born to Assimilate Thoughts about the Vlachs*, New York, 2003.
Banarji, J. *Agrarian Change in Late Antiquity Gold, Labour and Aristocratic Domination*, Oxford, 2001.
Barker, E. *Macedonia Its Place in Balkan Power Politics*, London, 1950.
Barros, J. *The Corfu Incident of 1923*, Princeton, 1965.
Bedlek, E. *Imagined Communities in Greece and Turkey Trauma and Population Exchanges under Ataturk*, London, 2016.
Birtles, B. *Exiles in the Aegean*, London, 1938.
Bivell, V. *From War to Whittlesea Oral Histories of Macedonian Child Refugees*, Melbourne VI, 1999.
Boskovic, A. *The Other Side of the Window: Gender and Difference in Prespa, Republic of Macedonia*, Brasilia, 2000.
Boskovska, N. *Das Jugoslawische Makedonien 1918-1941 Eine Randregion zwischen Repression und Integration*, Vienna, 2009.

Bowman, S. *Jewish Resistance in Wartime Greece*, London and Portland, 2006.
Brailsford, H. *Macedonia Its Races and Their Future*, London, 1906.
Brancoff, D. *La Macedoine et sa Population Chretienne*, Paris, 1905.
Breuilly, J. *Nationalism and the State*, Manchester, 1993.
Bridge, F. *Austro-Hungarian Documents Relating to the Macedonian Struggle, 1896-1912*, Thessaloniki, 1976.
Brown, A. *Yugoslavia Life and Landscape*, London, 1954.
Brown, K. *The Past in Question Modern Macedonia and the Uncertainties of Nation*, Princeton, 2003.
Brown, P. *The Making of Late Antiquity*, Harvard, 1978.
Brown, P. *Through the Eye of a Needle*, Princeton, 2012.
Browning, R. *Byzantium and the Bulgarians*, London, 1975.
Broussalis, P. *The Prespa National Park*, Athens, 1975.
Buxton, N. *Europe and the Turks*, London, 1907.
Cameron, A. *The Mediterranean World in Late Antiquity AD 395-700*, Abingdon, 2012.
Cameron, A. *The Byzantines*, Oxford, 2006.
Capper, S. *The Shores and Cities of the Boden See*, London, 1881.
Capuano-Bogevska, S. *Les Eglises de la Region des Lacs Ohrid et Prespa*, Turnhout, 2015.
Carpenter, T. *The Miss Stone Affair America's First Modern Hostage Crisis*, New York, 2003.
Carr, J. *The Defence and Fall of Greece 1940-41*, Barnsley, 2013.
Carrier, E. *Water and Grass A Study in the Pastoral Economy of Southern Europe*, Glasgow, 1932.
Cary, M. *The Geographic Background of Greek and Roman History*, Oxford, 1949.
Cassavert, I. *Hellas in the Balkan Wars*, London, 1914.
Casson, S. *Steady Drummer*, London, 1935.
Chandler, G. *The Divided Land an Anglo-Greek Tragedy*, London, 1959.
Chepreganov, T. (Ed.), *History of the Macedonian People*, Skopje, 2008.
Chiclet, C. and Lory, B. *La Republique de Macedoine*, Paris and Montreal, 1998.
Chretien, J.-P. *The Great Lakes of Africa Two Thousand Years of History*, New York, 2003.
Close, D. (Ed.), *The Greek Civil War 1943-1950 Studies of Polarisation*, London, 1993.
Clucas, L. *The Byzantine Legacy in Eastern Europe*, Boulder. co, 1988.
Condit, D. *Greece A Case Study in Guerrilla War US Army Special Warfare Research Division*, Washington DC, 1961.
Cousinery, E. *Voyage dans la Macedoine*, Paris, 1831.
Crivelli, A. *Lake Prespa, North West Greece A Unique Balkan Wetland (Studies in Hydrobiology)*, Geneva, 1997.
Crosland, D. and Constance, D. *Macedonian Greece*, London, 1982.
Curcic, D. *Architecture in the Balkans from Diocletian to Suliman the Magnificent*, Princeton, 2014.
Curta, F. *The Edinburgh History of the Greeks C.500 to 1050*, Edinburgh, 2011.
Curta, F. *Borders, Barriers and Ethnogenesis: Frontiers in Late Antiquity and the Middle Ages*, Turnhout, 2005.
Curtright, L. *Muddle, Indecision and Setback British Policy and the Balkan States August 1914 to the Inception of the Dardanelles Campaign*, Thessaloniki, 1986.
Cvijic, J. *Remarques sur L'Ethnographie de la Macedoine*, Paris, 1907.
Cvijic, J. *La Peninsula Balkanique*, Paris, 1918.
Dacie, A. *Instead of the Brier Concerning Yugoslavs*, London, 1949.
Dakin, D. *The Greek Struggle in Macedonia 1897-1913*, Thessaloniki, 1966.
Dakin, D. *The Unification of Greece 1770-1923*, London, 1972.
Danforth, L. and Van Boeschoten, R. *Children of the Greek Civil War Refugees and the Politics of Memory*, Chicago, 2012.

Deliso, C. *Hidden Macedonia*, London, 2007.
Dervishi, N. *Ethnokultura e Fushegropes se Ohrit*, Skopje, 2005.
Destani, B. and Elsie, R. (Ed.), *The Balkan Wars British Consular Reports from Macedonia in the Final Years of the Ottoman Empire*, London, 2014.
Destani, B. and Elsie, R. *The Macedonian Question in the Eyes of British Journalists (1899-1919)*, London, 2015.
Dimov, D. *The Macedonian National Question (1875-1924)*, Skopje, 1986.
Douchy, C. *La Guerre Turko-Grecque de 1897*, Paris, 1898.
Dury, C. *Rural Economy and Country Life in the Medieval West*, Columbia, SC, 1968.
Dzino, D. *Illyricum in Roman Politics 229BC-AD 68*, Cambridge, 2010.
Eudes, D. *The Kapetanios Partisans and Civil War in Greece 1943-1949*, London, 1972.
Evtimoff, S. *Les Serbs et la Macedoine*, Geneva, 1929.
Evyenidou, E. (and others), *The Monuments of Prespa*, Athens, 1991.
Falls, C. *Military Operations: Macedonia*, London, 1933.
Fine, J. *The Late Medieval Balkans*, Ann Arbor, 1985.
Fine, J. *The Early Medieval Balkans*, Ann Arbor, 1991.
Foivou, G. *History of the Second Civil War 1945-1949 (3 Vol)*, Athens, 1979.
Frary, L. *Russia and the Making of the Modern Greek Identity 1821-1844*, Oxford, 2015.
Frayn, J. *Subsistence Farming in Roman Italy*, London, 1979.
Frazee, C. *The Orthodox Church and Independent Greece 1821-1852*, Cambridge, 1969.
Friedman, V., Janev, G., Vlachov, G. *Macedonia and Its Questions Origins,Margins, Ruptures and Continuity*, Berlin, 2020.
Geist, M. *Mountain Sheep*, Chicago, 1971.
Gerolymatos, A. *An International Civil War-Greece, 1943-1949*, New Haven, 2006.
Giles, F. *Boundary Work in the Balkans*, London, 1930.
Gingeras, R. *Fall of the Sultanate The Great War and the End of the Ottoman Empire*, Oxford, 2016.
Glenny, M. *The Balkans 1804-1999 Nationalism, War and the Great Powers*, London, 1999.
Gounaris, B. (and others), *The Events of 1903 in Macedonia*, Thessaloniki, 1993.
Gounaris, B. *Steam over Macedonia,1870-1912*, Boulder, 1993.
Grazdenova-Bitrakova, V. *Golem Grad Prespa I and Prespa II*, Skopje, 2011 and 2015.
Greene, M. *A Shared World Christians and Muslims in the Early Modern Mediterranean*, Princeton, 2000.
Greene, M. (Ed.), *Minorities in the Ottoman Empire*, Princeton, 2005.
Grigorovitch, V. *Esquisse de Voyage dans la Turquie d'Europe*, Moscow, 1840.
Grunbaum, I. *Escape through the Balkans*, Lincon, NE, 1996.
Hacisalihoglu, M. *Die Jungturken und die Mazedonische Frage (1890-1918)*, Munich, 2003.
Hahev, C. *Makedonija 1941*, Sofia, 2003.
Haldon, J. *The State and the Tributary Mode of Production*, London, 1993.
Hammond, N. *A History of Macedonia, Historical Geography and Prehistory*, New York, 1981.
Hammond, N. *Venture into Greece With the Guerrillas 1943-1944*, London, 1983.
Hammond, N. *The Macedonian State Origins, Institutions and History*, Oxford, 1989.
Hammond, N. *The Allied Military Mission and the Resistance in West Macedonia*, Thessaloniki, 1993.
Harper, K. *The Fate of Rome*, Princeton, 2017.
Harris, D. and Hillman, G. (Ed.), *Foraging and Farming The Evolution of Plant Exploitation*, London, 1989.
Hart, J. *Women in the Greek Resistance 1941-1964*, Cornell, 1996.
Hassiotis, I. *Modern and Contemporary Macedonia*, Thessaloniki,1992.
Heather, P. *Goths and Romans 332-489*, Oxford, 1991.

Heydemarck, H. *War Flying in Macedonia*, London, 1924.
Hirschon, R. (Ed.), *Crossing the Aegean A Study of the 1923 Population Exchange between Greece and Turkey*, New York, 2003.
Hollingworth, C. *There's a German Just Behind Me*, London, 1943.
Horden, P. and Purcell, N. *The Corrupting Sea A Study of Mediterranean History*, Oxford, 2000.
Horden, P. and Nurcell, N. *The Boundless Sea Writing Mediterranean History*, Abingdon, 2020.
Iatrides, J. *Revolt in Athens The Greek Communist 'Second Round', 1944-1945*, Princeton, 1972.
Iatrides, J. and Wrigley, L (Ed.), *Greece at the Crossroads The Civil War and Its Legacy*, Philadelphia, 1995.
Inalcik, H. *An Economic and Social History of the Ottoman Empire 1300-1600*, Cambridge, 1997.
Ismirlaidou, A. *Koritsa 1850-1908*, Thessaloniki, 1997.
Ivanovski, V. *Chronology of the Events in Prespa (1912-1944)*, Bitola, 1995.
Ivanovski, V. *The National Liberation War in Western Macedonia (1941-1944)*, Skopje, 1973.
Jashkovski, D. *Bogomilism in Macedonia*, Skopje, 1975.
Jelavich, B. *Russia's Balkan Entanglements 1806-1914*, Cambridge, 1991.
Jovanovic, C. (and others) *Region Prespa*, Skopje, 2014.
Jovanovski, B. *Prespa*, Bitola, 1985.
Judah, T. *The Serbs*, Yale, 1997.
Kahl, T. *Ethniztat und raumlichte uerteilung der aroumunen in sudosteuropa*, Munster, 1999.
Karadedos, V. (and others), *Prespes Greek Traditional Architecture*, Athens, 1990.
Karamitsos, D. *History of the Greek New Territories,1897-1941*, Thessaloniki, 2016.
Karavidas, K. *Agrotika*, Athens, 1931.
Kassabova, K. *Border A Journey to the Edge of Europe*, London, 2017.
Kassabova, K. *To the Lake A Balkan Journey of War and Peace*, London, 2020.
Katsadorakis, G. *Mia Historia gia te Physe - kai ton Anthropo*, Prespa, 1996.
Kemp, P. *Healing Ritual Studies in the Technique and Tradition of the South Slavs*, London, 1935.
Kofos, E. *Nationalism and Communism in Macedonia*, Thessaloniki, 1964.
Kofos, E. *The Impact of the Macedonian Question on Civil Conflict in Greece (1943-1949)*, Athens, 1949.
Kofos, E. *Resurgent Irredentism Documents on Skopje 'Macedonian' Nationalist Aspirations (1934-1992)*, Thessaloniki, 1993.
Kofina, G.N. *Ta Oikonomia tis Makedonias*, Athens, 1914.
Kolisevski, L *Social and Political Development in the People's Republic of Macedonia*, Beograd, 1959.
Koliopoulos, J. *Plundered Loyalties Axis Occupation and Civil Strife in Greek West Macedonia, 1941-1949*, London, 1999.
Kolonomos, J. *Manastir without Jews Recollections of a Jewish Partisan in Macedonia*, New York, 2008.
Kondis, B. and Sfetas, S. *Emfilos Polemos*, Thessaloniki, 1999.
Koposkov, E. *Strana bes Nazvania*, Moscow, 2013.
Kornakov, D. *A Guide to the Macedonian Monasteries*, Skopje, 2009.
Kontogiorgi, E., *Population Exchange in Greek Macedonia The Rural Settlement of Refugees, 1922-1930*, Oxford, 2006.
Koroloff, L. *Drenoveni The Life and Decline of a Macedonian Village*, Pickering, ON, 2016.

Kos, M. *Appian and Illyricum*, Ljubljana, 2005.
Koukoudis, A. *Studies on the Vlachs*, Thessaloniki, 2003.
Jancar-Webster, B. *Women and Revolution in Yugoslavia, 1941-1945*, Denver, 1990.
Jovanovic, B. *Prespa*, Bitola, 1989.
Laiou, A. *Peasant society in the Late Byzantine Empire*, Princeton, 1977.
Laiou, A. (Ed.), *Economic History of Byzantium*, Washington DC, 2002.
Lafanovski, V. and Stoyjanovic-Lafanovska, l. *The Exodus of the Macedonians from Greece Women's Narratives about World War II and their Exodus*, Skopje, 2002.
Lampe, J. and Jackson. M. *Balkan Economic Hisotry 1550-1950*, Bloomington, 1982.
Leake, W. *Travels in Northern Greece (4 Vols)*, London, 1835.
Lees, L. *Keeping Tito Afloat The United States, Yugoslavia and the Cold War*, University Park, PA, 1997.
Ligeros, S. *En Onomati tis Makedonias*, Athens, 2008.
Lithoxou, D. *The Greek Anti-Macedonian Struggle 1903-1905*, Skopje, 2007.
Little, L. (Ed.), *The Pestilence of 541-750*, Cambridge, 2007.
Livianos, D. *The Macedonian Question Britain and the Southern Balkans 1939-1949*, Oxford, 2008.
Ljubovic, M. (and others), *Agriculture in Yugoslavia*, Sarajevo, 1968.
Loizos, P. and Papataxiarchis, E. (Eds), *Contested Identities: Gender and Kinship in Modern Greece*, Princeton, 1991.
Lory, B. *La Ville Balkanissime Bitola 1800-1918*, Istanbul, 2015.
Louka, E. *Water Law and Policy: Governance without Frontiers*, Oxford, 2008.
Lowry, H. *The Shaping of the Ottoman Balkans 1350-1550*, Istanbul, 2008.
MacDermott, M. *Freedom or Death The Life of Gotse Delchev*, London, 1978.
MacDermott, M. *For Freedom and Perfection The Life of Yane Sandansky*, London, 1988.
Maisson, A. *Documents, Contes et Chansons Slaves del'Albanie du Sud*, Paris, 1936.
Macfie, A. *The Straits Question 1908-36*, Thessaloniki, 1993.
Mangalakova, T. *Ethnic Bulgarians in Mala Prespa and Golo Brdo*, Sofia, 2004.
Marriott, J. *The Eastern Question A Study in European Diplomacy*, London, 1917.
Marantzidis, N. *Dimokratikos Stratos Elladas 1946-1949*, Athens, 2010.
Mather, W. *Muckydonia 1917-1919*, Ilfracombe, 1979.
Mazower, M. *Inside Hitler's Greece The Experience of Occupation 1941-44*, New Haven, 1993.
Mazower, M. (Ed) *After the War was over*, Princeton, 2000.
Mazower, M. *Salonika City of Ghosts Christians, Muslims and Jews, 1430-1950*, London, 2004.
McNeill, W. *The Greek Dilemma*, London, 1947.
McNeill, W. *The Metamorphosis of Greece since World War II*, Chicago, 1978.
Micheff, D. *La Serbie et la Bulgarie devant L'Opinion Publique'*, Berne, 1918.
Mitrev, D. *Pirin Macedonia*, Skopje, 1962.
Mitrev, T. *The United States of America and Macedonia 1834-1945*, Sofia, 1999.
Mitrevski, D. *Skopje Fortress Kale From Prehistory to the Early Ancient Period*, Skopje, 2016.
Moutsopoulos, N. *The Churches of the Prefecture of Florina*, Thessaloniki, 1966.
Michalopoulos, A. (and others), *Makedonia kai Balkania Xenophobia kai Anaptyxi*, Athens, 1998.
Mikulcic, I. *Heraclea Lyncestis Ancient City in Macedonia*, Skopje, 2007.
Mischkova, D. *Beyond Balkanism: The Scholarly Politics of Region Making*, London, 2018.
Mullett, M. *Theophylact of Ohrid Reading the Letters of a Byzantine Archbishop*, Aldershot, 1997.
Murphey, R. *Ottoman Warfare 1500-1700*, New Brunswick, NJ, 1999.
Myers, E. *Greek Entanglement*, Gloucester, 1955.

Myers, W. *People of the Storm God Travels in Macedonia*, Oxford, 2005.
Nakovski, P. *Makedonski Depa bo Polska*, Skopje, 1987.
Nexhipi, R. *Prespa dhe Manastiri neper Shekuj*, Kercove, 2003.
Nicholovoski, A. (and others), *The Cultural Monuments of the Socialist Republic of Macedonia*, Skopje, 1971.
Nicholovski, Z. *The Macedonian Diaspora*, Skopje, 2015.
Nielsen, C. *Making Yugoslavs Identity in King Alexander's Yugoslavia*, Toronto, 2014.
Nitsiakos, V. (and others), *Balkan Border Crossings*, Berlin, 2008.
Nitsiakos, V. *On the Border Transborder Mobility, Ethnic Groups and Boundaries on the Greek-Albanian Frontier*, Berlin, 2010.
Obolensky, D. *The Bogomils*, Cambridge, 1951.
Obolensky, D. *The Byzantine Commonwealth*, New York, 1971.
Obrembski, J. *Poreche 1932–1933*, Skopje, 2009.
Palairet, M. *The Four Ends of the Greek Hyperinflation of 1941–1946*, Copenhagen, 2000.
Palairet, M. *Macedonia*, Newcastle, 2015.
Pallis, A. *Reconstruction in Greece since the Liberation*, London, 1947.
Palmer, A. *The Gardeners of Salonika*, New York, 1965.
Palmer, S. and King, R. *Yugoslav Communism and the Macedonian Question*, Hamden, CT, 1971.
Papacosma, S. *The Military in Greek Politics The 1909 Coup d'Etat*, Kent, OH, 1977.
Papagos, A. *The Battle of Greece 1940–1941*, Athens, 1949.
Papazoglou, F. *Les Villes de Macedonie a l'Epoque Romaine*, Paris, 1998.
Paravantes, S. *Anglo-American policy and the Cold War*, London, 2020.
Parveva, S. *Village, Town and People in the Ottoman Balkans, 16th-mid-19th Century*, Istanbul, 2010.
Patagalean, E. *Un Moyen Age Grec*, Paris, 2007.
Pelikanidou, S. *Byzantine and Metabyzantine Monuments in Prespa*, Thessaloniki, 1960.
Pentzopoulos, D. *The Balkan Exchange of Minorities and Its Impact on Greece*, Paris, 1962.
Perry, D., *The Politics of Terror The Macedonian Revolutionary Movements, 1893–1903*, Duke, NC, 1988.
Petroff, L. *Sojourners and Settlers The Macedonian Community in Toronto to 1940*, Toronto, 1995.
Pettifer, J. (Ed.), *The New Macedonian Question*, London, 1998.
Pettifer, J. *The Kosova Liberation Army Underground War to Balkan Insurgency 1948–2001*, London and New York, 2012.
Pettifer, J. *The Making of the Greek Crisis*, London, 2015.
Phillips, J. *Macedonia Warlords and Rebels in the Balkans*, London, 2014.
Popovic, P. *Serbian Macedonia A Historical Survey*, London, 1916.
Poulton, H. *Who Are the Macedonians?* Indiana, 1995.
Probichevich, S. *Macedonia Its People and History*, Pennsylvania, 1982.
Pyanka, V. *Toponomastics of the Ohrid-Prespa region*, Skopje, 1970.
Qira, Z. *Cell Number 31*, New York, 1970.
Rabdale, J. *The Great Illyrian Revolt Rome's Forgotten War in the Balkans, AD 6-9*, Philadelphia, 2019.
Racev, S. *Great Britain and the Resistance Movement in the Balkans (1940–1945)*, Sofia, 1978.
Ramet, S. *The Three Yugoslavias State Building and Legitimation, 1918–2005*, Indiana, 2006.
Ramet, S. (Ed.), *Interwar East Central Europe, 1918–1941*, Abingdon, 2020.

Rae, H. *State Identities and the Homogenisation of Peoples*, Cambridge, 2002.
Reid, J. *Turkey and Turks: 'Being the Present State of the Ottoman Empire'*, London, 1840.
Reiss, R.A. *La Question des Comitadjis en Serbie du Sud*, Belgrade, 1924.
Richter, H. *Greichenland zwischen Revolution und Counterrevolution*, Frankfurt, 1973.
Richter, H. *British Intervention in Greece From Varkiza to Civil War February 1945 to August 1946*, London, 1985.
Rider, M. *Sheep and Man*, London, 1983.
Ristovski, B. *Macedonia and the Macedonian People*, Skopje, 1999.
'Rizospastis'H *Trixpon h epopoha toy Dhmokratikou Stpatou Ellatoy 1946-1949*, Athens, 1998.
Rossos, P.I. *Megali Pentaetia*, Athens, 1976.
Roucek, J. *The Politics of the Balkans*, New York, 1939.
Roucek, J. *Balkan Politics International Relations in No Man's Land*, Stanford, 1948.
Roudometof, V. *Collective Memory, National Identity and Ethnic Conflict*, Westport, CN, 2002.
Ruches, P. *Albania's Captives*, Chicago, 1965.
Ruches, P. *Albanian Historical Folksongs*, Chicago, 1967.
Sakkas, J. *Britain and the Greek Civil War 1944-1949*, Mainz und Ruhpolding, 2013.
Salmon, T. *The Unwritten Places Wanderings in the Mountains of Northern Greece*, Athens, 1995.
Sarafis, S. *ELAS Greek Resistance Army*, London, 1980.
Sarafis, M. and Eve, M. *Background to Contemporary Greece*, London, 1990.
Schama, S. *Landscape and Memory*, London, 1995.
Schmitt, O.J. (Ed.), *The Ottoman Conquest of the Balkans*, Vienna, 2015.
Schwanderer, G. and Spangenberg, A. *Prespa-Ohrid-Region*, Radolfzell, 2009.
Sfetas, S. and Kentrotis, K. *Oi Alvanoi ton Skopion*, Thessaloniki, 1995.
Sfikas, T. *The British Labour Government and the Greek Civil War 1939-1945*, Keele, 1994.
Skylitzes, J. *A Synopsis of Byzantine History 811-1057*, Cambridge, 2010.
Shapland, A. and Stefani, E. (Ed.), *Archaeology behind the Battlelines The Macedonian Campaign 1915-1919 and Its Legacy*, Aldershot, 2017.
Shaw, B. *Bringing in the Sheaves Economy and Metaphor in the Roman World*, Toronto, 2013.
Shea, J. *Macedonia and Greece The Struggle to Define a New Balkan Nation*, Jefferson, NC, 1997.
Sheppard, A. *Britain in Greece A Study in International Interference*, London, 1948.
Shoup, P. *Communism and the Yugoslav National Question*, New York City, 1968.
Sibinovic, M. *Prespa and Ohrid Lakes*, Skopje, 1987.
Simovski, T. *The Inhabited Places of Aegean Macedonia*, Skopje, 1998.
Simms, B. *Unfinest Hour Britain and the Destruction of Bosnia*, London, 2002.
Sinadinoski, V. *Anarchy in Macedonia Life Under the Ottomans, 1878-1912*, New York, 2018.
Skaric, S. (and others), *The Name Issue Greece and Macedonia*, Skopje, 2009.
Slupkov, I. *The Macedonian National Question in the Documents of the Communist Party of Greece 1918-1940*, Szczecin, 2018.
Sonnichsen, A. *Confessions of a Macedonian Bandit A Californian in the Balkan Wars*, New York, 1909.
Shklifou, B. *Dolnoprespanskiiat Govor*, Sofia, 1979.
Stavridis, P. *Moscow and Greek Communism 1944-1949*, Cornell, 1989.
Stebbing, E. *At the Serbian Front in Macedonia*, London, 1920.

Stoyanovski, A. (and others), *A History of the Macedonian People*, Skopje, 1979.
Smith, A. *Chosen Peoples Sacred Sources of National Identity*, Oxford, 2003.
Smith, A. *The Antiquity of Nations*, London, 2004.
Standring, K. *Prespa Walking Guide and Maps*, Agios Germanos, 2009.
Stathakopoulos, D. *Famine and Pestilence in the late Roman and early Byzantine Empire*, Aldershot, 2004.
Steinke, K. and Xhelali, I. *Die Slavischen Minderheiten in Albanien*, Munich, 2007.
Stephenson, P. *The Legend of Basil the Bulgar-Slayar*, Cambridge, 2003.
Stratilesco, T. *From Carpathian to Pindus*, London, 1906.
Sugarman, J., *Engendering Song Singing and Subjectivity at Prespa Albanian Weddings*, Chicago, 1997.
Swire, J. *Bulgarian Conspiracy*, London, 1939.
Tadic, J. (and others), *The Foreign and Yugoslav Historiography of Macedonia and the Macedonian People*, Skopje, 1970.
Talev, D. *Prespanskite Kambani*, Sofia, 1969.
Talevski, J. *The Borders of the Republic of Macedonia*, Bitola, 1998.
Tamis, A. *The Immigration and Settlement of Macedonian Greeks in Australia*, Melbourne, 1994.
Tamis, A. *Macedonian Hellenes in Oceania*, Thessaloniki, 2015.
Todorov, N. *The Balkan City 1400–1900*, Seattle, 1983.
Tomovski, K. *The Christian Architecture in Prespa*, Skopje, 1977.
Tranov, G. *Prespa*, Sofia, 1923.
Trifunovski, G. *Bitolsko-Prilepskata Kotlena*, Skopje, 1970.
Tsoucaras, C. *The Greek Tragedy*, London, 1969.
Turner, D. *Kiriakos A British Partisan in Wartime Greece*, London, 1982.
Upward, A. *The East End of Europe*, London, 1908.
Various authors, *Historia e Luftes Antifashiste Nacionalclirimtare te Popullit Shqiptar*, Tirana, 4 volumes, 1984–1988.
Vatikiotis, P. *Popular Autocracy in Greece 1936–41*, London, 1998.
Velimirovich, N. *Prayers by the Lake*, Chicago, 2018.
Veremis, T. *The Military in Greek Politics*, London, 1997.
Vickers, M. *The Albanians A Modern History*, London, 1997.
Vickers, M. and Pettifer, J. *The Albanian Question Reshaping the Balkans*, London, 2007.
Visninski, B. *Contemplating Macedonian Statehood*, Skopje, 1974.
Vlavianos, H. *Greece 1940–49 from Resistance to Civil War The Strategy of the Greek Communist Party*, Basingstoke, 1992.
Voigt, P. *The Greek Sedition*, London, 1949.
Voglis, P. *Becoming a Subject Political Prisoners during the Greek Civil War*, New York, 2002.
Vukmanovic, S. (General Tempo), *How and Why the Peoples Liberation Struggle in Greece met with Defeat*, London, 1950.
Vukmanovic, S. (General Tempo), *Struggle for the Balkans*, London, 1990.
Wakefield, A. and Moody, S. *Under the Devil's Eye The British Military Experience in Macedonia 1915–1918*, Barnsley, 2011.
Walker, M. *Through Macedonia to the Albanian Lakes*, London, 1864.
Walsh, R. *Narrative of a Journey from Constantinople to England*, London, 1829.
Ward-Perkins, B. *The Fall of Rome and the End of Civilisation*, Oxford, 2005.
Ward Price, G. *The Story of the Salonika Army*, London, 1918.
Wilkes, J. *The Illyrians*, Oxford, 1992.

Winnifrith, T. *Shattered Eagles, Balkan Fragments*, London, 1995.
Winnifrith, T. *The Vlachs The History of a Balkan People*, London, 1987.
Wittner, L. *American Intervention in Greece 1943-1949*, New York, 1982.
Wlodzimierz, P. *Toponomastikata na Ohridska-Prespanskiot Bazen*, Skopje, 1970.
Wood, W. and Mann, A. *The Salonika Front*, London, 1920.
Woodhouse, C.M. *The Struggle for Greece 1941-1949*, London, 1976.
Xatzhanastasiou, T. *Andartes kai Kapetanioi*, Thessaloniki, 2003.
Xhemali, V. *Forcat Kombetare ne Mbrotje te Shqiperise Etnike 1941-1945*, Tetovo, 2006.
Young, G. *Nationalism and War in the Balkans (by a Diplomatist)*, New York, 1915.
Zachariadou, E. (Ed.), *The Via Egnetia Under Ottoman Rule 1380-1699*, Rethymnon, 1996.
Zafeiropoulos, D. *To KKE kai H Makedonia*, Athens, 1994.
Zoi, N. *Nje Faqe Historie*, Korca, 2000.

Index

Agathoto 5, 106, 120
Agios Achilleos 2, 5, 16, 23, 126–7
Agios Germanos
   modern times 119, 121, 126, 133–5, 192
   Ottoman times 34, 36, 38, 40, 45, 56–7, 60–1
   pre-Ottoman 1, 5, 7, 16, 25, 28
   WW1-WW2 73, 84, 86, 92–3, 98, 109, 112
Antartiko 28, 56, 60
Artana 18, 52
Asamati 4, 15, 162

Bela Crkva 157, 164
Belgrade 35, 48, 52, 76, 79, 81–2, 85, 90, 92, 101, 118, 123–6, 181
Bezmisht 4, 41
Bilisht 39, 157, 194
Binovo 28, 40; *see also* Karies
Bitola; *see also Manastir*
   Ottoman times 32, 36–7, 39, 41, 43, 47–8, 54–5, 59–60
   post WW2 106, 118–19, 121, 123, 125, 131, 133, 136, 138, 146–8
   pre-Ottoman 4, 7, 13–14, 17–18, 27, 29
   WW1-WW2 67, 75, 77, 83, 92–5
Brajcino 4
Byzantium 13, 18, 23–4, 28, 49, 55, 58, 68, 85, 141, 160, 170, 176

Constantinople 4, 14, 18–21, 23, 25–6, 31, 33–6, 39, 45, 47–8, 52–3, 69, 72–3, 85, 106, 172
Corfu 67, 87, 104, 178
Corinth 20, 27, 34, 97, 101
Crete 34, 50, 54–5, 58, 61–2, 87, 103, 131, 161, 174, 176

Devoll 1, 15, 21, 35, 39, 132, 135
Dolno Dupeni 4, 57, 112, 119, 157, 180

Drama 73, 88, 93
Drenovo 28, 40, 53, 68
Dubrovnik 34–5
Durres 4, 18, 20, 22–4
Dyracchium 4, 18, 20, 22, 27

Edessa 23, 33, 40–1, 51, 93, 172; *see also Vodena*
Epirus
   modern times 130, 170, 177–80, 195
   Ottoman times 27, 33–5, 54–5, 61
   post WW1 67, 69–70, 72, 81, 85
   post WW2 92, 97, 104, 117, 121
Ezerani 4, 157

Fiorentina 32, 34–5, 38–9
Florina; *see also* Lerin
   modern times 123, 127, 131, 135–6, 140, 148, 152–3
   Ottoman times 34–5, 38, 40, 43, 52–4, 60
   pre-Ottoman 1, 9, 14, 16–17, 22, 27–8
   WW1-WW2 70–1, 73, 79, 87–8, 92–4, 98, 101–2, 109–10, 113

German 34, 56–7, 60, 84
Golem Grad 2–3, 14, 26, 39, 49, 56, 119, 164
Gorna Prespa ix, xi; *see also* Upper Prespa
Grazdeno 40, 48, 60, 86, 106, 112, 127; *see also* Vrondero
Grncari 4, 106, 118, 157

Heraclea Lyncestis x, 4, 13, 17–21, 27, 29, 34, 36, 163–5, 167

Ioannina 126, 195
Istanbul 18, 37

Kallithea 5, 7, 24, 35, 38, 40, 57, 74, 83, 98, 104, 120–1, 199

Karies 5, 28, 40, 42, 96, 121, 127; *see also* Binovo
Kastoria; *see also* Kostur
  modern times 119, 126, 131, 146, 148, 168, 176, 202
  Ottoman times 31, 33–5, 37, 42, 44, 54, 56, 58–9
  pre-Ottoman xiii, 1, 15, 27
  WW2 onwards 88, 94, 96, 98, 110
Kastoria, Lake 14, 34
Kilkis 73, 89
Konsko 4, 41
Korca
  Ottoman times 35, 40, 42, 52–3, 61
  pre-Ottoman 5, 15, 21, 27–8
  WW1 onwards 65–72, 75, 83, 87
  WW2 onwards 92, 95, 105, 123, 130, 132, 138, 142
Koritsa xiv, 15, 21, 27–8, 66–9, 71, 75, 92, 142, 170
Kosovo 7, 18, 42, 51–2, 76, 81, 83–4, 129, 134, 136, 141, 145, 148, 183, 201–2
Kostur xiii, 1, 27, 32–3, 35, 44, 54, 59, 161; *see also* Kastoria
Kotta 102, 196–7; *see also* Roulia
Krani xiii, 4–5, 16, 21, 28, 36, 57, 67, 83, 93, 106, 119, 157, 162, 164, 173
Kranonias 58
Kumanovo 75, 83
Kurbinovo 4, 127, 157

Laimos 5, 16, 40, 61, 73, 86, 112, 119–20, 133, 192
Lefkonas 5, 40, 57, 73, 83
Lerin 1, 14, 16, 22, 27–8, 34–5, 38, 52–3, 60, 71, 79, 101, 168, 170, 172, 179, 189; *see also* Florina
Liqenas xv, 4, 138
Ljubojno 4, 157
Lower Prespa ix, 19–20, 22, 51, 72, 102, 184

Maliqi, Lake 15, 35, 87, 132
Manastir; *see also* Bitola; *Heraclea*; *Toli*
  Ottoman times 32, 34–9, 41, 43, 47–50, 52–4, 56, 58–60, 62
  pre-Ottoman 4, 14, 18, 27–9
  WW1 onwards 66–7, 75, 81, 83, 93

Meliti 140, 178
Microlimni 5, 28, 40, 58, 93, 98, 104
Mikri, Lake 21
Monastir Gap 11, 27, 43, 65–6, 77, 93
Moschopolis; *see* Voskopoje

Nakolets 14, 26, 48, 50, 157, 162, 164, 173–4
Neverska ix, 9, 47–8, 50, 54, 80, 172
Nivica; *see also* Psarades
  Ottoman times 31, 39, 42, 50–2, 54, 56, 60
  pre-Ottoman 9, 22, 25–6
  WW1 onwards 68, 72–4, 77, 83, 86, 89
  WW2 onwards 91, 129, 164, 167, 171–2, 180
Novo Berde 18, 52

Ohrid
  Ottoman times 32–8, 41, 47–50, 52, 54, 59
  pre-Ottoman 4, 17–19, 21, 23–7
  WW1 onwards 65, 68–70, 75, 81–3, 90
  WW2 onwards 97, 125, 127, 131–2, 136, 145–6
Ohrid, Lake 4, 13–15, 29, 32, 41, 80, 85, 95–6, 103, 127, 133, 143–4
Orovnik 40, 56–7, 121
Orovo 44
Oteshevo 119, 157
Oxia 5

Pili xiv, 5, 7, 22, 48, 50, 71–3, 86, 95–6, 98, 106, 109, 120–1, 128, 130–1, 184, 188
Pindus Mountains 8, 91, 93, 96, 102, 104, 110, 161, 188, 192
Pisoderi 7, 16, 22, 40, 93, 152, 170, 188, 194
Pogradec 35, 70, 92, 133
Prespa *passim*
Pretor 16, 21, 34, 44, 67, 106, 158, 162, 164, 173
Prilep 7, 26, 35, 37, 54–5, 75, 83
Psarades; *see also* Nivica
  modern times 120–31, 133–5, 137, 140–3, 147–9, 151–3

Ottoman times   31, 39, 42, 44, 47–8, 50–1, 54
pre-Ottoman   4–6, 9–10, 22, 25–6
WW1 onwards   68–9, 71–4, 80, 83, 86, 88
WW2 onwards   91–3, 96–8, 101, 103, 106, 109–12, 114
Pushtec   xv, 1, 4, 15, 22, 41, 67, 70, 92, 95, 105, 115, 118, 126, 137–9, 157, 187
Pyxos   40, 44, 192

Radika, River   14, 85
Ragusa   34–5, 39
Resen
  modern times   118, 121, 124–6, 131–2, 136, 147
  Ottoman times   32, 34, 37, 39–43, 47–50, 56
  pre-Ottoman   ix, xi, xiv, 1–2, 4, 14, 18
  WW1-WW2   77, 93–4, 97, 105–6
Resna   ix, xi, xiv, 4, 32, 34, 39–41, 43, 47–50, 56, 59, 173
Roulia   102, 196–7; *see also* Kotta

Salonika; *see also* Thessaloniki
  Ottoman times   26, 33, 35, 40–3, 45–6, 49, 51–3, 56, 60
  post-Ottoman   66–7, 72, 118, 170–1, 173, 177, 180, 187
Saranda   20, 67, 70, 75
Serres   41, 73, 88
Skopje
  early history   7, 18, 33, 42, 51–2
  modern times   131, 133–4, 138, 146–53
  post-WW2   94, 119, 121–2, 125, 128
  WW1 onwards   66, 75–6, 84, 88

Skupi; *see* Skopje
Slivnica   4, 158, 169
Solun   15, 77; *see also* Thessaloniki
Stenje   4, 158, 164
Struga   34, 39–40, 73, 85, 132, 136, 147, 169–70, 175, 180

Thessaloniki; *see also* Salonika
  modern times   134–5, 140, 142, 146–7, 149
  pre-Ottoman   15, 20
  WW1 onwards   72–3, 77, 80–1, 86
  WW2 onwards   93–4, 101, 123, 128
Thessaly   5, 20, 26, 34, 54–5, 60, 73, 96, 110, 113, 121
Tirana   xv, 7, 91, 128, 130, 132, 139, 163
Toli   27, 29, 31; *see also* Bitola; *Manastir*
Tren   15, 28, 40, 157
Trepca   18, 52
Turnovo   106, 120

Upper Prespa   9, 18, 39, 50–1, 174
Uskub   33, 42, 51, 66, 75, 84; *see also* Skopje

Via Egnatia   4, 14, 16, 18–20, 22, 25–7, 29, 31, 33–5, 40, 70, 153, 165, 168
Vodena   23, 33, 40–1, 51, 172, 175; *see also* Edessa
Voskopoje   52, 69–70, 123
Vrondero   xiv, 5, 7, 40, 44, 60, 73, 86, 106, 112, 121, 127–8, 193; *see also* Grazdeno

Zaroshe   4, 83
Zhelevo   28, 56, 60